Aiding Students, Buying Students

Financial Aid in America

Aiding Students, Buying Students

Financial Aid in America

Rupert Wilkinson

Vanderbilt University Press
NASHVILLE

2005

© 2005 Vanderbilt University Press
All rights reserved
First Edition 2005

09 08 07 06 05   1 2 3 4 5

This book is printed on acid-free paper.
Manufactured in the United States of America

Library of Congress Cataloging-in-Publication Data

Wilkinson, Rupert.
Aiding students, buying students : financial aid in America /
Rupert Wilkinson.— 1st ed.
    p. cm.
Includes bibliographical references and index.
ISBN 0-8265-1502-9 (cloth : alk. paper)
1. Student aid—United States.
2. Student aid—United States—History. I. Title.
LB2337.4.W53 2005
378.3'0973—DC22

                                    2005016953

*For Mary, Camilla, Clara,
Matthew, and Richard,
who helped sustain this traveler
on a long journey.*

Contents

Illustrations

Acknowledgments

A fourteen-year project can rack up a lot of debts.

At the very start, two authorities on financial aid—Larry Gladieux and Bruce Johnstone—welcomed me into the field and sent me some key writing. Much later, Larry gave informed encouragement when it was much needed.

Among the many financial aid professionals and others who gave me quality time (listed in Appendix 3), four provided exceptional support extending way beyond their own institutions' affairs. Joe Case of Amherst befriended the project and me almost from the start and informed it at every point with his huge knowledge of modern financial aid and its recent history. Carol Hoffman, formerly of the Access Program (Lorain County, Ohio), read several draft chapters, made valuable comments, and hooked me into an e-mail service, the excellent National College Access Network, which made all the difference in keeping me up to date. Mary Morrison of Stanford fed me national surveys and reports I had missed and capped that with expert comments on the glossary (Appendix 4). Joe Russo of Notre Dame gave rapid responses on important issues and, as editor of the *Journal of Student Financial Aid,* published my first piece on the subject. I hasten to add that none of these good friends, or any others thanked in these acknowledgments, necessarily agrees with all my judgments and conclusions.

At the University of Sussex, Ted Tapper, an authority on the political economy of British higher education, was deeply involved in the project's issues; he also helped me find me find the right publisher. Other Sussex colleagues, too, gave help and encouragement: Bob Benewick, Colin Brooks, Steve Burman, Penny Chaloner, Steve Fender, Vivien Hart, Michael Hawkins, and Angus Ross. Sussex itself supported much of the work by enabling me to crisscross the United States as a study-abroad adviser and salesperson for the university. It is ironic that if I had been based at an American university, I would probably have been unable to visit so many American campuses over so many years.

Britain's Economic and Social Research Council gave financial aid to the project with two grants: one at the beginning for a pilot study of Amherst and Smith Colleges, and another one later for transcribing interviews. At the College Board, Mike Johanek, editor of the board's centennial collection of essays (*A Faithful Mirror*, 2001), encouraged the work by taking a long preview chapter from me. I also thank the board and Peter McCormick, editor of *College Board Review*, for letting me lift part of my *Review* article "Quarreling about Merits" (Winter 2004) for use in this book.

I wish I could thank by name all the college archivists and assistant archivists who expedited my research with efficiency and thoughtfulness. Prime among them must be Roland Baumann, archivist at Oberlin, where I did a big case study. Roland not only knew his stuff inside out but went beyond the papers with perceptive comments on Oberlin culture and politics, past and present. For special acts of kindness and help, I should also mention Tom Frusciano at Rutgers archives; Bill King at Duke; Mike Martin at UNC, Chapel Hill; Patrick Quinn at Northwestern; and Nanci Young at Princeton and later at Smith.

In my travels across the country, several friends repeatedly gave me shelter and much more—good company and local insights and contacts. I thank Diana Barringer, Mariana Berry, Susi Lanyi, Howard Nenner, Jane Sanders, and Pamela White. Howard, in particular, encouraged my work from the beginning; Susi provided a midwest clipping service; and Pamela helped devise the book's title.

But of course I had a home base camp too: my own family. Through the highs and lows of the project, my wife Mary gave a support that was creative and shrewd as well as loving. A stringent critic of academic prose, she spent many hours on my copy despite a big working week in her own career. Camilla gave all kinds of help, from advice on tricky paragraphs to knowing what to send where, if, as the British put it, I "stepped under a bus." Clara bid me ask the key questions more graphically: what I have always called the "Clara Questions" are on p. 11. Matthew, skilled at pruning dramatic scripts, amiably quoted William Goldman: "kill all your darlings." I tried to obey him—sometimes. Son-in-law Richard Walters gave generous time in computer-processing pictures and figures; he redesigned one of the charts and also supplied a marketing perspective on how colleges price themselves.

In revamping an early draft of the book, I received vital help from Tony Lanyi and Harold Wechsler. They read great chunks of it, prompted me to give it better focus, sent me important economic and historical articles, and cheered me on my way. I could not wish for better friends.

The same applies to Craig Comstock. Craig was my first editor, from college newspaper days, and he has read more of my writing over the years than is reasonable to expect of anyone. As my former agent, he gave me humorous but wise advice for my conversations with publishers.

At Vanderbilt University Press, my work met an exceptional editor. From his first reading of advance material, Michael Ames expressed an unusual range and depth of interest in the project. Demanding as well as supportive, with strong views about narrative flow, he has done a huge amount for this book. The book's complexity has also required much of Dariel Mayer, in charge of production and design at VUP, and George Roupe, the highly professional copy editor. Working with both, and with Sue Havlish on marketing, has been a pleasure, at least for me.

A salute, finally, to the people who gave rise to this book—to all students, past and present, who have struggled economically to go to college and graduate. The book, perforce, does them only partial justice because it concentrates on the attitudes of aid providers, not the experiences of aid recipients. Of course those experiences come into the story, but that is not the same as writing a book on working through college as a poor student or seeking and getting (or not getting) financial aid. The historian David Allmendinger did do this for early-nineteenth century New England, and there has been some good writing at various times on the experiences of poor students, including memoirs by former students themselves. But they deserve a full history.[1]

Rupert Wilkinson
February 2005

Prologue
A Gift Goes Awry

Ann Radcliffe of London, the widowed Lady Mowlson, was not a likely candidate for fleecing. A devout Christian and active philanthropist, she was also a tough-minded investor who ran her large fortune with acumen and attention to detail.

In 1641, the year our story opens, she was sixty-five. Her late husband, Sir Thomas Mowlson, M.P., a rich merchant and former lord mayor of London, had been a big donor to religious and educational charities. So had her father, Anthony Radcliffe, Master of the Merchant Taylors guild, which had endowed a school in London (the Merchant Taylors School of today) and scholarships for poor students at Oxford. Both men, like Ann, were part of a powerful tradition of educational philanthropy that flourished among the guilds and merchant families of Stuart England. Such people gave generously, but they knew how to take care of their money. Ann herself was not slow to set her lawyers on delinquent debtors or get involved personally in investment problems.[1]

This was the donor who gave the biggest gift to America's first college fund-raising mission, which reached England in September 1641. Harvard College had been founded five years before. The College needed help, surrounding parishes needed help, and some English philanthropists like Radcliffe, with a puritan (or low Anglican) faith, were interested in the struggle to build a Godly civilization in the wilderness. The mission's chief fund-raiser, the Reverend Thomas Weld, was a Harvard Overseer (trustee), and his promotional pack included a twenty-six-page treatise, "New England's First Fruits," a vigorous progress report ranging from the missionary challenge of the Indians to the curriculum of Harvard College. Weld himself, active in Massachusetts affairs, was an aggressive puritan advocate and salesman. He had already written from Massachusetts a lyrically upbeat letter to his former parishioners in England, professing his Christian love for them while extolling the superior achievements and abundant blessings of the new life.[2]

We do not know what Weld and Radcliffe said to each other when they met in 1643, but he must have impressed her. She gave £100 to Harvard, its income to be used for the "yearly maintenance [of a] poor scholler," preferably a "kinsman" if he be "pious" and "well deserving." It was America's first scholarship, and Radcliffe agreed that it should go initially to Weld's own son, Joseph, a Harvard junior studying for the ministry. She had all of this—her "good and pious intention"—drawn up as a covenant and signed by Weld, who immediately sent the money back to Massachusetts.[3]

Young Joseph did not hold his scholarship for long. Within a few months he and a classmate, James Ward, were found guilty of stealing gunpowder and money (about twice his scholarship stipend, which paid most of his college expenses) from two Cambridge houses including the home of his uncle. As instructed by the court, President Henry Dunster publicly thrashed the young burglars and expelled them. (Disgrace notwithstanding, Joseph Weld went on to become a Fellow of Magdalene College, Oxford; Ward was readmitted to Harvard and later became a minister at Ipswich, Massachusetts.)[4]

Ann Radcliffe could not have foreseen the delinquency of her scholarship's first recipient. But why did she let it go to the fund-raiser's own son? The Reverend Weld's parish of Roxbury was rated a "good living": he was only poor compared to rich Boston merchants. We must remember that Radcliffe would have known much less about Harvard and Massachusetts than the usual run of her English charities. She may well have preferred to start the ball rolling with the son of a minister whom she had met and trusted. There were, at the time, no bureaucratic tests of need and merit; it was an age of personal patronage as well as extended family loyalties: hence her preference for aiding a "kinsman." Giving to poor students destined for the church was part of her tradition, and it was often assumed that the sons of ministers were poor enough to qualify. It would be easy to believe this of ministers in a pioneer colony. She was not to know that ministers in the first few decades of the Massachusetts colony were richer on average than their counterparts in England.[5]

Eleven years later, Radcliffe's covenant with Weld did briefly help protect the scholarship fund from misappropriation. In the college's early years the General Court (Massachusetts legislature) acted as treasurer for Harvard and it therefore held the endowed scholarship funds. In 1655 the college urgently petitioned the General Court for money to restore its buildings from a "ruinous condition" and for other needs. The House of Deputies (the lower house) proposed using the scholarship monies for those purposes. The Magistrates (upper house) resisted this as illegal.

But that was not the end of it. In 1713, the Radcliffe-Mowlson fund, which had paid no income for scholarships since the 1680s, was turned over to the college administration, which promptly merged it with its general funds. Over the next 180 years, the Radcliffe gift was occasionally recognized by the award of scholarships, but it was generally used for other purposes. Its name was virtually forgotten till the late 1880s, when a researcher, Alan McFarland Davies, exposed the sorry saga. In a fit of honest guilt, the president and fellows of Harvard took $5,000 out of general funds in 1893 and restored the Lady Mowlson scholarship. The following year Ann's name was honored in the newly chartered Radcliffe College for women.[6]

The temptations and cross-pressures that played on the Radcliffe-Mowlson gift operated on other aid too in Harvard's early years. Supporting needy students had, from the start, been part of a popular pride in Harvard and general respect for learning—hence the "corn scholarships" (1645–55), funded from the sale of corn contributed by townships in Massachusetts and Connecticut. Due to cost and hard times, the corn contributions soon waned, but well before then President Dunster was asking the New England Confederation Commissioners (advisers on collective security and welfare) if Harvard might spend the corn money for general purposes. No, said the commissioners, unless no "poore pious and learned youth . . . be present." In the end about a third of the corn money went to student aid; most of it was used to pay Harvard's teaching "fellows."[7]

The story of the Radcliffe and corn scholarships was prophetic. Harvard always aided needy students, but spending on student aid had to compete with other college purposes. In the eighteenth century, Harvard let financial aid fall behind other priorities, especially the funding of faculty, as its academic ambitions developed.[8] Later the tide turned, but it was often a struggle for financial aid to keep up with rising costs and charges.

THE MOST OBVIOUS SIGNIFICANCE of the Radcliffe scholarship story for the history of student aid is the difference between then and now—between the pioneering gift made to a struggling, New World college and today's annual outlay of well over $100 billion, involving thousands of providers led by federal and state agencies and the colleges themselves.[9] There is also the contrast between the informal and vague accounting that misgoverned the Radcliffe gift and the complex bureaucratic and computerized systems by which most student aid is dispensed today. Again, in our own, more secular age, most aid is not religiously motivated, though well into the twentieth century divinity schools often charged little or no tuition. Conversely, explicit ideas of democratic opportunity that sanction most student aid today did not develop till the nineteenth century.

Despite all this, the story of America's first scholarship has three overlapping strands that run through the history of student aid into our own time. All of them involve motives and purposes.

Variety of Motives

Ann Radcliffe herself had at least three motives for giving the scholarship: the virtue of helping students who were supposedly poor and "well-deserving"; taking care of kinfolk; and promoting Christian enlightenment. Harvard College, too, had a range of almost inseparable motives, from advancing the institution to producing graduates who would benefit "the Country." (President Dunster actually hoped, ineffectually, that graduates would pay back their scholarships "in convenient time" if they left "the colonies.")[10]

Spending on Needy Students versus Other Spending

The questionable neediness of Joseph Weld and the subsequent diversion of the Radcliffe fund and others symbolized the struggle of "need-based aid" (in today's language) against other spending purposes. Until the 1960s, grant aid to students was seldom given solely on the basis of financial need; other student attributes, and personal connections too, helped determine who got the money. Student aid as a whole, moreover, has often had to contend against other college budget lines—from buildings to faculty—and, more generally, against other targets of social and philanthropic spending.

Mission and Market

Mission was manifest in the "good and pious intention" of Ann Radcliffe's covenant with Harvard and, indeed, the whole missionary nature of Harvard's founding. But Harvard's early scholarships were also a matter of practical economics. The appeal for student aid was a way of getting donors to give money to the college. The scholarships also became a way of promoting enrollment, not just by making it easier for needy students to attend, but by signaling good will and social responsibility.

Mission and market have been entwined ever since. Mission involves high moral and social purpose. It focuses on students and society as well as the individual college—on extending social opportunity, for example, as well as enhancing the college's educational quality by buying diverse talents. Market focuses more exclusively on the needs of the college, on what it has to do to survive and advance by attracting money and students—*enough* students to maintain viable enrollment, and the *right* students according to the college's identity and place in the market. These overlapping purposes resonate with a familiar dualism in American history and culture, the conjunction of strenuous moralism with business pragmatism.[11]

PART I

The American Way of Student Aid

1

Setting the Record Straight

This book tells the story of student aid in America. It explores the many reasons aid providers have had for assisting students. In doing this, it illuminates current problems and policies. The book focuses in particular on what is now a rich set of highly selective private colleges, but it connects their history to that of other institutions. (Many of today's elite colleges themselves started out as hardscrabble ventures catering only to white males.)*

Today, over half of all undergraduates in America get some form of financial aid: grants and scholarships, student loans, and work-study jobs. In recent years, more than three-quarters of first-year students at private four-year nonprofit colleges have received nonrepayable grant aid.[1]

Yet neither grants nor median family incomes have kept up with the escalation of costs at four-year colleges since the early 1980s. "Unmet need"—the gap between a student's resources plus aid and the cost of college—is generally greater for lower-income students, though they tend to go to cheaper colleges. Student aid itself has shifted: loans have grown faster than grants over the past two decades. New reports stress that many "college-qualified" young Americans are not going to college, due in part

---

*The term "college" is used throughout to refer to the undergraduate schools of universities as well as colleges without graduate schools. This book is not about graduate assistance and fellowships. Nor is it extensively about athletic scholarships, which have usually come out of separate college athletic budgets—though athletic aid has been controversial since the early 1900s and there have been issues about athletic claims on general scholarships for leadership and character.

to lack of money and fear of debt. All this has been happening at a time when the financial payoffs of a college education have risen, widening the economic gulf between college graduates and others. At stake is America's pride in being a "land of opportunity" as well as a successful "knowledge economy" with a highly educated workforce.

In spite of the shift to loans, grant aid has for decades been the fastest-growing item in the budgets of many colleges as their rising costs and charges qualify more students for aid because of financial need. At the same time, state governments and private colleges alike have been spending more and more money on "merit" scholarships not based on need. Most aid is "need-based," but even here, in a climate of bargaining and competition, private colleges often sweeten their aid offers to favor "strong" or "desirable" applicants rather than the neediest. By the late 1990s, too, private colleges increasingly differed in how they assessed student financial need.

All this has made some experts fear that the will to provide wide access to college through aid—indeed the very concept of need-based aid itself—is in mortal danger. The fear is compounded by estimates that a coming surge in the traditional college-age population (an increase of more than 16 percent in eighteen- to twenty-four-year-olds over the next ten years) will be disproportionately among lower-income families—half of them Hispanic.

These concerns are serious, but some of the claims get the history wrong. Several writers, sharp ones at that, have contributed to the myth that merit scholarships, not related to need, dominated grant aid until after World War II. More recently, the boom in merit scholarships has produced an opposite claim: that merits are very new.[2] In fact, both need-based and merit-based aid have long pedigrees in America, though need-based aid ("beneficiary aid" as it used to be called) is older, and merit scholarships acquired bitter enemies when they first became prevalent in the late nineteenth century.

Policy analysts as well as journalists have also portrayed the market-discount use of aid—increasing college revenue by pulling in more students—as a modern loss of innocence.[3] In fact the idea goes back at least to the early nineteenth century, and there were vestiges of it from the beginning, as we saw in the prologue. Although nineteenth-century college presidents often regarded student aid as a charitable outlay, funded by donors, they also "remitted" some charges as a price discount to keep up enrollments as well as help "worthy" students.

The tendency of grant aid to lag behind rising college costs is, again, much older than many people realize. Private-college deans worried about it in the 1950s during a period of tuition inflation. The lag occurred at different colleges throughout history as they looked to tuition increases as well as donations to fund new programs and facilities.

All student aid embodies choices, and many of the choices go back a long time. Whether explicitly or not, aid policies have always had to answer more than one of the following questions:

Who should get the most aid? Needy students? *Very* needy students? Virtuous students? (By what standard?) Able students? (How judged?) Students of a particular race or faith? (Which?)

Why aid them? To give the disadvantaged a break? To ease the burdens of the middle classes? To encourage effort and realize talent? To keep up college enrollments? To recruit diverse students to learn from each other?

Who should provide the aid? Individual donors and private foundations giving to colleges and students? Colleges themselves out of general income, including the fees of full payers? Governments using public funds? College graduates, paying back loans after college?

To SEE HOW THESE questions were answered in the past is to learn how we reached where we are today.

Elite Colleges

Who gets to college and who graduates are pressing questions, but one should also ask who gets to attend the best-funded and most prestigious colleges. Research in the 1990s indicated that the payoff in subsequent earnings of going to the most selective and well-endowed colleges, compared with going to "lesser" colleges, was particularly marked for low-income students.[4] Their previous disadvantage, it seems, gave their college education more leverage on their life chances, compared with richer peers who already had advantages and connections. Elite colleges nearly always provide far more resources per student, as well as valuable contacts after graduation. Elite-college leaders themselves have recently confessed that they are not doing enough to enroll low-income students—or middle-income students. Between 1985 and 2000, high-income freshmen increased from 46 percent to 55 percent of entering classes at the nation's 250 most selective colleges.

The question of access to these colleges touches an old anxiety, going back to the nineteenth century, that the social order may be getting more stratified and dominated by a closed upper class. Growing income inequality in the 1980s and 1990s sharpened the worry, intensifying historic American fears of falling apart as a society and falling away from a past promise of democratic virtue.[5]

Consider two propositions about student aid at highly selective, high-priced colleges—one by an imaginary friend of the system, one by a critic.

Friend: The system is a splendid combination of fairness and good finance. Along with successful fund-raising, it enables quality institutions to charge high prices to those who can afford it while opening their gates to those who can't.

Critic: The system is a model of self-deception. It enables leaders of institutions for the rich to feel good by letting in a few poor kids while charging such high tuitions that even some upper-middle-income students have to get the "generous" gift of aid.

Both statements have some truth; the record of elite private colleges is two-edged. On the one hand, their history has included many efforts to be more open—in spite of snobbery, racism, and sexism—and in modern times their high tuition has impelled them to make big grants to needy students. Since the 1950s they have led moves to base all aid on financial need; to guarantee meeting all need (that is, to make up from their funds any difference between college costs and what they estimate a student can afford or find from other sources); and to make special concessions to low-income or first-generation college students by reducing the loan or work components of the students' financial aid "packages."

Yet today the nation's richest, most selective, and highest-tuition colleges (these three up-market traits tend to go together) have more students who are able and willing to pay full charges (despite the fact that the charges are higher) and fewer low-income students than other colleges.[6]

As we will see in the next chapter, a complex of historical factors—cultural, demographic, and market—brought about this paradox. In a sentence, "name" colleges became more academically selective and in-demand across the country at roughly the same time (after the 1940s) that richer students became more likely to have strong academic records.

This shows that student aid cannot be separated from admissions policies and deeper cultural factors, but pricing itself does matter. "Sticker shock"—the deterrent of high tuition—discourages some low-income students from applying, even though they do not have to pay full price. High tuition also dismays many middle-class students who qualify for little or no grant aid under the stringent assessments of financial need operated by many private colleges.

PRIVATE COLLEGES, OF COURSE, do not monopolize elite sectors of higher education. In the colonial era, there was no clear distinction between private and public institutions. The difference mainly evolved in the nineteenth century. Until the 1820s, for instance, the Massachusetts legislature paid intermittent subsidies to Harvard, and it elected Harvard's board of overseers till 1865.[7] From the nineteenth century on, leading state and private universities related to each other in various ways, sometimes complementing each other and sometimes competing. Student aid figured in the way they staked out their respective markets.

Since the 1960s, state flagship universities have acquired richer student bodies as they have sought to become more academically selective and prestigious. It is often harder to get admitted by a state flagship than by the average, relatively unselective private college charging higher tuition. And by the early 1990s, if not earlier, the median family income of students at a state flagship was usually higher than at the general run of private colleges in the same state.[8]

This is not irrelevant to private colleges, even leading ones. For decades they have feared a "middle-class melt" of students to state universities. The challenge has grown as state institutions have developed elite honors programs for selected students, including special seminars and other activities. These programs are often attached to merit scholarships.

The Nature of Student Aid

Among the many studies of student aid, I know of none that has really defined it and laid out its different types.

Student aid, by definition, is targeted on some students as distinct from a general low-cost provision for everyone, such as low or free tuition. At the border between the two are arrangements open to all but designed for the needy: cheap dining "commons," for instance, or student-run "co-op" dormitories.

The low- or free-tuition approach to wide access is most obviously associated with state and community colleges. Many state universities founded in the nineteenth century were historically free-tuition, especially in the Midwest and after annual state appropriations were firmly established. In 1922, seventeen out of thirty-one state universities responding to a national survey charged no tuition to state residents, though they usually levied some other fees and most had started charging higher fees to students from out of state.[9]

Among highly endowed private colleges, Berea College in Kentucky has led the way in giving free tuition instead of targeted aid, while requiring work from all its students in return. With a tradition of service to Appalachia, the college takes no student above a low-income level and restricts 80 percent of its admissions to students from an Appalachian "territory." But Berea, and a few colleges like it, are deviants.[10]

Low or free tuition has not always, though, been an alternative to giving substantial aid. In the early nineteenth century, young provincial colleges such as Amherst and Bowdoin charged lower tuition than older universities while providing a lot of aid too. In our own time, private colleges that charge lower tuition but are not in high demand tend to give more grant aid (tuition discounts) as a proportion of their fees to get more students to come their way.[11]

The most obvious exceptions have been private black colleges, which have lacked, or believed they lacked, a class of customers able and willing to pay the same full tuition as at white colleges. So black colleges have kept their fees very low rather than discounting them heavily with their own grant aid. Since the 1970s, however, they have relied on expanded federal and state student aid, as have other low-tuition colleges, and they have also developed merit scholarships.[12]

Elsewhere, at different times and places, there have been policy disputes about the balance between tuition levels and aid. Should tuition be kept low, benefiting a large class range of students, some of whom could pay more? Or should the college boost tuition while giving much more back in aid to low-income students? Supporters of the second course have included budgetary conservatives, anxious to save money by targeting it, as well as liberal champions of the poor.[13]

ALL THREE MAIN TYPES of student aid—grants or fee reductions, loans, jobs—go back to medieval times. Strictly speaking, loans and jobs are only "aid" if they provide something students cannot usually find so easily on the open market. Student loans should count as aid if they are provided on special terms: low or zero interest rates or extended periods for repayment. Student jobs are aid if they go to specific students or the college helps students find them off-campus.

When speaking of grant aid, it is common to distinguish *need-based aid* from *merit scholarships,* or "merits," not based on financial need. In practice, the distinction has not been so clear-cut. Scholarships aimed at needy students have usually been scarce enough to require impressive qualities of one kind or another to get them. The dual meaning of the word "scholarship" helped justify this. Going back at least to sixteenth-century England, the word connoted both *provision* and *prize*—help for poor students, recognition of special merit.[14] Carried over to the New World, the two meanings connected with two watchwords of American culture: *opportunity* and *reward.*

Scholarships for needy students have frequently demanded special merit in requiring the holder to maintain better-than-average grades in college. Often, too, the grant amounts given have been *scaled* according to the student's initial academic record, and this has become far more common and fine-tuned in the past few decades. Grant aid awarded solely on need or income, without rationing or scaling according to anything else, was not widely established till the 1960s, with the advent of federal "educational opportunity grants" and the expansion of grant aid at elite private colleges. Most need-based aid should be called need-*related* aid.

But need considerations have also affected merits. Some defenders of merits have claimed that these awards often go to needy students. The truth of this claim has varied, but a hybrid form of merits, developed by eastern colleges in the 1930s, is indeed sensitive to financial need. All recipients, chosen entirely on ability, receive a basic award, but the amount is scaled up according to the student's finances. When the National Merit Corporation created its famous awards in the 1950s, this was the formula it went for. A number of scholarship-giving foundations use it today.

Besides financial need and merit, a third, broad basis for aid has been *service,* including past service by the student or a parent as well as future service by students in occupations for which their education will prepare them.[15] Service-oriented aid may or may not require financial need or special merit. It includes the many scholarships given in the past to ministerial students as well as children of ministers: both were often assumed to be needy. In the nineteenth century, state programs also included aid for Civil War veterans (past service) as well as support for teacher training (future service).

A modern mix of past- and future-service-based aid is the North Carolina Sheriffs' Association scholarships for state-university students majoring in criminal justice. Preference goes to children of sheriffs and deputy sheriffs, especially those killed in service. (States commonly give "slain policeman" scholarships, aiding children of police or firefighters killed in the line of duty.) Past and future service also figures in scholarships for minority students in disadvantaged areas; they sometimes favor students who have been active in organizations and civic activities in the hope that they will become community leaders.

Student aid for service has included loans as well as grants, and the two have sometimes gone together. In the eighteenth and nineteenth centuries, some college scholarships for ministerial students required recipients to pay back their grants—converting them, in effect, to loans—if they did not enter the ministry within a specified period. Conversely, various federal loans have had a "forgiveness" clause, turning the loans, or part of them, into outright grants for graduates entering public-need occupations such as teaching in inner-city schools; the categories have varied over time.

The very first federal student loans were in fact for service: the 1942 Student War Loan Program was designed to get students as quickly as possible into various fields, mainly sciences and engineering, deemed crucial to the war effort.[16] Many states, too, give loans to students training for public-service occupations such as school-teaching and nursing.

Most student loans, though, have not involved service. This was true both before and after the 1960s, when federal lending largely replaced lending by colleges themselves. And despite the long history of student loans, college authorities have not always agreed about them. Since the early nineteenth century, critics have seen extensive student loans as an unhealthy burden on students and graduates and a shirking of responsibility by parents. Proponents have seen them as a good investment by students, consistent with self-reliance, and an efficient way of extending financial aid at minimum cost.

GRANTS, LOANS—AND JOBS. Throughout American history, many students depended on paid jobs to get through college, whether or not the college provided them. In the eighteenth and early nineteenth centuries, colleges sometimes adjusted their calendars so that students could work on farms at the busiest season or take long winter breaks to teach school. A hundred years later, work was still so important that college authorities often referred to needy students as "self-supporting students." In 1926, according to a federal survey, a sixth of all college and professional students depended solely on work to finance themselves; at black colleges it was 37 percent.[17]

From colonial times, colleges provided some employment of their own to students—from bell-ringing to clerking—but at the end of the nineteenth century they became more active in helping students find jobs on and off campus. By then, "working one's way through college" (a distinctively American phrase) was well in tune with official values of self-reliance and a democratic right to better oneself through hard effort. College administrators, indeed, started referring to student employment as "self-help," and this term came to include student loans too, as it still does in financial aid jargon. America thus developed what foreigners might call a bureaucratic double-talk: "aid" could include "self-help"!

Like loans, however, student jobs have not always been celebrated. For students themselves, they were seldom joyous or prestigious. Administrators, too, have sometimes feared that heavy workloads were impairing student health and general well-being as well as academic effort. In spite of these concerns, most financial aid packages for students today include term-time employment and assume summer earnings.

Providers and Purposes

In 2000–01, 37 percent of grant aid came from the federal government, 15 percent from the states, and the rest (just under half) from colleges and philanthropy. Nine-tenths of student loans and many work-study jobs were federally sponsored.[18] Before the 1930s, by contrast, colleges and private donors provided most student aid.

Motives and rationales for aiding students have obviously varied according to the type of provider, though most have subscribed to extending opportunity to "worthy" students. Federal and state programs have frequently cited the needs of society for more education and training. Colleges have listed their awards and benefits to *look* democratic and to get the quantity and quality of students they want.[19]

To give a sense of different purposes, we can take a snapshot of the private donors (mainly of scholarships but also of loan funds) that have proliferated over time. They include direct donors to students as well as to college scholarship funds. They range from church groups and alumni (both important historically in building college endowments) to corporations and unions, from the Armenian Students of America to the National Council of State Garden Clubs, which offers scholarships in environmental studies as well as horticulture. Among a host of private-donor purposes, two broad ones stand out: taking care of "one's own" (Armenian Americans, for example, or union families) and recruiting talent and leadership for a particular business, profession, or way of life.

Individual donors have often given or made bequests as an extension of themselves, favoring students from their hometowns, religious groups, or preferred fields—sometimes rendering the aid almost unusable, as in the case of the University of California scholarship for a Jewish orphan planning graduate study in aeronautical engineering. More somberly, creating scholarships has been a way of responding to grievous loss by an act of renewal, be it a family memorial for a son or husband lost at war, a neighborhood award in memory of a killed schoolchild, or scholarship fund-raising for families of the victims of the September 11 terrorist attacks.[20]

In all this variety, giving to student aid is part of the country's civic tradition. It is particularly American in its individualist thrust—helping individuals to get on.

So FAR THE PURPOSES behind student aid may seem clear enough, but motivations are not always so simple, and one motive may mask another. Since the 1950s, for example, elite-college presidents' annual reports and fund-raising literature have often justified student aid less in terms of social justice than as a way of removing the financial barriers to getting good students and reaping the educational benefits of a diverse study student body. When student aid comes increasingly from a college's general funds, including rising tuition fees, it is more politic to tell full-tuition payers and alumni supporters that they are subsidizing outlays that enhance the institution and benefit all its students than to tell them that that they are paying for class philanthropy.[21]

Yet the presidents' reports hint here and there that social fairness and democracy are motives too. They often highlight numbers showing an increase in the public-school proportion of entering freshmen. In the realm of public rhetoric we often assume that altruistic postures conceal personal and institutional self-interest. It can, though, be the other way about. Pragmatic motives, albeit sincere in themselves, may mask altruism. Doing good is sold as hard-headed realism.[22]

Historically, the purposes of student aid have been obscured by reticence about social class. Even when the aid was explicitly need-related, college administrations and private donors described its targets in personal terms: "worthy students with slender means," "needy and deserving students," and so forth. The truism that America's culture of individualism is thorny soil for the language of class has applied with special force to colleges. As Martin Trow observed, Americans have sought higher education more to escape a lower-class identity than to collectively affirm it.[23]

Of course there have been exceptions. In the late nineteenth and early twentieth centuries, middle-class concern about "plutocracy" and poverty led college administrators to use social-class categories in discussing the different types of students who should be admitted and aided.[24] And in recent decades, as going to college became more common, admissions and financial aid officials have often used the cultural term "first-generation college," and not just "low-income," to describe lower-class or working-class students. (It still took an administrator with an unusually vivid turn of phrase to tell me, in the mid-1990s, that she targeted extra aid on "blue-collar as defined by me—no unemployed Ph.D.s!")

Class language has usually been starkest in debates about *government* aid, as this has clearly involved political ideology and the uses of public money. From the 1940s GI Bill to today's tax credits and state merit scholarships, politicians and commentators have argued about the socioeconomic groups that should benefit from various programs.

Historically, however, American political language has often elevated sectional and ethnic categories above class ones. At the college level, too, when policy makers have explicitly identified social groups, they have done so more easily in ethnic and racial terms.[25] In financial aid as well as admissions, this could mean excluding rather than favoring a group. In 1914, following the expansion of New York's upwardly mobile Jewish population, Columbia set up special scholarships to attract students living outside the city. Like other colleges' scholarships aimed at rural and western areas, the Columbia plan was meant to stem a campus influx of urban Jewish "undesirables"—an image that merged social class with ethnicity.[26] There was likewise an anti-immigrant thrust in scholarships restricted to "native-stock" Americans.

Today, financial aid policies have followed "affirmative action" admissions in favoring, not excluding, specific minorities. This started with African Americans in the 1960s and was extended to others in the 1970s.

As we will see later, private colleges have enjoyed more freedom from legal attacks on affirmative action than have state colleges and government programs. On most campuses by the 1990s, however, the goal of "diversity" had largely come to mean *racial* and *ethnic* diversity, or more precisely, getting more nonwhites and Hispanic Americans.

The reasons for favoring specific minorities show how the rationales for a financial aid policy can accumulate, once the policy is established. In the wake of the civil rights movement, admissions preferences and extra aid went to African Americans out of guilt and a desire for social justice, a wish to make up for the oppressions of racism. This motive has continued, but preferential policies have acquired other justifications, based on the educational value of enrolling underrepresented minorities. Interviewing elite-college administrators in the 1990s, I found that they justified extra minority aid most often as a way of enrolling diverse students to learn from each other and of training them—both minority and mainstream students—to be leaders and get on with each other in a multicultural society. Sometimes they also mentioned the idea of using merit scholarships to recruit minority role models of college achievement.[27]

There was also, though, a financial incentive. Although minority students *tend* to be poorer than others (thereby needing more aid), not all of them have low incomes. It often costs less to enroll more minority students, even with generous grant aid, than to enroll more low-income students in general, *all* of whom need a lot of aid at a high-tuition private college.

Racial and ethnic diversity, in other words, is often cheaper than class diversity per se, as well as being more visible.[28] This brings us to the complex relationship between ideology and economics in the motives for aiding students.

Mission and Market

The prologue identified three strands in American student-aid history: the sheer variety of motives for student aid, the struggle between need-related aid and other educational spending, and the entwining of "mission" and "market." This third theme needs more discussion. Mission and market are part of a wider duality of ideology and economics that runs through student-aid history. In government, for instance, the democratic mission of extending and equalizing educational opportunity finds an economic rationale in the idea of developing "human capital." The specific terms "mission" and "market," however, apply most forcibly to private nonprofit colleges. They have social and educational purposes (mission) but can only survive by attracting customers and donors and balancing their books (market).*

Even within the same institution, different officials can put different emphases on mission and market. Visiting a private liberal arts college in North Carolina in the late 1990s, I asked two administrators involved

---

*For economists, there are three main differences between modern private nonprofit colleges and profit-seeking firms, beyond the element of profit itself. First, a college's student *customers* are also *suppliers,* contributing to the college's educational product, in that students educate each other—though some do this more than others! Secondly, colleges have not only a *customer* market but a *donative* one: donors of endowment and gifts. Corporations have a second market too—investors—but it is more closely tied to expected financial performance in the customer market. The third difference shows most finely at the "quality" end of the markets, where neither college nor company seeks to increase its customers (student enrollment) by lowering the full price. BMW seeks quality and prestige to build financial strength. Stanford seeks financial strength to build quality and prestige.

with scholarships why their needy students from North Carolina got better aid packages (more grant, less loan) than similar students from other states. The first administrator cited the college's "historic mission" to serve students of the state. The in-state proportion had gone down and they wanted to reverse this. It was not a matter of losing good customers overall; they had plenty of demand from the Northeast.

The second administrator answered differently: "the North Carolina students bring us money." To reduce cost differences between state and private colleges, the state of North Carolina gave two kinds of grant aid for its students at in-state private colleges—one for all the students and one for those with financial need.[29] In bringing this aid to the college, the recipients reduced the grant money that the college itself had to give to needy students from inside the state. Though these students still got larger grants overall than equally needy students from elsewhere, it was economic to recruit them.

The two responses to my question were not totally different. The first administrator, too, noted that the North Carolina aid relieved the college budget, while the second administrator conceded that the college's mission was a reinforcing factor. The first explanation, though, was essentially ideological and stressed the historic culture of the college. (As such explanations are prone to do, it resorted selectively to history, stressing one part of the college's original mission.) The second explanation was basically economic and pragmatic, concerned with the institution's market survival and prosperity. It was not devoid of values: its line of thinking tends to respect competitive vigor and the strong financing of educational quality. But it rested more on practical bookkeeping than overt ideology.

In this case, the two leanings supported the same policy, but that does not always happen. Aid for students with very large financial need has often cost the college too much to help many of them. Private colleges, particularly, have often used aid to help several "low-need" students, each needing *some* aid, rather than one "high-need" student needing a lot of aid. Sometimes they have done this on purpose, but often the system has simply worked that way, by giving too little aid to attract or retain high-need students or, more recently at selective colleges, by screening them out academically.

I should not imply that the "mission" part of what colleges do is confined to extending opportunity. For centuries, achieving excellence—variously defined—has been a driving purpose at leading colleges. The consequent upgrading of faculty and plant costs money, and this can be at the expense of need-related aid, as we saw in the prologue story about early Harvard.[30]

MISSION AND MARKET AFFECT almost all private colleges, but they do so in different ways according to the college's selectivity—its ability to be choosy about who it admits. The United States today has just over fifteen hundred private, nonprofit institutions, enrolling about a third of all four-year college students. About eighty of these—colleges that have become highly selective, well-endowed institutions—are the main subjects of this book, and about twenty well-known ones are featured in the book's case studies and vignettes.[31]

Some economists have claimed that a small group of very highly selective institutions differ from the rest in that they give student aid for essentially nonmarket reasons—out of social responsibility and to obtain the educational benefits of a diverse student body. If they gave no aid at all, so the argument goes, they could find enough outstanding, full-paying students to fill their classes without losing academic quality. By contrast, most colleges *have* to discount their prices with grant aid to some or many students in order to keep up their enrollments or, in the case of more selective colleges, to get enough students with the academic quality they need to maintain their market position.[32] For almost all private colleges, relatively high tuition signals quality, so even "low-tuition" private colleges usually pitch full tuition higher than many of their students are able or willing to pay, and then offer special grant-aid discounts.[33]

This argument, I believe, underestimates the interplay between mission and market that has evolved over time for even super-elite private colleges. Many of these, as already noted, were humble-born, using aid like any other colleges to attract students. Today, though, a small band of colleges—most of the eight Ivies and probably less than ten others—could, theoretically, find enough good students, as measured by test scores, high-school grades, and other attainments, if they gave no student-aid discounts. They would not, however, recruit such a range of "interesting" students. They would, likewise, produce a less diverse student body, socially and racially. This would alienate customers (prospective students including full payers) as well as alumni and other donors—not to speak of existing students, faculty, and public opinion in general.[34]

Aid-supported diversity, in other words, is not just an ideological and educational value; it has become a market asset too. For a nationally visible college to look too socially exclusive or "lily white" would, over the long term, be to risk economic punishment as well as political opprobrium. In their own way, top colleges are part of a market system.

Private and Public

In spite of the market element, much of the aid deployed by private colleges comes from government. Most aided students at these colleges receive a bits-and-pieces mix of support from the college itself (at least a job, if not a grant) combined with state and federal assistance and perhaps an "outside" scholarship from a private donor. This entwining of private and public aid has a history.

State aid programs started in Massachusetts and Maryland just after the Revolution, whereas federal aid did not appear till after World War I, with a program for disabled veterans. Before the twentieth century, state scholarships and loans were often tied to specific institutions, including the great hybrids, Cornell and Rutgers, with their public and private sections.[35] Much later, when general state aid programs started to become more common, private-college lobbies helped to shape the programs to make sure they got a piece of them and the expanding opportunity they would create. In the 1950s, Pomona was so active at the birth of California's state scholarships that it lent "faculty wives" to the new state scholarship commission to do the computing of students' financial need. By the end of the 1970s, well over half of state grant aid was going to students attending private colleges in their home state.[36] State governments have justified aiding private-college students as a way of keeping talent in the state, giving poorer students more choice of college, and saving money by avoiding the cost of building more state-college capacity.[37]

Federal aid has always gone to private- as well as public-college students, and federal aid programs and private institutions have influenced one another as a result. In the 1940s, veterans getting aid under the GI Bill went disproportionately to the best-known private and state colleges as well as to trade schools. Since the GI Bill paid all tuition and more at any college, "Why go to Podunk College when the government will send you to Yale?" as *Time* magazine put it.[38] The GI Bill had a big impact on elite private colleges and the way their leaders thought about admissions and student aid.

Conversely, when the Johnson administration created the first full array of federal student-aid programs in the 1960s (grants and money for student jobs as well as an expanded loan program), it borrowed ideas and formulas from the private sector. The first director of the new Division of Student Financial Aid in the U.S. Office of Education was a Pomona dean, J. Edward Sanders, a leading figure in the financial aid community. Sanders, significantly, went on to found the Washington office of the venerable College Entrance Examination Board in 1966. The Board, as much a private-college association as a testing body, realized it needed a new presence in Washington to watch and influence federal student aid and other programs.

The connection between elite, high-tuition colleges and public aid should not, though, be exaggerated. Due to ceilings on public grants and income eligibility, federal and state grants cover a bigger proportion of costs at low-tuition colleges, and low-income students are more numerous there.

Excluding ROTC scholarships and veterans aid, federal grant aid may pay about a fifth of a student's expenses at an elite college where total costs exceed $35,000 a year—if, that is, the student has a family income under $25,000 and so qualifies for maximum federal aid.[39] State aid varies a lot between states. Though most of it is need-related, it generally gives more help to middle-income families than federal grant aid does, but it is usually confined to students attending college in the state, whereas highly selective private colleges recruit most of their students from out of state. At these colleges, state and federal aid combined is likely to be under a tenth of all need-related grant aid received by students. The great bulk comes from the colleges themselves.[40]

Public aid is still important, though, to these colleges and their students. As already mentioned, most student loans are federally sponsored. College administrators say that federal and state grants enable them to take better care of their neediest students while concentrating more of their own aid on middle-income ones. Actually, a study in the late 1970s and 1980s suggested that increases in federal aid led private colleges to expand their own aid—perhaps by bringing in more low-income students who still needed college assistance.[41]

Story Line

The next chapter (Chapter 2) explains the contours of student-aid history. How important was aid in different periods, and whom did it reach? How did the whole evolving system of American higher education impact on student aid? An increasingly important part of this environment was the federal government. Chapter 3 tells how it became a major aid provider.

The second part of the book focuses on the evolution of elite private colleges and their interaction with the public sector. Chapter 4 shows how a tradition of helping poor students developed in England, crossed over to colonial America, and then spread into a host of movements after the Revolution. During the nineteenth century, a profusion of colleges got involved in student aid, from small church colleges struggling on the frontier to new state and city institutions.

From the late nineteenth century through the 1920s (Chapter 5), a drive by the most ambitious colleges to raise standards combined with worries that mass organization and too much welfare might weaken the individual. This produced a movement for basing scholarships on "merit," not need, while extending loans and jobs to needy students. Between the 1930s and 1950s, however, grant aid for the needy regained the moral high ground (Chapter 6). The devastations of the Great Depression, followed by postwar educational liberalism, inspired leading colleges to cooperate in distributing aid more systematically according to family means.

In the 1960s and 1970s (Chapter 7), meritocracy arrived. Sitting atop a mass higher-education system, elite colleges became, *for the first time,* highly selective academically. They used aid to get talent and diversity, but their high scholastic standards were barriers to the disadvantaged.

Chapters 8 and 9 take the story into our own time. Starting with a case study of Oberlin College in the 1980s and 1990s, Chapter 8 analyzes the penetration of student aid by new market techniques and a new spirit of competition. Federal antitrust action against college "collusion" on aid practices (detailed in Appendix 1) reinforced this. Chapter 9 describes how elite colleges compromised with these forces while trying to roll them back.

Part III, a concluding essay, sees student aid as an evolving social and political system, with weaknesses but also possibilities for the future. It ends by proposing government and campus action that will make advantaged institutions more open to disadvantaged people—not by stepping outside history but by tapping into past experience.

2

Aid in History:
Who Got It, What Shaped It

The Reach of Student Aid

The history of the reach of student aid involves two sets of questions. First, how big was grant aid in different periods, compared with student expenses and college budgets (most aid before the 1940s was *college* aid), and what proportions of students got it? Secondly, *who* got the aid, and how adequately? We will focus here on grant aid and socioeconomic groups.

Answers to these questions can only be tentative because the data are spotty. There are no long-term studies tracing the amounts of aid given by a college—let alone whole groups of colleges—in relation to college budgets, total student costs, or family incomes.[1] Different studies and data, mostly for particular dates or limited periods, give different criteria against which to measure grant aid—full tuition, for example, or total college spending.

Published trend data on grant aid in relation to student budgets do not begin till the end of the 1920s. In 1929–30, grant aid per student in all colleges was a tiny 2.5 percent of total charges and living costs. In the 1930s Depression, charges fell and grant aid rose, but in 1939–40 it was still only 3.6 percent of charges and costs. The big change came with the GI Bill. In 1949–50 student grants were over half (55 percent) of all charges and living costs. As the wartime veterans' benefits tailed off, the percentage fell to 14 percent in 1959–60 (still much more than in the 1920s and 1930s). It then grew again, as new federal programs, including Social Security, took effect.[2]

It is tempting to conclude that student grant aid was of no account till after World War II. This would be wrong. Until the 1940s, admittedly, low tuition at some colleges and off-campus jobs found by students themselves were probably more important than grants and loans in widening college access. But the data reported above for the 1920s and 1930s masked big differences between colleges. At the end of the 1920s, many gave no scholarships at all, but that was far from true everywhere. A survey of thirty-five Methodist colleges in 1930–31 (including Albion, De-Pauw, Dickinson, and Ohio Wesleyan) found that eight had no endowed scholarships, but the median college in the group gave grant aid to just over a quarter of its students. The grants averaged 40 percent of tuition, though much less of total costs.[3]

Among colleges founded before the late nineteenth century, at least some shared a common sequence. At early stages in their history, they gave extensive grant aid to maintain or expand enrollments. As they found larger and richer clienteles and put more money into faculty and plant, their aid spending declined but rose again at various points in the twentieth century under new pressures to widen access and catch talent.

At Harvard in the early 1700s, following a buildup of endowed schol-

Figure 1. Grant Aid as a Percentage of Total Charges and Living Costs Per Student, 1929–1970[1]

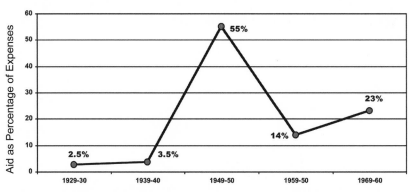

Graph and percentages derived from data in Carnegie Commission, *Higher Education: Who Pays? Who Benefits? Who Should Pay?* (New York: McGraw-Hill, 1973), page 32. Percentages based on all students, whether or not they received aid. Graph lines do not show fluctuations between ten-year points.

1. Full tuition and fees, plus living and incidental costs.

arships, between a quarter and a third of students received grant aid covering about half of their expenses, if they were frugal; there was also aid from jobs and loans. At Amherst, 39 percent of its first thirteen hundred students between 1821 and 1845 were ministerial charity students who got free tuition amounting to about a quarter of basic expenses. At New York University (founded 1831), nearly half of students were aided in the mid-nineteenth century, some getting free tuition. None of these aid levels was sustained.[4]

In the twentieth century, an unusual report by Swarthmore's president David Fraser showed a dramatic fall and then rise in scholarship spending there. In 1903 Swarthmore (founded 1865) returned 25 percent of its charges back to students as scholarships. The president of the time, Joseph Swain, had just started an admissions drive that would double Swarthmore's enrollment from 209 to 420 students in ten years, and he needed financial aid to do it. As Swarthmore's reputation and applicant pool grew, the college held back on aid, sinking to a low of 5 percent of charges in the early 1920s. The percentage then more than doubled because of a new honors program involving merit scholarships, followed by increased need for student aid in the 1930s. After a brief plummet in World War II, student aid as a proportion of charges climbed through various ups and downs to just under a fifth in 1980 (still less than the 1903 level).[5]

Figure 2. College Spending on Grant Aid as a Percentage of Full Charges[1]: Swarthmore College, 1903–1984

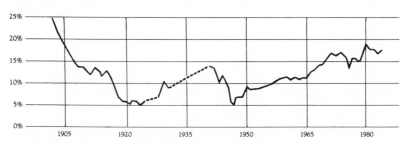

Graph reproduced from the President's Report 1983–84 (Swarthmore College), page 3, courtesy of Swarthmore College. Broken lines are for years with no data.

1. Tuition and fees, room and board. They represent *gross* revenue: what the college would have received if all students had paid full tuition without college grant aid.

This is not to say that Swarthmore perfectly mirrored other colleges. In broad outline, however, it followed a pattern seen elsewhere: high spending on student aid early in the college's history, though not necessarily at the very start; then decline; then a rise again in the modern era, often starting before the 1930s but accelerated by the Depression and rising even more after World War II.

HISTORICALLY WE KNOW LITTLE about trends in the shares of student aid that went to different social classes. There are no general studies of who got what aid till the late 1960s. (There is indeed, to my knowledge, no published data on rates of attending college by social class till after World War I.)[6]

In 1966–67, just after new federal aid programs were set up, the poorest quarter of college students had 94 percent of their estimated financial need met by aid—44 percent of it by grants. The second-poorest quarter got much less of a deal from either the government or their colleges. Only 38 percent of their need on average was met by aid—15 percent of it by grants. Similar proportions went to the upper-middle quarter of students. In both cases the students would have to make up the gap by extra borrowing or working or draining their families to an extent not expected by official estimates of ability to pay. The top quarter of students had virtually no need (it was estimated that they could pay full charges at whatever college they went to), but they still got some aid, mostly in loans.[7]

A study of college students in the late 1980s and early 1990s found again, not surprisingly, that lower-income students got more assistance from grant aid, but higher-income students received aid too, especially at private colleges. This was due in part to merit scholarships but also to high tuitions, which made more families eligible for need-related aid. At private colleges in 1992–93, grants from all sources—including federal and state—cut tuition on average by 45 percent for low-income students, 29 percent for middle-income students, and 11 percent for high-income students. The lower-income students also tended to go to colleges where full tuition was cheaper. At public colleges in 1986–87, average grants to low-income students actually exceeded full tuition; they covered some living expenses too.[8]

Let us now jump back a century for comparison: the data, such as they are, do not go further back. Did grant aid reach poor students as

fully as it has since the 1960s? The short answer is no, but rising costs
and academic work loads after the 1950s made it harder for students to
work through college—at least a private one—without grant aid or family
support.[9]

At leading private colleges in the late nineteenth century, tuition was
a third or less of tuition, room, and board (compared with three-quarters today). In a detailed magazine survey of aid for female students at
thirteen private and state colleges in 1891, Alice Hayes found fifty-seven
scholarships open to women that awarded more than full tuition. Nineteen provided full costs, but several of these were usually not awarded in
full. Hayes's article, "Can a Poor Girl Go to College?" concluded that
scholarships seldom did much for the "penniless" woman student compared with those who had the money for most of their college expenses.
(The situation was harder for women than men, who had more student
job opportunities and also more endowed scholarships. But barriers to the
poor operated for male students too. For example, colleges often gave no
aid to freshmen, waiting till the students had "proved themselves" before
providing scholarships or loans.)[10]

Hayes's study gives wider meaning to unique data on early female
classes of Smith College in the late 1870s and the 1880s. Partially published by Sarah Gordon a century later, it gives more information about
social class in relation to grant aid and admissions than anything published on an American college before or since.

We must allow, of course, for the particular circumstances of Smith at
the time. Opened in 1875, it was a new kind of enterprise—the women's
college. It might therefore be expected to deter non-professional families
unused anyway to higher education. On the other hand, it offered a protective, though not cloistered, environment for women students. It attracted, in fact, numerous applicants from different backgrounds. Its first
president, L. Clark Seelye, welcomed a measure of social diversity and
was quite sensitive to the needs of poor students but he also valued "well-
bred" refinement. "Special Students," admitted without examination for
no credit, did not enjoy full status: they were apt to be older and poorer
and to live off campus.[11]

In eight classes, 1881 to 1888, just over half the students (54 percent)
stayed all four years and graduated. Daughters of artisans and manual
workers were actually more likely than most to graduate: they numbered

9 percent of the graduates but less than 3 percent of the nongraduates. The small numbers suggest why. It would take extra determination and aptitude for a working-class girl to go to Smith, and these traits would help carry her through.

Nearly all the grant aid went to the four-year graduates; "Special Students," it seemed, did not qualify, and the aid was targeted on those determined to graduate. Thirty-one percent of them got grants, and 62 percent of these were full tuition ($100), amounting to just over a quarter of tuition, room, and board ($350), throughout the four years. On all this, Alice Hayes was right. Scholarships gave limited help in getting through college.

Within these limits, Smith aid did favor the less advantaged. Throughout the period, all Smith scholarships were officially designated for "meritorious students who would otherwise be unable to meet the expense of a collegiate education." President Seelye and a trustee committee also remitted the tuition of other "indigent but deserving" students who were "well prepared" to enter.[12]

As the table below shows, among the four-year graduates, half the daughters of "manual and office workers" got grant aid (either scholarships or tuition remissions), compared with a third of the "middle classes," comprising a broad range of backgrounds, from farmers, small merchants and sales agents to government officials, engineers, and schoolteachers. Just over a quarter of the "higher professional and executive" class—lawyers, doctors, ministers, professors and company managers—received grant aid, but most of this went to students with fathers in the less-well-paid professions: ministers and professors. In sheer numbers, the daughters of ministers and merchants received the most grant aid, as there were more of them.

Smith's student aid, in sum, was progressive in that it went disproportionately to lower-class and lower-income groups, as well as fatherless students. The justice, though, was rough. Daughters of clerks, cashiers, and schoolteachers—low-paid occupations—got very little grant aid; the reason is not clear, as we do not know the precise mixes of need and merit required to win a scholarship or get reduced tuition. In all occupational categories there were many students who were not aided. The gaps proved at least that a poor student without a scholarship could work her way through Smith, as she would usually have to. At $350 a year, Smith tu-

Table 1. Smith College Students Graduating 1881–1888: Enrollment and Grant Aid, by Father's Occupation

Father's occupation	Number of students	Students receiving grants	Percent of students receiving grants	Average grant dollars over 4 years[1]
Managers	27	3	11	245
Doctors	17	2	12	350
Lawyers	20	2	10	225
Ministers	47	23	49	366
Professors and high school principals	5	2	40	440
Total higher professionals and executives	116	32	28	
Business agents	1	0	0	
Engineers and architects	2	0	0	
Farmers	16	7	44	286
Government (low level)	7	4	57	315
Merchants and dealers	53	18	34	308
School teachers	7	0	0	
Sea captains	4	2	50	400
Total middle class	90	31	34	
Artisans	15	8	53	350
Clerks and cashiers	6	1	17	400
Mechanics and machinists	7	5	71	320
Total manual and office workers	28	14	50	
Other/varied	2	0	0	
Father deceased[2]	60	19	32	
Occupation not known	35	6	17	
All students	331	102	31	

Table based on student records in Smith College Archives; see notes 10 and 12 for this chapter. Average-grant data was collected only for specific occupations.

1. Tuition, room, and board over 4 years was $1400 (4 x $350).

2. May include some with living father but giving no information on him.

ition, room, and board was about three-quarters of the average earnings of semiskilled industrial workers, 40 percent of the income of clerks and ministers, and a fifth of what artisans could usually make.[13]

Progressive tendencies notwithstanding, most grant aid went to the upper and middle classes, as they made up most of the students. This was broadly in line with two findings, two centuries apart, from Harvard. A study of Salem, Massachusetts, in the 1740s through the 1760s found that the families of local Harvard scholarship students were poorer than other Salem Harvard students but richer than most Salem families. In the 1950s and 1960s, concerned Harvard deans found the same to be true of Harvard scholarship students compared with other Harvard students and national median family incomes.[14] In both periods, scholarship aid required financial need, yet compared to the general population, almost all Harvard students, indeed college students as a whole, were *relatively* rich.

Student aid could only go so far against stubborn social facts. Around the turn of the twentieth century, 6 or 7 percent of students at Michigan, where tuition and fees were forty dollars a year, had fathers who were manual workers. At Harvard, where tuition was $150, living expenses were higher, and many needy students did not get scholarships, the working-class proportion was about the same. The barriers to going to college were clearly cultural as well as economic.[15] Even vocationally oriented state universities had official entrance requirements, referring to textbooks and scholastic knowledge, that would look formidable, if not alien, to many ordinary folk.

From colonial times, most colleges recruited small numbers of artisans' and poor farmers' children, but it was something else again to put college and curriculum on the map for canal workers and factory hands—the great mass of wage labor that developed in the nineteenth century. In the Chicago of 1924, long after the worst exploitation of immigrants by the meat packers, semiskilled workers were four times as common among all men aged forty-five or more than they were among city-resident fathers of University of Chicago freshmen. Unskilled workers were fifty-six times as common in the former group than the latter.[16]

IF DEEP SOCIAL AND economic forces affected the output end of student aid—limiting its reach and impact—they also worked at the input end, shaping the whole system of higher education that generated student aid.

Constants

Underenrollment

Throughout American history, colleges have tended to be underenrolled, according to their own definitions of full capacity. This is certainly true of what are now private colleges, but it was also true of state colleges in the nineteenth and early twentieth centuries. Until well into the twentieth century, very few colleges of any kind set a limit on admissions numbers.[17]

The root cause of this was a mixture of permissive government, market risk-taking, religion, and geography. The diffusion of college-chartering powers among the states, many of them requiring minimal academic standards through the nineteenth century, enabled ambitious college builders to dot the landscape with brave new campuses. Religious freedom, too, encouraged a growing assortment of churches to build colleges, often in underpopulated areas, as they sought to spread religious enlightenment into the frontier. In the expanding big cities of the early twentieth century, demand surged for local colleges—but many colleges were not located in big cities.

The result is that through most of American history, college capacity exceeded demand. This was particularly important for colleges that did not enjoy fat endowments or state subsidies. To stay in business—and some didn't—private colleges had to charge fees, but they used financial aid to mitigate their prices when they could.[18]

The link between precarious enrollments and financial aid has continued into our own time. In the late 1980s and 1990s, more than half of public four-year colleges and some 60 percent of private ones accepted at least three in four of their applicants. These colleges are vulnerable to demographic and market shifts—a decline, for example, in the traditional college-going age group. They would be still more vulnerable without the price flexibility of financial aid.[19]

It is true that in the past fifteen years a surge of high-quality demand for top colleges has made them extremely selective: no problem there in filling spaces. By then, though, the pattern was set: it had become a way of life, as we have seen, to use financial aid to get the students a college believed it needed, whether or not aid was required to keep up total numbers. Even at the very top, financial aid is bound up in anxiety about losing good students to competitors. When Princeton, flush with scholarship money and concerned about losing low- and middle-income students, announced massive aid increases in January 1998 and January 2001, it sent shock waves through the Ivies and other elite colleges. They in turn expanded their aid.

Upgrading

American colleges, like individuals, have answered the call to upward mobility. Amherst, Bowdoin, Dartmouth, all known in the early nineteenth century as poor boys' colleges, had acquired a rich-boy reputation by the mid-twentieth. This was part of a general pattern. Colleges have tended, whenever they can, to move up and out, away from relatively poor, local or provincial constituencies to richer pickings further afield. College leaders and faculty, ambitious to build expensive quality and play on a larger stage, have been drawn to the prospect of an extended market, providing more customers and a bigger pool of talent.

The growth of a national college market in the twentieth century accelerated the trend, but it existed long before then. The trend was strongest among private colleges, not required like public ones to provide wide access for state or local populations. Since the 1960s, however, more and more state universities, encouraged by research-oriented faculty, have raised their undergraduate admissions standards at the expense of wide social access.[20]

The pattern has never been monolithic or simple. In the eighteenth and nineteenth centuries Harvard built wealth and social status by serving a *local* Boston upper class.[21] When it became less exclusive socially, it became *more* selective academically by recruiting students from across the country, as did other Ivies. Here the routes to moneyed status and academic selectivity ran in different directions, at least for a time.

Conversely, between the World Wars the free-tuition College of the City of New York (CCNY) was arguably the country's most selective college as a result of strong local demand from bright, lower-income Jews. By staying local, as it had to as a municipal college, CCNY attained high academic quality though not high social prestige. In our own time, too, many colleges—private as well as public—have found market niches by sticking to local and in-state students, offering them well-tailored services at quite low prices.[22] Yet even colleges like Roosevelt in Chicago (private) and Temple in Philadelphia (public), with strong traditions of serving a local working class, have opened second, suburban campuses catering to more middle-class students as well as white working-class students whose families have moved out from the inner city.[23]

The general move up and away from local constituencies has involved financial aid in several ways. Aid enabled colleges to compensate somewhat for the general move by retaining or reestablishing local ties, including those enshrined in their founding charters. Some colleges gave local scholarships almost from the start. Others, like Worcester Polytechnic Institute and its neighbor, Clark University, which were founded in the nineteenth century on the basis of free or low tuition, replaced those tuition policies with fixed numbers of free places or scholarships for local students when they moved to a wider market and higher charges.

In modern times, colleges have paid conscience money for their wider ambitions by setting up new aid programs for local students, sometimes singling out those who have shown leadership and community involvement. Motives vary. The programs may be part of a larger drive to renovate and spruce up a run-down surrounding neighborhood, a way of recruiting more minorities, a response to local political pressures, a genuine wish to "put something back into the community," or all of these. Depending on their circumstances, colleges can also get direct payoffs from special aid for local or in-state students. It may help them to beat off strong state-university competition and capture state aid money (as we saw in the last chapter), or even save on tight dorm space by paying students to commute (Fordham's Metro grants).

Not all colleges react in this way, and some have a mixed record on local access and aid. In the 1990s, Oberlin College, a rich and highly selective institution in a poor, rust-belt Ohio county, Lorain, did not encourage transfers from local community colleges. Its one need-related scholarship giving extra help to Lorain County students was instigated not by the college but by its donor, the widow of an Oberlin professor.

In the late 1990s, though, Oberlin faculty started a cooperative teaching program for disadvantaged high schools across the state. And from 2001, the college offered free tuition to entrants from Oberlin High School, which was polarized between many disadvantaged low performers and some academic high-fliers. The move was part of a wider program to improve the high school and build middle-class support for it. The program was prompted by shame at the school's rock-bottom state ratings; it also aimed to make the school more attractive to Oberlin faculty parents.[24]

In the South, loyalty to a whole region has encouraged colleges to off-set their national ambitions with state or regional scholarships. Certainly this is so in North Carolina, where Wake Forest gives extra grant aid to "natural constituents"—first-generation college students from the region with high financial need. The category recognizes that Wake Forest was founded by Baptists in 1834 for "plain folk" of the area long before the university was enriched by Reynolds tobacco money. Similarly, in 1985, the Duke family foundation that subsidizes Duke University gave it two scholarship programs for residents of North and South Carolina—merit scholarships for community leadership and need-based "loan replacement grants" to reduce student loan burdens. The wish to balance "high stand-ing as a national institution" with loyalty to "south-eastern roots" was an old story at Duke, but it has recently been of more concern to the Duke Foundation, with a family history of giving to the region, than to Duke trustees and faculty.[25]

The wish to move up to a larger stage has itself required financial aid spending. Although a national market offers a wider pool of talent and af-fluence, it also draws in more colleges, competing against each other for the most desirable students. Pitching their full-tuition fees at ambitious levels, colleges find there are not enough students to go around at those levels, so they need to expand the supply with financial aid discounts. The move away from local constituents may reduce the number of low-in-come students at these colleges, but the colleges still need financial aid to get middle-income students who cannot or will not pay full price.

Big Changes

Going to College

The most obvious historical change affecting student aid has been the huge rise in demand for college, leading in turn to a rise in demand for student aid and a mushrooming of student-aid programs.

In 1800 about 2 percent of men aged between fifteen and their early thirties are estimated to have gone to college for some period—the age of going to college varied a great deal. The rate of going to college took off in the 1890s, as society became more bureaucratic and organized more formally its ways of learning and of selecting people for promotion. By 1900, 4 percent of eighteen- to twenty-one-year-olds were at college; by 1940, 16 percent; by 1970, 48 percent. These figures include two-year community college students but omit the growth in older undergraduates after the 1960s.[26] (Women did not go to college till the nineteenth century and did not do so as much as men till the late 1970s. Through the twentieth century, though, their enrollment increased faster than men's except in the 1930s Depression and in the 1940s, when returning male veterans took some places away from them.)

The low rates of going to college in early America do not mean that higher education was unimportant then or entirely isolated from the people. As historians Joseph Kett and Daniel Walker Howe have argued, the idea of widespread self-improvement through learning—and not just material improvement—was well established by the late eighteenth century. Liberal intellectuals were more apt to espouse that idea than "the common man," but it was taken up by politically minded artisans and others. In addition to the small numbers that went to college, diverse men and women moved in and out of academies and seminaries that did not award degrees but often provided an intrepid mix of elementary and college-level courses.[27]

There were also variations by time and place. In the 1850s, around the farm town of Alfred, New York, a good half of young women took college-level courses at Alfred Academy and University, largely to prepare for school-teaching, though few graduated.[28]

For men, colleges were always an important route to ministerial careers, and in the early Republic most high national officeholders had been to college at least briefly, even under the antipatrician Andrew Jackson. Both inside and outside the curriculum, colleges trained future leaders in rhetoric and public discourse.[29]

All this, though, was small stuff compared with the advance of higher education in the twentieth century. Just why and how college education became the main gateway to "good jobs" is beyond this book's scope, though obviously it was part of the professionalizing of middle-class occupations.[30]

There were two implications for student aid. First, the trends helped to justify student loans. Borrowing for college was increasingly a good investment, with a career payoff. Secondly, the sheer growth of college education meant that student aid acquired a larger constituency of support, and the increased importance of college education for careers strengthened the case for student aid. From a democratic standpoint, the case became all the more pressing as social-class differences in rates of going to college did not diminish, though more people from all classes went to college and graduated.[31]

Poor Students, Rich Students, Good Students

As briefly noted in the introduction, the big increase in going to college has involved another sea change, creating more tension between the purposes of student aid.

Before World War II, college presidents often said that *poor students tended to be better students.* Even when they were less prepared for college than their richer contemporaries, they more than made up for that by a "hungry" attitude to study (to use a word from a later age). These claims were not just impressionistic; they were supported here and there by telling statistics.[32]

In the 1950s, all this began to change. *Richer students now tended to be better students,* at least in the way that students were usually judged academically. Since the 1940s, when scholastic aptitude tests became more important for getting into college, especially prestige ones, SAT scores have correlated with family income.[33] (They may well have done so before but it did not make so much difference in the GI Bill era of the late 1940s when a wide social range of student veterans did well at leading colleges.) Nor is it just a matter of high scores on standardized tests, which have often been accused of class bias. Merit scholarships or other programs for the academically talented tend to enroll higher-income students even when they are not just based on test scores.

The correlation between wealth and academic ability is not the same at all colleges. It depends to some extent on a college's market situation and the nature of its intake.

Colleges that have a tradition of recruiting strong students from a nonwealthy middle class or of losing the brightest rich students to more prestigious competitors can find that their best performers are middle-income or upper-middle-income rather than high-income students. Across the whole college population, however, middle- and upper-class students tend to do better academically than lower-class students.[34]

Why the great shift? In sum, poor students are now less apt to be an especially dedicated, select group, while more of the richer students have applied their resources to serious academic study.

For most of American history, going to college was so unusual a path that the few poor students who took it were apt to be specially motivated, with some cultural tools for taking on the syllabus. The image of the poor scholar as a Bible-literate farm youth was not pure myth, but there were other versions too, some already mentioned: the working-class students at Smith in the 1880s whose graduation rate was so high, and the Jewish students at CCNY.

Richer students, by contrast, tended—with many exceptions of course—to be "collegians," seeking fun and a veneer of cultivation rather than heavy academic engagement.[35] Their enjoyments could be intellectual, especially when student literary societies flourished in the late eighteenth and early nineteenth centuries, but the growth of fraternities and sororities reinforced a collective hedonism for those who could afford it. Right up to the 1930s, college administrators depicted rich students as frivolous, poor ones as serious. From the poor student's standpoint, academic life could compensate for being outside the main undergraduate social scene, even if the scholarly diligence of the poor attracted disdain from richer students.[36]

When this pattern changed after the GI Bill generation, it did so for two reasons, operating on different social-class levels, though both reflected the growing size and importance of higher education. As more of the population went to college, higher education drew in a greater range of ability among lower-income students, most of whom would not have gone to college at all in earlier years. It still took extra grit and aspiration for poor students to get to college, but lower-income students were less confined to those who were specially dedicated and qualified.[37]

Many more from the middle and upper classes were going to college too, but here another change was afoot. A new "cognitive elite" emerged, geared to passing tests and doing well in college.[38] In buckling down to serious study, the middle and upper classes reflected the rise of professional and academic culture, which attached high prestige to analytical power and commanded the good jobs. As part of this culture, elite colleges became more demanding and selective academically. In the 1950s and 1960s they helped to forge a new meritocracy, which recruited and rewarded middle-income public-school students, sometimes to the discomfiture of old Ivy League and prep-school families.

These families, however, soon read the game. Out went the "gentleman's C"; in came extensive test-coaching, enhanced college-prep courses in well-funded schools, and at home the use of money to cultivate every talent and experience that might give an edge to that college application. Thus equipped, the old upper class quickly joined the new suburban middle classes in dominating the cognitive elite.[39]

These social shifts did not create total conflict between helping needy students and recruiting academically able ones. For even the most selective college, attracting lower-income applicants widened the talent pool and offered the educational benefits of a diverse student body. Some elite colleges have tried to interpret "academic ability" as widely as possible, to recognize high potential within cultural disadvantage, and then give the financial support needed. Finding and nurturing such talent is not easy, however, especially not for most elite colleges as presently constructed. Just as academically selective admission policies tend to favor the non-poor, so do financial aid policies that reward academic merit, whether or not the aid is also geared to need.

Financial Aid Goes Professional

The trends to professionalism that helped produced a "cognitive elite" affected all aspects of higher education including financial aid itself.

Dispensing student aid has become more specialized and more based on intricate analysis. Well into the nineteenth century, when college administrations were still tiny and personal patronage flourished, the president himself or a deputized professor might hand out jobs and waive or defer tuition, often relying on ministers and others to recommend candidates for scholarships. From the late nineteenth century, an assortment of parties—deans and registrars, student job bureaus, scholarship committees, and alumni societies—became involved in financial aid. At Smith College around 1930, a knowing high school principal or counselor could seek scholarship aid for a student from any one of three college offices; whether the offices kept complete tabs on each other is not clear.[40] Not till well after World War II did most campuses concentrate all financial aid (grants, loans, jobs) under one expert administrator.

The move to a new professionalism in financial aid was part of a bundle of changes. Systematic packaging—providing aid to different students in carefully worked-out mixes of grant plus loan and/or job—developed alongside detailed means-testing ("need-analysis"), which assessed how much an aid applicant should pay. And as leading colleges became more selective, they were able to be more proactive in seeking the mix of students they wanted—"building a class." For that purpose it was useful to combine all aid with admissions in newly styled offices of "admissions and financial aid."

In spite of these shifts, less than half of all colleges (41 percent) in the early 1960s had centralized financial aid offices, and little more than a third (36 percent) had full-time or nearly full-time financial aid directors. They were most common at high-tuition colleges and big universities, especially where there were many student loans. At other colleges, the admissions director or dean of students often doubled as financial aid chief.[41] Today it is a rare college that does not have a full-time financial aid director, handling not just grants but loans and student employment (at least federal "work-study" jobs).

It was government that made the difference. The creation of big federal aid programs in the 1960s and early 1970s, providing all three types of aid, required a central and highly expert office on each campus to handle a mountain of federal rules and reporting requirements. At Smith College, to cite it again, the financial aid office doubled its professional staff in the 1970s, mainly because of the expansion of federal loans and other government aid programs. By then, student-aid officials had found a distinct professional identity. In the 1960s they set up regional associations and then the National Association of Student Financial Aid Administrators.[42]

In the 1980s and 1990s, the financial aid profession underwent further change, especially at private colleges struggling to compete in the marketplace. Financial aid officers became deeply involved in "enrollment management," supplying student data and analysis to help the administration attract and retain the students it wanted.

The welfare function did not go away. "My job," a financial aid director told me in 1994, "is 50 percent calculator and 50 percent Kleenex." At all American colleges, the student-aid administrator takes a responsibility for students seldom found in other countries. That responsibility is at least a *cognitive* responsibility: colleges may not meet all student need, but they try to *know* where and how big the gaps are. Only in America have student-aid administrators made the word "gap" into an active verb, meaning "not to meet all need"—not filling, in other words, all of the gap between a student's resources and college costs. By "gapping" students, they imply that permitting some "unmet need," as the jargon puts it, is a conscious if regrettable policy. Even failure can sound masterful.

It has not always been that way. Through much of American history colleges provided what aid they thought they could without keeping a close eye on student financial sources. In time all that changed. The 1930s Depression gave college leaders and government officials good reason to take interest in student finances, and after World War II, the escalating student population, coupled with steep rises in private-college costs, impelled colleges and governments to worry more about the economic welfare of students. If nothing else, high tuition concentrates the mind on who can afford what.

The federal government, clearly, was a big player in the professionalizing of student aid. This was just one aspect of the federal role in student-aid history. We turn to the larger, federal story in the next chapter.

3

Enter Uncle Sam

Unlike the states, the federal government has supported higher education via student aid more than by direct subsidies to colleges. From time to time, colleges have pressed the federal government for general grants to institutions, but their success has been mainly limited to aid for predominantly black, Hispanic, and Native American ("tribal") colleges.[1]

In 2001, state governments spent just under $64 billion on direct appropriations to public colleges, compared with $4.7 billion on student aid. The federal government provided nearly $51 billion in student aid— about $11 billion of it in grants. It spent approximately $20 billion on direct grants to colleges, but almost all of this went to specific institutions for research and other programs.[2]

Some economists have praised the indirect method of subsidizing higher education through student aid. They say that assisting customers who can vote with their feet by choosing where they go does more for the health and competitive vigor of colleges than giving colleges direct and regular subsidies.[3]

Historically, however, the federal focus on student aid has had more to do with political tradition than concern for college performance. Direct subsidy implies control, and this runs against deep-seated American distrust of central government power, especially in the sensitive realm of education—"the lives of our children." Aid to individual students, with no restrictions on choice of college or program, has been less vulnerable to suspicion of federal power. But the difference is only relative. Federal aid to students, too, has evoked conservative fears of being controlled and weakened by remote authority. The history of federal student aid is, in good measure, the story of struggles against those fears, enlisting different motives and interests to overcome them.[4]

Federal Ventures (1919–1950s)

Two different but compatible theories explain how and why federal aid appeared on the scene in the twentieth century. The first theory is not confined to the United States; it applies, for instance, to Britain, Germany, and Australia. As society modernizes and develops sophisticated professions, higher education becomes more prized, and political pressure builds up to make it more widely available. The national government starts spending big money on student aid, but this competes with other demands on government levied by a complex society, from high-tech defense to prisons and pensions. Faced with taxpayer resistance as more and more students go to college, the government turns some of its mounting student-aid costs back onto students in the form of loans rather than grants.[5]

The second theory is distinctive to America and its traditional distrust of federal power. To overcome this distrust, enacting major federal student aid programs has usually required a climate of national crisis to which the new programs can be linked as a remedy.

Even then, conservative fears that federal giving may sap individual self-reliance have promoted loans or "work-study" jobs against outright grants—except for military veterans, who have supposedly shown their mettle. Stipends for disabled veterans seeking job training were the first federal student-aid program, established in the social turmoil and labor unrest following World War I.[6]

It took the 1930s Depression to produce a wide-reaching federal aid program, and even then it only funded student employment, though grants and loans were mooted in the early days. Run by New Deal agencies—the Federal Emergency Relief Administration and later the National Youth Administration—the program was aiding about one in eight college students by the late 1930s as well as needy high school students. The aid for college students was parceled out via the colleges according to numbers enrolled. The government evolved rules and guidelines to ensure—quite successfully—that the program expanded the enrollment of students who really needed the money. All colleges qualified, despite arguments on one side that only public colleges should get the aid, as their students were poorer, and on the other that it should be targeted on higher-cost private colleges to help them in hard times and make them more affordable.

There were arguments, of course, about how the program should be run, how recipients should be selected (by a student's character and promise and not just sheer need?), how much red tape should be inflicted on the colleges, and even whether private colleges should accept at all the "intrusion" of federal aid, including government inquiry into student finances. Defenses of the program ranged from the claim that it would reduce the number of "dangerous" radicals on the streets to concerns about wasted abilities. The program's own mission statements included the aim of keeping up the supply of well-trained people who would contribute to the country's economic and social development—an idea that would surface again in the 1940s and 1950s.[7]

THEN CAME THE "GI Bill of Rights," as its lobbyists dubbed it— the Servicemen's Readjustment Act, signed into law in July 1944. The GI Bill was not just about education: it provided some unemployment pay and federal guarantees for cheap mortgages, a provision often credited with fuelling the huge growth of suburban homes after the war. But its most celebrated gifts were educational: not only stipends for family maintenance and books but, effectively, full tuition anywhere. Anyone who had served three months or more in the uniformed military qualified for twelve months (much more than the academic year) of GI-Bill college assistance, *plus* the same period that the veteran had served. An initial exception to this blanket coverage, removed in December 1945, was that veterans over twenty-four years of age had to show that the war had interrupted their education.[8] At its peak in 1947, just under a half of all college students were on the GI Bill.

The huge size of the federal wartime budget made the GI Bill's funding look relatively small and manageable. In 1944–45, the GI Bill's first operating year, total spending on veterans and on education and "manpower" development was just under 6 percent of all federal outlays.[9] In fact, GI Bill planners tended to underestimate the numbers who would go back to college. Later GI bills, starting with the Korean War, were more limited, giving fixed stipends but not full tuition except at very low-tuition colleges.

The 1944 GI Bill also had a lot of history and tradition on its side. Ever since the Revolutionary hatred of British redcoats and standing armies, Americans had seen themselves as an antimilitarist nation, despite admiring combat prowess.[10] Geographical isolation from other big powers, with their aristocratic, martial traditions, reinforced America's civilian identity. Serving in the military was respected but often thought abnormal, not something to be taken for granted. Parsimonious governments did not always reward veterans well, but the idea persisted that those who defended the flag at times of national peril (even the rebel flag in a civil war) deserved special gratitude.

After the Civil War, veterans' pensions became the centerpiece of welfare spending. This led to a more general emphasis on old-age pensions, but they did not replace educational aid to veterans. Several states provided it after the Civil War and again after World War I. By the mid-1930s, many states had also created special student-aid programs for the children of servicemen killed in the war. Veterans' lobbies were active players in this history, including enactment of the GI Bill itself.[11]

Other books have traced the intricate politics that produced the final bill. Its godfathers included liberal government planners who saw the bill as part of a wider postwar reconstruction not confined to veterans. A more potent force, however, was a very different set of interests, largely hostile to New Deal liberalism, including the American Legion and the newspapers of William Randolph Hearst. This camp insisted on making veterans a special case, a position that augured ill for those who later wanted to extend federal student aid to nonveterans. In the 1950s, indeed, the Legion attacked federal aid to education not connected with the military.[12]

From the early 1930s, President Roosevelt himself had opposed special benefits for veterans, not wishing to have his broad program for recovery from the Depression cut up and depleted by special interests at a time when much of the population was suffering. In the war, however, he shifted ground, declaring that the "greater . . . sacrifice" made by American servicemen deserved special attention.[13] Supporting a GI Bill provided a sweetener to go with lowering the draft age to eighteen; it also recognized the groundswell building up in Congress. By February 1944, Congress had before it 641 bills for veterans' assistance.[14]

A concern common to many supporters of the GI Bill was the fear of a return to economic depression and mass unemployment after the war. Training and educating GIs to make them more employable, rather than letting them flood the labor market, made humane good sense. The Depression specter of an unemployed veteran selling apples on the street corner was a frequently invoked image.[15]

The GI Bill's student aid, however, was service based, not need based. Only one government report, that of the Osborn committee, publicly considered basing the aid on financial need. It rejected the proposition, and rejected offering student loans rather than grants, on the grounds that both would discourage many of the ablest veterans from going to college. The country needed them back in school to "overcome the educational shortages caused by the war."[16] (It was later estimated that about 20 percent of the veterans who went to college would not have done so without the GI Bill.)

Notwithstanding the bill's silence on financial need, its ethos came increasingly to favor the underdog as different versions of it jostled their way through Congress. A medley of legislators, including northern conservatives and southern populists, waged an effective and remarkably explicit class war against plans to restrict the bill's student aid to winners of competitive scholarships or those who had already started further education.[17] As it turned out, middle-class veterans who had already started higher education or intended to were the most likely to go to college on the bill, but campuses did acquire more working-class and "plebeian" students.[18] And despite white southern fears about empowering black veterans, the final bill did extend opportunities to African American males. Women generally lost out, as they were so small a fraction of the armed services. They made up less than 3 percent of GI Bill students.[19]

The GI Bill's most clear-cut legacy was to open the way for subsequent, if smaller, veterans' aid bills, culminating in the Montgomery Bill of 1985, the first veterans' aid program for peacetime soldiers.[20] In 1976–77, when new federal aid to nonveterans (Pell grants) was well established, Vietnam War and other veterans' benefits still came to nearly half of all federal spending on student grants. Outside the military, the GI Bill produced no direct heirs, and viewed statistically over the long term, the upsurge in college enrollment after World War II was only a blip in an expansion that was occurring anyway.[21]

We should not, though, underestimate the bill's dramatic effects. The bulge in college enrollments triggered by the GI Bill, and the academic success of the veterans as serious students, showed that far more of the population could do good work in college than many experts had thought possible.[22] In the early stages of the GI Bill legislation, intellectual opinion had divided as to whether an influx of veterans would lower college standards. The veterans did increase demand for more vocational courses, but their diligence and ability strengthened the case for widening college access through financial aid—ultimately federal aid. For the rest of the century, champions of federal student aid were apt to cite the GI Bill as a noble precedent.

IN THE MEANTIME IT was no easy matter to build an effective consensus behind federal aid to nonveterans. The story of the U.S. President's Commission on Higher Education bears this out.

Established by Harry Truman in 1946 and largely composed of public- and private-college presidents, the commission was chaired by George Zook, president of the American Council on Education, the umbrella organization of American college associations. In the war Zook (who had worked through the University of Kansas as a hearse driver) had helped extend the coverage of the GI Bill to all veterans with some service. The idea for the commission came out of government and academic liberal thinking about educational inequality and wasted human resources. (A 1944 study proposed federal grants for needy high school students.)[23]

The commission's reports, published in 1947 and 1948, estimated that half the college-age population was capable of two years of college, and a third could do four years or more. The gap between this and reality—15 percent of eighteen- to twenty-one-year-olds in college—meant failure, in the commission's eyes, to live up to American democratic ideals and a "loss of talent—our most precious natural resource." Condemning college discrimination against blacks and Jews, the commission also stressed inequalities of educational opportunity between classes and communities.

The commission strongly supported the view that modern life had a social and technological complexity that required more education and created more demand for it. The start of the cold war made all this more urgent. Likewise, the defense of liberties required an "alert [and] educated citizenry." That idea went back to Jefferson, but the commission believed that the "citizenry" now needed higher levels of understanding to cope with the diversity of America's peoples and its new immersion in world affairs.

Among its various proposals for enlarging and renovating higher education, the commission called on the states to extend and enrich their two-year community colleges, with help from federal grants to public institutions. It also proposed federal scholarships for at least a fifth of non-veteran undergraduates, as well as graduate fellowships. Far bigger than today's Pell grants, the scholarships would vary according to the student's financial need up to eight hundred dollars (then about 80 percent of Harvard tuition, room, and board). Treading carefully around state-federal relations, the commission outlined a formula allocating the scholarships to the states on the basis of the number of high school graduates and eighteen- to twenty-one-year-olds in each.

For states with low high school graduation rates, the commission tentatively proposed giving high school scholarships to bring up the rates. State agencies would select all recipients, first on financial need and then on other factors including "the applicant's ability, character, [and] sense of responsibility."[24]

The Zook Commission reports, when published, garnered substantial support, including endorsements from *Life* magazine and the *New York Times*. Most college presidents, of private as well public institutions, approved of federal scholarships—more than of direct federal aid to their institutions. Some leading college presidents and educators, however, attacked the educational expansionism that underpinned the commission's call for federal student aid. The main criticisms were that inflating the college population would lower standards and encourage vocationalism while (according to other critics) producing too many graduates to be employed; that federal aid to public colleges would mean too much government control and would handicap private colleges; and that the commission trusted too naïvely in education to solve everything.[25]

President Truman publicly endorsed the commission reports, and his administration tried twice to introduce a scholarship bill, albeit scaled down from what the Zook Commission proposed. By then, however, Truman was preoccupied with the Korean War, and key administration officials were divided over student grants versus loans—which the Zook Commission had dismissed as unpopular with students.[26] Along with numerous bills for federal student aid in the late 1940s and 1950s, the administration bills did not get through Congress. Community colleges, the item perhaps dearest to the commissioners' hearts, continued to multiply but not with federal help.

Conservative forces in Congress were a big obstacle to federal student aid. A leader of the resistance was Graham ("Judge") Barden, a crusty Democrat from North Carolina and dictatorial chairman of the House Committee on Education and Labor. Although he had been a key legislative proponent of the GI Bill, he generally hated the idea of federal aid to education as he did most federal initiatives involving liberal causes. (Curiously, he was the official House sponsor of the administration's unsuccessful 1950 aid bill. One suspicion was that he introduced the bill to placate his wife, a former schoolteacher and local library trustee, before killing it in committee.)[27]

When the champions of federal student aid finally got a bill passed—the National Defense Education Act of 1958 (NDEA)—they did so by focusing on the science and technology needs of a nation increasingly worried by what seemed to be the superior rigor of Soviet schools. The shock waves in 1957 caused by Russia's launching of Sputnik, the first space satellite, were deliberately used by aid advocates, though many of them had wider social purposes than beefing up the nation's sciences. In fact high-level proposals for science scholarships as well as graduate fellowships went back to 1944, but NDEA only got passed by substituting a loan program for a scholarship program.[28]

In the policy disputes that led to NDEA, the scholarship proponents, led by liberals within the administration and Congress, largely followed the Zook Commission script, though they divided on several issues, including how much weight to place on student merit versus financial need. The opposition, which included some of the elite-college establishment, feared excessive federal control of education and questioned whether student grants would be cost-effective. Some midwestern state-college leaders believed that federal scholarships would draw talent away to eastern private colleges. Congressional conservatives, in particular, distrusted anything that might undermine student initiative and readiness to make sacrifices for a college education. (No such concern was voiced about students with rich parents.)[29]

The act, as finally passed, made various provisions for teaching development and graduate fellowships, but its centerpiece was the undergraduate loan program. A college could received loan money according to its enrollment size, provided it chipped in a dollar for every nine dollars in federal loans. The loans were interest-free through one year after graduation, then 3 percent per annum. The college chose the loan recipients, but they had to have some financial need, and the college was supposed to prefer students with "a superior academic background" who wished to teach school or those whose "academic background [indicated] a superior capacity or preparation in science, mathematics, engineering, or a modern foreign language." Including languages met the concern that Americans needed to be better equipped to understand and operate in a dangerous world.[30]

Passed just after the heyday of McCarthyism, NDEA required loan recipients to swear an oath of allegiance to the United States and sign an affidavit disclaiming revolutionary connections. Some leading colleges objected to these requirements as discriminatory and refused to take part until the affidavit requirement was withdrawn in 1962. Some college presidents also wanted more direct aid to the colleges themselves. In the meantime, several colleges substituted or expanded their own loan funds instead of using the NDEA funds.

NDEA did retain a grant element: loan recipients could get up to half their loan forgiven by teaching in the public schools—10 percent off for each year of teaching up to five years. This attracted women and roughly cancelled out the male bias of the preference for sciences and technology.[31] The stress on "academic background," however, discouraged colleges from using the loans to help disadvantaged students; extending educational opportunity took a backseat to NDEA's concept of national needs. Even so, a beachhead had been established for federal student aid and a subsequent expansion of student loans.

Federal Aid Established (1960s–Present)

Seven years after NDEA, a very different student-aid bill was enacted: Title IV of the 1965 Higher Education Act. It gave money to colleges for Educational Opportunity Grants (EOGs) for low-income students with "exceptional financial need." The colleges in return were required, rather vaguely, to make "vigorous" efforts to find such students. Title IV also created a new subsidized loan program—interest-free through college and reduced interest thereafter—for low- and middle-income students.[32]

The previous year, under the 1964 Economic Opportunity Act, the College Work-Study program had revived the New Deal's funding of student jobs, and by 1968 there were three special schemes (the Trio programs) for encouraging disadvantaged students to go to college.

These measures set up the basic pattern of federal aid that is with us today: grants and outreach programs focusing on low-income students, loans and jobs for many more.

The 1960s programs were part of President Lyndon Johnson's "War on Poverty," but they had roots in the previous administration. John F. Kennedy had tried to get a federal need-based scholarship program but had failed: he had a weak position in Congress, and as the first Catholic president, he was vulnerable to suspicions that he might use federal aid to education to breach the constitutional separation of church and state. The church-state issue was not new: it had bedeviled aid to education bills in the 1950s. Other opposition to Kennedy's scholarship proposals was much the same as in the 1950s, too, though more stress was now put on their cost.[33]

Despite this failure, the Kennedy administration left an important legacy: it officially recognized the problem of poverty amid affluence. Appalachia had been vividly featured in Kennedy's 1960 election campaign, and the Kennedy White House was receptive to a growing stream of analyses and exposés of poverty-related problems, including the need for "retraining" the disadvantaged. The civil rights movement may have been a spur: in the spring and summer of 1963, it moved onto northern streets with protests against unemployment and low wages as well as direct discrimination. By that autumn, President Kennedy had told his staff that he wanted major antipoverty legislation the following year.[34]

On succeeding the assassinated president in November 1963, Lyndon Johnson seized the campaign against poverty as a way to make his mark in history. His landslide election victory in 1964 made the ambition possible. Johnson's approach to poverty stressed empowerment of the poor themselves, including educational opportunity. It was a theme that connected with his own past, as he had borrowed money to go through teachers' college, had taught poor Mexican Americans, and had later served as Texas director of the New Deal's National Youth Administration.[35]

Most of the planning for Johnson's student-aid programs came before the black urban riots that started in 1964, but the emergency atmosphere of the riots helped get the programs enacted. So, more generally, did the civil rights movement, by highlighting the issue of equal opportunity. The civil rights movement gave federal student aid a new moral high ground, though Johnson and others also justified it as a national economic investment.[36]

Meanwhile, the sheer growth of higher education, especially state and community colleges, gave credence to the belief that almost everyone should be able to go to college and that government aid could help make it possible. Although the new EOGs were far smaller than GI Bill benefits, they could halve the cost of going to a free or low-tuition community college. (Ironically, the community-college lobby itself was cool to EOGs, preferring direct federal subsidies supporting free tuition across the board. This position was no flash in the pan, as we will see.)[37]

The Higher Education Act, like the whole poverty program, raised expectations. Equity-oriented social scientists, who flourished in the 1960s, soon saw the gulf between aid and reality: poor people and black people remained far less likely to go to college than the white middle class. The Carnegie Commission's report *Quality and Equality* (1968) noted that 50 percent of high school graduates with "high ability" but low family income did not go on to college—a loss to the nation as well as a failure of social justice—and that EOGs reached only 225,000 students, less than 4 percent of all undergraduates.[38]

There were also differences and inequalities between colleges and between states in how EOGs were allocated, and students did not know if they would get EOGs until colleges had admitted them.[39] In early 1969, a government report, mainly written by the economist Alice Rivlin, Assistant Secretary of Health, Education, and Welfare, proposed a big new program of direct grants to students, enabling all to "pursue a postsecondary education."[40]

In 1972, the ideas of Rivlin and others bore fruit. By then, the financial costs of the Vietnam War were no longer escalating, and the campus rebellions against the war, which had antagonized many members of Congress toward students, had subsided. The result was the Basic Educational Opportunity Grant (BEOG), later named the Pell grant after its chief congressional architect, Senator Claiborne Pell of Rhode Island. It was the first major federal aid program not born in emergency, though we could see it as a second-stage product of the 1960s turmoil.

All students with low and lower-middle family incomes qualified for a BEOG. By 1975 one in five college freshmen was getting one, as well as many students at vocational trade schools. The grants were scaled according to family income and some kinds of assets but could not exceed 50 percent of total college costs. (The limit was raised later to 60 percent and then eliminated in 1992.) The grants were scaled down for part-time students. Actual amounts depended on annual appropriations by Congress, but the original "authorized" maximum of fourteen hundred dollars (more than actually appropriated) was supposed to approximate average costs, other than tuition, of going to a community college. As if to prepare for BEOGs, the growth of community colleges had accelerated in the late 1960s.

The original EOGs of 1965 were renamed Supplemental Educational Opportunity Grants (SEOGs). Colleges processed both grants but had more leeway, within limits, to select which needy students got what amount of SEOG money. Today colleges vary in how they distribute SEOGs, but they were intended, in part, to help make private colleges more affordable for low-income students.[41]

In 1975, a third federal grant program, the State Student Incentive Grants (SSIGs), started providing money for state aid programs on a matching basis, "dollar for dollar." Later renamed, inelegantly, the Leveraging Educational Assistance Partnership (LEAP), SSIGs encouraged states to set up general need-related scholarship programs. At the start of the decade, most states did not have them; by 1979, they all did.

Federal spending on SSIGs was relatively small (always under 4 percent of the amount spent on Pell grants), but SSIGs represented a distinctively American, and federal, way of doing things: using financial incentives based on numerical formulas to influence and encourage rather than command and control. SSIGs were in fact more successful at seeding new programs than expanding big preexisting ones.[42]

The federal measures that culminated in the SSIG program were a victory for proponents of government aid to students over those who wanted direct assistance to colleges (some wanted both). In the debates and maneuvering that led to the Pell grant legislation—the 1972 Higher Education Act Amendments—there was genuine concern that extensive federal student aid would encourage colleges to raise their prices in order to take advantage of the added purchasing power given their customers.

Direct federal support for colleges, on the other hand, might enable them to hold down their prices.[43]

Ten years later, during the Reagan administration, Secretary of Education William Bennett claimed that expanded federal student aid did indeed cause "'greedy" colleges to jack up their prices. Subsequent studies were divided as to whether this happened at public colleges; it did not at private colleges, where federal aid was a smaller part of charges.[44]

SINCE THE MID-1970S, TWO other themes have stood out amid the twists and turns of recent federal-aid history: conflict between class interests and the growth of federal loans, prompting efforts to make the loans less onerous. One argument for expanding federally guaranteed loans of different kinds was that the private loan market would not by itself provide enough for students because of their lack of collateral. But that did not answer the question of whose loans should be subsidized.[45]

Following the government's effort to target aid on low- and lower-

Figure 3. Financial Aid Outlays, 1974–2000, by Major Types of Aid (in billions of constant 2001 US dollars)

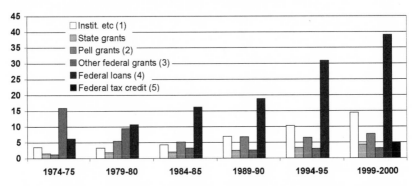

Based on data in College Board, *Trends in Student Aid 2002* (New York: College Board, 2002), pages 7 and 19. Excludes federal work-study funds paid to colleges, and non-federal loans.

1. Grants by colleges and private donors.
2. Pell grants began 1973–74.
3. Includes aid allotted via states and colleges, veterans and other military-related aid, and social-security college aid for surviving dependents (until it was phased out in the mid-1980s).
4. Includes unsubsidized loans (still under general market interest rates).
5. Started 1998-99.

middle-income students, the upper-middle classes sought relief too. Federally subsidized loans had in fact been designed for them as well as for poorer students. Unlike Pell grant recipients, students taking these loans did not have to be below a certain income level; they just had to show financial need. An upper-middle-income student at a high-cost private college could qualify.

In 1978 the government went further. To head off expensive demands for tax credits on tuition costs, which would favor richer students, the Middle Income Student Assistance Act opened subsidized loans to all students, regardless of need. (This was actually a replay of 1965, when need-related subsidized loans were themselves a political alternative to tuition tax credits.) In 1981, the Reagan administration, driving hard to cut the federal budget, got the financial need requirement restored.

Pell grants, too, were subject to class struggle and changing eligibility as middle-class interests tried to make them available to more middle-income students. This meant that Pell appropriations were spread thinner to more students.[46]

Underlying these battles was the long-term erosion of all Pell grants compared to college costs and the relative shift in federal aid from grants to loans. This caused worries that, among other things, high debt levels would steer graduates away from low-paying social-service careers.

To ease the burdens, the Clinton administration introduced two initiatives in 1992–93. Through community service in AmeriCorps, participants could earn a stipend plus a college grant or credit against student loans. Secondly, an "income-contingent" loan plan, already piloted at ten colleges, gave students the option of paying off their loans at a rate determined by their subsequent income. After twenty-five years, any remaining loan would be forgiven.

Both schemes were controversial and still are. Aimed to stem a supposed loss of community spirit in the land, AmeriCorps has earned more praise for its call to social service than for helping students. The grant or loan credit ($4,725 in 1993 and the same ten years later) did not seem a great bargain for a year's work at near minimum wage.

The program was funded to cover less than 2 percent of college students. Five years after it started, only half its participants had used its educational benefits.[47]

Income-contingent loans have been discussed since Milton Friedman proposed them in 1955. Duke and Yale experimented with them in the 1970s, but in one form or another they are centuries old. Some economists fear they will attract mainly low earners and be expensive to finance, as many borrowers won't pay much back—a proposition that will take time to prove or disprove. Among financial aid officers there has also been a worry that the extended periods for repaying the loans will lead students into huge accumulated interest repayments. Few students in fact have opted for them.[48]

There is a deeper charge against federal student aid as a whole: it has not reduced educational inequality. Bigger proportions of low-income high school students and of black students go on to college now than did in 1970, but their chances of doing so have not increased relative to richer students and white students, and their chances of getting bachelor degrees have actually fallen behind the others.'[49] Expert commentators on federal student aid seldom criticize the basic concept of Pell grants. They do fault their level of funding, though some would put more emphasis on outreach programs gearing low-income youth to college.

Class issues also figured in the matter of family tax credits for college expenses. The Clinton administration finally introduced them in 1997, with wide congressional support, in response to college price inflation. Costing over half as much as Pell grants, the new benefits were better armored than Pells because they did not depend on annual appropriations.

Critics of the tax credits argued (and still do) that they mainly benefited middle-class students, with significant taxable family income, who would go to college anyway. And low-income students, dependent on grant aid, had to subtract their aid from the college costs that could be covered by the tax credits. Tax-credit defenders noted that the credits were "progressive" in the tax-law sense, fading out entirely for families with gross adjusted incomes above $100,000. Clinton's secretary of education, Richard W. Riley, observed that over half the tax-credit recipients had family incomes under $50,000. Politically, the administration saw the credits as an alternative to tax cuts, not as a substitute for more grant aid.

Critics of the tax credits mainly wanted to get more low-income and disadvantaged students into college. Defenders did not oppose this, but they were equally worried about the heavy burdens of paying for college on middle-income students who were eligible for little or no need-related aid. Here, as ever, student aid had no one purpose.[50]

Looking Back and Across:
Federal Aid and College Aid

Before the 1960s, federal student aid consisted of a series of discrete initiatives. Most were aimed at specific groups considered unusually needy, deserving, or useful and were hatched in urgent circumstances—postwar demobilization, the Great Depression, the Sputnik "crisis." The Zook Commission's proposals in the late 1940s for a wider, more permanent program of federal scholarships produced no direct results, mainly because of congressional opposition, though the commission's reports enriched public discussion of college access and student aid.

The legislation of the 1960s and 1970s put federal aid on a wider base. It combined all three forms of student aid—grants, loans, and support for student jobs—and it did so when many colleges were moving to grant-loan-job packages for their students. The new federal programs, taken as a whole, were also more widely targeted than ever before, with the exception of Depression-era work-study aid. Although a particular concern about black youth and urban disorder had helped bring about the 1960s EOGs, federal loans and some of the grant aid went to a broad band of middle- and lower-income students. As a result, federal aid initiatives did not depend as much on emergency conditions as they had before; government aid now had wide support.

What old and new federal student aid did have in common were values that combined equalizing opportunity with social utility. These appeared, of course, in different mixes, but even the National Defense Student Loan Program, which stressed national security goals (social utility), required recipients to be needy (equalizing opportunity). The GI Bill, it is true, did not require financial need, but its main architects thought of it as extending opportunity to those who would not otherwise have thought seriously of going to college.[51]

THE IDEAS ABOUT STUDENT aid and access embodied in federal programs involved the private sector. None of the programs excluded private-college students, and private-college leaders participated in congressional hearings and general debate on federal student aid. In return these leaders felt they had to justify in public-interest terms their own admissions and financial aid policies.

They had, at the same time, to balance the public-interest dimension with the demands of market survival and competition in a way that the federal government did not. Merit scholarships are a good example of this. In the late 1990s they were less than 1.5 percent of all federal grant aid to undergraduates and were often tied to specific fields such as science and health care.[52] Compared with individual colleges and states, which compete for talent, the federal government has not had *competitive* incentives to introduce merits. There has been no national "brain drain," prompting special rewards to keep college talent at home. From a national standpoint, federal merits go to students who could and would attend college in the United States anyway, though they may attract them into one field rather than another, as is often their purpose.

But market motives for student aid at the college level have not just been a matter of competition. Before the twentieth century, the market survival of many colleges, public as well as private, depended more on getting students in their area to go to college per se than on luring them competitively to one college rather than another.

This is very old. It goes all the way back to the forbears of American colleges, England's original universities. While benefiting from church subsidies, private endowments, and a royal franchise, medieval Oxford and Cambridge had to justify their existence by attracting a good number of students (including many who would not automatically seek further education) and then train them for the priesthood, law, and public administration. We begin the next part of this book by going back to that era, to the English origins of American student aid and a period in which public policy and college purposes were tightly entwined.[53]

PART II
The Way of Elite Colleges

4

The Roots of Student Aid

In England and elsewhere in Europe, the idea of aiding poor students—especially "clerks" or church students—was well established by the thirteenth century. When the city fathers of Oxford lynched some clerks in an ugly town-gown episode in 1209, the penalties levied on Oxford by the pope included semiannual grants and an annual feast for poor students, as well as curbs on student rents and food prices.[1]

Aid for medieval students came from many sources—the crown, bishops and dioceses, local benefactors, and colleges themselves. And before universities were fully established, rival "masters" offered tuition discounts to get more students to take their lectures.[2]

Types of aid varied, from free places given in return for doing college chores to access to kitchen leftovers or a license to beg like a mendicant priest. Some fee remissions foreshadowed today's "income-contingent" loans: recipients were supposed to pay them back if they came to "fatter fortune."

Why provide all this? The starting point was Jesus' care of the poor and afflicted, linked to the idea of supporting pious learning. Wealthy philanthropists found a niche here, funding the studies of "chantry scholars" who would then pray for their benefactor's soul. More importantly, the church looked on poor students as a pool of future priests and administrators; the church ran much of the country's legal apparatus, but priestly work did not attract the rich and well-born.[3]

Student aid, though, seldom reached the poorest. It required basic literacy, and some scholarships explicitly excluded villeins (serfs). Loans were interest free, in line with the church's ban on usury, but they often required the deposit of a book—a costly item in those days—or a goblet, a cloak, or a piece of furniture.

The commonest beneficiaries were the ambitious sons of tradesmen and yeomen (small farmers), relatives of clergy, and those who caught the eye of a local patron. Richer students sometimes took along servants and poorer comrades and subsidized their studies; they might be useful later if they rose to high office.

The results of all this were uneven. Educational opportunity depended on luck, on where you lived and who you knew as much as on merit and need. By the early 1500s, too, in France as well as England, there were plenty of complaints that colleges were giving free places to the wealthy and privileged, though upper-class students seldom deigned to graduate.[4]

Yet the tradition of aiding poor students had staying power, surviving England's transition from Catholicism to Protestantism. In the late sixteenth and early seventeenth centuries, the typical donor of endowed scholarships was a rich merchant or lawyer, devoutly evangelical, who gave as an act of constructive Christian charity, earning social respect in this world and good marks in the next. Such people believed that giving to schools as well as colleges could help aspiring and promising youth to rise out of "vicious" poverty and ungodly ignorance. They believed, too, that assisting poor scholars, often bound for the church, could build an educated and active clergy, shining light into dark places.[5]

Colonial Colleges

These ideas carried over to the New World—directly so as several scholarship donors to America's first college, Harvard (founded in 1636), were London merchants. Well into the nineteenth century, the college looked on student aid as a way of attracting "useful" talent to the ministry.[6] Church connections could even trump financial need in determining who got aid. Samuel Mather, class of 1723, son of the famous church leader and writer Cotton Mather, had a scholarship given by Thomas Hollis, a London Baptist merchant, which required both piety and need. Piety he had in plenty—he told tales on classmates for reading "vicious" works— but needy he was not.[7]

In general, though, Harvard's grant aid went to poorer students. Its biggest scholarship donors in the colonial period were far more apt to require that recipients be "poore" or needy, preferably kinfolk, than to stipulate piety or future service in holy orders.[8] The college itself did not confine its grant aid to ministerial students as some other colleges did in their early years. It saw aid more widely as a way of recruiting poor and promising students to become enlightened leaders against "barbarism, ignorance, and irreligion."[9]

In addition to endowed scholarships, student aid at colonial Harvard included college loans and jobs. A seventeenth-century Harvard student might do clerical work, wait on table, monitor attendance at prayers, be a chapel bell-ringer, mind the college fire engine, or serve as a "scholar of the house" (building superintendent). The college usually gave these jobs to those who needed them, but a useful and pleasing fellow could stack up several. Jonathan Ince, class of 1650, met all his expenses by mending pots and pans while doubling as president's secretary and college butler (head servant).[10]

This array of jobs, coupled with the scholarships and loans, helped Harvard expand its social reach. In its first two decades, its students came almost entirely from the professional and propertied gentry. By the 1670s, a good third were the sons of artisans, tradesmen, small farmers, and a few seamen and other workers.[11]

But the trend did not last. As we saw in the prologue, grant aid (and probably other aid too) fell back in the eighteenth century. The college concentrated its spending and fund-raising on getting more faculty to teach a growing range of subjects. Financial aid did not keep pace with increased enrollment.[12]

Somewhat the same thing happened at Dartmouth. Eleazar Wheelock, a Congregationalist minister, founded the college in 1769 as a biracial (Indian-white) institution for training Indian missionaries as well as generally combating the "ignorance and irreligion" of a "remote" and "poor" region, New Hampshire. White and Native American students worked together clearing land and erecting buildings. Half of them were "charity students," getting free tuition in return for later service as missionaries. By the 1790s, however, the missionary and interracial zeal had run out (Wheelock died in 1779). Expensive upgrading, as at Harvard, combined with parlous finances, induced the college to find more full payers and discontinue free places and the admission of Indians (always a minority anyway). The college did, though, reduce tuition for needy students and let them defer their payments.[13]

THE IMPORTANCE ATTACHED TO aid also varied from one institution to another. Like the leaders and patrons of Harvard and Dartmouth, the founders of America's second oldest college, William and Mary (founded 1693), believed strongly in student aid. From the outset, the college gave free tuition and maintenance to ministerial students, supposedly chosen for their "poverty . . . ingeniousness, learning, piety, and good behaviour," who would take Christianity to the "barbaric Indians."[14]

By contrast, Yale (founded 1701) and the College of Rhode Island (later Brown, founded 1764) gave almost no grants. They provided a few student jobs but concentrated more on keeping down costs and charges for everyone with a simple curriculum. In Yale's case, annual subsidies from the Connecticut legislature helped make its charges less "burthensome."[15]

King's College (later Columbia, founded 1754) was different again. Of America's nine colleges in the late eighteenth century, only King's could meet all its running costs from investment income.[16] Yet it kept its charges unusually high—well beyond the reach of manual workers and small farmers—and gave little if any aid. The Anglican merchants and lawyers who controlled King's had no wish to build a proselytizing ministry, and they felt numerous and prosperous enough to keep the college for their own sort.[17]

This was not for lack of other ideas. Edward Antill, a founding donor to King's, wanted to fund a special corps of talented poor boys. Set apart within the college, in a sort of honors program giving "a more liberal Education," they would go forth after graduation to find others like them whom they could prepare for college entry. This would produce a "succession of men" for high office and promote "a general taste for polite learning." Antill argued that few rich students had "great abilities" or diligence, whereas the college's power to give opportunity for poor youth—and take it away—gave it a carrot and stick with which to keep them "close to their studies."[18]

Antill's ideas got nowhere with the college, nor did similar proposals by others. Not till after the Revolution, when the college's governors became more diverse and outward looking, did the newly named Columbia

College cease to be a top-priced institution—partly because of competition from the College of New Jersey (Princeton).[19]

THE MEDIEVAL IDEA OF recruiting poor students (only males of course) for the church and social leadership played out differently at different colonial colleges. Much depended on the finances and markets of each college, but much depended, too, on the values of college founders and supporters. Many had a paternal and pragmatic sense of justice: they wanted to select and support "deserving" poor students so they could be more "useful" to society. This attitude would never die (in different language it drives much of student aid today), but it would be challenged in the nineteenth century by more expansive demands for educational democracy and opportunity, ultimately for women as well as men.

The Impact of the Revolution

The American Revolution did not revolutionize student aid. Certainly it did not do so via students themselves. The upheaval made students more turbulent and more intolerant of college rules and traditional deference, but their protests were often led by well-heeled "blades" whose outlook was not particularly egalitarian, at least not in a socioeconomic sense. When Harvard prescribed in 1786 a simple uniform for its students and banned the wearing of silk, to "lessen the expense of dress" and promote "home manufactures," it required stiff fines to enforce the rules, and over time the requirements were eroded.[20] (This was not the last time that students would resist sumptuary rules designed to curb extravagant differences of dress.)

Indirectly, though, the Revolution did promote student aid—in two ways. First, the Revolution, and the Louisiana Purchase that followed it in 1803, released a burst of settlement west of the original colonies, no longer constrained by British controls and French power. The expansion featured colleges even more than people. Most colleges founded between the Revolution and the Civil War appeared west of the former colonial territory, whereas most of the population remained within it.

As already mentioned in Chapter 2, the Revolutionary value on religious freedom and equality encouraged a variety of churches to flourish. Each of them wanted to have its own colleges, and many were eager to train ministers and other graduates to promote Christian civilization on the frontier. The result was a proliferation of colleges amid a sparse population. To survive, the colleges had to charge low prices and provide "charity" aid and easy credit.

The second link between the Revolution and student aid was ideological. Hereditary privilege and "aristocratic" exclusiveness were discredited. Instead, the new republic was often seen to require an educated citizenry and a good supply of leaders, provided by schools and colleges open to rising talent. These ideas figured strongly in the founding of colleges during the early decades of the republic, but they persisted through the nineteenth century[21] In this context, scholarship aid was at least as important *symbolically,* aligning colleges with republican, antiaristocratic virtue, as for anything it did materially for students.

No one college reflected all the trends bearing on student aid after the Revolution, but Williams College, founded in 1793, exemplified several, before it fell on good times later in the century. Williams really started in 1791 as a "free school" endowed for fifteen pupils, the legacy of Colonel Ephraim Williams, who was killed fighting the French in 1755. Stationed at Fort Massachusetts, the province's far western outpost, Williams established the endowment in gratitude to the local village, West Township, which had provided him with recruits. The endowment also required the township to change its name to Williamstown.

The Free School in Williamstown did not open till after the Revolution, but it was then quickly transformed into a college, a cheaper alternative to Harvard, the only other college in the state. In applying for a state charter as Williams College, the Free School trustees said they wanted to bring a "liberal education . . . within the power of the middling and lower classes of Citizens." This was very like the founding ideas behind Maine College (Bowdoin), established a year later, but the trustees had wider ambitions too: they hoped to attract "young gentlemen from every part of the Union." The Free School became, in effect, a fee-charging academy affiliated with the college—a change that violated Colonel Williams's will in the eyes of some townsfolk.[22]

Violation or not, early presidents and faculty of Williams genuinely cared for poor boys as well as needing them to keep up enrollment. In 1799, President Ebenezer Fitch worried about the loss of students "who leave us thro' mere poverty." Major relief did not appear till 1811 when Woodbridge Little, a local cleric turned lawyer and a founding trustee of the college, gave Williams its first big gift, followed by a legacy (he died in 1813). The Little endowment provided "charitable aid," giving full support, not just tuition, for poor students of good moral character intending to prepare for the ministry, "whose talents promise eminent usefulness to their profession." Williams was not a sectarian establishment, but like most other colleges of the time, its presidents were ordained ministers, and its faculty was overwhelmingly Congregationalist. Little himself was unusual among scholarship donors in wanting to make sure that the very poorest student could go to the college. His endowment provided extra support in cases of "peculiar need" if highly merited.[23]

In the early decades of the new century, Williams was threatened by competition from even newer colleges, not only Amherst (founded 1821) in western Massachusetts but colleges in Vermont and New York. Enrollment in the 1820s and 1830s fluctuated between just over 130 and less than 90. The problem was the very modern one of how to get enough students who could pay full fees while helping those who could not. The Little endowment's concentration on full support for poor students reduced the number of students it could help (probably never more than about 15 percent of enrollment, if that).[24] In 1822, an anxious president Edward Dorr Griffin asked his trustees, "How shall we provide for the increasing number of poor & pious youth who have their eye toward our college?" Faced with falling enrollment in 1836, the president and his five professors took substantial pay cuts, over half of which was spent on remitting tuitions.

From the 1840s on, Williams's market improved, at least financially, as growing numbers of prosperous families in New York, Albany, and other cities came to look upon college education as a mark of refinement. There was a noticeable shift in the Williams student body from the "half-bumpkin, half-scholar figures" described by Nathaniel Hawthorne at Williams in 1838 to fashionably dressed young men. Mark Hopkins, Williams's longtime president (1836–1872), was pleased to get students from modest country backgrounds, but he was also proud to recruit from families of "high standing."[25] As the college grew and acquired new facilities (including fraternities in 1857), student aid did not keep pace with expanding enrollment and rising charges.

The same happened at other colleges, and it amounted to a process of cyclical change. In the early nineteenth century, institutions like Williams and Amherst were the new, cheap colleges; by the late nineteenth century they had abandoned that role to a newer wave of state and urban colleges, though they never renounced all claim to social democracy.[26] Running through this history of change was a medley of fears, hopes, and experiments involving student aid. Three overlapping themes stand out: the search for enrollments and markets, religious and spiritual variations, and movements for educational democracy and opportunity.

Finding a Market

We saw in Chapter 2 that American colleges were often founded ahead of demand. The heyday of this was the first half of the nineteenth century.

The expansive optimism of early nineteenth-century college founders resembled that of the great continental railroad builders. In both cases, the investment rested on faith that customers, with some inducement, would follow. Many colleges were founded in communities that had no elementary or secondary school: as late as 1900 less than 7 percent of thirteen- to eighteen-year-olds were in school.[27] Colleges often created their own in-house feeder schools, "preparatory departments," and through most of the century, pupils in these departments frequently outnumbered students in the degree-giving "collegiate" or "academic" divisions. Despite these buttresses, colleges were often miniscule. Average college enrollment did not reach a hundred till the 1880s.[28]

93 (1840)
116 (1850)
120 (1860)
wrong!

The impulse to build colleges in a raw environment was largely religious, but it was also fed by local community ambition, spawning what Daniel Boorstin called "the booster college."[29] Colleges were often started by an alliance between an energetic clergyman and leading citizens, eager to advance their community in cultural repute as well as trade. Booster colleges and other grassroots movements for higher education in the nineteenth century exposed a remarkable dualism in the culture. Respect for advanced education (the power of learning as well as the traditional trappings of academe) coexisted with an anti-intellectual preference for the "school of hard knocks" over bookishness, for experience over "useless" and even "dangerous" theorizing.[30]

This mix of attitudes meant that enthusiasm for founding colleges was not matched by desire to attend them. Yet colleges usually depended on student tuition fees in the absence of large and reliable subsidies from government and private donors, though gifts were important too. Ironically, this very dependence on tuition revenue made colleges more ready to discount or defer (lend) tuition payments, to make sure of getting

enough students who would pay at least something. Enrollment problems, similarly, often encouraged colleges to offer advanced placement to
students, admitting them as sophomores or even juniors.[31]

Student aid was also a way of raising money for the college from donors. This led many colleges, and not just obscure ones, into "perpetual"
(or "proprietary") scholarship schemes. These schemes flourished especially from the 1830s to the 1850s. For a specified sum, often five hundred
dollars, a college would sell to the donor and his heirs or nominees (the
rules varied) the right to a tuition-free place at the college in perpetuity.
On the face of it these plans looked more viable than other get-rich-quick
schemes that flourished at mid-century, appealing to an American mixture of curiosity, practical enterprise, and gullibility. In a period when college tuition commonly ranged from twenty to sixty dollars a year, a five-
hundred-dollar donation was the equivalent of a lot of tuition revenue. It
seemed almost costless, too, as the perpetual-scholarship holder did not
necessarily replace a tuition-paying student. In the long run, however, the
schemes locked colleges into a flow of students, not necessarily needy or
meritorious, who were financial deadweights.

The schemes also failed because colleges usually adopted them to get
out of financial straits: the money vanished into operating costs rather
than going into major new investments enhancing the college's quality
and standing. Colleges that fell for the schemes usually ended up decades
later buying back the scholarship rights (an expensive business) or using
legal ruses to cancel or get round them.[32]

A more prudent market use of scholarships aimed at a coattails effect,
cultivating sources of students who might enroll along with the scholarship winners. In the late 1820s, Columbia was offering a free tuition place
to any preparatory school sending it five students in a year. In 1830, Columbia's trustees, alarmed at the imminent founding of a rival University
of the City of New York (later NYU), expanded these scholarship offers
into a city goodwill policy. They gave two full-tuition scholarships apiece
to the High School of New York City, the city corporation (city government), the General Society of Mechanics and Tradesmen of New York
City, and the Clinton Hall Association for worker education.

Columbia also offered two ministerial scholarships to every church
denomination in the city.[33] The university, by and large, was never a very
churchly institution, but it could not ignore the importance of the ministry as a college market.

Religious Variations

Student aid, it will now be obvious, was an important meeting point between colleges and churches. Through assistance for ministerial and other "pious" students, colleges used churches to find a market and raise money, while churches used colleges to train clergy and promote religion. The fact that so many college presidents were clerics reinforced the relationship.

At Presbyterian Princeton, a trustee-faculty report in 1896 showed that market motives and religion could still be a potent mix at the end of the century. According to the report, the college's tuition "remissions," amounting to a $100 discount off $150 full tuition and mostly paid for out of general funds, strengthened the college financially and spiritually as well as attracting academically superior but needy students. Without the aid, the report estimated, Princeton would lose at least a hundred students to "less expensive institutions." At fifty dollars each, this was the pay of three professors. On the spiritual front, two-thirds of the aid went to ministers' sons and ministerial students. They supplied a core "evangelical" community at a time when the faculty had become more secular and specialized (and, they might have added, more and more students were not Presbyterians).[34]

Not that colleges and churches always agreed about student aid. Some denominations took time to be persuaded that ministers should be college graduates. Despite the Baptists' Rhode Island College, Baptists and Methodists generally took longer than other major sects to accept college training for ministers, believing in the primacy of spiritual experience and the importance of being close to the people.[35] In 1854, Rev. W. E. Pell of the North Carolina Education Society, a Methodist body formed to "assist young men" studying to become traveling preachers, wrote in some annoyance to President Braxton Craven of Normal College (later renamed Trinity College and then Duke University). The society, said Pell, was supporting students for too long at the college and without enough consultation. To do the church's work, the students did not usually need to take the full array of subjects required to graduate. Pell recognized, though, that some college study was useful training for his itinerant ministers, and he allowed that in "special cases" students might merit support from the society "until they graduate." Ironically, President Craven himself had just completed a year of fund-raising for the society.[36]

Whatever the frictions, church-college alliances gave opportunity to students. This is graphically shown by David Allmendinger's study of students from poor New England farms in the first half of the nineteenth century. Though often fired by religious revivalism, they also sought training for the ministry to get away from restrictions at home and move up the social ladder.[37]

A boost for these students came from the Congregationalists' American Education Society (AES), an important actor in Allmendinger's history. Though it operated mainly in New England, the AES was America's first large-scale student-aid organization, transcending the efforts of local charities and individual donors. Founded at Boston in 1815, it had a competitive thrust, facing off a feared expansion of Catholicism while asserting the authority of the college-trained Congregationalist minister against less-educated Baptists and Methodists.[38] At its peak in 1838, the AES was aiding over eleven hundred students in academies and colleges; one in seven New England college students was a beneficiary.

AES aid initially consisted of grants, but after the financial slump of 1819, a shortage of funds forced it to shift to loans. It also became more bureaucratic. Abandoning personal visits to students, it issued students detailed forms ("schedules") for recording their workloads, expenses, and off-campus earnings, to make sure they merited and needed aid. In 1829 both the loans and the bureaucracy provoked a public attack from James Carnahan, the new president of Princeton. Despite Princeton's Presbyterianism, it had several students on AES aid. Carnahan cared deeply about assisting poor students, if they were carefully selected, but he objected to the intrusion of the AES's impersonal, fact-finding forms. As for student loans, the church was the students' "parent, their guardian," and parents should *give* to their children, not "bind" them with "legal bonds" to repay. To do that was to undermine family duty and gratitude.[39]

In the early 1840s the AES went into decline. Many of its loans were not repaid, as the recipients remained poor; the society actually canceled the loans of graduates who went into poor churches or became missionaries. As the country became more secular, the AES found it harder to raise funds. It reduced its beneficiaries drastically and returned to giving grants. In 1874 it merged with another charity and began to shift away from student aid in favor of direct gifts to colleges.[40] It was, nonetheless, the forerunner of modern, systematic approaches to student aid. Carnahan's criticism of its loans and red tape had a modern ring too, but basically he was defending an older pattern, based on personal and informal contact between donors and students.

RELIGIOUS SUPPORT FOR "POOR and pious" students was not confined to training future ministers. It was part of a recurring conflict in many colleges between a puritan paternalism—the strict demands of a devout president and faculty—and the hedonism of well-heeled young students. Yale president Jeremiah Day reflected this conflict in the 1830s when he sought donations for new "charity" scholarships. He looked to families that had had to practice "self-denial," to give the college the right "moral and religious . . . tone." When rich students were too concentrated together, they were prone to laziness, "vice," and conceit about their "accidental advantages."[41]

The famous evangelist Lyman Beecher explored more fully the links between virtue and college access. Beecher was one of a generation of revivalists who called for a moral overhaul of society led by an alliance between ministers and prominent laypeople. In 1815 he published a tract "on the importance of assisting young men of piety and talents in obtaining an education for the Gospel ministry." Two decades later his widely read *Plea for Colleges* (1836) took a broader view of what was needed. It drew on Christian principles for both justice and order.

As Beecher saw it, the moral and mental uplifting of society required more college-educated leaders, recruited by a wide net for talent—just as Jesus, one might add, found his apostles among ordinary fishermen made "fishers of men," who in turn would cast their nets widely. Beecher was a Yale graduate but he was also the son of a blacksmith; he wanted a moral meritocracy but he opposed it to exclusive privilege, and he did so in the language of an American Revolutionary patriot inveighing against royal power: "Colleges and schools . . . break up and diffuse among the people that monopoly of knowledge and mental power which despotic governments accumulate for purposes of arbitrary rule, and bring to the children of the humblest families the select talents and power of her entire population." College life itself, he hopefully declared, was a great equalizer where rich and poor could meet. At the same time, religious discipline could prevent republican freedom from degenerating into a leveling radicalism of insurrection and hate. Religion, in short, should control educational democracy as well as endorsing it.[42]

For Lyman Beecher personally, religious discipline merged with physical exercise and practical work—happy axmanship on big piles of wood—which in his view invigorated and sharpened the mind. Combined with his political views, this made him an active supporter of "manual labor" academies and colleges.[43]

The "manual labor" movement waxed and waned in the 1830s, but in one form or another, its ideas never died. In practical essence a student-support system, it was fueled by a rich mixture of spiritual and social concerns. Originating in Switzerland, the idea of the manual-labor community was given a more religious tone by Washington Gale, a Presbyterian minister. Gale started small, with free tutoring plus room and board for six students who in return worked his New York farm. He then institutionalized the idea, founding the Oneida Institute, a manual-labor academy, in 1829 and Knox Manual Labor College in Illinois (today's Knox College at Galesburg) in 1837. By then the system was widespread: students defrayed much of their costs by supposedly healthy and productive work, two to four hours a day, at college farms and workshops. Under the original system, it was required of all students.[44] (Literally, therefore, it was not targeted student aid in its original form, but as we will see, it soon ceased to be comprehensive, and it is part of student aid's cultural history.)

Rationales for manual labor varied, even in the same state. In Ohio, the Episcopalians' Kenyon College presented it simply as student support, whereas evangelical Oberlin imbued it with a host of hopeful meanings.[45] Depending on the college, the system was seen as a way of keeping students out of mischief, a source of student self-reliance, and a toughly practical training for ministers and missionaries (against Methodist circuit riders who claimed that college was an effete irrelevance).

The most elaborate theory of the system came from Theodore Weld, its great evangelical promoter. For Weld, manual-labor education served a divinely ordered personal unity—the interdependence of mind and body—matching an ideal, "republican" unity of society. Not only did the system bring education "within the reach of the poor" but it bred respect for physical labor and promised to close the "chasm" between an educated class and manual workers.[46] Weld wrote at a time when a growing distance between employers and employees was sharpening concerns about equality and community. Artisans' home workshops, employing apprentice lodgers, had become little factories using labor from outside.[47] In keeping with the times, the manual-labor system was both democratic and entrepreneurial. Bringing student jobs in house and making everyone do them was supposed to put all students on the same footing while sustaining productive enterprises that would help the college economy. The rural isolation of so many colleges, miles away from big labor markets, gave added incentive for creating student work programs.

But they did not succeed. Inexpertly planned and operated, the college farms and workshops lost money, especially after the financial panic of 1837. Many students did not like having "to make brooms and barrels for the good of [our] souls," and as there were often not enough jobs to go round anyway, the schemes soon became voluntary. By the 1850s almost all had petered out.[48]

Despite failure, the idea of integrating study with practical work, providing student support but much more than this, reappeared in different forms and mixes in the nineteenth and twentieth centuries. Some versions were more overtly religious than others, but all involved a search for personal and social unity. The oldest variant was Mount Holyoke's "domestic work" system (1837–1913), but elements also showed up in the movement for agricultural education, the creation of state college farms, and much later, in the 1920s, the "Antioch program," alternating academic study with off-campus work.[49]

Today, the spirit of the old manual-labor schools is most evident in a handful of private colleges that involve all their students in work programs in return for reduced charges. Their historic leader is the Christian but antisectarian Berea College in Kentucky, whose network of craft shops and other enterprises goes back to the 1890s.[50]

Democracy and Opportunity

It was inevitable that evolving concepts of social democracy would rub off on education. The nineteenth century featured a series of movements and demands to extend higher education to new classes and groups. Slavery abolitionists even succeeded, precariously, in founding colleges based on racial coeducation—Oberlin from the 1830s, and Berea in the 1850s, though vigilante threats soon caused Berea to suspend operations till after the Civil War when black colleges were created. The first major scholarship program for black students was established in the 1850s by

Charles Avery, a rich Pittsburgh businessman who was also a Methodist minister.

The strongest push for wider college access occurred in the emerging public sector, but it affected private colleges too. It had two strands. The first, a concept of selective access was embodied in the scheme for public education in Virginia, proposed by Thomas Jefferson in the 1780s and again in 1816–18. Starting with three years of free primary school for "'every person" (whites only), Jefferson envisaged a series of draconian selecting-out stages by which the talented poor, those who survived each stage, would continue to get free schooling. At the apex of the system, ten poor boys a year (no girls) of "superior genius [and] disposition" would go to free-tuition places at the College of William and Mary.

Although Jefferson wanted to spread knowledge among the people, to make them "safe . . . guardians of their own liberty," this approach to college access was to select and support a chosen few rather than expand the whole higher-education system. Jefferson, in fact, did that too in going on to help found the University of Virginia, but he argued anyway that his selective education plan would "activate a mass of mind . . . double or treble what it is in most countries."[51]

Despite this appeal to a young nation's ambitions, Jefferson's plan looked too radical and expensive to get through the Virginia legislature. Legislators also felt that Jefferson was too "atheistic" to be entrusted with the scheme, while William and Mary's brand of religion was too Anglican—a view held by Jefferson himself. But the idea of highly selective scholarships for the needy meritorious did not die. When Harvard's President James Conant, a century later, created a new college program of "national" scholarships, he made much of Jefferson as an educational democrat.[52]

The second strand in the drive for wider access was a crusade to expand higher education itself. Populist expansionism, to give it a name, originated in resentment against Federalist Party elites in the 1790s. It was most fully expressed by Jonathan Turner's call in 1851 for an "industrial university" in Illinois, to be governed by a public "Board of Trust." Turner, and others like him, attacked the domination of colleges by a small professional class. They wanted the traditional, classics-heavy college curriculum extended to include agriculture and other practical subjects, so as to be useful and open to a wide spectrum of people. Turner called them the "industrial classes," all those engaged in "agriculture, commerce and the [mechanical] arts." Their core was that medley of small producers and skilled workers that formed, three years later, the new Republican Party.[53]

Turner's ideas were echoed in the 1850s at a variety of institutions, from the short-lived "people's colleges" of upstate New York—founded by local businessmen, artisans' associations, and farming improvement societies—to the North Carolina Methodists' Normal College (later Trinity and then Duke), whose prospectus rejected "the delusion" that a "finished education" and the "treasures of Science" could only benefit "professional men" and not "the Merchant, the Mechanic, and the Farmer."[54]

The most dramatic product of populist expansionism was the 1862 Morrill Land Grant Act, passed in the Civil War. It gave each state in the Union proceeds from the sale of federal public lands according to the number of U.S. senators and representatives the state had. The state, in turn, had to give the money to one or more colleges, new or existing, provided their teaching included agricultural and "mechanical" subjects. The state colleges, created or augmented by the Morrill Acts (there was a second one for the south in 1890), combined practical courses with liberal arts and sciences and charged little or no tuition. They also provided student aid, usually through work on the college farm, and sometimes also through state scholarships, parceled out to each county or state-assembly district so as not to discriminate geographically.

The spirit of all this was voiced by the businessman-politician who gave the founding endowment for Cornell University just before it received the (much smaller) New York land grant. "I would found an institution," Ezra Cornell famously declared, "where any person can find instruction in any subject." The university's organizers announced that it would be open as cheaply as "welfare and efficiency" allowed to "poor young men and . . . young women . . . without distinction as to class, locality or previous occupation."[55] In a deal with New York state, Cornell got the land grant in return for giving a full-tuition scholarship (about a fifth of student expenses) to one student a year from each assembly district. At one point, in 1880, 41 percent of Cornell students had these scholarships, and from 1874 till well into the twentieth century, all students in the university's state agriculture school got free tuition.[56]

PRIVATE CHURCH COLLEGES, TOO, included champions of low-cost access, as we saw most notably in the manual-labor college movement. Kenyon, for example, was founded in 1829 by Philander Chase, Episcopal bishop of Ohio, to "enable children of the poor" to escape from the "comparative ignorance [compelled by] straitened circumstances," to become schoolteachers "throughout the vast valley of the Mississippi" and to "rise by their merit and wisdom into stations hitherto occupied by the rich." Chase's plan stressed the college's "unexampled cheapness" for all the students (not a wild boast at under seventy-five dollars a year for total expenses), but the low-fee policy was supplemented by jobs on the college farm and some scholarships for theology students and clergymen's sons.[57]

Politically, student aid was also caught up in attacks on public colleges themselves. Opponents of state universities pictured them as citadels of privilege, favoring one class or section of the state, despite their claims to inclusiveness. In the 1870s and early 1880s, the University of North Carolina's state scholarships, awarded by county panels supposedly on the basis of need, "moral character," and "usefulness," were criticized by some for going in fact to the rich, and by others for taking students away from poor church colleges.[58] Private-college presidents sometimes joined anti-intellectual farmers in decrying state colleges as godless institutions; they also feared them as competitors, though not all state universities were cheap, especially in the south. This, again, involved student aid. For a good hundred years, from the 1830s on, there were many who earnestly argued that money was better spent on student aid at existing private colleges than on building new public ones.[59]

Throughout these antagonisms, few leaders or publicists directly attacked the idea of extending college opportunities, in one way or another, to poor students. Private citizens might harbor undemocratic thoughts about wide access to higher education, but stating them from a public position was another matter.

Certainly this was so in the Jacksonian 1830s and 1840s. The historian S. Willis Rudy makes a nice distinction here in describing opposition to a New York City bill of 1847 creating a free municipal academy (the origins of City College). Conservative Whig newspapers attacked the Free Academy on several grounds: it would cost the city too much; its powers were too vague; it would threaten other schools and colleges, for whom scholarships could provide all the access needed by the common people. The editors did not, though, criticize the bill on elitist grounds. They left that to readers' letters, one of which declared that financing the academy's free tuition would be a levy by "the pauper class . . . upon the active, industrious (and if you please, affluent) portion of the country."[60]

The main obstacles to radical extensions of higher education were more indirect and institutional than this. Few colleges could afford massive student assistance; even state universities received limited public support till well into the twentieth century. There were academic barriers, too. Most colleges, even ones that had diversified the curriculum, required Latin, and often Greek too, as well as substantial mathematics and algebra for entrance to their degree programs. To do otherwise, by orthodox standards, was to be less than a real college. That was one reason so many colleges had preparatory departments in the absence of widespread secondary education. The fact remained that preparing for such requirements was a formidable commitment for a poor student.

In reality, then, most students who went to college had some cultural and economic advantages—a background orienting them to learning Latin and Greek and help, or at least encouragement, from family and friends. Even Thomas Jefferson's scholarship plan for poor boys accepted this. Though he believed that "nature" had sown its talents "as liberally among the poor as the rich," he assumed that most college places would go to those whom "the wealth of their parents . . . shall destine to higher degrees of learning."[61]

As we saw earlier, this kind of privilege was attacked by efforts to add practical subjects to the curriculum and extend it to the "industrial classes." The attempt to diversify and democratize the curriculum actually took off in the 1820s. It was not confined to public colleges and practical courses: it could mean teaching languages, mathematics, and other academic subjects as optional alternatives to the old classics-centered syllabus.

There was also much resistance. Courting popularity by adding new subjects devalued, it was claimed, the balanced rigors of the old curriculum, and for small, hard-up colleges it was expensive to do so, at least until more students were attracted. Outside the state colleges, curricular conservatism dominated until the "electives" system developed by Harvard's Charles William Eliot from the 1870s.[62]

College attitudes toward the curriculum did not correlate perfectly with attitudes toward student aid. Jeremiah Day at Yale, who sought more charity scholarships, was the author of the famous "Yale Report" of 1828, which defended the standard, conventional curriculum. Conversely, when President Francis Wayland of Brown championed a modernized curriculum in the 1850s, he argued that attracting diverse students with relevant programs was a more effective answer to Brown's falling enrollment than buying them with aid, though in effect he did that too. By and large, however, extending the curriculum went with lowered financial barriers. From Cornell's founding in 1865 to Stanford's in 1891 with free tuition, those who wanted to diversify the curriculum as a training for "practical life" tended to stress a wider social reach, including coeducation for women.[63]

AMONG THOSE PUSHING FOR greater social inclusion were the philanthropists who founded urban institutes and colleges, offering different mixes of vocational and academic training to working-class men and women. They were part of a succession of reformers who sought to humanize and control what seemed to be a growing urban jungle. If they could not reach everyone, at least they could give hope to and uplift those who could take the opportunity.

Several of the new urban institutes, like New York's Cooper Union for the Advancement of Science and Art (founded 1851) gave free tuition.[64] Not all, though, had the endowment to sustain this. Temple College in Philadelphia, for example, moved quickly from free tuition to more selective student assistance while retaining its basic mission. Temple, a nonsectarian Christian establishment, was founded in 1884 with church support by Russell Conwell, a Baptist minister who had made a small fortune on the lecture circuit with a motivational success talk. His founding aim was to help young laboring men and women become "practical and effective Christians," serving themselves and their fellows by acquiring a "taste" for higher learning and entering professional life. After a few years of free tuition, Temple charged a low sixty dollars a year for its daytime collegiate programs, and forty dollars a year for more vocational ones (especially courses such as millinery and dress-making for women). Conwell adjusted fees according to individual "circumstances" but concentrated support on evening students with daytime jobs. In the early years, these students paid just five dollars per annum for three courses.

Conwell was a democratic conservative. He decried a growing division of society between rich and poor. Through education he wanted young people to break the "aristocratic fetters" that held them down. He himself had been raised on a poor hill farm in Massachusetts and said he had felt the sting of poverty at Yale. At the same time, he admired rich individuals as achievers and believed that most people did not have to be poor: the Temple idea was to help the aspiring to help themselves.[65]

Access Issues: A Century at Harvard

Temple had some success in attracting skilled workers, sales clerks, and the children of small proprietors, but few moves to extend higher education had much effect on the waves of poor immigrants that swelled America's population in the mid and late nineteenth century. (A notable exception was City College's enrollment of New York Jews from the 1890s.) For most immigrants, struggling to make do in rough jobs, college was worlds away, and the anti-Catholicism of many Protestant promoters of student aid did not help. Catholic colleges multiplied in response to Irish immigration, but in some cities Catholic power may have reduced educational opportunity by keeping out free public colleges.[66]

Among non-Catholic colleges, Harvard had the biggest proportion of Catholic students by the early 1900s (9 percent in 1908), but that was small in comparison with Boston's large Irish population, and in other respects too, Harvard's record on access was mixed.[67] The world of Harvard was, of course, very different to that of Temple and other inner-city colleges, but its relative exclusiveness was never uncontested. The history of Harvard in the nineteenth and early twentieth centuries was full of argument about democratic access, how to define it, and how to fund it in competition with other spending purposes of the college. Much of the arguing had a modern ring, pitting those who wanted charges held down for everyone against those who would concentrate subsidies on the poorest.

Until the late 1870s, Harvard was the country's costliest college. Its tuition, room, and board in 1830 was around $180 a year, compared with about $100 at Dartmouth and $80 at Hamilton.[68] A long-term decline in student aid relative to the college's enrollment became acute in 1824 when the Commonwealth of Massachusetts cut off its subsidy to Harvard, which had been initiated in 1814; a quarter (twenty-five hundred dollars a year) had been earmarked for scholarships. The reduction of poor students worried a committee of overseers (trustees) in 1826: it warned that

Harvard "was not designed by the founders to be an establishment for the rich alone." The very next year, however, another overseers committee declared that the college should not "exhaust its resources for the support of a large number of indigent persons [who] might become useful and respectable in some other course of life."[69]

Even among those who wanted to lower Harvard's financial barriers, there were sharp divisions. From the 1830s to the early 1850s, these followed political party lines. Jacksonian Democrats, a minority among the overseers but strong in state politics, championed a broad section of the populace, neither rich nor very poor. A Worcester newspaper editorial summed up their attitude in 1846. It was "notorious," declared the writer, that Harvard's "extravagant" spending debarred all but "some of the rich and charity scholars." The "great class in between them—essentially the people—are excluded by the high tariff . . . imposed upon learning."[70] This camp favored a general cut in tuition rather than a big increase in targeted aid.

On the other side were former Federalists and Whigs, more accepting of class differences, provided they went with opportunities to rise. They tended to favor high tuition to pay for quality programs and facilities, while wishing to raise more money to help poor but bright students. Lowering tuition across the board would be a wasteful boon to the rich. President Josiah Quincy, who took this view, also believed that increased grant aid to poor students would more than pay for itself by increasing enrollment and thereby revenue from room rents. He was conscious, too, of competition, including Yale's ministerial scholarships. In 1838, following the establishment of Amherst with low fees and free tuition for church students, Quincy organized a big loan fund subscribed by wealthy friends of the college.[71]

Despite Quincy's belief that student aid could make money, Harvard relied on gifts and bequests rather than its own general funds to provide scholarships. In the late 1840s and early 1850s, Samuel Eliot, Harvard's treasurer and chief fund-raiser, organized a major drive to raise money for student aid. Eliot had become more and more aware of a contrast between the "rapid accumulation of wealth in Massachusetts" and the needs of faculty and poor students. Tactfully but persistently he called upon the "liberality" of Boston's elite to ensure that "the means of cultivating talent and diffusing knowledge [would] not be withheld from" their great university. Many purposes of the college lacked money, he said, but none was more important than aiding "indigent and deserving students."[72]

Eliot scored some successes. They included Harvard's first alumni class scholarships and, thanks in part to his lobbying, forty state scholarships a year to be shared between Harvard, Amherst, and Williams.[73] The big changes, though, came under his son, Charles William Eliot (president 1869–1909).

CWE

Ambitious to build a university of diverse excellence, President Eliot believed strongly in recruiting both the rich and the poor and a large stratum between. Provided they were able and vigorous, the banker's son and the mechanic's son had much to give Harvard and much to receive. He was less sure about the academic potential of women, especially at the start of his presidency, when he saw their admission to university courses as an "experiment."[74]

On the matter of tuition and aid, Eliot gave something to both pre–Civil War camps—the tuition-cutters and the student-aiders. Tuition, hiked from $104 to $150 just before he took office, was frozen for forty-five years: Harvard gradually ceased to be a top-priced college. In 1904, three overseers publicly proposed that Harvard eliminate a worrying deficit by raising tuition 50 percent to $225, spending half the increase on scholarships. Supported by a majority of the faculty, Eliot successfully resisted the proposal on the ground that it would "impair [Harvard's] democratic quality, and in the long run . . . diminish its influence." It would drive away a "large class," polarizing the student body into "the well-to-do, and the aided."(Three years later the university conjured away its deficit by distributing central overheads to departments, which apparently had the funds to absorb them.) The episode echoed a similar row at Berkeley in the 1890s.[75]

On the student-aid front, Eliot did support a continuing drive for new scholarships. By the late 1870s, 14 percent of students had scholarships; more strikingly, the scholarships averaged $235 each, much more than tuition though less than Harvard's high room charges. Unfortunately, the growth in scholarship funds then fell behind expanding enrollment, especially from the late nineties. By the early 1900s only 6 percent of students had scholarships, and most of them were withheld from freshmen, though the president also gave aid here and there from special funds on the request of a student's professor. To get grant aid a student was supposed to be needy, but as the aid got scarcer, it became more like a prize for the academically chosen, as indeed it was meant to be; the neediest did not necessarily get it. The only exceptions to the high academic bar for scholarships were some local ones restricted to students from a small area.[76]

As elsewhere throughout the century, the main support for the needy was paid work, supplemented sometimes by college loans. Eliot claimed at the start of his presidency that "scores of young men" earned or borrowed "every dollar they spend here," and that situation did not change. Harvard's bureau for student employment was unusually dynamic, with links to the area's numerous employers, though there were always more job seekers than places.[77]

The result of all this was a limited amount of social democracy. The small minority of Harvard students whose fathers were manual workers inched up from an estimated 7.3 percent in the early 1870s to 7.8 percent in the early 1900s. In pursuit of high academic standards, Eliot cultivated ties with leading prep schools, but he also encouraged public-school admissions. Harvard's student body was not as "preppie" as Yale or Princeton's. To make Harvard admissions less socially exclusive, Eliot eliminated Greek from the entrance requirements, but his overall raising of admission standards was criticized—by the president of Princeton, no less—for disadvantaging rural and small-town students from modest schools.[78]

Socially, Eliot's very tolerance of freedom and diversity produced a result not far from the polarization he warned against—a gulf between the quasi-private, "Gold Coast" clubs at the apex of college social life and poorer students who commuted or lived on campus (the Yard). Poor boys, Catholics, and Jews could find niches at Harvard, but it was easier for them to feel fully accepted in the diverse, urban milieu of the University of Pennsylvania, though even Penn had its redoubts of snobbery and anti-Semitism.[79]

HARVARD'S EXPERIENCE DEMONSTRATED THE significance and limits of student aid in the nineteenth century. Tuition fees and student aid were twin focus points for debate about who should be encouraged and helped to go to college. Student aid, including work and loans as well as grants, was used to extend the class reach of college, but social justice was never its sole purpose. President Eliot wanted scholarships to relieve financial anxiety and thus aid serious study, but he accepted that they should be few enough to be prizes for achievement.[80] At other colleges during his long presidency, and indeed among some at Harvard, a movement gathered to base scholarships entirely on achievement and not on need. Harvard's leaders would resist this, but there were agreements as well as differences between the two positions as their protagonists moved into a new era.

Ann Radcliffe of London, donor of America's first scholarship (to Harvard in 1643) was raised in a tradition that combined pious giving with making money and protecting it. The Merchant Taylors guild, of which her father had been Master, grew from a medieval religious and social "fraternity [of] tailors and linen-armourers," making the padded tunics worn under armor, to a powerful merchants' association that gave extensively to charity, including the support of poor scholars.

On the Merchant Taylors' coat of arms *(opposite)*, two "rampant" camels, signifying trade with the east, frame knightly mantles and field tent, as made by the tailors. The holy lamb atop the visored helmet represents the guild's founding dedication to St. John the Baptist. The Latin motto declares that through concord, small things grow. *Courtesy of the Master and Wardens of the Merchant Taylors' Company.*

Samson Occom, a Mohegan Indian, studied the Bible with the Rev. Eleazar Wheelock in the 1740s. His abilities encouraged Wheelock to found an Indian school and then Dartmouth College (1769) for Indian and white missionaries. Ordained a Presbyterian minister, Occom raised money in England for Wheelock's projects, but much of the money for Indian scholarships went to white students. Occom resented this, but it was hard to attract Native Americans to white men's institutions. *Courtesy of Dartmouth College Library. Undated engraving.*

Thomas Jefferson proposed extensive free schooling for white Virginians in the 1780s and again in 1816-18. At the apex of the system, ten poor boys of "superior genius and disposition" would get free places at the College of William and Mary every year. The state legislature said no to the scheme, but the idea of using aid to select poor students of talent did not die. The University of Virginia (another brainchild of Jefferson) gave this statue to William and Mary (Jefferson's alma mater) for its 300th anniversary in 1993. *Image of the Jefferson Statue, University Archives, Swemm Library, College of William and Mary. Sculpture by Lloyd Lillie. Photograph by Karen McCluney.*

Fannie Jackson Coppin graduated as "class poet" in 1865 from Oberlin, America's first co-educational college and the first to admit black students regularly. Born a slave, Coppin worked through college, helped by an aunt's savings from work as a domestic and scholarships from Oberlin and the African Methodist Episcopal Church. She went on to become a distinguished high school principal in Philadelphia. *Courtesy of Oberlin College Archives, from a 1865 class album.*

Pauline Durant, whose husband Henry founded Wellesley College, started the Wellesley Student Aid Society in 1878, soon after the college opened. For decades, the Society's grants and loans, funded by alumnae, gave more support to needy students ("calico girls") than the college did. Pauline and Henry were religious evangelicals. After he died in 1881, she fought a losing battle as a Trustee against the secularizing of the college. In 1896, against her opposition, Wellesley ended "domestic work" (student jobs shared by everyone) and raised tuition. *Courtesy of Wellesley College Archives. Undated photograph by Taylor and Brown.*

At Yale's 1911 Commencement, President Arthur T. Hadley (on the right) strode forth with U.S. President and Yale graduate, William H. Taft (center) and former Yale President Timothy Dwight. Hadley, Yale's first non-clerical president, was a distinguished economist and brilliant if eccentric teacher (during one lecture he jammed both feet into a wastebasket and continued speaking while trying to free himself). He wanted scholarships to be awarded *only* for superior work, with loans and jobs for needy students; but this idea met resistance from alumni donors and a redoubtable student-services chief, Cornelius Kitchel. *Images of Yale Individuals, Manuscripts and Archives, Yale University Library.*

Stanford Trustee Herbert Hoover instigated major financial changes at the university between 1912 and 1920, including a move from free tuition to tuition fees coupled with extensive loans. As a geology student in Stanford's first class (1895), Hoover had worked through college and set up a co-op student boarding house. Two years out of college, already a successful mining executive, he was anonymously lending money to Stanford students. A Quaker humanitarian, the future U.S. President believed that the best charity was to promote self-help—hence loans rather than grants. *Courtesy of the Herbert Hoover Presidential Library. Photograph by Wilfrid Jenkins, 1914.*

If Herbert Hoover had seen this photograph, he would have been pleased—as a Stanford student in the 1890s, he started up a laundry service. In the twentieth century, American colleges sponsored "student agencies" in which students sold goods and services to other students. This Yale laundry van was featured at the front of a 1929 government booklet, "Self-Help for College Students." *U.S. Department of the Interior.*

The 1944 GI Bill, providing 90% of all student grant aid as late as 1949-50, brought a flood of veterans onto campuses. It caused a dorm crisis, dramatized in 1947 at the University of Wisconsin by a campus tent and a placard appealing for "rooms to rent." The cramped domestic scene (University of Maryland, 1949) shows a student veteran with his "dependents." Wives and children qualified for GI Bill allowances, but 97 percent of GI Bill students were men, as the primary benefits required service in the uniformed military. *Courtesy of Special Collections, University of Maryland Library and Wisconsin Historical Society, image WHI-3338.*

Harvard dean John U. Monro was the chief architect in the 1950s of a "need-analysis" system, closely assessing student finances and costs to allocate aid where it was most needed. He was a founder of the College Board's Scholarship Service, helping colleges to administer "need-based aid." But Monro also loved to teach and he had a long-standing concern about African American opportunity. In 1967, he left Harvard to teach and develop freshman courses at black colleges in Alabama—Miles and Tougaloo. *Courtesy of Harvard University Archives. Photograph by Harvard News Office, 1957.*

Halfway down a ski slope in 1969, Senator Claiborne Pell (D., RI) had an idea. He saw a way of using tax data to allocate new Federal grants to students according to income and need. Pell delivered the idea to his staff on a ski-lodge placemat. The eventual result was the Pell grant program, centerpiece of Federal scholarship aid. A quietly effective legislator, he once quipped, "the secret is always to let the other man have your way." *Senate office photo, c. 1990, possession of Pell family. Photograph by U.S. Senate Photographic Studio.*

Ada Comstock Scholar Corky Robinson and other Smith College students await their professor, December, 1988. Started in 1975, Smith's Ada Comstock program admits older undergraduates, many with children, whose college education has been "delayed or interrupted." "Adas" are diverse but they tend to need a lot of aid. The program is named for Ada Louise Comstock, an influential Dean of the College, 1912-23, who strove to empower women as leaders. *Courtesy of Smith College Archives. Photograph by Bob Stern.*

5
Merit and "Self-Help"

From the late nineteenth century, scholarships based on academic performance and not on financial need—what today we call "merit scholarships" or "merits"—became more common, more publicized, and more argued about. They were known variously as "open competition," "prize," and "honors scholarships." From the late 1890s, too, colleges got more systematically into the business of providing and finding student jobs, and this was followed by new ideas about student loans. All these trends reflected big shifts in the way that middle- and upper-class Americans ran their society and thought about it.

The rise of large-scale bureaucracies, in business as well as government, meant that success was increasingly *organizational.* For a few heroic individuals, this meant the founding of corporate empires, or leading reform movements to curb them, but for more and more people (mainly men of course) success meant winning promotion *within* an organization.

Politically, conservatives and reformers of different stripes worried about stark contrasts between rich and poor, plutocracy and the masses, and feared that middle-class folk would be squeezed between big capitalism and organized labor. After a new wave of immigration in the 1880s, urban poverty and squalor caused widespread concern, but so did the question of how to preserve individual creativity and self-reliance in a dense social structure.

Historic beliefs that America had been and should be a nation of individualists made a fertile ground here for social Darwinist ideas. Social Darwinism took different forms, but its main adherents believed that too much provision for social welfare, indeed too much of civilization itself, threatened nature's "selection of the fittest," shoring up the unfit rather than rewarding the fit and vigorous through competitive struggle.[1] The challenge for those social Darwinists who wanted to preserve a humane and democratic society was how to organize individual effort and achievement—replicating the struggle for survival in a state of nature—in a way that extended social opportunity without diminishing individual initiative.*

The inaugural address in 1899 of Yale's president Arthur T. Hadley, a political economist, connected many of these concerns to student aid and other college policies. In this speech, and a later article in *The Century Magazine,* he expressed distaste at the rise of "luxury" and "conspicuous differences of wealth" among Yale students. Up to a point, he said, it was inevitable and useful for poorer students to have to live with these differences, but if the wealthy set became too dominant, poorer students would feel "their powers repressed" and college life would lose its "traditional spirit of democracy and loyalty and Christianity." His solution was to promote a college community of hard work based on a demanding common curriculum, where rich and poor worked together, lived together, and met on "an equal footing."

Hadley's ideal college democracy was no welfare state. He believed that "beneficiary" grants, targeted on the needy, were "demoralizing" to recipients and reduced them to an inferior state of "pauperization" (a word he used twice, though rather vaguely, in his inaugural address). He believed, too, that some claims for aid on the basis of need were "fraudulent." He called instead for widely available long-term loans at low or no interest and expanded employment of students, giving, he hoped, real service to the college and "the wider world." Outright scholarships, on the

---

*As many writers have observed, upper-class fears of urban softening and restriction were expressed in organized athletics (about which leading college presidents were ambivalent) and romanticizing the frontier. In 1901, Union College demonstrated that even in New York state, the "Wild West" could serve new-style organizational efficiency. Discovering a large number of unpaid student bills, due as much to laxity as to charity, a new assistant treasurer—a former debt collector—had himself sworn in as a special deputy sheriff. When students filed past his counter on "tuition-payment day," he placed his revolver in conspicuous view. Receipts are said to have quadrupled in three years. Dixon Ryan Fox, *Union College* (1945), 28–29.

other hand, should be merits, "distinctly in the nature of a prize for really distinguished work."[2]

Hadley's vision of a common community and curriculum, in contrast with Eliot's diversity of living and learning, was not fully realized. He and his allies got rid of the socially exclusive "Sophomore Societies," built more reasonably priced dormitories, and held down tuition and other charges, but he could not, of course, abolish all social cliques, and he did not do much to prevent the Yale curriculum from acquiring optional alternatives, each attracting different types of student. Student-aid loans and employment were expanded, but he accurately foresaw obstacles to turning scholarships into merits.[3]

What he did do, philosophically, was to weave all three major types of aid—grants, jobs, loans—into a double-barreled attack on social division and on habits of dependency caused by getting something for nothing. His was not the most conservative position on financial aid: in the 1870s even student loans had run into fire from some Columbia trustees and others on the grounds that they would raise poor youth to a station for which they were not suited.[4] It was more common, however, for conservatives to praise, at least in principle, the idea of beating one's way upwards, while fearing, like Hadley, that gift aid would undermine the effort.

This anxiety continued well into the 1930s, and outside college life it has survived in worries about welfare "handouts." Although Hadley's fear of "pauperization" was rooted in the social anxieties of his era, it resonated with longer-term traditions of American individualism, pitting self-reliant achievement against "demoralizing" dependency.

The Rise of Merits

Merit scholarships were not new, but until the late 1860s they were seldom clearly designated as such in college literature. It is sometimes hard to know if financial need was required, especially when scholarships were dedicated to specific secondary schools or sponsored by church congregations.[5] The birth dates of clear-cut merit programs also varied a lot between colleges. Williams had no merits till 1895; Oberlin had none until the 1920s and no major ones till 1930.[6]

A pioneer of the new merit movement was Cornell. The state scholarships it established in the 1860s, in return for getting the New York land grant, were based not on financial need but on scholastic ability as demonstrated in local examinations. Cornell and New York's education authorities developed public examinations as a way of recognizing the meritorious—an approach soon followed by civil-service reformers in their fight against the promotion of officials through personal patronage and corrupt deals. Cornell's first president, Andrew White, wanted wide social access to the university, but he also sought excellence throughout the educational system. As he and others saw it, exam-based *"competition"* for scholarships (his italics) would "stimulate the earnestness" of schoolteachers and administrators as well as their pupils in preparing for college.[7]

The same idea drove scholarship legislation for New Jersey's landgrant university, Rutgers. The state established awards for Rutgers in 1864 on much the same basis as Cornell's.[8] Like Georgia's HOPE scholarships and other programs in recent years, state scholarships were seen as lodestars leading the public schools to better things. And unlike most college "merit" scholarships today, the early state awards were meant not so much to compete against other colleges for good students as to get anyone of ability to go to college at all, especially among college-suspicious farmers. When New York started its Regents scholarships in 1914, a program not confined to Cornell, they too were based on competitive examinations, though they were allocated disproportionately to isolated rural areas.[9]

But Andrew White's enthusiasm for competitive scholarships was also fired by institutional ambition. The awards, he believed, would "attract to us a most valuable class" of future leaders in "action and thought [holding] high positions . . . throughout the country."[10] Cornell's state scholarships continued to be merit based through the 1940s, but its development as a uniquely hybrid university, combining state and private schools, may have encouraged the private side to continue the merit tradition, leaving it to the public side to promote cheap access through low or free tuition. (Tuitions for different Cornell colleges started diverging in 1875.) Until the 1950s the main scholarships advertised in the catalogs of the private College of Arts were merits.

Elsewhere, too, colleges introduced merits to help upgrade themselves academically or start themselves off with high standards. Some of this involved a new spirit of bureaucratic precision, aiming to ginger up performance with formal requirements and distinctions. In 1895 Dartmouth changed its main, need-related scholarships from a uniform $75 to $85, $75, or $50 depending on the student's grades; it also issued new rules requiring scholarship-holders to maintain grades well above passing. (These rules became commonplace in the next century.) At about the same time, Dartmouth established four "prize" scholarships, again of differing amounts ($150, $125, and two at $100) for the four top students in each class. (Dartmouth tuition at the time was $100; total charges were $252 to $391, depending on facilities.)[11]

The 1890s also saw the founding of the University of Chicago, designed with Rockefeller money to be a powerhouse of excellence. William Rainey Harper, the first president, worried about student living costs and set up cheap part-time courses for teachers and railroad workers, but the main publicized scholarships were "honors" merits, and little aid went to freshmen, though that was not unique to Chicago. In his report of 1899, Benjamin Terry, dean of Chicago's "Senior College" (juniors and seniors), declared that the university's "bounty" should be awarded only on the basis of "high merit," not "indigence." (Terry's sense of justice ran to bureaucratic rigor and consistency rather than social opportunity. Too often, he said, departments gave scholarships as a result of "'lobbying' by an ambitious student or last-minute scurrying around to find a candidate" rather than a "systematic" assessment of students' work. This was "unfair . . . to the students.")[12]

Toward the end of Harper's presidency in 1906, more tuition remissions, often requiring work in repayment, went to students "who would not otherwise be able to attend the University." Harper's successor-to-be, Dean Henry Judson, justified them on the grounds that they expanded enrollment and thereby revenue. Before this, however, the main impetus for need-related aid seems to have come from outside the administration—from women in city alumni and civic clubs pursuing a role of care-taking and uplift rather like that of Jane Addams at Hull House, the famous Chicago center providing educational and other programs for poor immigrants. Well into the 1930s, the scholarships advertised in the university's catalogs were overwhelmingly merits.[13]

In the 1920s, other colleges brought in merits for strategic academic purposes. Swarthmore's president Frank Aydelotte used them as part of his successful war on student athleticism and antiacademic values. His new honors program, providing special seminars and flexible requirements for a select company, was attached to a raft of "honors" scholarships, whose holders therefore paid less and got more.[14] On the West Coast, the scholarships offered by the new Scripps College for women (founded 1926) were entirely merits; even its need-related loans were restricted to students of "marked ability." Scripps's leadership was interested not in wide social access but in establishing an academic identity that was both demanding and distinctively for women.[15]

At the end of the decade, even Oberlin, by tradition a staunch believer in "beneficiary" (need-related) aid, accepted ten merits from Amos Miller, a prominent alumnus and Chicago lawyer, on condition that the college gave ten more. The motives again included academic upgrading— literally so, as just three years before the faculty had undertaken a review of grading policies to tighten them up.[16] In all these cases, merits were not just a way of buying good students but of signaling, to other students and the world at large, that the college stood for academic excellence.

The secularizing of colleges may have assisted the merits movement. This process weakened the constituency of "poor and pious" students as major claimants for need-related aid. Churches themselves, at least the more upper-class ones, were not immune to the lure of merits. Writing to Kenyon's president in 1879, the Episcopal bishop of Pittsburgh applied his brand of Victorian "muscular Christianity" to the matter of scholarships:

> I am very decided in my opinion that scholarships ought to be always prizes. . . . I hesitate about speaking confidently as to the condition of "need" coming in. But I very much incline to the idea that competitive prizes should be open to all who will compete. This makes prizes honorable in every sense and they would generally be won by the plucky, talented, religious youth, who seeks the ministry. Anyhow, we don't want many who could not, or would not win. College youth for years past have said—with some reason—that the future parsons in their classes, whose piety was their sole merit, were generally feeble fellows, without pluck, force, or brain. Exact *excellence* . . . and we will win men worth ordaining, and other men will esteem the ministry more fully and seek it at their own cost. [emphasis in original][17]

Although ministerial scholarships had often called for "promise" and talent, the writer here was abandoning a traditional assumption that poverty and piety made for earnest dedication deserving aid. He could have been writing about scholarships for any profession. Need-related ministerial scholarships did not end (far from it), but by the late nineties in some quarters they were reputed to "pauperize inferior persons."[18]

The merits movement did not go uncontested by those who wanted to restrict scholarships to the needy. Andrew White showed he was aware of this in the defensive way that he extolled Cornell's merits in official university statements of the 1880s. While believing that the state scholarships should be awarded "for merit and not as a dole to poverty," he declared that "in the experience of Trustees and Faculty . . . a system based on merit alone" would mainly benefit "students of small means." It was a "well-known fact" that in all colleges "the great majority of the best scholars come, not from the wealthy class, but from those whose circumstances have forced them to feel the need of thrift and energy." In addition, a trustee committee was looking at the "applications of needy and meritorious students" who did not win state scholarships, "remitting tuition to those who really deserve and need" aid.[19]

Two decades later at Yale, the fate of President Hadley's pitch for making all scholarships into merits revealed the resistance. Before and after he took office in 1899, donors gave endowed scholarships, some restricted to needy students and some not, without great change in those proportions. The university continued to give need-related "beneficiary" aid, about a third of it from general funds, and unlike Harvard's aid, it generally included freshmen. Some of it was earmarked for ministerial students, and this, coupled with new alumni fund-raising for local and working-class youth, probably helped protect the whole system of need-related grants. The main innovation in Hadley's time was a formula whereby beneficiary grants varied after the student's first semester according to his academic performance *and* his degree of need (as assessed by the student-employment bureau). This scaling of aid by *both* merit and need was as unusual for the time as it is commonplace today.[20]

The system's architect was Cornelius Kitchel, an old Yale hand who—unusually again for the time—ran all three branches of student aid: jobs, loans, and scholarships. A critic of heavy student loan burdens, Kitchel believed that Yale should provide cheap access through scholarships in the absence of a fully fledged state university. Not till he left office in 1909, to be replaced by an official more in tune with Hadley, did the administration succeed in turning some awards for upperclassmen into loans by calling them "repayable" scholarships.[21]

As already suggested in the case of Yale, alumni could be a force for need-related aid, opposed at least tacitly to merits. Like other parts of society, college alumni became more organized in the late nineteenth century. This in turn led to admissions recruiting by alumni clubs, whose members often knew the local candidates and their financial needs. This did not always square with college administrations, which were more likely to demand that new students prove themselves academically for a semester or two before getting scholarship aid. At Wellesley, the college administration excluded first-year students from its aid, even its co-op dorms, until the 1920s when it introduced "freshman" merit scholarships. By contrast, the alumnae-supported Students' Aid Society was established in 1878 (just three years after the college opened) on the idea that it was as important to educate "calico girls" as it was to educate "velvet girls." Its grants and loans were need based, they were available to first-year students, and they required no special academic distinction. Not that there was open war between Wellesley alumnae and administration. Pauline Durant, who founded the society, was the wife of the college's founder, Henry Durant. The college treated the two approaches as complementary[22]

IF CHAMPIONS OF MERITS had to recognize the claims of student need, their opponents recognized the value of achievement through competition. A leading example was Frederick Barnard, president of Columbia from 1864 to 1889. Against resistance by conservative trustees, Barnard pressed for "truly catholic" admissions, including women and former black slaves. In 1865 the university started admitting tuition-free "any student of good moral character and industrious habits" who could satisfy the president and treasurer that he could not pay the fees. At the end of the 1870s, when the trustees had established twenty-five full-tuition "prize" scholarships (merits), Barnard criticized them in his annual report. He virtually called merits a bribe, asserting that they lowered the "moral tone" of a college by "appealing to a mercenary motive." There were other incentives—"honorable distinctions"—that could be used to spur "noble ambition" for knowledge.[23]

In the same report, though, Barnard proposed an end to the old free-tuition policy. Whereas the merits were under-applied for, applicants for need-related free tuition had increased: a fifth of the college and a third of students at Columbia's School of Mines were now getting it. Student attitudes, he averred, had changed from reluctance to seek charity to a tendency to exaggerate financial need in making a claim. In addition to tightening the assessment of financial need, Barnard called for a fixed number of need-related scholarships. They should always be outnumbered by applicants, so that they could be awarded by competitive examination. Barnard later softened his position: the free-tuition policy continued for needy students with specified grade levels (60 percent in an entrance examination, 70 percent thereafter), but his attitude was very much of his time—the humane but stringent moralist, setting carefully constructed hurdles, based on competitive achievement as well as tested need, to promote virtue and stem greed.[24]

In attacking merits, Barnard explicitly defended Harvard from an unnamed "authority" who had criticized that university for not using them to "stimulate excellence." Harvard, in a way, had preempted merits by refining the academic criteria for its need-related scholarships. By 1830 and maybe earlier, Harvard was scaling its scholarships according to the recipient's scholastic "standing." And as already mentioned, to get any scholarship at all, a needy student usually had to be outstanding.[25]

Despite this vigorous compromise between need and merit, President Charles William Eliot was whipsawed by different critics of Harvard's scholarship policy. From one quarter he reported "frequent complaints" that those who won the scholarships often had much less financial need, if any, than those who did not. (If poorer students were apt to do best academically, this was only a tendency.) Others, however, worried that scholarships confined to the needy impaired self-respect and, as a correspondent put it in 1910, the year after Eliot left office, "favored mendicants." There were also those, like Barnard's antagonist, who believed that merits were needed to spur non-needy students as well as needy ones to achievement. In line with this, the proportion of major Harvard scholarship donors who specified financial need fell sharply after the 1860s, though the proportion explicitly requiring academic excellence did not rise till the 1920s.[26]

In defense against introducing merits, Eliot produced data showing that many students achieved high honors without scholarships. The university also created honorary scholarships without money for outstanding, non-needy students. Meanwhile an Overseers committee investigated whether some of the university's endowed scholarships should legally " be open to general competition." The committee found that most scholarship donors had specified need and none had explicitly not required it. The university, implied the committee, should stick to requiring need in all its scholarships.[27]

Yet Eliot himself shared in fears of the time about aid and dependency. He wrote in the 1890s of the "insidious danger [of] giving scholarships too freely," and he too used the word "pauperization," especially against clerics whose free ride at divinity school too often became, in Eliot's view, a lifelong habit of seeking gifts and "half-fare" concessions.[28]

These fears were not a passing obsession. Encouraging a scholarship donor in 1920 to give a merit, President William Neilson of Smith, no friend of wealthy privilege and luxury, regretted that most scholarships in America were "conditioned upon poverty" and thereby "associated more with indigence than with ability or learning."[29] In fact, most of Smith's own scholarships required need, but they were few enough to require superior merit. Like others before and after him, however, Neilson seemed sure that the charity image of need-related scholarships obscured the achievement of winning them.

Work

In his ten-year report of 1903, Chicago's president William Rainey Harper gave a colorful list of the jobs that the university employment office had helped find for many students. They ranged from clerking to debt-collecting, checking and lighting street lamps, reading to old people and minding the young, and working in stores and suburban railroad stations and newspaper offices.[30] The very name, "bureau of self-help," given by Yale and some other colleges to their student employment offices at the turn of the century, headlined the two forces shaping student aid: the rise of bureaucratic organization, and concern for self-reliance versus dependency.

The creation of college offices to administer campus jobs and give information about off-campus employment started in the mid-1890s.[31] It reflected the growth of administrative systems, in colleges as in business and government, and the development of networks between institutions—in this case between colleges and employers as well as with the YMCA, which operated student job-finding agencies. Finding jobs for students was also needed as a defense against other trends of organized society. Teaching school for part of the year, once a mainstay for hard-up undergraduates, provided fewer openings as it became professionalized, and union power in some areas threatened to block off other jobs as well.[32] On the other hand, the growth of a student "rich set" on many campuses, state as well as private, opened up markets for poorer students to find employment—from laundry service to special tutoring for exams.

Not all of these were college approved, but colleges did support the expansion of student agencies whereby students worked as campus representatives for merchants and manufacturers.

Educationally, college administrators tended to respect working through college as good for building character, independence, and ability to manage. It was hard, of course, not to believe in student employment when it sustained part of a college's clientele and furnished cheap labor, but ideology should not be discounted. To avoid giving too much charity, some colleges instituted "service scholarships," requiring work in return for grant aid.[33]

Not everyone took this view of working through college. When friends and alumnae of women's college Smith formed a Students' Aid Society in 1897 to raise funds for student loans, they did so partly to reduce the strain for students of combining academic work with employment.[34] Theories of feminine frailty, common at the time, made the matter a health issue, but the concern was not restricted to women. In the 1920s especially, as more research was done on college students, there were sharp disagreements as to whether student jobs impaired academic study and stunted the student's social life and personal well-being.[35]

Colleges and their student cultures varied a lot in their hospitality to working students. The more sensitive supporters of student employment recognized the subtle and not so subtle snobberies that could operate against such students. Still, official doctrine as well as sheer economic necessity perpetuated the idea of working through college.[36]

Looking to Loans

In January 1920, Stanford University (founded 1891) ended its free-tuition policy, which had been made possible by the founding largesse of Senator and Mrs. Leland Stanford. (The senator died in 1893, but his widow remained an active force in the university.) In its fledgling years, Stanford had felt vulnerable to competition from the tuition-free University of California at Berkeley, but once it was established, it could compare itself to other leading private universities, where tuition ranged from $150 to $250. Stanford's new tuition started at $120, but the following year, 1921, it was pushed up with little warning to $225.[37]

Even in 1919, Stanford had levied an "incidental" fee of sixty dollars for nonacademic services, but charging tuition was attacked in the student and local press for excluding many who would be unable to afford it. In reply, trustee Herbert Hoover, an architect of the new policy, published a brief for it. He portrayed a university caught between financial deficits in the wake of wartime and postwar inflation, the dearth of new endowments from a young alumni body, and high aspirations. Hoover stressed the university's goals of expanding enrollment and improving faculty salaries and "scientific equipment" commensurate with a "world reputation."

Hoover claimed that when the university and its friends sought more endowments to preserve free tuition, they had run into criticism that those students who could afford to pay were not "carrying their share of the load." He estimated that two-thirds of the students could pay the new tuition, a judgment borne out in his view by the number of students with automobiles and, he added archly, "the receipts of [local] ice cream parlors." For the remaining 30–35 percent of students, Hoover outlined a scheme of seven-year tuition loans at 5 percent interest. (With the tuition hike the next year, the terms were liberalized to no interest for seven years, 6 percent thereafter.)

Mrs. Stanford herself, said Hoover, had long believed that completely free tuition lowered students' "sense of responsibility." From his own experience when he had tried to borrow money as a Stanford student, he thought that a loan was more compatible with self-respect than being one of a "specially designated," needy group getting free tuition. Having to borrow to pay tuition was not an "infringement of democracy" but an investment in the improved "earning power that comes from university training." There would, however, be a grant fund for particular hardship cases.[38]

The effect of these changes on the social mix of Stanford students is not clear, but alumni did respond with scholarships. The move to tuition did not seem to affect undergraduate enrollment, but it fell by just over 5 percent following the big tuition hike in 1921.[39]

Although Hoover was not the first to assert that students themselves might prefer borrowing to gift aid, the Stanford move heralded new thinking in the 1920s about tuition charges and student loans.[40] Three developments promoted this. As leading colleges competed more and more on a national stage, the cost of their ambitions to upgrade facilities and get the best faculty threatened to outrun the growth of gifts and endowments. Secondly, increased acceptance of college "training" by employers gave a market value to that training, which in turn seemed to justify

Hoover's conception of student borrowing as an investment in "earning power." Thirdly, business leaders promoted the slogan "welfare capitalism," centered on the idea of the socially responsible corporation, providing employee benefits while making money. This encouraged the belief that "sound business practices" could be adopted by other institutions too: the corporate model was safe for America.

The result of all this was considerable discussion among college presidents and others about the possibility of charging tuition equal to the full cost of education—a policy so far made unnecessary by subsidies from donors. Some champions of this idea were not much concerned about equity for poor students, but most proposed lending to students so that they could pay full costs later if they could not do so immediately, just as businesses extended credit to customers.[41] Consumer credit and installment buying were big developments in the 1920s.

A prominent exponent of this approach was the New York realtor and philanthropist William E. Harmon, whose student-loan agency, started in 1922, was one of some seventy-five student-loan foundations—over half of them church-based—operating nationwide by the late twenties.[42] Harmon's thinking about student loans was moral as well as financial (he also funded city playgrounds and the use of religious movies in church services). In Harmon's view, colleges and students alike should be self-supporting, the former by charging full costs, the latter by borrowing, if need be, full-cost tuition. Handling such loans would rid students of dependency on "semi-charitable" scholarships and train them in "business obligations." Nor would it disqualify the poor. At the colleges where his foundation had student loans, those with the most students of "very limited means" had the best record of repaying.[43] His colleges included Yale, in line with President Hadley's promotion of loans earlier in the century, though Yale did not charge full costs.

A broader case for charging full costs through loans was made about the same time by Trevor Arnett, business vice president of the University of Chicago and a published authority on college finance. Opinion on student loans was changing but divided at Chicago. In the mid-1920s its leaflet "Aids and Awards" still declared that "the University does not encourage students to borrow [though it] may be wise" to do so a short time before graduation and "remunerative employment."[44] Arnett took a different view. He recognized the "democratic" objections to charging full costs, and he appreciated that college education was not just a personal investment: it was a "community asset." He considered, nonetheless, that its benefits were "primarily personal." Students, therefore, should pay the full costs of their education, though not the costs of faculty research. Loans could enable students to pay when they could do so most easily.

This approach, Arnett believed, would educate the public about the real costs of education and deter the frivolous student. At the same time it would constrain colleges to keep down costs while removing their dependence on donors, who in general he saw as a reactionary lot despite his own close ties with Rockefeller philanthropy. Gifts and endowment should be concentrated on university research and some scholarships for the specially meritorious.

Arnett pursued his plan through the 1930s when he was a high Rockefeller foundation official. As late as 1940, he argued that loans did more for student "independence and sturdiness of character" than did scholarships. He also claimed that some colleges, old and new, implemented his plan, but in general he was reduced to hoping that it would be gradually implemented over the long term.[45]

In the 1920s, a small group of colleges, including Cornell, Bryn Mawr, and Smith, came up with a less thoroughgoing plan for recovering full costs: they sought extra contributions from those parents who could afford it. At Smith, President Neilson wrote in May 1925 to all parents of the graduating class, asking them to give a thousand dollars if they could. This was the difference between four years of tuition, room, and board at $750 a year and four years' full cost at $1,000 a year. Neilson told the parents that half of them could pay this quite easily: most of that half had sent their daughters to boarding schools charging on average twice as much as Smith did. Responses to Neilson's request were mixed, and he did not try it for long. Nor did the other colleges.[46]

Although neither approach, Arnett's or Neilson's, achieved their aims, both were prophetic. In the long run, colleges would rely more and more on student loans, albeit federal ones, to finance their markets. Private colleges would also push up full tuition to recover as much of their costs as possible from their wealthier students. In the meantime, however, the double impact of depression and war would undercut the idea of higher charges while shaking up the whole culture of student aid.[47]

6

Seeking Equity and Order

The 1930s Depression gave colleges good cause to worry about getting enough students. It also produced sharp disagreements about financial aid policy and the role of the federal government. In general, economic devastation followed by war led to a new stress on aid for the needy. It produced the first formal intercollegiate system for assessing need and monitoring student-aid policies.

Depression Differences

America's undergraduate population fell by about a tenth in the early 1930s, both in absolute numbers and as a proportion of eighteen- to twenty-one-year-olds, before resuming its long-term growth. Enrollments at some private colleges took a sharp knock, causing worries about loss of student quality as well as revenue. The student population as a whole shifted to state and commuter colleges, where low charges counteracted a general lack of scholarships; most gave none.* Some "subway colleges" and others actually increased their enrollments.[1]

Crosscurrents of policy and opinion were particularly strong at pri-

---

*The late congressman Carl Elliott, from a poor Alabama hill district, told of camping out as a student in the University of Alabama observatory. The only "financial aid" came from a groundsman who illegally wired his cooker into the college electricity. Later, he got a job as a grader from a sympathetic professor. His experiences, contrasting with those of the snobbish fraternity smart set, stimulated his later championing of federal student-aid bills. Elliott and D'Orso, *The Cost of Courage* (1992), chap. 3.

vate colleges. As economic trauma shook traditional practices and beliefs, colleges and their leaders reacted in different ways. Many faculty and students collected and gave money for emergency student aid. Colleges often deferred tuition payments (a form of temporary loan) and increased their scholarship spending from general funds. Low-cost "co-op" housing became more common, too, at both public and private colleges. At the same time, some colleges limited their intake of students needing aid—a new resorting to what would later be called "need-conscious" or "need-aware" admissions, though Trinity College (later Duke) had done it back in the 1890s, also because of financial crisis. Some eastern colleges became more dependent on old upper-class money to supply full payers.[2] Many colleges, including elite ones, lowered admissions standards to keep up enrollments, but at Cornell, as elsewhere, there were worries that student jobs might interfere with study. The catalog discouraged all students except those with "great determination" and strong health from taking jobs: academic work must come first.[3]

Conservatives continued to fear that too much aid would create dependency, a "gimme" attitude as one put it, especially if the aid came from the federal government.

Although most colleges gratefully accepted the new federal "work-study" funds for student employment, some of the richer colleges preferred to use their own money. Smith's president Neilson started with the program but left it, claiming it inflicted too much red tape for too little money.

At Princeton, on the other hand, the alumni magazine flayed Williams and other elite colleges for not accepting federal aid, whatever they thought of Roosevelt's New Deal administration. That Williams had gone into the red expanding scholarship aid from its general funds was no excuse. The editors debunked three specters of government aid at Williams and other colleges: extravagant "Santa Clausing" by the government; dangerous federal control of the colleges; and the admission of too many unqualified students in a move toward mass higher education—a fear that surfaced again in early stages of the GI Bill.[4]

Disputes were not confined to the role of government. A row that broke out at Northwestern in 1935 pitted several deans, led by the education school's Ernest Melby, against President Walter Dill Scott and a powerful personnel director, Elias Lyman. The deans tried in vain to get Scott to spend much more on need-related scholarships. Melby's side ar-

gued that this spending would more than pay for itself by increasing enrollment as well as maintaining student quality. A contrast was drawn
between serious students struggling to make ends meet in the Depression
and rich socialites from the collegiate culture that had developed in the
twenties. Melby's portrait of the poor, dedicated teacher-trainee was a secular version of the old church-student ideal.[5]

At Swarthmore, different ideas developed more harmoniously, as be-
fitted a Quaker establishment. The faculty chose to cut their own pay to
fund new scholarships, taxing themselves progressively according to sal-
ary level. President Frank Aydelotte endorsed this but quit the federal
work-study program. He recognized that many colleges could not afford
to do this, but he disliked the program's tendency to "sap [student] self-
reliance"—as if it gave cash hand-outs rather than jobs. In 1938–39 (no
earlier) Swarthmore started without fanfare to scale its merit scholarships
according to individual student need. When the Depression ended in the
early forties, Swarthmore just as quietly dropped the "need" element (at
least the catalogs stopped mentioning it), but it returned after the war.
The same happened at the University of Chicago.[6]

Bridging "merit" and "need" by awarding a flat-rate scholarship on
merit and then, if necessary, scaling it upwards according to need had
already appeared in a new set of regional scholarships. Often called "national" scholarships, they were targeted on the west and south by elite
northeastern colleges.

The regional scholarship idea went back to Princeton and Yale just
after World War I, egged on by western alumni and competing with each
other to become more national in reach. Not all regional scholarships required "need," and different colleges put different weights on academic
ability, athleticism, and "character," variously defined.[7] Depression hard-
ships, however, impelled college leaders to think more closely about how
to recruit talented students by putting aid where it was needed. At Harvard, President James Conant noted that existing scholarships usually
paid no more than "a half or a quarter of a student's expenses." Conant
himself was no fan of "working through college": he thought it depleted
academic study, so the Harvard National Scholarships were designed to
replace a student's need for employment with grant aid.[8]

Created in 1934, the Harvard Nationals gave all scholarship winners
one hundred dollars but scaled the amounts up according to need, in
some cases to full expenses. They reflected Conant's attachment to the

educational ideas of Thomas Jefferson, including his belief that talent was widely spread through society. Conant was particularly concerned about the disadvantages of distance for rural and small-town youth (Jefferson's yeoman) living far from any college. In fact, a third of early Harvard Nationals went to private-school students, and for some officials at Harvard and elsewhere, as already mentioned, scholarships for rural and western youth helped keep down the intake of urban Jews. The scholarships were a more discreet, if less powerful, method of doing this than religious/ethnic quotas, which, once exposed, aroused liberal fury.[9]

Despite this darker side, regional scholarships supported the idea of the nationally democratic university. A Princeton policy paper on scholarships in 1936 argued that private universities could be more national than public universities, which had to serve local constituents. "To train for life in a democracy," the paper asserted, a great private university should include "a cross-section of that democracy both geographic and economic."[10] In practice the cross-section was limited. Seven percent of Princeton students' fathers in 1936 were blue collar or low white collar, compared with 64 percent of the male work force. At Harvard, only two of the 161 National Scholars enrolled between 1934 and 1940 were working class (both the sons of truck drivers). And as late as 1951 black Americans constituted less than 1 percent of students at leading American private and public colleges.[11] Still, the idea that geographic and social diversity was *educational* complemented Conant's belief in recruiting outstanding talent, unimpeded by geographic and financial barriers. Both ideas supported the development of scholarships reaching across the country, awarded for scholastic achievement but scaled by need.

Although the regional scholarships were aimed to expand a college's pool of applicants, they did not stop a bidding war for academic and athletic talent, which remained in short supply. Western students, indeed, met the new interest of eastern elite colleges by "shopping around" for scholarships, but bazaar behavior was not confined to western students and eastern colleges. There were charges, remarkably like today's, of materialistic bargaining by students and inflated buying by colleges. By the late 1930s, Harvard, Yale, and Princeton were trying to control the competition by discussing shared applicants on the telephone and agreeing not to outbid each other for them. The Midwest, too, saw some fleeting efforts at price control by groups of colleges.[12] A seed was sown for more formal cooperation on scholarships after the war and ultimately to what the Justice Department would call a price-fixing conspiracy.

Beyond the GI Bill

During the war years, college enrollments fell as military service and civilian war work drew off young people. Financial help, however, came to many colleges in the form of campus education and training programs for service personnel, especially the navy's V-12 program and the army's Specialized Military Training program.[13] The return of full employment also meant that fewer families had financial need, enabling colleges to spend less on aid. Male and coed colleges cut their aid spending still further in the early postwar years when large numbers of their students were veterans supported by the GI Bill.[14]

When the veteran influx and GI Bill money tapered off in the late forties, elite male colleges felt it most, as veterans had concentrated there and they charged higher prices than the big state universities, where veterans had also concentrated. Thrown back onto their own scholarship funds, these colleges faced three conflicting challenges—from rising costs, new demands for access, and intensified competition. The cost spiral caused by postwar price inflation led colleges to raise tuition sharply. At the same time, the GI Bill experience helped generate demands for wider social access to college, including elite institutions.[15] The good work done by veterans in college led influential educators—James Conant among them—to revise their views about how many Americans could handle advanced college courses. Opinions differed about the numbers that should go to college, but wartime and cold war thinking generally supported the idea that a strong American democracy required wider educational opportunities.[16]

All this put pressures on colleges to provide more aid for needy students. The veteran record undercut the prewar belief among campus conservatives that grant aid weakened the individual, though that idea persisted among some legislators, as we saw in the history of the 1958 National Defense Education Act.

The third challenge, making it harder to deal with the first two, was the return to a bidding war for good students as well as athletes. This was expensive, as it involved competitive scholarships that often exceeded the student's need or went to well-to-do students who had no need at all. The main combatants were ambitious elite colleges reaching across the country to compete with each other as well as with local colleges. To save travel time, their admissions officers tended to visit the same big suburban high schools and prep schools, neglecting smaller rural establishments. It still cost them more to recruit students from afar, as they had to add travel costs to the grants they offered.[17]

The scholarship bidding war depleted college budgets in general and financial aid funds in particular. It was also part of a volatile admissions scene in which students applied to increasing numbers of colleges, without stating their preferences. Colleges had not yet reached the stage of haggling with students and altering individual offers, but they found themselves pushing up their award levels in light of what they heard their competitors were doing. For the liberal college administrator who wanted to put aid where it was most needed in an orderly fashion, the whole business was stressful, undignified, and inequitable.[18]

At Swarthmore a liberal president, John Nason, responded quickly to these trends. Nason had to deal with a conservative, and indeed racist, section of "managers" (trustees) from the South and border counties. During World War II Nason had opposed military training programs as inconsistent with Swarthmore's Quaker tradition. When a majority of the managers overruled him, Nason declared that in that case Swarthmore—and other colleges—should take a lead in serving the war effort against a racist enemy. The college trained Chinese officer cadets, provided financial aid for Japanese American students who had been interned, and more cautiously (and under student pressure) admitted its first black student in 1943.[19]

Soon after the war, Nason moved to scale Swarthmore's Open Scholarships—merits—according to need as they had been temporarily in the Depression. Nason did this to widen the net for good students, in addition to making the college more socially inclusive. Already concerned about competitive bidding for students, Nason wanted the Open Scholarships, then fixed at $650 for all winners, changed to a sliding scale of $100 to $1,000 so that he could match offers of $1,000 elsewhere, provided that the student needed it. (Total tuition, fees, room, and board at the time was $1,050.) Some managers, loyal to the idea of a fixed scholarship geared solely to excellence, demurred at this, and the managers' executive committee could not reach a consensus. Nason and his supporters then made an end run. They got the plan referred to a special managers committee, which led to approval by the full board in June 1947.

The Swarthmore community was still divided on student aid. In the early 1950s, the board chairman, Howard C. Johnson, though a conservative on many things, including race, spoke out publicly for need-scaled merits as a response to bidding wars. Some alumni, on the other hand, wanted Swarthmore to minimize student aid, believing the college could attract enough good, full payers without it.[20]

Swarthmore did retain some full-tuition merits, but other colleges in the 1940s and 1950s inserted "need" requirements in all their scholarships. The language of college catalogs shifted too: they were more apt to describe scholarships as "financial aid" than as prizes.

By THE EARLY 1950S, leaders in the private-college sector recognized that student aid needed a major review. This was addressed by the Commission on Financing Higher Education (not to be confused with the 1947 President's Commission on Higher Education, the Zook Commission, discussed above). Presidents of leading private universities dominated the commission's membership. The commission was funded by the Rockefeller Foundation, and it sprang from worry about the financial future of colleges, especially smaller private ones. An advance commission report in 1951 focused on cost inflation, which was outstripping college endowments.[21]

The commission's main report, *The Nature and Needs of Higher Education,* was accompanied by three major staff studies, which drew on history as well as sociology. Published in 1952, all four reports contained policy proposals and featured student aid prominently.[22]

The main report was an expression of cold war liberalism. It did not mention the communist foe, but it made frequent references to freedom and the importance of having diverse institutions outside government control. Its historical account of American higher education was patriotic and upbeat. The size and variety of the system, it claimed, had given plenty of opportunity to poor students of talent. In the commission's view, this was more important than ever and under threat from rising costs. As the leader of "free nations," America had a special duty to develop, through education, the wisdom and enlightenment of its citizens.

The importance of "trained experts" was mentioned too, although one of the staff studies, by Byron Hollinshead, put more emphasis on the practical need for advanced education in a complex modern society.

Despite its stress on citizen enlightenment, the Rockefeller Commission proposed much less expansion of higher education than the Zook Commission.[23] Noting that far more of the population went to college in America than in Britain, France, or Germany, the commission wanted an increase in the college-going proportion of "young people" from 20 percent to 25 percent, not counting veterans. Although this meant expanding by a fifth, the commission believed that college-standard work was beyond the capacity of most Americans.

But *who* should go to college? Here the commission was more radical than it seemed. Arguing that 40 percent of the top quarter of youth did not go to college—as measured by test scores—it wanted to get as many as possible of these into four-year colleges, replacing some students who did go to college but had "little or no intellectual interest" and often dropped out. (This echoed a more explicit class challenge by James Conant, who asserted in 1943 that lower-class ability should change places with upper-class mediocrity: more upward mobility required some downward mobility too.)[24]

On student aid, the commission started by saying that the "economic barrier [was] usually exaggerated": a person with enough "determination" could put himself through college, and aid was increasingly tailored to need. They allowed, however, that "for some students the economic barrier [was] a formidable one."[25] They decried merits and bidding wars and said (politely) that colleges should improve their teaching to provide for a wider variety of students.

The commission's staff study by Byron S. Hollinshead made more of economic disadvantage affecting motivation. It also claimed that existing college scholarships were too small to "be of much help" to very poor students. Like Alice Hayes on women's scholarships in 1891, and indeed like the commission study by staff director John Millett, Hollinshead found that most aid went to students who could nearly afford their college without it.[26] In his own research and thinking, Hollinshead combined a sense of social justice with a practical concern about wasted human resources that went back to World War II.[27] On the subject of merits, though, Hollinshead (who remained president of Coe College while serving as a commission staff consultant) was ambivalent. Calling merits "scarcely defensible," he immediately added that he liked the idea of subsidizing "all those in the top 5 to 10% of ability . . . to develop the nation's highest talent," without the complexities of assessing need.[28]

Despite the proposed increase in college places, the commission reports were what we might call neo-Jeffersonian rather than expansionist. They called for a selection system based on ability and achievement, removing barriers of money, race and gender. To finance this, they looked to increased scholarship giving by alumni and corporations. None of them faced the paradox that to attract more alumni gifts it would often seem necessary to favor college applicants from rich alumni families.

The reports differed on federal student aid. The commission's own report rejected it, predicting that it would involve government controls imposing too much uniformity on the system. The staff studies, on the other hand, making more of economic barriers to opportunity, called for federal scholarships, provided there were safeguards against excessive federal control.

Hollinshead's report, in particular, explored collective action. To contain college costs he proposed that neighboring colleges avoid duplicating expenses by doing more course interchanges and other forms of cooperation—a forerunner of the college-consortium model today. He also proposed a central, but not governmental, commission to administer corporate scholarships and advise companies on how to set them up.[29]

This idea became a reality. In the early 1950s an increasing number of companies created scholarship programs. Their wish to nurture and attract "brainpower" was reinforced by cold war fears of government intrusion. In education as in other spheres, a strong independent sector meant a strong America, world champion of private enterprise. To advise firms on how to run their "sponsored" scholarships, the Educational Testing Service (ETS), founded in 1947 by the College Entrance Examination Board and other nongovernment bodies, created an advisory program called Sponsored Scholarship Service.[30]

A better-known venture was the National Merit Scholarship Corporation, established in 1955. National Merit was seeded by grants from the Ford Foundation and Carnegie Corporation, but it was designed to attract scholarships from company sponsors. The foundation and educational administrators who created National Merit worried about the "talent loss" of "highly able students" who did not go on to college after high school. National Merit's founding president, John Stalnaker, a psychologist and former college dean who had also run Pepsi Cola's scholarships, stressed that businesses and research laboratories needed widely educated recruits, not just specialized technicians. The "loss" of such talent stemmed from "lack of motivation" for college as well as lack of money.[31]

The National Merit solution was to organize a Jeffersonian pyramid of examinations and interviews across the country, offering the winners the honor and financial reward of a college scholarship. All winners received a minimum scholarship of $100, rising to $1,500 according to need. The college taking each winner also got a grant from National Merit to cover added costs.[32]

At a time when America's high schools were under fire for teaching "life adjustment" and a general dumbing down, the new scheme stressed scholastic rigor and attention to talent—just as Cornell's Andrew White in the 1880s had hoped that competitive scholarships would promote academic effort in the schools. Stalnaker and his associates believed, too, that the systematic procedure for choosing National Merit winners would help set a better moral "tone" for corporate scholarships than the notion that a "bright youngster today has a market price and can be paid to go to college"—a reference again to a bidding war.[33]

National Merit's architects also believed that, despite ETS's advisory service, the cost and complexity of choosing scholarship recipients was putting off many would-be scholarship donors who did not want to give just to individual colleges. National Merit largely did the job for them. In its first year, nineteen corporations participated, and 525 scholarships were awarded. This was tiny compared with the needs identified by the Rockefeller Commission, and soon after National Merit started, a leading admissions director, MIT's Alden Thresher, criticized the whole system for rewarding "highly motivated" students who were headed for college anyway rather than searching for "unknown talent." In tapping corporations rather than government, however, National Merit was in tune with the Rockefeller Commission's preferences. Stalnaker himself opposed federal scholarships.[34]

Getting Together

In 1954, a year before National Merit started, private colleges set up their own central agency for handling student aid. The College Scholarship Service (CSS) was a new offshoot of the College Entrance Examination

Board (College Board). A complex financial aid clearing house and information bureau, CSS provided its member colleges with a common "methodology" for assessing how much a student and his or her family could be expected to pay for college. It also told its members what each of them had offered in aid for the same admitted student. It had no power to ban merits and bidding wars, but in subtle ways it operated a "shame culture" against both.

Several forces converged to bring about CSS: long-term developments within the College Board, a new professional and liberal ethos among elite groups of admissions officers, and a reaction against bidding wars.

Wresting order from chaos was a founding mission of the College Board. Leading college presidents had created it in 1900 to replace a cacophony of different college entrance requirements with one admissions examination.[35] The exam business soon led to scholarship business. In 1907, the board started providing competitive examinations for several scholarship sponsors, including the Pennsylvania Railroad and the American Railway Master Mechanics. After World War II, College Board's scholarship services increased in line with the growing number of company sponsors such as Westinghouse and the Grumman Aircraft Corporation—though their scholarship requirements often called for "leadership" as well as academic ability. Pepsi Cola, which used College Board testing from 1945, set aside extra scholarships for black students in states where schools were segregated, while in general favoring the prototypical "Organization Man," later made famous by William Whyte. Winning candidates had to have earned the "respect of classmates" and be voted "most likely to succeed." The idea was to excite high school interest in college as well as lowering financial barriers to college.[36]

At this point a new generation of admissions and other campus officers appeared (though not yet a distinct financial aid profession). Many of them had close links with the College Board. Influenced by the GI Bill, they were heirs to the liberal side of World War II America, the planners and administrators who wanted to make postwar society a better place. They were also comfortable with quantitative analysis, an approach encouraged by wartime logistics and personnel testing. They were not all adept statisticians, but they were open to numerate arguments and plans.

A leader of the new wave was Harvard's John U. Monro, a principal architect of CSS and chair of its first executive committee. As a boy, Monro had been a day student on scholarship at Phillips Academy, Andover, and then gone to Harvard, again on a scholarship. After working in the Harvard news office and on the *Boston Transcript* as a reporter, he became a wartime naval officer, serving with distinction in the Pacific. He returned to Harvard after the war as an adviser to veterans. He did special studies of the veterans and helped his boss, Wilbur Bender, director of veterans affairs and later dean of admissions, devise methods of selecting ex-GI students who were more sensitive to their potential.

In 1950 Harvard's provost, Paul Buck, a big player on the Rockefeller Commission and a strong administrator (he also had a Pulitzer Prize in American history and a Great Lakes ordinary seaman's certificate), moved to centralize student aid. He gave Monro three days to create a financial aid office, handling student jobs, loans, and upperclassmen's scholarships. Monro did it and became its first director. Freshman scholarships remained separate for a while, but its director worked closely with Monro.[37]

Monro combined an antiestablishment streak with a deep desire to nurture ability among the disadvantaged. He believed, too, in "helping the student to help himself" and "helping him pay his way"—the titles of two of his articles. To make Harvard's grant aid go further, especially after the GI Bill money ran out, he and others persuaded the college to follow the prewar example of Yale and MIT in promoting student loans.[38] He also expanded student employment—and student workloads. He created Harvard Student Agencies, an umbrella organization providing premises and backup for a wide range of student businesses. For students with extra need not covered by scholarships, Monro offered extra work, known around the office as "JUMjobs" after Monro's initials.[39] All this, however, was part of a systematic effort to calculate more precisely what students could afford to carry, both in college costs and in workloads. And behind that lay an ardent wish that Harvard's social base should not contract when the veterans had left.

World War II was the catalyst for Monro's commitment. At the end of the 1950s, in a rare burst of ideological emotion, he contrasted the destructiveness of war with the "awakening" and "strengthening'" that education could bring to "each young person." He believed that "education is at the heart of our democratic process."[40]

The war also focused these concerns on race. While doing navy training in Chicago just after the attack on Pearl Harbor, Monro became interested in the city's black communities. Affected by a racial episode later in the war, he was dismayed on return to Harvard to see only two black faces in an early postwar class yearbook. To generate African American applications, Monro visited inner-city Chicago high schools and worked with a "Negro" scholarship foundation.*

The results were not dramatic. The Harvard class of 1961 contained just 7 black students among its 1,156 members. Monro himself regretted that Harvard had not appointed a senior black administrator to help make the college more congenial to black students. In 1967, he resigned as dean of the college to devote the rest of his life to teaching English and mathematics and developing freshman studies at small black colleges.[41]

Monro was not the only elite-college administrator to seek more black students in the postwar years. By and large, though, race did more for financial aid reform than vice versa: African American disadvantage symbolized wider inequities of class and education. Racism itself existed among CSS planners. As late as 1960, Northwestern's admissions director, C. William Reiley, an active participant in the talks that led to CSS, was color-tagging black, Jewish, and Catholic applications to contain the numbers admitted.[42]

CSS came from more, indeed, than liberal sentiment. It was also a form of price and cost control. Already, in 1939 and 1945, Ivy League universities had signed agreements aimed, in part, to limit the competitive buying of athletes. This did not stop the bidding war for academic talent, nor athlete-buying outside the Ivy League. The University of Pennsylva-

---

*On the carrier U.S.S. *Enterprise,* Monro was "damage control" officer, in charge of postattack repairs. The navy was ahead of the army in trying to integrate the races, and the ship's executive officer issued an order that personnel of different races should be treated the same. Monro, by his own account, disobeyed the order. To protect a young black seaman, a "carpenter's mate," from southern whites in the crew who were dead against his bunking with them, Monro offered him a cot in the carpentry shop and he took the offer. Later, in a firestorm following a *kamikaze* attack, the seaman showed exemplary valor, rescuing live ammunition from the flames. The "chiefs" (senior noncommissioned officers) then came to Monro and said their men would like the seaman to bunk with them. Monro said he didn't know if he would want to but he put it to him and he accepted. According to Monro, the young carpenter was the first African American that he got to know well, and the memory came back sharply to him when he saw the Harvard yearbook. Monro interview by author, Tougaloo College, Nov. 1992. On the navy and race relations, see Doris Kearns Goodwin, *No Ordinary Time* (1994), 521–24.

nia continued to buy athletes till a change of presidents and another Ivy League agreement in 1954, but by the 1950s more and more elite colleges saw the need for collective self-restraint.[43] Liberal arts colleges, in particular, feared that the Ivies and other rich universities would out-buy them. The Ivies themselves, offering an expensive range of quality programs, had more to fear in the long run from price competition for good students than from competition in the substance of what they offered. Harvard, indeed, hinted that it might heat up the bidding war and out-buy other colleges if steps were not taken to damp the bidding down.[44] The liberal axiom and founding tenet of CSS, that students should not have to consider price in choosing a college, suited the market situation of both the weaker and the stronger colleges that created CSS.

Whatever the economics, the actual formation of CSS came out of social ties between college admissions directors, backed at key points by their presidents and supported by history: northeastern colleges had conferred on admissions standards and other matters from the early nineteenth century.[45] A coterie from the Ivies and other elite male colleges (not yet coed) was especially important. Its members often dined together after conferences, and they even gave themselves group nicknames, the "Order of the Misunderstood" and the "Liars and Friars," reflecting, it seems, the pressures from different constituencies that weighed on admissions people.

Collusion

Most of them, maybe all, believed in basing all aid on students' financial need, but they found they were calculating that need very differently. This made it difficult to hold a firm line against offering competitive scholarships. Two administrators, Eugene (Bill) Wilson of Amherst and Donald Eldridge of Wesleyan, took a lead in pressing for a College Board review of the scholarships situation and a common financial information form for applicants.[46]

In 1952, the Seven Sisters College Conference of leading northeastern women's colleges requested a College Board study of admissions and scholarships. From early in the century, the Seven Sisters had made common cause on several fronts. Seeing themselves as elite underdogs compared with the male Ivies and leading male liberal arts colleges, they banded together to get full recognition by educators and financial donors. In 1943 the Sisters started cooperating in offering scholarships across the country, though their midwestern alumnae groups divided sharply at the time on whether the awards should be need-related grants or merits. By the early 1950s, need-related aid had won, and Seven Sisters officials were well used to conferring on matters ranging from admissions to student welfare.[47]

Responding to the calls for a collective review of financial aid, the College Board commissioned Dean Edward Sanders of Pomona, a former education professor, to spend several months visiting colleges across the country in the fall of 1952. Sanders' report, exposing the bidding war and likening its ethics to buying athletes, led to an urgent College Board "symposium" in the spring of 1953.[48]

Sanders and Monro gave the key addresses at the symposium. In a way, Sanders's comments were more radical. A storekeeper's son from Arkansas, Sanders had worked his way in the 1920s through Hendrix College (AR), an unusual southern college for the time, as it was racially integrated.

Sanders wrote and spoke thoughtfully about colleges and students. At the symposium he took a dim view of national recruiting drives by colleges. Like the Rockefeller Commission's Hollinshead, he did not believe that recruiting students from far afield produced a more truly diverse student body. Bowing to reality but with tongue in cheek, he proposed that the railroads, followed by airlines and bus lines, subsidize the national traffic in students by funding scholarships as a tax-deductible, marketing expense. More seriously, he called for collective action to reduce the scholarship competition, including a "common procedure for determining financial need."[49]

Monro's paper to the symposium offered just that. He laid out in detail the system he had developed at Harvard for deciding what students and their families could pay, adjusting aid accordingly. Like modern "need analysis," it resembled tax law, with sliding scales for handling income, assets, different kinds of expenses, and family size. Monro also showed the student budget he used in figuring financial need: tuition, room and board, medical fee, a figure for "personal and miscellaneous expenses," and a variable one for "two round-trip railroad coach trips home each year."[50]

Adjusting aid according to assessed need was not new. The Woodridge Little endowment at Williams provided for this in 1811. Yale and Princeton did it in the early twentieth century, and regional and other scholarships of the 1930s often scaled merit aid according to need, as we have already seen. Most grant aid, though, was either-or: a needy student either got or did not get a scholarship of a fixed amount.

After World War II, more colleges looked at ways of assessing and scaling financial need, and the Rockefeller Commission reports of 1952 explicitly suggested the use of income-tax returns.[51] Monro's scheme, in fact, included the use of federal tax returns, and it was probably the most sophisticated plan to date. Its purpose was to avoid giving some aided students too much and others too little. The Monro plan became a blueprint for intercollegiate cooperation, not just as a practical procedure but as a statement of equity.

Following the symposium, Sanders and others organized a West Coast College Board group of colleges for the express purpose of entering into a scholarship agreement. Thirteen colleges signed it in January 1954. The signatories promised to separate "honors at entrance"—accolades without money for high achievements—from "scholarship grants awarded in amounts proportionate to . . . financial need," as reported on a common financial aid application form. Academic merit could only figure here as a way of selecting needy candidates for "limited scholarship funds" (i.e., as a rationing device). Endowed scholarships, whose conditions required that they be awarded without regard to need, should be marginalized as "exceptions," in a separate part of the application form. The West Coast colleges undertook to promote the agreement's need-oriented principles among schools, corporations, and the general public.

Meanwhile, back east, the Seven Sisters tried to go even further. At a meeting in October 1953 a majority of the seven wanted to sign an agreement to compare individual scholarship offers to the same student before they were made, so as to keep them more or less the same. Several of the Sisters were already doing it informally by phone, as were other colleges, and the following year the seven agreed to do it more formally.[52]

Despite these initiatives, or maybe because of them, an ad hoc committee of College Board members, meeting in October 1953, could not agree whether a new central agency was needed for handling scholarships. Monro himself doubted that it was administratively feasible to start the new agency off on a national rather than regional basis. It took a group of presidents of New England colleges—Amherst, Bowdoin, Dartmouth, and Harvard—to put through College Board the proposal for a new agency with a national clientele. The board established the CSS in the spring of 1954, and ninety-seven colleges signed up to use it in its first year.[53]

The early CSS did essentially what the College Board still does today.[54] It provided a common financial information form for applicants seeking aid at member colleges. Originally called the Parents' Confidential Statement, it largely followed the Monro blueprint, and it was quite like a tax return, though it contained one or two questions the IRS would not have dared ask—an item on year and model of car lasted till the 1973 version. After some checking for consistency, CSS sent the applicant's data to each member college that the applicant had applied to. It also gave the colleges a manual on how to use the data in calculating what the family could afford. Two years after its founding, CSS started giving members its own calculations, but it was still left to college administrators to fine-tune their assessments of what families could pay and to gauge what students needed to live on.

After deciding what aid, if any, to give an admitted student—including loans and jobs as well as grants—the college reported all this information to CSS, which passed it on to other colleges offering a place to the same student.[55]

CSS did not assume that all colleges could meet all need, in part because there was no agreement as to how much a student could be expected to carry in loans and campus jobs. Nor was CSS a command organization. Unlike the West Coast agreement, its rules did not formally restrict merits. It operated, rather, through information, on the premise that member colleges would prefer not to make big bids for students, out of line with financial need, as long as they *knew* that their peers were not stealing a march on them. A college that did step out of line would be exposed by the reporting system and subject to opprobrium from the others. CSS backed up this ethic by training financial aid officers in "need analysis" and doing studies of student and family resources. This fed back into the need analysis formula and made it more sensitive, including (much later) to independent students who had no money from parents and might be parents themselves.

The CSS system did not wipe out merits and competitive bidding, but it did reduce them. CSS was dominated even more than its parent body, the College Board, by elite colleges where the bidding war had been hottest and which had the most scholarships. (In 1954, the year CSS was founded, the 155 members of College Board, about 11 percent of all four-year colleges, gave out 41 percent of all college scholarship money.)[56]

THE BIRTH OF CSS reflected its era in two respects. On one hand it was shaped by the rise of humane social science. Its organizers really did believe that quantitative analysis, applied sensitively, could extend college access by putting aid where it was most needed. Monro himself did not like the idea that CSS was mainly a defense against the bidding war; it was an agency of positive enlightenment. He was also wary at first of corporate scholarships, seeing them as an invasion of college admissions until General Motors and other sponsors agreed to gear their awards to financial need.[57]

In spite of its anticommercialism, though, CSS reflected an age of oligopoly. Industry's dominant corporations, less challenged than today by foreign firms competing in price as well as quality, tended to substitute what economists called "marginal product differentiation"—styling and gadgets—for price competition. In their high-minded way, America's elite colleges were doing the same. Of course they offered more than gadgets, but in getting together to end the bidding war, they were exerting producer power against the ability of customers to shop around for price bargains, even if they were also extending access to middle- and lower-income customers. CSS's founders hoped, indeed, that the new system would encourage groups of colleges to make binding agreements about awards (i.e., prices and discounts) as Seven Sisters and the West Coast group had already started to. Within a decade that hope would become a flourishing reality along with other aspects of the CSS approach to financial aid.

7
Choosing the Best

The most important three periods in American higher-education history were, arguably, the early nineteenth century (the break-out period of college expansion), the 1860s (birth of the state land-grant college system), and the mid-1950s to mid-1970s.

Today's mold of higher education was largely set in that last period. American higher education became at once a mass system and a highly stratified one. Big differences opened up between the scholastic selectivity of elite colleges and the rest. In the upper reaches of the system, colleges increasingly competed for an academic status based on published faculty research and getting "bright" students.

The effect on access to elite colleges was double-edged. The search for good students, supported by increased financial aid, fanned out through a wide range of the middle classes, but heightened academic admissions standards were a barrier to the disadvantaged.

The new selectivity caused three kinds of friction for elite colleges. First, alumni felt increasingly frozen out as the power of "connections" lost ground to the reward of meritorious achievement in college admissions. In fact, the two sides of the conflict accommodated each other. The colleges needed alumni gifts and bequests to help fund ambitious programs and, indeed, financial aid itself. Alumni families, for their part, put more into academic endeavor, as we saw in Chapter 2. Admissions offices continued to favor "legacies" ("alumni kids") though less than before: as admissions standards rose, "legacies" had to do better to get in.[1]

The second conflict involved civil rights and the drive by almost all colleges to enroll more black students. These students tended to do worse than whites on standardized admission tests such as SATs, and less well in college than whites with the same SATs.[2] From the mid-sixties, leading colleges tried to make their admissions criteria more sensitive, tapping for "potential" shown in adverse conditions. They also experimented with preenrollment courses and other programs to remedy cultural disadvantage. Worries persisted, however, especially among some faculty and alumni, that standards were being lowered for minority students.

The third conflict involved money and access. Attempts in the late sixties and early seventies to enroll more low-income students—not just black ones—caused a clash between financial aid spending and the costs of competitive excellence—offering a "richer" range of courses and recruiting distinguished faculty. When push came to shove, "excellence" won. In the late 1970s, efforts to seek and support disadvantaged students fell back. Student "diversity" remained a college value, but it was cheaper to achieve it by enrolling minority students, not all of whom had high financial need, than by enrolling large numbers of low-income students.

Along with these big shifts, elite colleges took a lead in developing new financial aid practices. These had their own bureaucratic momentum, but they were part of a changing academic culture.

Systems Beget Systems

Between the mid-1950s and the mid-1960s, colleges moved to a *packaging* concept of financial aid. They systematically helped students assemble packages of grants, loans, and jobs, taking into account what they got from scholarship foundations and state and federal government. By 1965 most colleges were doing this, providing students with at least two of the three main types of aid. A survey of financial aid administrators, 1962–1964, found that over 90 percent favored government loans and agreed that term-time jobs were "good for students."[3]

A big factor here was the federal government's National Defense Student Loan Program, started in 1958. This involved many more colleges in student loans, but the trend had actually started a few years before. The ethos of the new College Scholarship Service, explored in the last chapter, had much to do with it. Like CSS's method of "need analysis," packaging grants with loans and jobs was a way of stretching aid as far and effectively as possible in meeting student need. Many colleges offered their own loans along with federal ones until the 1970s when the great expansion of federally subsidized loans largely took over. Students themselves were readier to borrow, as more and more jobs required a college education and loans were more publicized.[4]

This is not to say that opinion was unanimously in favor of loans. The skeptics even included Pomona's dean Edward Sanders, a founding father of CSS. Sanders and others like him thought that big student loans encouraged parents to avoid making sacrifices for their children's education and landed young graduates with debt just when they were starting out to make their own homes and families.[5]

In other ways, too, CSS ideas did not always dictate how to handle aid. As a result of the federal requirement that colleges allocate National Defense loans only to students with financial need, many colleges signed up with CSS for its system of "need analysis."[6] In 1961 the 950 colleges subscribing to CSS officially adopted "Principles of Financial Aid Administration," including a statement that financial aid should not exceed a student's need. By 1970, the "Principles" were also stating that the *mix* of a student's aid package and its amount of "self-help" (loan and job) should be based on the student's financial "circumstances."

But these declarations were not binding; they were "guidelines."[7] Many colleges, including some CSS signatories, gave merit scholarships not based on need and altered the package mix so that specially desired students—top scholars or athletes, say—received what would later be called "preferential packaging": bigger grants and less "self-help." They did this, of course, to compete for desired students, despite the complaint that weaker students were less able to cope with heavy job or loan burdens.[8]

As we saw in the preceding chapter, the basic CSS system reduced but did not end the practice of competing for students through merit scholarships and aid that went beyond need. To reduce the practice still further, CSS helped colleges form cooperative "overlap" groups. The idea was that colleges in each group would give "relatively equal aid offers," based on student need, to common ("overlapping") applicants. By the mid-1970s, CSS was supplying financial data on applicants and their aid offers to twenty-four groups of two or more colleges—in all, nearly 150 colleges across the country.[9]

The style of cooperation ranged from phone calls between two or three colleges to set-piece conferences. Some groups simply affirmed common policies including the proscription of merits. Some tried to agree on the "expected family contribution" (EFC) that they would charge a shared "admit" (admitted student) to whom they were offering grant aid. Other groups just swapped information after the fact about what they had charged and offered. Since full tuition, room, and board, etc. varied somewhat between the colleges in a group, it made more sense to agree on approximate EFCs than scholarship amounts, as the latter would depend, or should depend, on total costs of attending the college. One or two groups also tried, though, to control the package mix between grants and "self-help," to prevent or limit the practice of giving extra grant money to specially desired applicants.[10]

Few of the overlap groups lasted long against competitive pressures to favor hotly desired students. The most enduring and organized overlap groups were the Ivy-MIT group and an allied group of selective New England colleges. Both groups emerged from informal consulting about how much to charge and aid those applicants for aid whom more than one college had admitted. By the end of the 1950s, financial aid and admissions directors of the two groups were meeting twice a year in conferences that included joint sessions as well as separate group meetings.

The two groups lasted till 1991, when the U.S. Department of Justice started its antitrust action against the Ivy-MIT group for price-fixing.[11] Their strength, compared to other groups, was a matter of culture and geography as well as economics, as we saw in the previous chapter. Concentrated in a small region with strong traditions of elite private education, they shared well-defined pools of applicants and a habit of talking with each other about common problems. Their officers confidently believed that superior institutions should not have to spend money on price discounts (scholarship grants) for students who did not need them. The quality and repute of their colleges should be enough to get the richer students they wanted at full price. This would husband aid money for good students who really needed it—provided that none of their number broke ranks.

There was also the question of athletics. The Ivies and some other elite colleges, mainly in New England, had originally come together as athletic leagues. Athletics remained important to many of them, but their administrations and faculty did not like athletic scholarships, and unlike a Duke or Stanford, which did give these awards, they did not compete in football or basketball with big state universities that bought athletes. They still faced, though, pressures from their own coaches and some alumni to give special deals to athletes—sweetened aid packages, if not outright athletic scholarships. Policing each other's aid offers helped them to resist—more or less—those pressures.[12]

IN THE MID-1960S ANOTHER policy movement got under way at leading colleges—a shift to what is loosely called "need-blind" admissions but should really be termed "need-blind/need-met." Under this policy a college admits students without regard to how much they can pay, and then meets all their estimated financial need after allowing for state and federal aid and, in some cases, scholarship aid from private foundations.

Need-blind/need-met admission involves financial risk because it rests on a *bet* that it will not land the college with more financial need than it can fund. This made colleges chary of declaring it their policy till they were sure it would stick. Yale was one of the first to implement it as official practice in 1964. By the late 1960s a handful of private colleges were doing it. Their number swelled in the 1970s and early 1980s, but some of them failed in some years to keep to it.[13]

The main alternative to a need-blind/need-met policy had hitherto been the usual practice but now acquired a name: "admit-deny." Admit-deny colleges admitted students without regard to their need but denied grant aid to some needy students—usually weaker ones—when the financial aid budget did not have enough funds for them. The gap might or might not be filled by loans and campus jobs.

A second alternative was to contain financial aid by "need-aware," or "need-conscious," admission, as it was later called: putting a cap on the number of needy, or very needy, students the college admitted.[14]

Establishing a need-blind/need-met policy required a new confidence that financial need could be filled by well-organized packages of aid, using loans and campus jobs to supplement grants. There also had to be a clear idea of what constituted "meeting need." Guidelines surrounding the new federal loan and work-study programs were important here in defining the maximum loan and workload that could reasonably count as part of financial aid. In actual dollars, too, the advent of federal grant aid helped some colleges make the final jump to meeting all need.[15]

The new academic selectivity of elite colleges was also a factor in going need-blind/need-met. Denying aid to some students but not others became more painful when all seemed "such great kids."[16] Avoiding the problem by need-aware admission was no happier a solution. In the liberal campus climates of the 1960s and early 1970s, administrators who deliberately turned away needy applicants had to keep quiet about it to avoid trouble from faculty and students.[17]

Need-blind/need-met admission, by contrast, signaled social inclusiveness and openness to all talents. It was specially attractive to high-priced colleges, anxious to show that they had not cut themselves off from mainstream American.

By the 1980s, need-blind/need-met admission had become a moral and academic status symbol—and an economic one too. The private colleges most able to afford it had large endowments and many students paying substantial fees. For all the democratic symbolism of need-blind/ need-met admission, high academic admission standards excluded most high-need students. Academic selectivity helped colleges go need-blind/ need-met by limiting their exposure to lots of aid-expensive customers.

Need-blind policy still carried financial risks, and these increased in the early 1970s at the very time that it also became more valued for its good public relations. During this period, middle-class objections to high tuition threatened to cause an exodus from private to state colleges. When the CSS and its member colleges tried to ease the problem by reducing their estimates of what families could afford to pay, this made more families eligible for more aid, putting more strain on financial aid budgets.[18]

Other college priorities, too, thwarted need-blind/need-met policy. This was even true at rich Princeton in the late 1960s and early 1970s. President Robert Goheen (1957–1972), the son of a Presbyterian medical missionary in India, had helped lead Princeton away from a culture of snobbery centered on its "eating clubs." Goheen and his successor, the economist William Bowen, issued a series of statements endorsing need-based aid for clearly defined reasons. As Bowen put it in 1976, "providing access to Princeton without regard to financial circumstances" was good "in its own right" (social fairness and opportunity) and good for the institution. The "friction of different perspectives" made for better education, and by reaching out for "the best minds and most promising individuals," Princeton would position itself to "educate future leaders" in a society whose leaders were already becoming more diverse.[19]

In the 1960s Princeton practiced an "admit-deny" policy and was hoping to achieve full need-blind/need-met admission, mainly through its large and growing scholarship endowments.[20] It was ready, however, to subordinate those hopes to a major policy move in keeping with the times: admitting women. The move entailed *adding* a thousand women to Princeton's thirty-four hundred male students in 1969. Increasing enrollment rather than reducing the number of men was more painless politically—but not financially. As at many colleges, tuition income did not cover all teaching and administration costs, so the university relied on income from gifts and endowment to make up the difference. Increasing enrollment would reduce this income per student.

To prepare for financial trouble, President Goheen approved a plan developed by a faculty economist, Gardner Patterson. This entailed fundraising for more scholarships, combined, if necessary, with need-aware admissions (admitting only richer women, and fewer poor males), plus budget cuts elsewhere. In the end, the need-aware measures were not deemed necessary; existing faculty and facilities absorbed the extra students much more than had been expected.[21] Had it come to a choice, though, Princeton would have put gender diversity above class diversity.

From 1970 on, Princeton achieved full need-blind/need-met admissions in almost all years. In 1971, however, amid cost inflation and a budget deficit, the university provisionally admit-denied fifty-one applicants by putting them on a financial aid waiting list. Struggling to be as fair as possible, the admission and financial aid directors offered grant aid to all "admits" from a "poverty background" and selected the admit-denied group so that it matched the admission ratings (admissions desirability) of those offered grants.

In the end, the budgeting problem evaporated, but not so comfortably as it had in the move to admit women. An extraordinary fund-raising drive by the Undergraduate Association (student government) produced grant aid for two of the fifty-one. Eighteen went elsewhere, and the remaining thirty-one were offered grant aid when a number of admits who had been offered grants did not enroll.

To prevent such a scenario happening again, the dean of the college, backed by the admissions office and involved faculty, called on the university (as they already had) to make financial aid its "highest priority." The administration, of course, had other spending priorities too: that was the rub. In the late 1970s, however, Princeton increased its financial aid spending from general funds, over and above specific scholarship gifts and endowment.[22] Others, too, were doing this.

Academic Elitism

The precarious progress of need-blind/need-met admissions was a small but telling part of a dramatic change in American higher education and society. The 1950s saw a sharp increase in the proportion of young adults getting college degrees, especially among high test-scorers. This was amplified by the postwar "baby boom," which expanded the traditional college-age population in the 1960s and 1970s.[23]

These trends brought together two themes we have already met—populist expansion and Jeffersonian selection. Among unselective community and state colleges, enrollments rocketed. Students taking degree courses at junior colleges multiplied more than sevenfold between 1950 and 1970.[24]

At the other end of the scale, elite private colleges expanded their student bodies somewhat, but their applicants increased more. In the early 1950s Stanford accepted more than three in four applicants; by 1965 it was taking one in four. Harvard moved from two in three in 1952 to one in three in 1960. The scholastic quality of elite-college applicants rose as well. Top students became more concentrated at top colleges.[25]

In the public sector, too, many universities became more selective academically in the 1950s and 1960s. The burgeoning enrollments of two-year community colleges were no threat to this. On the contrary, in California, home to 40 percent of all community-college students, ambitious leaders of the University of California system regarded community colleges and lesser four-year state colleges as a protective buffer zone. They satisfied democratic demands for widely accessible higher education while enabling UC campuses to be more selective. Some community-college students transferred upwards, but most did not go past two years. The same happened elsewhere.[26]

STUDENT DEMAND *ENABLED* ELITE colleges to be much more selective academically, but the colleges also chose to go this way rather than massively expanding their enrollments or making more of nonacademic qualities in selecting their students.

Enter *meritocracy* (not to be confused with "merit" scholarships, which may or may not be involved). Strictly speaking, a meritocracy is a governing elite whose members are selected according to their demonstrated ability (by merit of achievement) rather than social background or group type such as class, race, or gender. The kinds of ability rewarded may be more common in some groups than others, and the meritocracy, such as it is, may not be the only influential elite in the society. In fact, meritocracy is seldom pure: in almost any social system, who you know and where you come from can open doors.

The advance of meritocracy is bound up with the growth of expert professions and large-scale bureaucracies, with systematic procedures for selecting and promoting people. Hence the link to academia. *Knowledge*, well displayed and used, is a professional person's portable capital; it also offers a way of objectively assessing "merit," be it in college work or a civil service exam. Colleges and universities, for their part, have nearly monopolized the certifying of advanced knowledge through an array of degrees and diplomas.[27]

None of this was wholly new: the system had been in the making for decades. It was crystallized, however, by a change in the dominant culture of higher education. Christopher Jencks and David Riesman, writing in 1966–67, called it "the academic revolution." Again, this was not wholly new. The rise of a highly professional faculty, championing closely measured academic achievement among themselves as well as students, began in the late nineteenth century. It accelerated, though, in the 1940s and 1950s when wartime and cold war America discovered the uses of "brainpower," from anthropology (understanding the "national character" of enemies and the habits of allies) to nuclear physics.[28]

The link between faculty research and a college's status, and the growth of a national market in well-published professors, strengthened the voice of faculties in college affairs. In admissions, the faculty wanted, by and large, more students like themselves: academically motivated, not necessarily rich, Jews and Catholics as well as WASPs. At expensive colleges, that meant more financial aid. It also meant rolling back the anti-Semitism that still existed at many prestigious institutions.

Major universities, favored by government research grants, led the trend to a new academic culture, but they were followed by others.[29] Even liberal arts colleges, without big science labs and graduate programs, found a niche in the new culture. By offering superior undergraduate teaching, an ambitious liberal arts college could become an effective preparatory school for graduate work elsewhere. A good example was Wesleyan in Connecticut, which received an infusion of research-oriented faculty who had worked in wartime intelligence and other agencies. Aided by a lucrative endowment, Wesleyan transformed itself between the 1940s and 1960s from a provincial, traditionally Methodist college to an elite institution with a more diverse and highly selected student body.[30]

Elite colleges varied, however, as to when they became more academically selective. The top Ivies themselves differed here. Harvard's big postwar move to widen the net for academic talent really started in the early 1950s, some ten years before comparable efforts at Princeton and Yale, where a clubby conservatism was more broadly entrenched.[31]

Even at Princeton, though, a new reliance on SAT scores in admissions beginning in 1942 rewarded "scholastic aptitude" rather than a knowledge of subject matter that favored the best secondary schools. By the 1960s, SATs and their ilk had run into criticism for "cultural bias," especially against disadvantaged minorities, but the tests did open elite colleges to a wider pool of talent.[32]

SATs

Test scores and other numerical measures—high-school grades and class rank—weighed most heavily at the big state universities, which lacked the money and staff to evaluate individual applicants more deeply. At leading private colleges, admissions staff spent a lot of time evaluating a candidate's mind and character. Some of this was still academic: an attempt to distinguish curiosity and thoughtfulness from mere test-taking skills. But it also became part of a wider social engineering, putting together a range of abilities and talents (including athletic ones) while cutting some slack to alumni families. All this happened, though, on the crest of rising median SAT scores for those admitted, and the scores did correlate with academic ability.[33]

The link between student academic quality and the need for financial aid was explored most intricately in the mid-1960s by Humphrey Doermann, Harvard's admissions director. Statistical studies of Harvard's admitted students and applicants comprised the bulk of his analysis, using SAT and family-income data. But he also focused on three other, very different private colleges that were upgrading themselves academically: the venerable Illinois liberal arts college, Knox; the University of Puget Sound, Washington, already selective but trying to beat off state-college and eastern competition; and the prominent black university, Fisk, not selective (it admitted 96 percent of applicants) but academically ambitious.

On the basis of these and other studies, Doermann believed that more and more colleges were following each other in "lockstep" competition for "the bright and prosperous"—students with high SATs *and* the money to pay full private-college charges, which had gone up faster than average family incomes. The number of these students had grown, and richer students tended to have higher SATs, but there were not enough of them to go round, especially as leading state universities were entering the fray. The message was plain. If ambitious private colleges were not going to rein in their rising costs, they would have to spend more on need-related financial aid to get enough students at the academic levels they wanted.[34] And spend it they did.

Hope and Dismay

Many liberal academics in the 1960s believed in a "happy coincidence," as Jencks and Riesman skeptically put it, between academic professionalism and educational democracy. Selecting students on their intellectual merits would provide "equal opportunity" and "social mixing."[35] This outlook was very much that of Kennedy-style pragmatic liberalism. Doermann's statistical studies fitted right into it: he couched a personal concern for equalizing opportunity in a facts-and-figures appeal to colleges' self-interest.

Doermann worried, though, that private colleges might cut back on the big grants that "able but low-income" students needed, if the colleges could not get enough money from scholarship fund-raising or full-tuition payers. His data also showed that between 1956 and 1966 the median family income of Harvard scholarship holders stayed just above that for all recent high school graduates. Harvard's grant aid spending did increase a lot, but much of that increase was absorbed by raised charges.[36]

Doermann was not alone in his findings. Another Harvard admissions officer, Richard King, had already reported, in 1957, that only 18 percent of Harvard scholarships (under 5 percent of all Harvard undergraduate places) went to students in the lower half of American family incomes—this after a good five years of the refined, need-related aid system developed by John Monro. In his final report, covering 1952–1960, Harvard's dean of admissions and financial aid, Wilbur J. Bender, claimed that an expanding wedge of highly qualified "middle and upper-middle income" students was displacing "the commuter group" and other low-income students, despite his efforts to diversify the student body in many directions.[37]

In the view of Bender and King, toughened academic admissions criteria, coupled with rising tuition (causing what would later be called "sticker shock"), were excluding and deterring low-income students. Elsewhere, too, admissions insiders lamented in the early 1960s that most private-college aid went to students who did not have great need and would go to college anyway. More should be done to make the whole prospect of going to college, including getting student aid, a living reality to disadvantaged youth.[38]

Responding to these worries, leading colleges tried to reach down to lower-income students. Some of their effort focused on groups with particular academic promise. At Yale in the early 1960s, a much-discussed target was Bronx High School of Science, which had a pool of serious students propelled by Jewish values on achievement through learning. In the late 1960s, Amherst started targeting "blue-collar" and "middle-income" transfer students, many of them veterans, "whose intellectual ambitions [had] been aroused" at community colleges.[39]

There was also the matter of race. At institutions as far apart as UC Berkeley and Northwestern, the meritocratic liberalism that in general demanded higher academic standards and (in Northwestern's case) had to repel anti-Semitism also pressed for more racial diversity. At Yale and other eastern colleges, high admissions ratings for students with "character" and "leadership," once virtually a code for preppie styles, were extended to the ghetto survivor who looked like a future leader in a multiracial society. A drive started by Dartmouth in 1968 to enroll more black students as well as Native Americans and poor white New Englanders more than doubled the proportion of freshmen in the bottom quartile of national family incomes, from 4.1 percent in 1966 to 9.4 percent in 1971–73.[40]

Dartmouth's founding mission (to train Indian as well as white missionaries) gave it special cause to seek Native Americans, but the widening of racial targets occurred elsewhere too. The initial focus on black students, instigated by the civil rights movement and reinforced by black-student activism and the assassination of Martin Luther King, Jr., in 1968, spread to other minorities and disadvantaged groups. This happened in financial aid as well as admissions. In providing more aid for disadvantaged groups, colleges often started with special deals for black students (bigger grants and exemption from "admit-deny" policies). Some of these colleges then expanded their special benefits to include Hispanic and other disadvantaged groups, tapping money from federal and state programs.[41]

IN SPITE OF THESE advances, by the late 1970s many selective colleges had lost the confidence and will to prepare disadvantaged students for their academic rigors, a task that proved more difficult than some had imagined. As the liberal optimism of the 1960s faded, special education programs for these students were cut back. Instead, elite colleges competed more and more for middle-class minority students with good academic credentials and lower financial need, though they had already started doing this in the mid-sixties.[42]

The result showed itself even at Harvard, where grant aid spending had kept up with rising tuition more than at most private colleges in the state. In the 1960s, outreach efforts by admissions staff had increased the lower-income proportion of high-scoring applicants. Between 1960 and 1970 the presence of blue-collar workers, clerks, and sales workers among Harvard students' fathers had expanded to about one in five. By 1979 they had dwindled to one in nine, a much larger fall than in the national workforce.[43]

Across the nation too, between 1975 and 1980, the proportions of freshmen from manual-worker families and noncollege families fell more sharply at "highly selective" private universities and "very highly selective" private liberal arts colleges than at other four-year institutions, private or public.[44] Leading private institutions were more able than most to attract high-achieving middle-class minority students as a way to get "diversity." They also had the highest admission standards and tuition fees, usually necessitating big student loans that deterred low-income students.

By the end of the 1970s, the search for ethnic diversity had replaced anti-Semitism and racial discrimination at America's leading private colleges. In class terms, the picture was not so progressive. The introduction of need-blind/need-met policies and the expansion of financial aid had done little that lasted for low-income students at these colleges.

8

New Strategies

College Chooses

In late 1993, Oberlin College, Ohio, bit the bullet, or abandoned its principles, according to one's point of view. It decided to limit its intake of needy students by instituting "need-aware" admissions. It also established a major new program of merit scholarships not requiring need.

Under financial pressures and the influence of new market-driven strategies, other colleges made similar moves, but they were not made easily. Oberlin's journey dramatized the troubled history of student aid in the 1980s and 1990s, especially among elite colleges that were somewhat weaker than the market leaders. The leaders in turn were given pause by what the others did.

Oberlin, it must be said, was never a typical liberal arts college. Known throughout its history as a nursery of social activists—from abolitionism in the 1830s to 1850s to pacifism in the 1930s and gay rights and other issues today—it was the first American college to coeducate men and women to degree level and admit black students on a regular basis. Both took place soon after its founding in 1833. On race as well as gender, it was not immune to prejudices of the larger society, but it eschewed fraternities and sororities, and its ethos—among students as well as administrators—generally valued social openness.[1] (Harry Colmery, the liberal lawyer who largely wrote the GI Bill, was, fittingly, an "Obie.") In 1964, with Rockefeller Foundation money, Oberlin became one of the first colleges to organize precollege campus programs for inner-city high school students.[2]

Oberlin has also identified itself with academic and artistic excellence. Since the 1920s, unusually high proportions of students have gone on to get Ph.D.s; it has an outstanding art museum; and its famous Conservatory of Music, founded in 1865, enrolls some 400 of its 2,800 students.[3]

As much as any college, therefore, Oberlin has felt a dual commitment to access and excellence. Both obviously cost money—the first for financial aid, the second for faculty, facilities, and again financial aid, to widen the talent pool of applicants. By most standards, Oberlin has had a big endowment and a prestige that commands high tuition fees, but the pack it has wanted to run with—a group of elite colleges, mainly in the Northeast—has richer alumni and larger endowments per student.[4] And in the 1970s, Oberlin lost some of its distinctive image when the Ivies and other elite male colleges started admitting women and made special efforts to recruit black students and other minorities.

These challenges were not unique to Oberlin. Women's colleges, too, were threatened when male colleges went coed, and in a culture of constant upgrading and competition, many college administrations spend a lot of time eyeing stronger institutions as well as those coming up from below.[5] Liberal arts colleges as a whole became more anxiously competitive in the 1980s as the number of high school graduates leveled off—a trend made worse by a longer-term shift among four-year college students toward vocational subjects rather than arts and sciences.[6]

Faced with these pressures, Oberlin did not cut prices: to do so would signal weakness and require cutbacks in what it offered. Instead, it followed the tuition increases of its peers and market leaders. From the early 1980s private-college tuition fees began to go up faster than most family incomes. We will look later at the reasons for this, but it meant that more students qualified for more financial aid on the basis of need. Oberlin, which had ostensibly been practicing "need-blind/need-met" admissions and financial aid in most years from the early 1970s, saw the scholarships item in its "Educational and General" budget grow from 12 percent in the early 1970s to 20 percent in the early 1990s.[7] Yet the college was offering less-generous financial aid packages (smaller grants, bigger loan burdens) than its stronger rivals. In part because of this, Oberlin became less attractive to students and therefore less selective. Between 1971 and 1991 its "admit rate" (proportion of applicants offered places) rose from 44 percent to 68 percent in the College of Arts and Sciences. (The conservatory did better; it took 35 percent in both years.)[8]

Through the 1980s and early 1990s, Oberlin's planners twisted and turned as they tried to maintain quality without sacrificing historic obligations to needy students. They considered different admissions and financial aid strategies, one favoring the best students, another the neediest. By the early 1990s Oberlin was giving preferential packages (more grant, less loan) to outstanding students on aid, but indirectly it was also "gapping" (not meeting the full need of) all aided students, except the very poorest, by adding 10 percent to what the standard national means test indicated that they could pay.[9]

In 1989–90 Oberlin, like other colleges, tried targeting its publicity on rich suburbs, to attract more good applicants who could pay full fees. Though the actual selection process would stay need-blind, if Oberlin ended up enrolling more full payers and fewer needy students, it could afford to give the needy better aid. (The same argument is used for need-aware admissions, but "geo-demographic targeting," as the jargon had it, operated at an earlier point in the admissions effort.) For whatever reasons, the tactic did not work. The proportion of Oberlin students getting grant aid stayed at about 45 percent.[10]

Oberlin administrators also debated whether they should get back into giving merit scholarship not based on need. The college had given this up in the 1950s, but as it fell behind in the competition for high-scoring students, the pros and cons of merits (were they fair? would they work?) were debated.[11] In 1985 the conservatory, competing for top performers against lower-charging, independent music schools with big endowments and smaller overheads, was allowed to introduce merits. Seven years later, the main College of Arts and Sciences tried targeting some merits on middle-income white and minority students who were not quite poor enough to qualify for need-based aid.[12] The "experiment," as it was called, seemed to pull in some superior students, but the results were inconclusive.

IN TWO INTENSE MONTHS of meetings and memos, November-December 1993, the College of Arts and Science's General Faculty Planning Committee, chaired by religion professor Grover Zinn and supported by senior administrators, persuaded majorities of the college's faculty, trustees, and, it seems, students that Oberlin's financial and academic health needed a fresh approach. An enlarged program of merits would be established, supposedly paid for by "new money" (i.e., special fund-raising, though that proviso did not stick). The college's admissions would become need-aware, reducing somewhat Oberlin's intake of the weakest high-need students, but Oberlin would save its soul by protecting "under-represented minorities" from need-aware exclusion and by giving better aid packages, especially to minorities.[13]

To help administer and control the need-aware policy, an admissions rating scale would award a small number of points to a full payer, more points to a black or Hispanic or Native American, *or* a good athlete, *or* an alumni "legacy" (no added points for being in more than one category), and the most points for high test scores (SATs or ACTs) and high-school grades. "Personal" qualities got some points too, as did "early decision" applications (early commitment to Oberlin).[14]

Need-aware admission at other colleges is not usually operated this way, but Oberlin adopted the scale to make sure that its admissions staff, imbued with "Obie" traditions of access, would comply. The only row over the scale occurred when a black trustee, William Robinson, com-plained that racial considerations had not been adequately met. He got the points for minorities boosted.[15] The social-class implications were less discussed. Privately some faculty worried that "race [had] hijacked class," as one put it, but it was largely left to a political scientist with a British socialist background, Chris Howell, to make that point publicly.[16]

One faculty member, American historian Gary Kornblith, queried the cost rises that had prompted the need-aware policy in the first place. Oberlin, he said, should ask if it really needed such an expensive range of programs and courses. His challenge got nowhere. Most faculty valued need-based aid and wide social access to Oberlin; at one point they voted for a one-year pay freeze to support the aid budget. They wanted even more, though, to teach good students in a rich variety of courses, with ample time and backup for their own research.

Eight years later, at the start of a new century, Oberlin was in better shape. Its admit rate in fall 2001 was down to 39 percent for the College of Arts and Sciences (27 percent for the conservatory). This was due in part to better aid packages and perhaps to merits, as well as an upturn in the number of graduating high school seniors. The admissions office re-ported happily that a tenth of incoming students were black—the highest in a decade—and that 13 percent of the freshman class were first-genera-tion college students. This was probably higher than at most other elite colleges, many of which had also moved to need-aware admissions.[17]

In the investment boom of the 1990s, Oberlin's endowment nearly doubled, but the college did not go back to need-blind admissions. Ideally, its administrators said, it would like to do so, but there was too much pressure on the budget to develop quality programs and facilities and make faculty pay competitive. In the early 2000s, Oberlin increased its admissions preference for full-pay and nearly full-pay students as its gift income and endowment fell off in the recession and escalating health insurance and other costs produced budget deficits—a situation made worse as the recession produced more student distress calls for financial aid.

In many respects, the college remained a "left-wing" institution. It attracted liberals and activists, and its work-study jobs for students included community work off campus. Nevertheless, in basic enrollment and student-aid policies—including need-aware admissions, merit scholarships, and stiff loan requirements—Oberlin responded to financial and market pressures in much the same way as more conservative colleges.[18]

Cost Surge, Price Surge, and Demanding Parents
Managing Aid in Interesting Times

In the economic hurly-burly of the 1980s and 1990s, liberal arts colleges were particularly vulnerable. Their overheads consumed more of their budgets than at larger institutions enjoying economies of scale, and they often had difficulty attracting as many men as women. The more selective ones, however, ended up prospering as Oberlin did, and their financial aid history in the period was quite similar to that of leading private universities.[19]

A crucial part of that history was the rise of college costs and prices. Other writers have explained why tuition, especially at elite private colleges, has tended to rise more than prices in general. Among other things, colleges are labor-intensive (since when have they won high ratings for big student/faculty ratios?) and in pursuit of research excellence they have cut faculty teaching loads.[20]

From the early 1980s, increases in full tuition at private colleges—the biggest part of their charges—started to exceed not only price rises in general but the growth of most family incomes. The surge leveled off at a new high in the mid-1990s after it ran into political protest.[21]

As the economist Charles Clotfelter has shown, the main reason for this price surge, at least among top colleges, was not a "cost push" by any particular kind of expense. Rather, they increased their prices and general spending *because they could get away with it*—not to make money in itself but to buy the best of nearly everything. In the 1980s and 1990s median family incomes increased very little in real terms (measured against the cost of living) but the top 25 percent of families enjoyed a big rise in their real incomes at the same time as their average family size fell sharply and they became more ardent about getting their children into "name" colleges. Tapping this wealth and enthusiasm, elite private colleges pushed up full tuition—by more, indeed, than the income rise of the top 25 percent, but not as much as the top 5 percent of families. Between 1981 and 1992, leading private colleges increased tuition by somewhat larger percentages each year than private colleges in general, but the rest followed.[22]

Economists have been confusing, if not confused, as to whether increased financial aid spending was a cause or result of this trend.[23] Mainly it was a result. As at Oberlin, the tuition hikes meant that families further up the economic scale qualified for financial help. Colleges claimed a spurious virtue in giving more aid when in fact their prices had drawn even upper-middle-income families into need-related aid. At the same time, financial aid *enabled* colleges to charge high full tuition by providing price discounts to those students who could not or would not pay full price.

To some extent, admittedly, financial aid was a genuine cost factor (an "independent variable," as economists put it) in driving up college prices. In the 1980s and early 1990s, zero growth in the number of college applicants stimulated more spending on marketing and financial aid to compete for students, and a decline in the real value of federal grant aid shifted financial aid burdens onto college budgets. Although that aid was a small part of college assistance at expensive colleges, their leaders sometimes saw themselves as "dogs eating their own tails"—aid costs driving up tuition charges, which in turn required more aid, and so on. Financial aid, they feared, would gobble up all tuition gains.[24]

This picture was overdrawn. As long as a college could find some customers able and willing to pay a higher full price, it was worth it, financially, to charge that price even if the college had to discount it (give grant aid) to more customers. At most private colleges in the 1980s and 1990s, annual increases in *net* tuition dollars per student (tuition revenue *after* deducting college grant aid) were still above general inflation, especially at the most selective colleges.[25]

These results were partly achieved by containing financial aid—although in a sense that meant punishing the victim. Besides packaging more loans, private colleges as a whole left more financial need "unmet." Between 1988 and 1999, the proportion of estimated student need at these colleges not covered by aid (including loans and work-study jobs) grew from 12 percent to 21 percent.[26] Till the mid-1990s the main brunt of this fell on lower-income students: net charges at private colleges (what students paid after deducting all grant aid) rose faster for poorer students than richer ones. This was not true in the mid to late 1990s, but between 1992 and 2000, increasing proportions of private colleges' own grant aid went to middle- and upper-income students, especially the latter.[27]

The more expensive and selective colleges usually met all need, but in the 1990s a procession of them joined Oberlin in restricting their intake of lower-income students through need-aware admissions. At the very top it took a massive investment boom for some highly endowed colleges to make big increases in grant aid.

Despite those concessions, the whole process whereby rising college costs and prices led to curbs on financial aid reenacted an old struggle between college spending priorities—programs and facilities versus student aid for wide access.

Controlling financial aid, however, had to be done subtly; crude cutbacks would not wash. For one thing, the continuing value on "diversity" featured minority students, who tended to need more aid. For another, even rich parents and students sought the satisfaction—psychic as well as financial—of getting a special deal, and a good one at that. The father, earning $330,000 in 1997, who berated a North Carolina college for offering his not-brilliant son the lowest of three merit scholarship levels, was no freak.

In part, this just meant that higher education was joining an American mainstream culture that honored the tough-guy bargainer and expected almost no one to pay full sticker prices. But that culture was itself changing. Middle-class parents were less ready to sacrifice for college—to defer buying a new car or pass up an elaborate vacation or generally reduce high levels of consumer debt. Among the upper and upper-middle classes there seemed to be a new "sense of entitlement," coupled with a fear of not winning and a narcissistic wish to "look good."[28] Even the federal government, in the form of the Justice Department, sanctioned the new climate of bargaining and competition when in 1991 it broke up the "overlap" colleges' agreements on charges and financial aid.[29] The culture persisted through boom and recession, and it governed suppliers as well as customers: the strong demand for entry into "name" colleges did not diminish competition among those colleges to get "the best."[30]

All this favored the growth of "enrollment management," analyzing what it took, in care as well as financial aid, to attract and retain different types of students. A key part of this was allocating financial aid cost-effectively according to the college's goals. The role of financial aid in attracting needy and diverse students was not forgotten, but it was now meshed more finely with other aims, according to the college's circumstances.

One aim was saving or even making money—"optimizing tuition revenue" in the jargon. Historically, as we have seen, student aid—like any discount—had sometimes made money for under-enrolled colleges by bringing in more customers. Now it was discovered that even a fully enrolled college could increase its tuition revenue by manipulating financial aid, or "leveraging" as it was sometimes called. Basically this meant using aid to attract and enroll low-need or even no-need students (via small merits, for example), displacing high-need students who would have required more aid.[31]

Leveraging was just one part of some finely tuned admissions and financial aid policies that evolved in this period. All of them involved ethical as well as practical questions. Elite private colleges often tried to resist or modify them, but each was a track by which market forces penetrated more deeply into student aid. Today these policies are very much with us; they are not just historical.

Going Need-Aware

I discussed in the last chapter the open-checkbook exposure of need-blind/need-met admissions and financial aid. Colleges practicing it sometimes avoided beating the bushes for low-income, aid-expensive applicants: too many students with high need would break their financial aid budgets. And always there was the suspicion that ostensibly need-blind colleges did some peeking and cheating, quietly preferring the richer of two applicants if neither was stellar. When Smith led elite colleges away from need-blind admissions to an openly need-aware policy in 1992 (while still meeting all need), it was wryly praised for "at least being honest."

It is hard to know how much of the suspicion was justified and how much was jealous paranoia, heightened by the special nature of student aid. When a system purports to be altruistic but is also a competitive market mechanism, it is easy to suspect its integrity. Be that as it may, being need-blind was—and is—no guarantee of being *rich*-blind. Some colleges that have publicly espoused need-blind/need-met policies have also, more quietly, favored students from rich and well-connected families, not necessarily alumni, who are thought likely to give or help raise big money.[32]

Despite these compromises, being need-blind while meeting all need remains "an article of faith," as an Ivy dean put it, for about thirty highly selective colleges that are rich and strong enough to hold the line.[33] Here it still enjoys a cachet, symbolizing commitment to meritocratic excellence. The one Ivy university, Brown, that held out against need-blind admission was repeatedly criticized by schools, alumni, and students; in 1975 and 1992, minority students occupied its administration building. The investment boom of the 1990s and a new president moved it to take the plunge in 2001.[34]

Colleges moving in the opposite direction, from need-blind/need-met to need-aware admissions, encountered different amounts of student protest. The most successful resistance was in the early 1990s at Amherst and Wesleyan, where it got to the trustees. At both colleges the trustees were persuaded to think again about abandoning a fully need-blind admissions policy. The price in both cases was reduced grant aid, meaning higher loan burdens for the unrestricted number of needy students enrolled by the colleges.[35] Amherst and Wesleyan had enough market strength (customer demand and financial resources) to continue need-blind/need-met admissions without thinning their grants to an unacceptable level, but many other colleges were not so well fixed. Like Oberlin, they had to persuade their various constituencies, including students, that going need-aware was a painfully necessary way to keep solvent, pay for good faculty and facilities, and take care of the needy students they did admit.

The system they usually adopted was much like Brown's; put simply, it works like this: The admissions office selects applicants regardless of financial need, going down its wish list till it reaches a point quite low down the list. It then goes need-aware, choosing the rest of the class from a swing group of less-desirable but still admissible applicants. Here it will usually prefer no-need or low-need applicants over somewhat stronger high-need ones to keep within the aid budget, but it may also use the swing group to balance the class, favoring men, say, or intended physics majors if these are scarce. Many colleges use their admissions waiting lists the same way; some indeed are need-blind only till they start admitting students from the waiting list.

Colleges going need-aware often say that it affects about 4 to 8 percent of their admissions. That may not, however, be a negligible proportion of their lower-income students. At most highly selective private colleges, even without need-aware admissions, well under 20 percent of students come from families in the nation's bottom half of incomes.[36] There can also be a "student quality" problem in abandoning need-blind/need-met admissions. For colleges with deep pools of good and well-to-do applicants, it may not much matter: the substituted students may not be much worse than the students they bumped. In the mid-1990s, however, some colleges held to need-blind/need-met policies largely because they did not have a reserve of rich substitutes who could meet their standards.[37] Other, less-selective colleges could not even contemplate need-aware admissions; they did not have enough applicants of any kind to pick and choose.

When selective colleges did abandon need-blind/need-met policies, they usually chose need-aware admissions coupled with meeting all need rather than the converse "admit-deny" method of containing financial aid: admitting need-blind but denying grant aid to some students who needed it. The reasons for this choice emerged at heated meetings of the National Association of College Admission Counselors (NACAC) in the early 1990s.

Dominated by high-school college counselors and some admissions officers from unselective colleges, NACAC passed resolutions demanding that colleges practice need-blind admission even if they could not meet all need.[38] Backers of the resolutions argued that colleges should not "play God." They should let students decide whether or not to attend a college without getting the aid that the college figured they needed. Who could know what resources a student might find—a personal loan from a family friend, say, or a gift from a grandmother that would not show up in the college's assessment of family income and assets? It was also deceitful and wounding to reject a student without saying that the reason was financial rather than academic. Need-aware colleges rarely leveled in this way: even today their admissions literature seldom mentions the policy.

But the need-aware defenders held an honesty card too. Admit-deny policy could be a cruel sham, saying in effect to a poor student, "We'd

love to have you, but who knows how you can afford it?" At Mount Holyoke back in 1968 the student Afro-American Society made just this point
when it called on the college to reject black students if it could not give
them the aid they needed. (The demand worked: Mount Holyoke, which
was practicing admit-deny at the time, tried to accept and fully aid all admissible black applicants.)[39]

There was also a real welfare and administrative problem with admit-
deny, especially at expensive colleges with demanding academic workloads. High-need students admitted but denied sufficient aid tended to
fall behind in their studies because of working at extra jobs to make ends
meet, while pestering the financial aid office for more assistance.

Viewed in this light, need-aware admission, enabling a college to
meet all need, seemed a more responsible policy.[40] It could also help a
college's selectivity rating. Applicants admitted without enough aid were
more likely to turn down an admissions offer, and this in turn meant that
a college had to make offers to more of its applicants. As so often with
financial aid, market matters were seldom far from social and academic
ones.

Merit Issues

Merit scholarships, on the face of it, are the opposite of need-aware admissions: they involve spending money rather than saving money. As we
have already seen, though, merits can be a form of financial leveraging.
They can save money or at least not cost too much, by substituting students with low or no financial need—the kind who tend to win merits
due to superior academic preparation—for students who need a lot of
aid. Even a student receiving a full-tuition merit costs no extra money if
he or she replaces a student needing aid up to full tuition or more. A well-
publicized merit program can also attract other good applicants even if
they don't win merits, though they can be wasted if given to students who
would have enrolled anyway.[41]

Since the 1970s, merits have become a larger part of student aid at
private colleges. By the late 1980s, nine in ten colleges gave them, and
in 1999–2000, according to one estimate, over a third of private-college
grant aid did not require financial need. This included athletic scholarships, but most was based on academic record or "special talents."[42] Be-

tween 1992 and 2000, the proportion of private-college students getting merits jumped from 18 percent to 31 percent. A similar surge occurred in the public sector, as state governments and colleges sought talent more competitively. The trend to merits was particularly strong among midwestern liberal arts colleges, facing strong competition from state universities as well as the attractions of the East and West Coasts.[43]

Merits have also crept up the college pecking order as more and more selective colleges have been drawn into a bidding war for outstanding students. The main resistance has been at the top: the Ivies and about twenty-five other prestigious and highly selective colleges, mostly in the Northeast, have stayed with an elite tradition of restricting aid to the needy.[44] While even Harvard and Yale lose students to merit-giving institutions, ranging from Boston University to Rice and the University of Virginia, the merit-resisters attract so many good students that they do not have to buy them with offers that might trigger a merit bidding war among themselves. (In a sense, they already give merits to everyone: they choose all their students more stringently than most colleges pick merit winners, and then give big subsidies across the board from their rich endowments.)[45]

NB

Since the early 1970s, when there were signs of a new bidding war for students, there have been widespread anxieties about the long-term value of expanding merit aid, even when it pays off for individual colleges in the short term. In recent years, however, public-interest arguments about merits have largely focused on their growth at the state level. Among private colleges, merit critics have been more vocal than merit defenders about the interests of society and students in general, as opposed to individual colleges. Merit defenders seem to assume that whatever enhances individual colleges is good for society.[46]

The two sides have seldom had a real debate on these issues—not in public at least—so let's have one. Mike Merit and Alison Antimerit (genders assigned arbitrarily) make most of the arguments heard in the last twenty years.[47]

> Alison: Merits are an unfair waste of money. They mainly go to well-prepared middle-class students who would get to the right college anyway.
> Mike: Not from the college's point of view. Unless it has enormous prestige and selectivity, enabling it to scorn merits, it often needs them to attract

superior students. These students give a lot to the education of other students. And they raise the college's *U.S. News* ratings, which then attract more good students.

Alison: But by using money that could go to need-based aid, merits reduce the student body's social diversity—and diversity is educational too.

Mike: Merits needn't come out of the same pot as need-based aid. A college can buy good students like it does any educational resource—library books or extra faculty. And some scholarship donors prefer to give to "sheer excellence" through merits.

Alison: You know, though, that merits often bump the poor by enabling a college to enroll more well-prepared students and fewer disadvantaged ones. And when you talk of *buying* good students, you're describing exactly what the president of Columbia, Frederick Barnard, called "mercenary" inducements back in the 1870s. You're expecting students to work hard and choose colleges for what they get offered in money, not the education itself.

Mike: But rewarding achievement with money is an old American tradition. And why shouldn't richer students as well as poorer ones consider special price discounts (merits in this case) in choosing colleges as they would anything else. Many colleges, anyway, meet the "mercenary" charge by linking merits to special programs like research with a professor or a summer's study abroad.

Alison: That actually makes merits more unfair. A favored few, usually not the neediest, pay less for getting more.[48] Merits are also invidious because they are mainly based on what the student did *before* getting to college. A student paying full tuition may do as well in college as a classmate with a merit discount.

Mike: That used to be a concern in the 1980s, but students now don't seem to mind. They're used to paying different prices for all sorts of reasons. Like airline tickets.

Alison: You said it!

Mike Merit and Alison Antimerit share strong educational values, but Mike is essentially a market-minded conservative, while Alison is an equity-oriented liberal.

The Alison camp, however, has not been above market arguments. In the 1980s and early 1990s, it often claimed that merits signaled market weakness (having to buy students) and were less cost-effective as a way of luring good students than investing in better programs. To "turn a head," as the phrase went, a college had to spend exorbitant amounts of merit money. In the late 1990s, the growth of merits reawakened a fear voiced in the early 1950s, that competitive bidding for students would wreck colleges finances. Some critics also claimed that merit recipients, attracted to a college by dollars rather than the college itself, tended to be lukewarm alumni who did not respond to college fund-raising. Merits, in short, were bad business.[49]

Merit defenders have denied most of this. Merits, they say, can visibly strengthen a college, not weaken it, if they *go with* improved "substance and sizzle" in the college's programs. Smart targeting of merits, and experimenting with different amounts offered, can make them cost-effective in attracting good students. And the honor attached to a merit can flatter the student's parents and encourage them to become loyal donors to the college.[50]

Merit defenders have also invaded the opposite camp with their own appeals to liberal fairness. They produced three such arguments during the 1990s and early 2000s, though none of them was wholly valid.

1. Merits spread talent down the college pecking order.
The economists Michael S. McPherson and Morton Owen Schapiro have argued this since the 1980s. They concede, indeed stress, that merits are often wasted in competitive offers between peer institutions. But they also say that merits enable colleges to attract students who would otherwise go to more selective and advantaged colleges where they would not qualify for merits (if the colleges gave merits at all).[51]

This "drawing down" effect does indeed occur, though no research has been done to show how much it happens. The opposite can happen too: private-college merits can pull talent "up" from cheaper and less-well-funded state colleges.

In terms of social class, the drawing-down effect is often quite limited, because the talent moves between institutions with broadly similar social composition—for example, from the Ivies, giving no merits, to Duke or Tulane, which do give them. And when public colleges use merits to draw high-fliers away from elite private institutions, they tend to put them in special honors programs, reducing their benefit to other students.[52]

This said, merit scholarships probably do lessen the monopoly of talent by the richest and most selective colleges.

2. Merits lighten middle-class burdens.

Many merits go to students who qualify financially for little or no need-related aid but who have much more difficulty paying high tuition than do richer students. Merits ease the pain.

The relief, though, is uneven, as only some middle-class students get merits. In the 1990s, too, the growing proportion of high-income students at private colleges (those in the top quarter of all family incomes) who got merits overtook the proportion of middle-income students (two middle quarters). So merits gave increasing relief to rich students too.[53]

3. Merits can increase a college's tuition revenue, *funding more need-based aid.*

If merits, providing less than full tuition, attract added students to an underenrolled college, they will increase the college's tuition revenue because the added students will pay some tuition. As long as this added revenue exceeds the added costs of teaching and administering the extra students, the merits produce a real surplus. Some of this may be used to fund more need-related aid.

Merit aid, however, often pays off financially for a college not by adding tuition payers but by substituting advantaged students for high-need students, as Alison observed above. This is particularly apt to happen at more selective colleges that have full enrollment anyway, so that giving merits does not increase the total number of students. The end result is a cut, not an increase, in the college's spending on need-related aid—as is sometimes intended.[54]

MERIT AID HAS SHOWN itself to be a more complex animal than college officials realized in the early 1980s. At the most selective colleges, however, it is at best a necessary discrimination rather than an object of enthusiasm.

Preferential Packaging

Although most private colleges still give more need-related aid than merits, specially desired students often get a bigger grant in their financial aid packages, reducing the expected "self-help" (loan/job) component.[55]

"Preferential packaging" of this kind has caused much less public discussion than outright merits. This is partly because it still goes to needy students, but also because mere "packaging" sounds more trivial and arcane than outright merit awards—a matter of relative adjustment best left to college administrators.[56]

Yet preferential packaging is now an important element in the way most private colleges allocate student aid. Two-thirds of private colleges responding to a 1994 survey said they did it, and it seems to be gaining popularity.[57] (Fewer state colleges do it—a third in the 1994 survey— as they depend more on state and federal student aid outside their control. Charging lower tuition, they also have less pressure to reduce it with fine-tuned offers.)

Many private-college administrators find preferential packaging a good way of combining the *welfare* and *market* functions of student aid: it is confined to needy students while helping a college compete in the market for students that many colleges want. But preferential packaging is not always as fair and pure as it may look, though its complex evolution has masked the inequities. Preferential packaging has developed a big array of different types, each based on a student attribute. Each type favors and disfavors different income groups.

"Good students," not surprisingly, are the most likely to get preferential packaging at private colleges. In the 1994 survey, 91 percent of private colleges based at least some of their preferential packaging on academic merit. Fifty-two percent did so for minority groups, 39 percent for students with talent in the performing arts, 30 percent for those with athletic prowess, and 29 percent for lower-income students.[58] Preferential packaging based on academic merit or special abilities (sometimes called "merit within need") is less common among more selective colleges, but during the late 1980s and 1990s it reached up into the elite strata even more than merits did.[59]

Varying scholarship aid according to perceived merit goes back, as we saw earlier, to the nineteenth century, though it was not widely done then. In the 1960s and 1970s, when top colleges had become much more selective academically, many started meeting all need without discriminating between good and mediocre students—they all seemed good. The colleges therefore expected all needy students to carry up to the same specified amount of "self-help" (loan and/or job) before qualifying financially for a college scholarship. If their estimated financial need was less than the self-help figure, they received no college grant at all.

Some Ivies, however, did preferential packaging, due largely due to their tradition of giving generous "national" scholarships to needy high-fliers outside the east. Different Ivies phased these out at different times, but the weaker ones retained and even expanded this preferential packaging in the 1990s to compete against stronger Ivies as well as non-Ivy colleges offering merits.[60] They also did more ad hoc special deals, negotiated with star applicants, as we will see in the next chapter.

"Merit within need" packaging tends to favor middle-income students over low-income students, who are less apt to have outstanding academic records. Many of the questions about fairness and cost raised by merit scholarships apply to preferential packaging, too. Like merits, academically-based preferential packaging can benefit a college not just by attracting good students but by "optimizing" tuition revenue—either by increasing enrollment (if a college is underenrolled) or by displacing high-need, aid-expensive students.

Colleges that lack big endowments and depend for income almost entirely on tuition fees are more likely to value the revenue aspect of preferential packaging, especially if they already have many students needing substantial aid. Richer and academically ambitious colleges, which go for preferential packaging, are more apt to see the revenue aspect as a secondary benefit. When Smith College created its Dunn Scholars program in 1994—a preferential package that replaced student loans with extra grants—it did so mainly because of worries about losing outstanding applicants to other colleges. At the same time, Smith's dean of enrollment responded to fears about its cost by predicting (accurately) that the program would not reduce net revenue. Although each Dunn scholar cost the college more in grant money than a non–Dunn scholar with the same need, the program's overall effect was to enroll a larger number of strong low-need students, replacing weaker high-need applicants who would have cost the college more in grants than the Dunn scholarships.[61]

Not all these preferential programs have the same class bias. The most regressive versions are based primarily on test scores and/or exclude high-need students on the grounds that they get big grants anyway, or they entail *extra* loan requirements for the weakest ("low-rated") students without special concessions to those with high need.[62]

Some colleges, on the other hand, use such wide criteria for preferential packaging—stressing a student's potential and motivation as much as test scores—that they do not favor middle-income students over low-income ones. Both Oberlin and Mount Holyoke claimed to achieve this in the mid-1990s.[63]

UNLIKE ACADEMICALLY BASED PREFERENCES, improved packages for minorities—the next most common type at private colleges—go disproportionately to lower-income students.[64] Their usual beneficiaries are African, Hispanic, and Native Americans—groups classed as "underrepresented minorities," as far fewer of them get to four-year colleges than (non-Hispanic) whites. Some colleges include Asian Americans, especially in states where they are few. (Asian Americans as a whole are not underrepresented, though this is not true of all Asian nationality groups.)

Preferential packaging for minorities has been widespread among private colleges since the 1960s. Its growth and persistence reflects the strength of ethnic diversity values on campuses across the United States. Despite racist episodes and black-white friction—among college administrators as well as students—colleges became important redoubts for "affirmative action" (positive discrimination) in the conservative years of the Reagan and George H. W. Bush administrations. They have continued to be so.[65]

Several of the arguments for minority-based preferential packaging are the same as those developed for affirmative action in college admissions, as related in Chapter 1. More specifically to financial aid, proponents of preferential packaging for minorities argue that African and Hispanic Americans tend to have less credit access and fewer job contacts (even after college) than white Americans at the same income levels, and that Hispanic Americans are particularly averse to borrowing.[66]

Private colleges enjoy some safety from attacks on affirmative action. The legal cornerstone of these attacks is the Fourteenth Amendment requirement that the states give "equal protection of the laws" to all persons. In college admissions and financial aid, this applies most directly to state programs and public colleges.[67] Also, adjusting a package to attract a desired type of student is less obviously subject to the amendment's requirements than is a clear-cut minority scholarship. Still, some private-college leaders have been uneasy about the racial restrictiveness of minority-based preferential aid, especially its discrimination against disadvantaged white students. The concern involves basic fairness as well as a possible vulnerability to lawsuits.*

On both grounds, Oberlin and Smith, which had established minority packaging in the early 1990s and late 1980s respectively, were among several colleges that gave it up in the 1990s. Smith substituted special outreach and scholarship programs for disadvantaged students including minorities.[68] Stanford expanded its "Diversity" awards, concentrated on the usual three minority groups, into "Special Recognition" awards, which included other students too, especially those who showed ability in hard circumstances. The change reflected California's variegated ethnic mix and its bruising political battles over race-based admissions at the state universities.[69]

It should be added that some colleges like Oberlin that have abandoned minority packaging but operate a need-aware admissions policy, still protect low-income minority applicants from exclusion under that policy.

THE PREFERENTIAL POLICIES DISCUSSED so far have only had an indirect *tendency* to favor one or another socioeconomic group. Some policies do so directly. The most obvious type is "differential packaging," as it is known in financial aid jargon. Differential packaging uses extra grants to reduce the loan or job burden of students with low family income or high financial need. The exact categories vary from college to college and sometimes explicitly favor first-generation college students.

Differential packaging has been most common at the richest and most selective institutions, where it has existed since the 1960s. With relatively few low-income students, they can afford more easily than most the extra cost of differential packaging, and many of them are heirs to the

---

*At the time of writing, no court has ruled on preferential packaging for minorities. In my view, it violates the spirit of prevailing Supreme Court decisions on race and state university admissions because it uses group-based numerical formulas to decide who gets the preferences rather than weighing race along with other attributes of the individual student. See *Regents of the University of California v. Bakke* (1978), espec. Justice Powell, and *Grutter v. Bollinger* and *Gratz v. Bollinger* (2003).

original College Scholarship Service tradition of basing aid only on financial need.

Not all rich and selective institutions practice differential packaging, however. Since the early 1980s, between a third and a half of the thirty-one elite Consortium on Financing Higher Education (COFHE) group of private universities and liberal arts colleges reported reducing self-help levels for low-income or lower-class students. Elite colleges that do not do differential packaging look to their students' earning power after they graduate. All of them, they assume, will have a reasonable chance to pay back their loans. Colleges that differentially package, on the other hand, are apt to stress that big loans scare off poor families, and that low-income students may well have to contribute summer earnings to their families and go on contributing after they leave college.[70]

The most dramatic expansion of differential packaging was made by Princeton in January 1998. Already reducing student loans for poorer students, it now replaced all loan "expectations" with grants when family income was under $46,500 (just over the national median). Students with family incomes between $66,500 and $46,500 got their grants progressively scaled down. Two years later, Princeton replaced loans with grants for all its students on financial aid.

Over these two years Princeton also made big changes in how it assessed family assets, savings, student summer earnings, and other items in deciding how much students should pay. The result was that many students paid less. What had started as differential packaging for low-income students expanded into concessions that gave all aided students more aid and qualified more upper-middle-income students for aid too.[71]

Princeton did this in part because it could afford to, especially in the wake of the 1990s investment boom. It had, and has, by far the biggest endowment per student of any American college.[72] It also feared it was losing low- and middle-income students to competitors, including state universities. By 1997 its proportion of undergraduates qualifying for need-based aid had fallen below 40 percent, from the low forties five years before—an enviable state financially for many college administrations but not for a college sitting on billions and still sensitive about its exclusive image.[73]

Princeton's competitors did not spend much time praising its generosity. Instead they quietly grumbled that the moves were pure price competition and publicly declared that aided students should contribute financially to their education—ignoring the fact that Princeton still expected its aided students to hold down term-time jobs.

Policy responses to Princeton varied. Some elite colleges that already had differential packaging intensified it, reducing still further the loan burdens of their neediest students. Others increased grants across the board: Harvard halved the loan and job loads of all aided students between 1998 and 2001. Many more elite colleges reduced their assessments of student and family income and assets, especially home equity.[74] This largely benefited middle-income students and qualified more upper-middle-income students for aid.

Financial aid observers feared that colleges unable to afford big concessions to many students would instead use more merits and preferential packaging to cherry-pick their strongest applicants. This was far from the differential-packaging principle of concentrating aid on the neediest.[75]

IN THE MEANTIME, STARTING long before the Princeton moves, many colleges in the 1990s—including highly selective ones—adopted packaging policies that, one way or another, gave extra grant aid to *low-need* students. The favors went especially to those whose assessed financial need was small enough to qualify only for loans and jobs, as could happen when all aided students were supposed to carry a standard amount of self-help before qualifying financially for grants. Middle-class families complained that they were shouldering steep college costs yet getting no grant help. "You've given us nothing" was the cry. Among high-tuition colleges, it took a strong market position (high demand) and a stubborn attitude to resist this appeal.[76]

The 1990s saw colleges further down the pecking order develop complex discounting strategies that, again, directly favored students with low (or no) need: they included merit awards as well as preferential packaging. These policies concentrate on "yield" rather than need. They rest, that is, on calculations of how many students of a particular type will come to the college at a given price and discount. They focus on what a student is prepared to pay, not what he or she *should* or *could* pay.

The prime target is often the student with a good academic record and low or no financial need. In high demand elsewhere, this student usually gets the best package in relation to his or her financial circumstances.

These policies use sophisticated statistical modeling, often supplied by specialist consultants, and they have been greatly facilitated by the computer revolution. They also reflect a general business trend towards "market segmentation," in which analysts measure the amount of consumer buying ("yield" produced by different prices and marketing appeals among different types of customer). Airlines as well as colleges have used the term "need-analysis."

Complex, yield-oriented discounting is practiced mostly by less-selective private colleges that have little endowment and depend heavily on tuition revenue. Some elite colleges, though, have been important in its development—especially Carnegie Mellon, Johns Hopkins, and Rochester. Their analytical approach, stressing the price responsiveness of different types of students, has influenced other leading colleges, which have commissioned their own faculty economists to do studies of yield.[77]

Even so, elite-college managers have been disturbed by the yield approach and other practices discussed in this chapter. From need-aware admissions to the advance of merits to complex discounting, market stratagems have complicated the world in which need-blind admissions and need-based aid reigned together in moral supremacy. Elite colleges—creators of the College Scholarship Service—largely built that world, though later they led the way to need-aware admissions. In the 1990s, college administrators, especially financial aid veterans, expressed anxiety and ambivalence about the erosion, as they saw it, of "need-based values." The next chapter says more about these concerns and the way in which elite colleges tried to control the onward march of the market.

9

Containing the Market

Professional Angst

The departures from need-based aid met in the last chapter have been uncomfortable for financial aid officers and other college administrators. My interviews with them in the 1990s produced remarks about "unease" and "soul-searching," being "torn" by new policies, and wondering if "I am compromising my values." The disquiet appeared most strongly in discussions of "ethics" at professional meetings. In 1997 the College Board organized a whole conference on "Ethics in Enrollment Management and Financial Aid," though the main result was simply a call for more discussion and open disclosure of practices.[1]

The anxiety stems from the historic tension between market and social mission in college admissions and student aid. That tension was sharpened by the development of a modern financial aid profession, dedicated to allocating aid on the basis of need but increasingly dominated by the demands of sophisticated enrollment management. College financial officers belong to a national association that states that their first responsibility is to the needy *student,* but they are paid—and hired and fired—by college managers who require them to think first and foremost of the *college* and its standing vis-à-vis market rivals.[2]

The two viewpoints, of course, are not necessarily opposed, as we have seen historically. Taking good care of students is in any college's interests, and enrollment managers know it. But when veteran financial aid officers say, as they sometimes do, "I'm a Neanderthal" (or a "dinosaur"), they are saying, in a discreetly self-deprecating way, that their heart belongs to an earlier age when financial aid was more simply centered on need. Nor is this just nostalgia. Some enrollment managers as well as financial aid officers have admitted to me that they would prefer not to give merits or do academically based preferential packaging if they could count on other colleges not to do so either. But usually, of course, they cannot.

Ambivalence, then, is not confined to financial aid officers. Indeed, admissions officers have their own set of conflicts over the way colleges sell themselves.[3] In some institutions, too, admissions officers have been more enthusiastic about reaching out to disadvantaged groups than the financial aid office, which has to be concerned about balancing the aid budget. And at some colleges, the strongest voice for basing aid on academic record rather than financial need comes from faculty.

For many college officials involved in financial aid and admissions, there are ways of talking and thinking about it that massage ambivalence and make it easier to live with policies that favor the nonpoor.

1. Technical euphemism. "We brought down the discount rate" (grant-aid per enrolled student as a percentage of full tuition) sounds better than "we cut financial aid" or "we enrolled fewer high-need students." "We must look for more students with financial strength" sounds better than "we've got to get more rich kids."

2. "Others are worse." At colleges that give, say, small merit awards, administrators will sometimes point to other colleges that give bigger merits ("they just *buy* students"), or don't meet all need, or, worse still, are guilty of both.

3. Specters of social division. Over the past three decades private-college officials have echoed the fear of Harvard's president Eliot in 1904 that high tuition and expanded aid would lose the middle classes and polarize the college between two blocs—the rich who could afford high fees and the poor who would get the aid. The conclusion sometimes drawn today is that the middle classes rather than the poor need extra assistance to stem their flight to state universities where full tuition is lower. This flight in fact has not taken place at highly selective colleges (at least not before the recent recession), and low-income students do not form a large bloc at most private colleges.[4] A bigger but less-publicized problem at high-tuition colleges is the strain of being one of an impecunious few living among a prosperous majority.

4. "They come anyway." Selective-college administrators often say they get high yield (high rate of acceptance of admission and financial aid offers) from low-income applicants. They sometimes add that even when the financial aid packages include heavy loans, the grants for high-need students are so big that they satisfy the students. This ignores the many low-income students who do not apply to expensive colleges in the first place. But it is true that yield is often relatively low for students with strong academic records (who tend to be middle or upper income); these students have more offers from other selective colleges to choose from. It is tempting, therefore, to give them better financial aid packages.[5]

5. Cognitive anarchism. The more ebullient defenders of merits and other departures from need-based aid sometimes claim, "We don't know what need is anyway."

Determining how much a student or family can and should pay toward college costs is an inexact science. It requires detailed knowledge of individual circumstances and value judgments about the sacrifices that a family should be prepared to make.[6] But this does not invalidate the attempt to apply common standards, adjusted as sensitively as possibly to special circumstances, in deciding what a student or family should pay.

Since the 1980s, though, consensus about the value of common standards has weakened as colleges have gone their own way in assessing their students' financial need. This has encouraged some enrollment managers to challenge the moral superiority of the financial-need concept while still using it as a factor in fashioning student-aid packages. Other administrators, who believe more deeply in basing aid on financial need, have lost confidence in the collective health of their mission.

Elastic Rules, Slippery Deals

> *I hate to think of myself as a used-car*
> *salesman as some of us have to be.*
> —Financial aid director of a highly selective
> private midwestern university, 1994

Market stratagems described in the last chapter concentrate on defined groups of students. Since the mid-1990s, private colleges have also been more ready to cut special deals with individuals—to boost their initial aid offer to a strongly desired applicant who can show some financial need and cite better offers from other colleges. This practice is not new but it has been encouraged by a customer culture of bargaining and an industry of "how to get more" advice books, consultants, and Web sites.[7]

How some colleges have responded is equally important. By burying competitive special offers within the way they assessed student need, they discredited and obfuscated the whole system of student aid.

There are basically two ways of sweetening a financial aid offer to a student without exceeding the student's estimated financial need. The first is ad hoc preferential packaging: increasing the grant and reducing the "self-help" component (loan and job) of the package originally offered to the student. The second way is to raise the estimated financial need itself. This reduces the expected family contribution (EFC): the basic price charged to the student supposedly on the basis of what the student (and student's family if the student is a 'dependent') is deemed able to afford.

The most openly publicized version of the first way was started by William Elliott, Carnegie Mellon's vice president for enrollment, in the early 1990s. In its admissions and financial aid literature, Carnegie Mellon invites admitted applicants to submit copies of "competitive" offers from other colleges, and it says it *may* respond to these, budget permitting. Elliott even prints the number of recent "requests for review" and the number of "favorable responses." In 1998–99 about half the petitioners—the more desirable ones—got their grant raised, by an average of over three thousand dollars.

Elliott's operation is only unusual in that he publishes what he does. Many admissions and financial aid people disapprove of his blatant competitiveness, though his candor is in line with calls for open disclosure of practices. Elliott himself argues that his practice has its own equity. It "levels the playing field" for a student between different colleges so the student can choose a college without regard to price—an original mission, ironically, of the College Scholarship Service.[8]

In a more informal and limited way, Ivy universities did this in the 1980s. Yale, for example, would sometimes improve its offer to a strong candidate if Princeton or Harvard had offered more, but usually not to students with offers from less prestigious Ivies.[9] As cooperating members of an "overlap" group, the Ivies agreed quite closely on the EFC for students that more than one of them had admitted. This left the aid package—the mix of grant and self-help—as the place to sweeten offers to hot candidates.

Events in the early 1990s, including the antitrust breakup of the overlap groups, encouraged the Ivies and other elite colleges to move to the second way of competitively improving their offers: revising EFCs. MIT's settlement with the Justice Department in 1993, as well as subsequent legislation, prohibited colleges from agreeing on prices (EFCs) they charged to individual students and families; it also explicitly preserved the use of discretion ("professional judgment") in adjusting EFCs to special financial circumstances. Colleges whose admissions were not need-blind could not discuss the details of financial aid policy directly with each other. Or so it seemed. The law, in fact, was unclear about who could discuss how much with whom, but the threat of further antitrust action by the Justice Department—which would impose huge legal and information-gathering costs on colleges, as it had in the overlap case—caused a general fright among college administrators through the 1990s about cooperating on financial aid policy.[10]

In 1993–94, moreover, the government started a new "Federal Methodology" (FM) for assessing students' financial eligibility for federal grants and loans. At the same time, the College Board launched a separate "Institutional Methodology" (IM) for private-college aid. The more selective colleges in particular used IM, but they still had to use FM for the federal loans and grants that went into their students' aid packages. Amid initial uncertainties about how to use these methodologies, colleges found they were assessing financial need quite differently from each other.[11]

Accidental variations soon became deliberate. When seeking a desirable candidate, a college could sweeten its financial aid offer by altering its assessment of what the student and family could pay—"tweaking" EFC, as the euphemism put it—rather than altering the package mix. From the student's standpoint, lowering EFC rather than preferential packaging usually came to the same thing: it increased the grant. But it enabled the college to respond to competitive offers while appearing to stay true to need-based principles.

Many private colleges tell students who query financial aid offers that they are open to "new information"—about special family expenses, for instance—which may increase the offer. Using "professional judgment," a financial aid director will bend the rules in unusual cases—reducing, for instance, the standard assessment on home equity (usually 5 percent through the 1990s) if the family lives in an area with very high house prices relative to their income. Some leading colleges are adamant that they only make these adjustments in cases of genuine extra need, although competitive offers from elsewhere may have triggered the further inquiry. They say, too, that being open to these discussions helps the first-generation college student who may not be as savvy about filing for aid as middle-class families.

Some colleges, though, are aggressive in using "new information" to favor and compete for strong candidates. As one administrator put it, "There's no end of questions you can ask if you really want someone." Has the family had heavy medical expenses? Is it carrying an unusual amount of debt? Each question is reasonable in itself but not asked so persistently of everyone. This amounts to what one expert has called an "alms race" conducted through "preferential need analysis."[12]

Among highly selective colleges, the alms race appeared to increase after the overlap agreements were shut down and again after Princeton announced its first big financial aid boosts in January 1998.[13] Announcements by Harvard the following month that it would be "*competitively supportive*" (note the dual values) in responding to "attractive offers" elsewhere, were entirely based on flexible need analysis. The policy, which continued, was not totally loved within the university's admissions and financial aid administration. Some staff disliked it as "invidious," but it was later defended on the grounds, again, that seeking "new information" favored the disadvantaged student who lacked knowledge about the financial aid process. Evidence of this has not been shown either way.[14]

The worst manipulation of EFCs is what I call "methodology hopping." FM often produces a lower EFC than versions of IM used by private colleges. FM, in particular, differs from IM in not taxing home equity. Since the early 1990s, when FM was started, some colleges, including a few very selective ones, have favored specially desired students by jumping them from IM to FM.[15] At one West Coast college, the enrollment chief used this ploy to resisted a command from the trustees to end preferential packaging for minorities. The administrator literally complied but then moved minority students onto FM for college aid as well as federal aid. So the students continued to get extra grant money from the college.

Methodology jumping is deceitful because it is *bogusly formulaic*. The college purports to arrive at a basic price to the student (EFC) by a formula based on financial need, but it selects the formula on grounds other than need. Like preferential need analysis based on individual negotiation, it has made students, parents, and high school college-admission advisers wonder just how colleges allocate aid and has raised doubts in general about the probity and future of need-related aid.[16]

Counterattack

By the late 1990s, leading private-college financial aid directors, supported by their presidents and the College Board, were convinced that IM required revision. IM, they increasingly felt, was too hard on middle- and upper-middle-income families in relation to their "expectations" as well as "economic realities."[17] A family with a $60,000 gross income and one of two children in college might have to pay an EFC amounting to 15 percent of income plus 3–4 percent of assets. Concessions made by some colleges following the big Princeton move in January 1998 reduced the burden, but the concessions varied.

Financial aid directors worried in particular that IM's use of family assets penalized those who had built up savings for college expenses. This was old concern, but the influential economist Martin Feldstein gave it new voice in the mid-1990s: he accused need-analysis methodologies of punishing thrift and discouraging savings.[18] IM—and FM too—also seemed to favor some family situations rather than others, independently of real ability to pay, and to reward the family that manipulated its assets and spending so that it looked poorer than it was.

If these problems could be addressed, so IM revisionists hoped, the pressure for special deals might be reduced at both ends—among students and families, who would get aid offers that looked more reasonable, and among colleges, who would share a renewed confidence and consensus about what they should offer.

History was being replayed: the original College Scholarship Service (CSS) formula of 1954 had been a response to colleges using different need formulas as well as merit aid. Ultimately, the technical and detailed process of revising IM was about restoring "community" and "consensus," words used repeatedly by the revisers. It tapped into the two historic American fears mentioned at the start of this book—the fear of *falling away* from a past era of promise (the founding years of CSS) and of *falling apart* (as different colleges went their own competing ways in what they offered students). Neither fear was unfounded. In particular, the fear of falling apart and the wish to reestablish community was a reaction to the culture of aggressive competition that had become so prominent in college admissions.[19]

In the fall of 1996 there was a meeting of financial aid directors from colleges practicing need-blind admissions and thus qualified under post-overlap legislation to consult on aid policy principles. They drew up guidelines that started to revise IM and produced some agreements on how to apply it to individual cases.[20] Two comprehensive revisions of then followed. The first, called New IM, was hatched by a CSS committee, chaired by Wesleyan's financial aid director, Edwin G. Below. The second came out of the 568 Presidents' Working Group. This confederation of twenty-eight college presidents took its name from a key section (568) of the law that had allowed them to consult directly with each other on student-aid policy if their admissions were need-blind.[21]

Designed to take effect in 1999–2000, New IM resembled a detailed overhaul of tax law, raising and lowering liabilities and allowances in different places, and replacing some old categories with new ones. Most saliently—and put very simply—it enabled families to save more for college expenses without adding to the assets that increased their EFCs. It also made it harder for business owners to use losses and depreciation to minimize their "taxable" income.

At the same time, it dealt with perceived inequities that were not necessarily class based. Thus its provision for the college costs of a student's sibling reduced the *extra* allowance that old IM had given to a family with two children *simultaneously* in college. The CSS revisers did not believe that they should pay less than another family that also had two children going to college but had spaced them out so that only one was in college at a time.[22]

The revisers estimated that New IM would reduce EFCs for most "dependent" students, especially those with family incomes between $40,000 and $90,000 in 1998–99. (Most private-college students depended on some family resources.) Independent students—not dependent on family funds—would usually pay more. The revisers believed that they should concentrate more of their assets and income on college, but low-income students and those with children were generally protected from adverse changes.[23]

New IM, overall, tended to increase a college's financial aid costs, but it emerged near the end of the 1990s financial boom, when colleges with substantial endowments—the ones most apt to use IM—had seen big increases in their investment income. Some had already begun to apply pieces of the new methodology.

FOR ALL THE EFFORT that went into them, the CSS revisions did not seem to reduce special deals not based on need. The second revision attempt—by the 568 Presidents' Working Group—addressed this problem along with others. In the late 1990s, leaders of the Consortium on Financing Higher Education (COFHE) association of elite colleges shared their anxieties about threats to need-based aid. Their concerns included federal spending on tax credits, state trends toward merits, and what one president called a "short-term" focus on "satisfying consumers" rather than long-term social policy.[24]

COFHE members that practiced need-aware admissions kept out of the discussions, for legal antitrust reasons already explained, but the talks were joined by presidents from some non-COFHE colleges that practiced need-aware admissions and met all need. The result was the 568 group: presidents of twenty-eight colleges. It was chaired by Cornell's president, Hunter Rawlings, and served by a subcommittee of financial aid directors from member colleges.[25]

In July 2001, the 568 group presidents publicly endorsed a report from the subcommittee. The report combined a statement of "financial aid principles" with extensive proposals about how to assess financial need. Families, it said, should pay college costs according to their ability to pay and should do so equally on this basis. Colleges should tell applicants clearly how they measure ability to pay and what criteria they use in giving any aid not based "exclusively on need." In assessing what a family should pay, "professional judgment" should be used only to "recognize unique or extenuating financial circumstances," not to favor some students for other "institutional purposes."[26]

Taken as a whole, the report's statement of principles was an attack on preferential need analysis and methodology-hopping. In a comment on the statement, as reported by the *New York Times,* one of its signatories, MIT's president Charles Vest, claimed that "in too many instances aid [was] going to the squeakiest wheel, rather than to the neediest students."[27]

The report's analysis of how to assess financial need was as detailed as the CSS revisions. In some places the two agreed; in others they differed. Like the CSS proposals, the 568 recommendations tried to make it easier for families to save for college without penalizing their assets. The 568 revisions also reduced the maximum taxable value of a family's home—that is, the amount of home equity counted in assessing ability to pay college costs—from 3 times family income to 2.4 times. They proposed this, in part, to give colleges less excuse to reduce or eliminate the home-equity factor arbitrarily for desired students.[28]

Not everything was neatly settled. One of the many questions addressed by the 568 group was how to deal with a "non-custodial" parent (NCP) who would not pay his due share of a child's costs. The issue was not new (it had exercised Smith's president Jill Conway in the 1980s), but it had become more prominent with the rise in divorce rates and one-parent families. It was in part a gender issue, as the NCP was usually the father. Expecting a recalcitrant or vanished NCP to pay up could penalize the student as well as the custodial parent by setting a higher EFC than the student and custodial parent could afford. On the other hand, college administrations did not want to bale out delinquent NCPs. The 568 group issued some principles and guidelines but they found it a "vexing" problem.[29]

All in all, the 568 group's blueprint was an effort to establish a "consensus approach" to financial aid, leaving member colleges less opportunity and justification for playing favorites. The 568 group wanted to reduce burdens that seemed unfair to middle-income families, but its leaders were concerned as well about low-income students. At the time of writing, it is too early to gauge the effect of the 568 group revisions on the competitive uses of financial aid: they were not aimed to start till the 2003 admissions season. They are significant, though as a collective, elite-college effort to shape financial aid policies.[30]

The 568 group has not escaped suspicion that it may be or become another post-overlap cartel for squashing price competition.[31] Certainly the 568 "consensus approach" was an effort to *stabilize* prices, reducing the volatility of special deals. Unlike most cartel behavior, though, the 568 revisions lowered prices overall: in general they reduced EFCs and so cost the colleges more. If one still wanted to see the 568 confederation as a market-power interest group, the most plausible picture would be of a price-cutting strike against less-endowed colleges that could not afford such across-the-board cuts, as opposed to special deals here and there.

All this, however, is to underestimate the genuine concern about social equity, educational opportunity, and the responsibility of colleges felt by COFHE and 568 group leaders. As a motivating force, market did not totally trump mission.

It did, though, restrict the front on which mission defended itself. Although the 568 group also worked to extend the life of the "antitrust protection" law that enabled the group's discussions to take place, the 568 report concentrated on the need analysis and professional judgment that determined EFCs. It made no direct comment on merit scholarships or the more regressive forms of preferential packaging, although both often affected how much a family (not just the student) actually paid for college. In a National Public Radio discussion of the report, Hunter Rawlings, chair of the 568 group, made a point of not criticizing either merits or preferential packaging based on student "desirability."[32] His own university, Cornell, did this kind of packaging, and some of the 568 group gave merits. (They included Duke, whose financial aid director, James Belvin, chaired the group's expert subcommittee, though Belvin himself disliked merits.)

For all their range of detail, the 568 and CSS reports were essentially narrow-front, defensive actions against the market's invasion of an inner sanctum of financial aid—the professional system used to determine a student and family's ability to pay.

PART III
Reforming the System

In looking at the history of student aid, what lessons can we learn for the future? Let's start with the three main strands in the history: diversity of motives, the conflict between aiding needy students and other educational spending, and the interplay between mission and market.

Mixed Motives

Even within need-related aid, economic class justice—giving more opportunity to poor students per se—has not been the only motive. For those who value this kind of justice, there is good news and bad news. The good news is that other motives and allies—fellow travelers, as it were—can be enlisted to support aid for the needy. The bad news is that the fellow travelers may fall away or divert aid from the neediest.

Through much of financial aid history, the image of the poor and pious student, often bound for the ministry, was a potent force for "beneficiary" aid. This force obviously lost power in the more secular twentieth century, and long before that, it could have lopsided effects on educational opportunity. The Princeton report of 1896 (mentioned in Chapter 4), which stressed beneficiary aid in recruiting churchly adherents to the main college's Presbyterian culture, said only in passing that the science school had just one scholarship, whereas a third of the main arts college (the "Academic Department") received grant aid.

Again, in today's very different world of selective private-college admissions, the educational value attached to racial and ethnic diversity helps to promote need-related aid but tends to favor middle-class minorities, through admissions targeting and "preferential packaging" of aid, over low-income white students.[1]

Message for future policies: if you want to extend the social reach of student aid, by all means use other agendas but don't count on them too much or let them eclipse basic appeals to social fairness.

Aid for Needy Students versus Other Spending

College budgets have had two kinds of "other spending": merit aid not requiring financial need, and general college spending on programs (including faculty) and facilities. At elite private colleges, general spending has been the greater threat to increased access for needy students, especially very needy students.

Although merit aid has increasingly gone to richer students, it has always benefited some needy ones. How much it has depleted need-related aid rather than just adding to it is debatable. And the most prestigious colleges have resisted merit aid the most.

Programs and facilities, on the other hand, have competed with student aid for dollars since the seventeenth century. To push this point too far as a complaint would be absurd: funding access to good education would be meaningless and impossible if most of a college's budget was spent on student aid and little on the education itself. Nevertheless, student aid at leading colleges has often had to struggle against growing claims on the college budget from other quarters. The struggle has often been indirect, through rising student charges. As colleges upgrade their facilities and improve their programs with more and better-paid faculty, they have tried to recoup the added costs not just by fund-raising but by hiking tuition and other charges. Student aid has often done no more than keep up, if that.

At the same time, escalating prices can give a false impression of aid effort for needy students. When charges went up faster than most incomes—as they did at private colleges in the 1950s to 1960s and 1980s to 1990s—more students and richer students qualified for grant aid on the basis of need. At expensive colleges, by the early years of the twenty-first century, students with family incomes over $160,000 were qualifying for need-related grants, especially if they had brothers and sisters in college too.

Colleges in this situation often lamented virtuously that they were spending more and more on financial aid, when in fact they were just compensating for becoming more expensive and were not necessarily doing more for low- and middle-income students.

Message: spending on wonderful programs and facilities and spending on wide access are not totally compatible. "Excellence" should concede something to access and not just vice versa.

Mission and Market

The third theme in college financial aid history, the interplay between social/educational and financial/market purposes, is the most complicated, with numerous links and overlaps between the two.

An early link was sequential: mission motives led to market ones. In the early nineteenth century especially, as we saw in Chapter 4, the drive by religious denominations to advance themselves and enlighten the "heathen" frontier created more church-linked colleges than the student market could easily support. Although some colleges collapsed, financial aid of one sort or another—from informal loans to scholarship price discounts—helped others to survive. Educators earnestly believed in student aid as good in itself, but it was, still, a market response to religious and educational expansionism.

Financial and market motives can also directly exploit mission motives. Going back to medieval times, enlisting the wish of charitable donors to extend education and enlightenment has been a way of getting them to give to colleges, including gifts of scholarships and loan funds. Appealing to mission was a way of tapping a *donor* market and buoying, ✓ through donated aid, a *student* (customer) market.

As leading colleges became more selective, mission and market met on the drive to attract desirable students who would fit in with colleges' values while enhancing their reputations. Definitions of "desirable" differed between colleges and historical periods, but they did not necessarily impel colleges to seek the poorest students needing the most aid (be it grant aid or "self-support" in working through college). As we saw in Chapter 2, the *academic* incentive for seeking very needy students diminished after the 1940s when richer students tended to be better students, as "better" was usually judged.

This was offset only somewhat by the growing belief that student diversity was itself educational. A conflict developed between the "extend opportunity" side of college missions and the "seek excellence" side, as both cost money. In admissions as well as financial aid, this produced policies that favored well-prepared middle-class students with low financial need and a small number of high-need, aid-expensive students of exceptional promise.

Mission and market have also fused in technical processes. The refinement since the 1950s of need analysis, based on detailed financial data from aid applicants, was justified by a mission motive, the wish to distribute aid as fairly as possible where it was most needed. But need analysis also served a market purpose. As a college finance director remarked to me in the mid-1990s, imagine selling cars and setting a price only after many customers have revealed "vast amounts of financial information" about themselves. Even those customers who do not give information by not applying for aid are saying something about their ability to pay, though not necessarily their *willingness* to pay. All these data and nondata help colleges shape their price structures.

Since the 1980s, as we saw in the last chapter, the market has penetrated need analysis itself, inducing college administrators to find more financial "need' and give more aid when they really want a student who is in hot demand elsewhere. This trend illustrates a larger truth about the relationship between social welfare programs and market capitalism. As social programs (including need-related student aid) have expanded, the market has infiltrated them rather than retreating.[2]

In a sense, though, this is not new. For decades, the culture of the marketplace has affected financial aid methods. The rise of credit finance encouraged student loan schemes in the 1920s, elite-college agreements on pricing and aid echoed postwar trends in business oligopoly, and complex student-aid discounting in the 1990s reflected the growth of sophisticated market analysis in business generally. All this prepared the ground for further penetration of the market into student aid.

Message: the market is everywhere and long has been. It should be used but also watched and curbed.

Flawed Justice

Despite the market influences, financial aid has been called "Robin Hooding" and "America's only socialism," though it operates through pricing mechanisms.[3] No other country's higher education soaks rich families in favor of poorer families as much as the American system does. This is true at least of the country's private colleges and probably true of its leading state ones, too.[4]

The underlying principle is that no student should pay full costs, as higher education is a *public* good, benefiting the whole society; all students, however, should pay what they can up to a point, as higher education is also a *private* good, conferring important advantages on those who get it. To equalize access to these advantages, poor students should pay less than rich ones.

This rationale was not invented all at once: different parts evolved at different times. The idea that higher education benefits society as a whole is precolonial, though the supposed benefits later shifted, from religiously infused enlightenment to training for democratic citizenship and economic productivity. The belief that higher learning in general, as opposed to preparing for specific occupations, is a good economic and career investment for the individual got a boost in the 1920s from leaders like Herbert Hoover and Trevor Arnett with links to big business as well as the academy. It was not, though, till the early 1960s (the Kennedy era of virile brainpower) that theories of higher education as a "human capital" investment, earning returns for the individual as well as the economy, became doctrine among economists.[5]

The history of varied charges is, of course, the history of financial aid itself, going back to medieval times; but the growth of a strong private sector in American higher education expanded the range between top prices and those heavily discounted with grant aid. From the 1950s, particularly, the price stretch grew at the most prestigious and sought-after colleges as they became at once more academically ambitious and more concerned about social inclusion. To help fund expensive programs, they pushed up full tuition while discounting it to needy students.

The class justice in all this was never pure. Today, as in the past, richer students tend to go to richer colleges that spend more money on them—though they also tend to give more back as alumni, and in fact far more students with upper-middle family incomes and above go to public community colleges than is generally realized (over 40 percent of young first-years).[6]

The justice of the system is also flawed in that the personal payoffs of a college education have been used to justify high levels of borrowing and working by students as an investment in their future. The burden of this has fallen heavily on poor students; big debts deter them more than others.

Politically, the system's dependence on student aid to offset relatively high full prices produces pots of aid money into which diverse interests, not always the neediest, have dipped their spoons. There is not much difference here from pork-barrel and interest-group politics, for all the high-toned discourse about who should get scholarships. Even groups making genuine appeals to social conscience—World War II veterans, for example, and African Americans—have used these appeals as political levers to get special financial aid benefits.

Message: The American way of student aid rests on basically just principles, but its flexibility has led to inequities and raids by special interests. Life is never entirely fair, but public and college policies should reduce the inequities.

Elite Co-option

A harsher view of student aid is to see it as a form of *elite co-option.* This is a system in which elite groups selectively recruit just enough people from the rest of the population to suit their purposes without altering their culture and standards or dispossessing their own offspring. (There is some room for new blood as upper-class families tend to have fewer children.) The recruitment motives may vary: obtaining new talent, learning from different backgrounds, looking and feeling democratic, buying off groups that might make trouble. The actual gatekeepers and gate-openers—admissions and financial aid officers in the case of colleges—may genuinely believe they are serving social democracy, but, according to the theory, they are still defending cultures of privilege.[7]

The tendency of institutions to recruit their own kind reinforces this. Even in the 1960s, when elite private colleges tried to admit and aid a wider social range of students, their new policies reflected a power shift to a meritocratic faculty loosely allied with liberal administrators. Among students, the main beneficiaries were an extended middle class, resembling the faculty themselves.

Elite co-option is a slippery concept, as it does not neatly tell us how much an institution has to open its gates and change its culture to qualify as *not* co-optive. Under the GI Bill, for instance, college access and admissions criteria widened and campus cultures changed: students became more studious, which pleased the faculty. As in the 1960s, though, the main beneficiaries were middle-class students, most of whom would have gone to college anyway.[8]

For all its flaws, the theory of elite co-option can help us guard against exaggerated impressions of openness, especially when colleges have small but highly visible programs helping low-income students. Sometimes these programs exist alongside regressive aid policies that favor low-need students over high-need ones.

At Smith College, for instance, the Ada Comstock program for older women, started in the 1970s and supported by strong ties with community colleges, has earned and deserved good publicity. Although it is not a financial aid program per se, it tends to enroll low-income women needing a lot of aid. Between 1991 and 2000, however, Smith reduced the "Adas" from over 12 percent of the student body to under 8 percent, mainly on grounds of cost, despite big increases in Smith's large endowment for most of that period. And in the 1990s and early 2000s, Smith packaged its aid so that students with low academic admissions ratings (who tended to be lower income) were expected to carry extra heavy loans. This made more grant money available for higher-rated students. Smith's publicity, though, did not suffer much. Even within the Smith community, probably more people knew about the Comstock program itself than its diminished numbers and the arcane bias of Smith's financial aid packaging.[9]

Historically, the Smith example is not unique. Since the late nineteenth century, college catalogs have often listed an array of endowed scholarships and loan funds in addition to sections on "beneficiary aid." They inevitably stress the range rather than limits of what the college offers for needy students, though they do sometimes say that they have more supplicants than resources.

Message: Deception and self-deception can flourish among the most honest gatekeepers. Elite power protects itself in subtle ways.

Social Mobility and Inequality

However much student aid has opened college gates, it assists social mobility rather than directly equalizing economic conditions. This accords with traditional American values on equalizing opportunity to achieve unequal rewards. But inequality can put a brake on mobility. It is not easy to move upward from a deeply disadvantaged condition, especially when many of the disadvantaged are cut off from "mainstream" society. The United States has greater income inequality than most other developed nations, if not all of them, depending on the measure used, and contrary to popular belief, it has low to medium rates of upward mobility, again according to how you measure it.[10]

Where people live counts for a lot. Since the 1940s, poor families have become more segregated in neighborhoods with ill-funded schools and low levels of education.[11] This helps explain why rates of going to college and graduating have stayed so far apart for poor and rich students, and black and white ones, despite federal and other student-aid programs aimed at just this problem.

"Does financial aid come too late?" a question raised in the 1940s and again in the 1960s, has found a new currency among policy analysts.[12] There is no consensus, though, on the answer. Most experts agree that low-income Americans need a better economic and educational deal at an early age. They do not agree, though, as to how much the anticipated costs of college reach back into family life long before the college years, influencing whether or not a high school student prepares for college.[13]

Message: Student aid is embedded in powerful social forces. To extend educational opportunity, other policies must operate too.

What Can Aid Do?

I have stressed so far the constraints on student aid as a tool for extending opportunity. Aid has been pulled in different directions, while competing for funds against other educational spending. And it operates amid deep social and economic inequalities.

Yet student aid has not been powerless. Historically, it has enabled students to attend colleges they could not otherwise afford. This is particularly true if one includes under "aid" the provision of jobs by colleges and their general accommodation of "working through college." In the

1920s, several studies showed (when taken together) that working-class students were about as likely to go to a middling-prestige range of coed private colleges as to a similar range of state universities, charging much lower fees.[14]

In the late 1980s, when charges were far higher in real terms and it was harder to finance a full-time college education just by working, more low-income students with high test scores went to private colleges than to public ones. They did so in about the same proportion as all high-scoring students (though fewer of the richest went to public colleges). This could not have happened without financial aid.[15]

It is true that student aid has enabled many colleges to boost their full charges by providing discounts for those students who cannot or will not pay full price but are wanted by the college. Looked at long-term, however, this is again all part of a flexible pricing system in which private colleges charge what they can and state colleges vary too, though they are subject to state price controls. The effect has been to expand the whole higher education system by drawing in tuition revenue as well as donations and government subsidies.

But what of aid's direct effect on students in the short term? A stream of studies, mostly done since the early 1970s, have looked at different aspects of this question. With some exceptions, they have found that aid does encourage students—especially low-income ones—to go to college and stay the course.[16]

Student aid and net price (charges less grant aid) also help determine *which* college, and what type of college (public or private), students go to. The research, however, mainly focuses on students who have already applied to different colleges. It does not clearly show how often a generous amount of aid at a high-tuition college can get poorer students to apply there in the first place. This obviously involves a college's admissions and marketing policies as well as aid itself.[17]

The big aid increases at Princeton, recounted in Chapter 8, point this up. In the five-year period 1997–2002—starting just before Princeton replaced loans with grants for all lower-income students and ending two years after it did the same for all aided students—the percentage of entering classes with family incomes under $40,000 rose from 7.75 percent to 11.1 percent. This may look small, but it was actually a 43 percent increase. Yet Princeton stayed at the bottom of twenty-one top-rated private universities ranked according to the proportion of their students on federal Pell grants (who usually have a family income under $35,000).[18]

Much of this was probably due to Princeton's posh location and its lingering reputation for exclusiveness as well as extensive "early decision" admissions (see glossary). The question remains as to whether Princeton could have done more to attract low-income students with its expanded aid packages. The new Princeton aid did get general publicity, and the admissions office put out the message to schools that had produced Princeton applicants before. But it did not market the new packages aggressively at other schools, including disadvantaged ones.

Would that have made a difference? This is a question for all highly selective private colleges. In higher education generally, the more academically selective and demanding a college is, the fewer students it has from working-class and noncollege family backgrounds. This applies to public as well as private institutions, and it is not just because more selective colleges are more expensive. In mid-1990s Britain, when virtually no universities charged tuition and all were under public pressure to be more "inclusive," the proportion of students from blue-collar and lower-income white-collar families correlated closely with the university's academic prestige and selectivity.[19] The most obvious reason was class difference in academic preparation and expectations.

Yet if one controls for academic qualifications by looking only at high test scorers, low-income students in the United States have still been underrepresented at highly selective colleges—about a quarter less than their proportion of high-scoring students at all four-year colleges.[20] And beneath the high scorers, rich students are far more likely to go to elite colleges than are poor students. The reason, again, is not simply financial, though financial worries can be involved. Going to an elite college usually means going *away* to college—away from the local and familiar and away from an existing part-time job that may be contributing money to the family household. When the writer Richard Rodriguez was about to leave home for Stanford—the first in his family to go away to college—his mother asked him, "Why aren't the colleges here in Sacramento good enough for you?" She added, "you know your scholarship will never cover it all." That was back in the 1960s, but the same attitudes exist today. Hispanic families are particularly averse to college far afield, especially for their daughters.[21]

These realities are not enough to let selective private colleges off the hook of enrolling more low-income students. Since the 1960s, a multitude of "access" and " precollege" programs have spread across the country, supported in part by federal and state governments. These programs reach into disadvantaged schools to orient students to further education. They give information about financial aid and how to get it, and a third or more of them provide their own supplementary grants for college.

The programs often concentrate on getting students into local public colleges and trade schools. By contrast, less than a quarter of private colleges sponsor their own programs on campus for disadvantaged precollege students.[22] Though some local private colleges do a great job at serving first-generation students, it is tempting for the more selective colleges to write off disadvantaged students as unqualified for the rigors of their courses. Some elite colleges, too, do not give transfer students—including those from community colleges—their most generous financial aid.

Yet as far back as the 1950s, some leaders in private-college admissions worried about fishing too much for the same shiny fish in the same suburban pools. In the 1960s they pioneered new efforts to find talent elsewhere. Enthusiasm waned in the 1970s, as we saw in Chapter 7, but it never died out. In the 1980s and 1990s, institutions ranging from Middlebury in Vermont to the University of Southern California were bringing disadvantaged high school students onto campus for intensive classes, with aid offers attached for those who enrolled at the college.

In the late 1990s Smith's SUCCESS program did the same for disadvantaged students about to enter Smith who had shown much more intellectual ability than their test scores indicated.[23] Recognizing that able, disadvantaged students might have low test scores was all the more important, as middle-class families often buy test coaching that boosts their scores. Nor did the students' low scores hurt Smith's rating in the academic marketplace. In the influential *U.S. News and World Report* ranking of colleges, SAT and ACT averages contribute just 7.5 percent of the college's total rating. Class rank in high school, whatever the school, counts almost as much.[24]

In the recession of the early 2000s, Smith closed down SUCCESS for budgetary reasons (i.e., other spending priorities), just as Middlebury had closed down its science program for minority high school students in the early 1990s, two years after federal support ended.

Message: Disadvantaged students cost a lot in aid and preparation, but the academic barriers to enrolling and graduating more of them at the richest, most selective colleges are not insuperable. These colleges could do better.*

Prescription

Since the early 1990s, more and more policy analysts and commentators have called for renovations in student aid. While attacking some trends at state and college levels—especially the growth of merits—they have concentrated most of their fire on the federal government. They have pressed, among other things, for bigger Pell grants and better information about aid, linked with "outreach" to disadvantaged schools and families.[25]

The public experts have focused mainly on lower-income students and disadvantaged minorities. Some of them, indeed, have championed "economic affirmative action," extending racial preferences in college admissions and financial aid to all low-income students. Almost invariably, they have disapproved of federal tuition tax credits, along with state tuition savings schemes, for lightening middle-class burdens rather than getting more students—especially poor ones—into college. Unhappily for their cause, there have been few effective proposals for curbing tuition inflation. This is a powerful driver of tax credits.[26]

The call for wider access to college gets support from many studies stressing the economic and social benefits of higher education, for the whole society as well as the college graduate. The claims tend to underestimate the *credential* effect of higher education—the value of a college degree per se in getting a good job, as opposed to the productive value of

---

*On Feb 28, 2004, Harvard announced big grant increases for lower-income students, a precollege "Summer Academy" at no charge for academically able but disadvantaged Boston high school students, more outreach to schools where bright students "never [considered] applying," and more admissions emphasis on accomplishments in spite of "limited resources." Harvard president Lawrence Summers said that only 10 percent of students at the "most selective" colleges came from the "bottom half of the income scale" and that students taking test-prep classes might be "the least diverse in the country." The new aid policy, eliminating or reducing "expected family contributions," was based on research showing financial and social anxieties among Harvard's lower-income students, who often contributed summer earnings to their families, which in turn disliked heavy borrowing for college (Harvard News Office).

the education itself—but credentials are part of the reality of who gets what in society. Demands for more government spending on student aid and college access run up against demands for spending on primary and secondary schools, but several economists have argued—controversially— that colleges use federal money more effectively than primary and secondary schools and should offer more "remedial" programs to make up for what schools fail to do.[27]

There is also some disagreement among student-aid experts about federal aid and *type* of college. Should federal aid policies concentrate almost entirely on getting more students through public colleges? Or should government aid also help poorer students go to more expensive, well-endowed establishments?

Supporters of the first school of thought stress that aid dollars go furthest at low-tuition public colleges, where a government grant can cover a bigger proportion of a student's costs. And graduating from any college (as opposed to not being a graduate) makes more of a difference to future earnings than graduating from an elite institution. The economy also needs to get more students into technical postsecondary training below degree level. This too requires a lot of student aid.[28]

The second school—to which I belong—concedes that most federal aid should help provide basic access to college and other postsecondary training. Historically, however, federal aid has gone to students at all types of college. This has encouraged some federal programs to be cost-efficient in levering aid from other sources on a "matching grant" basis. The National Defense loans of the 1950s and 1960s required colleges to put in some of the loan money, and the State Student Incentive Grants to states, starting in the 1970s, required state contributions to scholarships that were usable at private as well as state colleges. (Similarly, Massachusetts's Gilbert scholarship program has given money to private colleges according to the amount of grant aid they themselves give to in-state students.)

Why do this? The buzzword is "choice," a root American value. It means here the democratic freedom of all students to choose the type of college that suits them best. More specifically, it means helping poor students to attend well-endowed, selective colleges that spend far more on each student than other colleges—providing smaller classes, more advising, and better facilities.[29]

If none of this matters enough to be an issue for public policy, then why is so much importance, pro and con, attached to racial preferences in college admissions? Affirmative action only applies to a selective minority of colleges that can pick and choose among applicants. Most colleges, private and public, do not have enough customer demand to be able to make ethnic choices.[30]

Recasting Loans

In turning to my own specific proposals, the best place to begin is with student loans, since they have become such a big part of aid for all aided income-groups. In 2001–02, loans—mainly federal or federally supported—came to just over half of all student aid.[31]

The movement for more loans started in the early 1900s, as we saw in Chapter 5, and the loan share of all aid has been rising since the 1950s. In recent years, three leading state universities—Maryland, North Carolina at Chapel Hill, and Virginia—have followed Princeton in replacing loans with extra grants for lower-income students. These are welcome, of course. So are the many "differential packaging" programs (extra grant, less loan for poorer students) at other colleges. But we can expect no general rollback of loans; the trend has been the other way. The challenge is to make loans less burdensome and less of a deterrent to lower-income and minority students.

Proposal 1: Cut interest rates on federal subsidized loans (awarded where students have financial need) to the rate of general inflation.[32] This would make them interest-free in real terms. If Britain can afford to do this, and envisage continuing when college students expand to 50 percent of the young adult population (the government's target), it should be a serious proposition for the United States.

Proposal 2: Establish a commission to review "income-contingent" loan schemes, including the current federal plan offered and the alternative plans and critiques of them put forward since the 1960s. The commission should assess whether a new income-contingent loan scheme could attract more students into it than the present one. The commission should consider, among other options, the "graduate tax" idea, using the income-tax system to collect repayments when the individual reaches a certain income level.

Since this would probably expand the federal government's role as a direct lender to students, as opposed to sponsoring and subsidizing loans indirectly through private lenders, the commission should identify likely political resistance to a graduate tax—including private lenders and perhaps the IRS (complaints about added work). These obstacles should not interfere with the basic design of a new system.

"Student/Program Grants"

"Campus-based" aid—federal or state money given to colleges to allocate according to set rules—goes back to the federal work-study aid in the 1930s Depression. The main federal campus-based grants today are the Federal Supplemental Educational Opportunity Grants (FSEOGs). These are the original 1965 "opportunity grants" for students with "exceptional financial need" and are now "supplemental" to Pell grants.

Rancor between "have" and "have-not" colleges has clouded the history of FSEOGs. A complex formula governs the distribution of grants to colleges, but it is skewed by how they were allocated more than twenty years ago. Elite colleges had disproportionate influence on the regional panels of experts that decided the allocation. As a result, the current distribution of FSEOG money does not allow enough for the growth of community and state colleges since the 1970s. So richer, more selective colleges—including state flagships—tend to get more FSEOG money to spend on fewer low- and middle-income students. The same applies to federal money given to colleges for extra loans (the Perkins program) and for work-study jobs. Though this helps expensive colleges to extend access, the distribution among colleges is based as much on historical accident and who got there first as on clear principles.[33]

A new program of campus-based federal grants would get past this and serve other objectives too, whether or not it eventually replaced FSEOG.

Proposal: Create federal "student/program grants," allocated to colleges according to the number of their undergraduates who are below specified income and asset levels (a different level for independent students). A required proportion of the grants would go to the students as financial aid. The college would spend the rest on academic backup and support for disadvantaged students. This could include intensive courses prior to first-year entry, as in Smith's SUCCESS program.

State programs such as New York's Higher Education Opportunity Program (HEOP), started in 1969, have the same dual mix of student aid and academic support. So did the original Pell grant plan, though the final legislation dropped the "cost-of-education" supplement that was to be paid to colleges according to the number of their Pell recipients.

Combining the two elements in one program recognizes the historical values of access and quality and the fact that both cost money. And if it increased the number of disadvantaged students at expensive colleges, it might lead those colleges to spend more of their own money on them, as the students would still need a lot of college aid to pay high tuition. HEOP seems to have had this effect in New York.[34]

Showing and Shaming

Getting colleges to extend access will require more than giving them money. This applies especially to the richest, most selective colleges, which have other expensive agendas and less need of government student aid, or *any* student aid, to fill their classes. Private colleges with the biggest endowments (including endowed scholarships) give less grant aid in proportion to their tuition income than do most others.[35]

All nonprofit colleges enjoy tax breaks as charities. Government and the courts as well as society in general have repeatedly declared that extending "educational opportunity" is a central purpose of American higher education.[36] It is reasonable, therefore, that federal and state governments should put public pressure on the richer colleges to open their gates wider.

The colleges would not be insensitive to this pressure. Since the nineteenth century, their leaders—like other elites in American society—have been anxious not to look too exclusive or undemocratic. In modern market terms, looking democratic, being part of the American mainstream, is good for publicity and public relations.

Among themselves too, elite colleges have respected social pressure. As we saw in Chapter 6, they created the College Scholarship Service in the 1950s not only to assess student financial need and process aid applications but to report on and shame member colleges that deviated from basing aid on need. The "overlap" groups of cooperating colleges did the same.

Proposal: The federal government should publish and publicize annual lists of the fifty richest universities and the fifty richest four-year colleges as measured by endowment per student. The two lists would be ranked according to each institution's percentage of full-time undergraduates with low incomes. Qualifying for a Pell grant might be used to define "low-income."[37] An addendum attached to the lists would give a paragraph on each institution, listing what it did in three areas: precollege programs for disadvantaged groups; special admissions ties to community colleges and "nontraditional" groups such as older and part-time students; and "differential packaging" of aid. The federal government would also work with the states to publish ranked lists of all private colleges and all public colleges (two lists) in the state.

The use of rating lists to (implicitly) praise and provoke is well established. College leaders frequently criticize the *U.S. News and World Report* ratings of college quality, but they do not ignore them, and they know their influence on reputations. Closer to my own proposal, in 2002 and 2004, the *Journal of Blacks in Higher Education* ranked elite universities and colleges according to their Pell-student percentages, and other Web sites displayed the results.[38]

The *Journal's* data showed that universities with about the same academic selectivity and location (urban or rural) varied considerably in their Pell percentages. Independently of these factors, an institution's commitment to enrolling poor students evidently counted. The new government rankings should encourage such commitment.

Revising Antitrust

While public ratings could encourage colleges to *compete* on access, revised antitrust legislation could help them to *cooperate* in limiting their aid awards not based on financial need.

Current antitrust law, as applied to colleges, is ham-fisted in dealing with the growth of merit scholarships and the historic wish of colleges to get together on common problems. Although the leaders of many colleges below the very top ones believe they need some merits for quality and market reasons, they also recognize that a merits bidding war with other colleges can waste money, often on students who don't need the help. Yet the statutes that followed federal antitrust action against the Ivies and MIT take an all-or-nothing position on the problem without being totally clear. They permit colleges practicing need-blind admissions to agree to ban merits altogether, but they do not say whether colleges can agree to *limit* merits. Contrast this with the fine numerical restrictions that member colleges of the National Collegiate Athletic Association are allowed to place on athletic scholarships given by Division I and II colleges.[39]

The law is also unfair in its requirement that cooperating colleges practice need-blind admissions. This lets in need-blind colleges that do not meet all financial need, but excludes colleges that operate need-aware admission, restricting their intake of needy students to make sure they meet all their need. It is true that when colleges moved to need-aware admissions policies in the 1990s, they sometimes (not always) reduced their intake of low-income students. But need-aware admissions can encourage a college to be more adventurous in getting disadvantaged, aid-expensive talent to apply: it knows that it can protect its budget, if necessary, by limiting its intake of less-talented needy students. In the recent Pell student surveys of top-rated institutions, the three liberal arts colleges with the highest Pell percentages—Mount Holyoke, Smith, and Oberlin—all practiced need-aware admissions. Mount Holyoke, like Smith, has a program for older women who tend to have low incomes, and Oberlin admissions officers have a tradition of welcoming low-income students.

Proposals: Extend the eligibility rules of the current antitrust statute so that agreements to ban or limit merits can include any college. These agreements should be deemed sufficiently well-intentioned to require no other sign of virtue such as need-blind admissions (which most colleges claim to do anyway). The law should explicitly permit the limiting, not just banning, of aid not related to need, as well as "preferential packaging" (bigger grants for specially desired needy students).[40]

These changes might not have an immediate effect, but like all the proposals offered here, they might encourage fresh and creative thinking about financial aid in the colleges—if, that is, the colleges are ready to do this.

Toward a More Knowing Campus

The professionalizing and sophistication of student aid have made it a world apart on college campuses. Even aid recipients often understand only the pieces of aid they get (if that), not the strategies and issues behind them.

This is not for lack of trying by administrators. College mission statements often include general remarks about student aid. Financial aid offices put out specific notices, leaflets, and Web site information. And committees on admissions and financial aid often include faculty and student representatives.

Still, the knowledge barriers are formidable. Many social science professors, people often concerned about who gets what and why in society, know vaguely that their institution does or doesn't practice need-blind admissions and does or doesn't give merits. But they don't know much about the issues behind these policies or whether the institution meets all need. As for preferential and differential packaging, "What's that?" they'd probably ask. I have no specific proposals to put here, just a general proposition. War, said Winston Churchill, is too important to leave to the generals. Student aid is too important to leave to the experts, or even to college presidents. Everyone on campus who cares about social fairness as well as the college's health and survival should take an active interest in student aid.

The 1990s did see the appearance here and there of low-income student associations, a response perhaps to growing income inequality in the 1980s and 1990s. They have seldom been as strong as minority student associations, partly because they lack the same backing from college administrations where offices for "multicultural" support are well established. They have also had to contend with the reluctance of many low-income students to define themselves publicly and collectively as poor and lower-class.

This said, there is work to be done by wider associations of students and faculty. They can scrutinize and publicize the student budgets—what students are supposed to live and thrive on—that financial aid offices use in determining need. And they can explore and air the whole experience of being on a tight budget among affluent peers.

The scrutiny of financial aid also needs a more incisive student press. This applies to admissions too. After interviewing college administrators, I have had some fun inventing "irresponsible" student newspaper headlines that I have never seen. "Financial aid rewards the smart rich." "Development office leans on admissions to favor big donors."

In the late 1920s and early 1930s, Harvard *Crimson* editor David Riesman (later to become a great sociologist) "made the University [his] beat," not just reporting official announcements but getting behind them.[41] Some able student editors have done this on financial aid—at Northwestern in the 1960s, Oberlin in the 1990s, for instance. But much more needs to be done here, and not just negatively—reporting creative initiatives as well as ethically dubious practices. Student aid, after all, is for students. It deserves its student investigators and writers.

Last Word

For champions of aid to needy students, and *very* needy students, this book has offered wintry reassurance. They are not alone in history: support for disadvantaged students has always lived a life of struggle. But this book is also meant to offer hope. To repeat Chapter 2, the history of student aid is a roller-coaster, not a straight line. From the standpoint of social equity and opportunity, there have been ups as well as downs. The important thing is to have new ideas in place for when new opportunities arise—for when a federal administration is willing and able to spend much more on student aid, and when leading colleges decide that imaginative programs for seeking and supporting obscure talent are worth as much as buying another celebrity professor or state-of-the-art design for the new student center.

Appendix 1. The Case of the Charitable Price Fixers: *United States v. Brown University* et al.

On May 22, 1991, the U.S. Department of Justice issued a "complaint" against the eight Ivy League universities and the Massachusetts Institute of Technology (MIT) for cooperating to eliminate price competition. They had violated, according to the Justice Department, the 1890 Sherman Antitrust Act, which prohibited any "combination . . . or conspiracy, in restraint of trade or commerce."[1]

The federal court case that ensued has prompted much legal commentary and economic analysis, but it has not so far been recounted from different sides of the issue (there were more than two) in a way that folds technical details into a human drama. We have already seen aspects of the case in different parts of student-aid history—from the 1930s to the present—but the full story needs to be told as one.

WE SAW IN CHAPTERS 6 and 7 how anxieties about a bidding war for students, using merit scholarships, led elite colleges in the 1950s to cooperate on how they assessed students' financial need and gave out aid. We saw, too, that a cluster of northeastern colleges took the cooperation furthest and most durably.

Agreeing to ban all merit scholarships, they sent their financial aid officers to big working conferences, meeting twice a year from 1958. Sitting at long tables, first at Harvard and then usually at the Wellesley faculty club, the college officers would try to agree on a basic price—"expected family contribution" or EFC—to be paid by each financial aid applicant getting admission offers from two or more colleges. EFC, in turn, was based on shared financial information about each applicant and a common "methodology" for assessing what a family could afford. For some of the sessions they divided into two groups, the Ivies and MIT in one group and a group of liberal arts colleges plus Tufts University in the other. They called themselves the "overlap groups," as they dealt with overlapping lists of admitted students.[2] The Ivy-MIT group, in particular, tried not only to agree on the EFC for each shared "admit" but to narrow their differences in the amount of "self-help" (borrowing and campus-job earnings) expected from most of their aided students.

In the 1980s, facing stiff competition from Stanford, which assessed student need more generously, the Ivy-MIT group launched the "High Stick Agenda" to attract Stanford into the club. ("High Stick" is a translation of the Spanish "Palo Alto," the town adjoining Stanford.) Unhappily for Stanford's suitors, the university's provost, James Rosse, was an antitrust economist with prescient doubts about the overlap groups' legality. Stanford did not join.[3]

On May 2, 1989, the *Wall Street Journal* published an article by Gary Putka about the overlap operations. "The Ivy schools," declared Putka, "are part of a price-fixing system that OPEC might envy."[4] This article was the main trigger of investigations by the Justice Department. After collecting mounds of paper from all the overlap colleges and many others, the Justice Department decided to attack the Ivy-MIT group first. The complaint in effect ordered the group to desist from price-fixing or face litigation.

The Ivy universities, but not MIT, immediately gave way. They signed a consent decree in which they undertook not only to cease agreeing on prices and financial aid packages for individual students but to discontinue their collective ban on "no-need" merit scholarships.[5] This ended all overlap activity; the non-Ivy colleges desisted too. At the same time, the Ivies set about winning back through legislation the right to agree on general policies on student aid. They sought a new law to give colleges some protection from the Sherman Act.

MIT refused to sign the consent decree. It decided to challenge in the courts the assertion that it had violated the Sherman Act.

Why the different responses? The Ivies said they complied to avoid big litigation costs. This certainly explains why the smaller, non-Ivy colleges discontinued their meetings. But that was not all. Unlike (or much more than) MIT, the Ivies had secretly conferred with one another about tuition fees and faculty salaries.[6] Big tuition increases had earned all colleges a bad press, and the Ivies knew that the Justice Department was investigating them for price-fixing on tuition and salaries as well as on charges to aided students. They felt vulnerable. In the consent decree they promised to desist from price-fixing agreements in all three areas. They put pressure on MIT to surrender too; at one point two Ivy presidents held a conference call with Charles Vest, MIT's new president, to persuade him to sign. It was later claimed that they did not know that the Justice Department would accept their signing of the consent decree without MIT.[7]

MIT, for its part, had special reason to resist. Engineering students tend to come from poorer backgrounds than liberal arts students. MIT had more students on grant aid than the Ivies, and its leaders had a particular passion for basing aid on financial need. As a student, "Chuck" Vest, the son of a state-college professor, had turned down a small merit scholarship on the grounds that he did not need it.[8]

MIT's big research business with the federal government was also a factor. The requirements attached to government research grants seemed to be getting more and more intrusive. As one MIT officer put it, "The time had come to draw a line." The same year as the Justice Department suit, MIT had to promise to pay back to the federal government $731,000 in allegedly excessive research overheads.[9]

MIT's stance was much admired by elite-college administrators, including many at Ivy colleges, and other people concerned about student aid. One of the smaller overlap colleges sent ten thousand dollars to MIT as a gesture of appreciation. But the issue was not one-sided. Indignation ran high in both camps. From the standpoint of MIT and its allies, the overlap meetings were a charitable operation, ensuring that financial aid was concentrated on needy students. The Justice Department had gratuitously invaded this process, imposing crude free-market principles of price competition that were designed to govern commerce, not colleges. MIT's champions also observed, with many a knowing smirk, that Attorney General Richard Thornburgh was about to run as a Republican for the Senate: attacking elite colleges was, in their view, a form of grandstanding.

From the standpoint of the Justice Department's Antitrust Division and its supporters, including some writers on college economics, the overlap colleges were a price-fixing cartel, acting in their own economic interests. That they were selling education and not automobiles should not hide the fact that they had formed a price ring to control charges and costs. This view went far beyond the personal agenda of the attorney general, and it crossed party lines: key Antitrust Division players had voted Democratic in the 1988 presidential election. There was, though, a personal element. A leading Ivy president had canceled a meeting with Thornburgh, apparently on learning that he would soon leave office. This had offended the attorney general and hardened his attitude toward the Ivies and MIT.[10]

As the dispute went through the courts, two questions emerged. First, did the Sherman Act's ban on combinations "in restraint of trade or commerce" apply to nonprofit colleges? Secondly, as the Sherman Act had often been used against companies trying to fix and maintain high prices, what effects did the overlap agreements have on charges to students?

The first question took everyone into uncharted waters: this was the first antitrust case on price agreements between colleges.* The second question produced a flurry of conflicting price studies. The Justice Department claimed that the overlap agreements enabled the colleges to jack up their prices to aided students and increase their overall revenue. MIT denied both claims. Although the opposing frontline attorneys had personal respect for one another, each side accused the other of bad statistics and bad law.[11]

In early September 1992, Chief Judge Louis C. Bechtle of the U.S. District Court in Philadelphia upheld the government complaint. The Sherman Act, he said, did not apply just to profit-seeking companies; case law had applied it also to professional associations of dentists, engineers, lawyers, etc. In selling education in return for tuition fees, MIT was engaged in commercial transactions. MIT had argued that the overlap agreements fulfilled the free-trade spirit of the Sherman Act by extending consumer choice: concentrating aid on students according to their need enabled more students to seek access to MIT. Bechtle discounted this argument; he followed previous antitrust cases in focusing on *price* competition.

Bechtle declared, however, that the complex studies of price effects commissioned by MIT and the Justice Department were unnecessary. By their own admission, MIT and the Ivies had met together to cut out price competition for aided students, and in collectively banning merit scholarships not based on need, they had deprived some students of "the opportunity to receive competitive tuition reductions." If rich MIT and its confederates were so committed to need-based aid, it should not require a collective police force

---

*Some antitrust cases had involved restrictions on National Collegiate Athletic Association (NCAA) scholarships. The consent decree did allow "members of a common athletic league," such as the Ivies, to agree to ban athletic scholarships not based on "economic need." The Justice Department had decided not to take on the added complex area of athletics, especially as the NCAA had had some success in the courts. In the view of the Antitrust Division, the best legal justification for allowing restrictive agreements on scholarships was that unfettered buying of athletes (by the richest athletic departments) might destroy the competitive balance needed to preserve the "product"—intercollegiate athletics. The Antitrust Division had mixed views of this argument.

to ensure that they spent a lot on it, even if they had to rearrange their budgets to meet the need of all students while also giving merit scholarships.[12]

MIT appealed the district court ruling, and a year later, in September 1993, the U.S. Court of Appeals, Third Circuit, gave a complex response. Its majority decision, supported by two of three judges, agreed with the district court that MIT was not immune to the Sherman Act. Although MIT actually subsidized all its students (from endowment income and gifts), so that none of them paid the full cost of an MIT education, it did not operate purely as a charity. Even its need-based student aid enhanced its allure in the marketplace by attracting talented students and providing the educational benefits of social diversity.

The appeals court conceded, however, that colleges were more removed from commercial firms than the professional associations cited by the district court, and it recognized the social importance of equalizing access to quality education. The court put much of this in Sherman-like terms, stressing the value of a "free exchange" of ideas. It likewise gave more credit than the district court to MIT's argument that the overlap agreements extended consumer choice and competition "by broadening the socio-economic sphere of its potential student body."[13]

The appeals court therefore remanded the case back to the district court, ordering it to discover through fuller analysis whether MIT could achieve the same social benefits—"equality of access to higher education and economic and cultural diversity"—without the overlap agreements. The third judge in the appeals case, Joseph Weis, Jr., dissented from the ruling. The Sherman Act, in his view, was never meant to apply to colleges; the district court decision should simply be overturned.[14]

Two months later, in late December 1993 and before the case could be heard again by the district court, MIT reached a settlement with the Justice Department (though several Justice officers did not want to settle). The settlement stipulated that colleges should not agree on prices and financial aid packages for individual students. They could, though, agree with one another to give aid only on the basis of financial need and agree on common principles of how to assess that need, *provided that* they admitted students without regard to what they could pay ("need-blind" admissions) and then met all "demonstrated" need. MIT accepted this proviso to affirm the social purposes of student aid and to hold the Ivies, if it could, to need-blind admissions. MIT thus preserved some policy principles, while the Justice Department succeeded in proscribing outright price-fixing.[15]

In the meantime, the Ivies' lobbying for legislation—seeking partial protection from the Sherman Act by statute rather than in the courts—had produced results. Starting with the 1992 amendments to the Higher Education Act, a succession of statutes anticipated and continued the main provisions of the MIT-Justice settlement. Unlike the settlement, the legislation did not require collaborating colleges to meet all student need, but it did require need-blind admissions, a condition fulfilled by all the Ivies except Brown.

The Ivies' pursuit of new legislation initially worried MIT, as it seemed to cast doubt on the legality of overlap under the Sherman Act. The 1992 amendments (Section 1544) therefore contained a proviso that the law would not affect pending antitrust litigation.

All the statutes carried "sunset" provisions, ending them at specified dates. The current version, the Need-Based Educational Antitrust Protection Act of 1997, has been extended to September 30, 2008, while requiring that the General Accounting Office of the Congress report by 2006 on the act's social benefits.[16]

MIT versus Department of Justice in Retrospect

As applied to commercial firms and associations, antitrust case law has usually not accepted benign social purpose or effect as a defense of collective price-fixing when that price-fixing is clearly intended.[17] MIT did not deny that it and the Ivies had combined to control their prices to aided students. (Neither MIT nor the Justice Department made much of the fact that differences in financial aid packaging—the ratio of grant to loan and job earnings—did cause price differences among the Ivies and MIT.)[18]

The case therefore turned largely on whether MIT's status as an educational charity, in contrast with the usual commercial targets of the Sherman Act, allowed social purpose and benefit (opportunity for needy students) to be a defense, and on the importance of the social purpose and the overlap agreements to each other. But the case also turned on the extent to which MIT and its allies sought and obtained economic and market benefits from price-fixing, despite the district court's initial discounting of economic analysis.

From this dual perspective, both MIT and the Justice Department had some overlap history on their side. The overlap meetings came out of a genuine wish to scale aid according to student need and to do so without being taken advantage of by a competitor offering a student more aid than he or she needed. As we saw in Chapter 6, the meetings germinated in a post–World War II democratic ethos shared by elite-college admissions and financial aid officers. As they often said, they wanted to take the price factor out of a needy student's choice of college.

On the Justice Department's side, the scholarship bidding war of the 1940s and 1950s was a price war that had cost all the colleges money. It had also created an administrative nightmare. Big swings and differences in the scholarships offered to bright students made it hard to plan admissions and financial aid. From this standpoint, the overlap agreements were an effort to maintain prices and an orderly, more predictable market.[19]

As the appeals court essentially recognized, MIT's students were not just consumers; they were also suppliers, contributing talent and diversity to the college's product (the educational experience). In aiding students, colleges were also partially *buying* students. For MIT the fairest and most cost-effective way to do this was by need-based aid, making the institution affordable to more students and thus widening the talent pool. Financial aid was a more or less fixed quantity that would be depleted if MIT had to buy non-needy talent with merit scholarships. This the appeals court accepted.

In the view of the Justice Department and the district court, financial aid was not "zero-sum." Merit scholarships did not have to come out of the same pot as need-based aid, even if traditional college budgeting assumed it did. The district court also implied that competing for high talent with merit scholarships (special discounts) was for colleges a natural way of doing business. Such talent would be unfairly deprived if it was not offered "competitive tuition reductions."

Behind these different viewpoints lay different values on competition and cooperation. For the Justice Department's Antitrust Division, competition, including price competition, was the surest way to invigorate and enhance higher education. For MIT and the Ivies, too, competition was important, especially in educational and research quality, but so was cooperation on some basic programs including student aid. As high-priced, high-spending institutions, the Ivies and other elite colleges had clear incentives to compete not on price but in what they offered. At the same time, they believed in the social value of need-based aid. Student aid, in short, was at once a business tool for attracting customers/suppliers and an instrument of social policy.

Appendix 2.
Research Strategy and Limits

The primary research for this book consists of archive work at 41 colleges and other organizations and conversations and correspondence with some 475 people from 129 institutions between 1990 and 2004 (see Appendix 3). I concentrated mainly on what are today well-endowed, high-tuition and highly selective private colleges and to a lesser extent on state flagships, but the research, especially interviews and secondary reading, covered a variety of other four-year colleges to put the elite focus into a wider context.

Archive Research

Archive work ranged from long historical sweeps, covering most of a college's history, to looking at a particular policy over a few years. Within a general search for data, I sought statements and episodes that framed issues and expressed policy values rather than trying to produce a comprehensive history of financial aid at all leading colleges.

Good light should not control where one looks for something, but richer colleges tend to have the best archives. The main archive materials used were catalogs and circulars; presidents' annual reports, sometimes including subreports from deans and office directors; papers of presidents and others; trustee minutes; and special admissions and financial aid reports, including sections of college strategic plans. These were supplemented by foundation and government documents, especially federal but including some state reports.

Much of the record, however, is incomplete, especially at the college level. Deciding who should get how much money and why is a delicate business, and college policies on the matter have not always been entrusted to permanent files. For example, the insertion of "need" into many scholarship requirements after World War II appears in college catalogs but seldom in archive policy papers.

Likewise, only here and there have I found a written record of disagreements over financial aid *within* a college administration or among trustees, faculty, and students. Administrative control of the written record has probably exaggerated consensus. In the interviews (see below), I did indeed uncover policy differences, but this is not a political science book or a study of organizational dynamics. I have not systematically investigated the maneuvering and clout of different players and groups involved in financial aid policy. Studies along these lines, specifically focusing on student aid, have almost all been at the federal level—on the GI Bill and later programs. The only exception I know of is Angeles Lacomba Eames's study of merit-aid policy-making at three midwestern colleges, 1996–2000.[1]

Affording College: The Limits of Historical Data

As noted in Chapter 2, we have little hard data before the twentieth century on what proportions of different social classes went to college, and we have little before the 1960s on what it cost different social groups to go to different kinds of colleges. Catalogs in the nineteenth and early twentieth centuries often gave college charges and sometimes indicated how much aid a student might get, such as free tuition or reduction of charges, but the catalogs I have read in this period seldom said how many students received such aid and did not repeat those data over time.

Existing studies of student economics in the colonial era and nineteenth century do not relate student charges and college aid to family and student incomes. Nor do they really tell us what a "self-supporting" student at a particular time and place could earn through the year by school-teaching and other jobs.[2] I did not attempt the valuable but huge task of finding such data, as my focus was on policy attitudes rather than results. But of course results reflect and illuminate policy. Hence my analysis in Chapter 2 of Sarah Gordon's unique data on aid to Smith College students in the 1870s and 1880s, which I set against national data on incomes of manual workers and others. Local data would have been better, but this, again, needs a separate study.

Interviews

As Appendix 3 shows, the number of interviewees varied from one to four at most institutions to forty-four at Smith and fifty-three at Oberlin—scenes of major policy developments in the 1990s. Because the interviews took place over more than ten years, they picked up trends and changes in the 1990s and early 2000s, especially as I revisited some colleges and reinterviewed some people—sometimes more than twice.

The most common interviewees were campus financial aid directors, and deans or vice presidents of enrollment (in charge of both admissions and financial aid). Other interviewees, depending on issues and time available, included admissions directors, deans of the college, senior administrators in finance and development, directors of institutional research, legal advisers, and some presidents and ex-presidents. Among retired administrators, a few had professional experience going back to the 1940s and 1950s. Interviewees also included faculty (especially historians of the college and faculty serving on relevant committees), students and alumni, and government officials involved in particular policies. I reinterviewed several financial aid directors and enrollment chiefs after they had moved to other colleges. This stimulated comparisons between institutions.

Because of the sensitive nature of financial aid, and my wish to tap personal opinions and attitudes, I promised my interviewees not to quote or cite them by name or position though their names would be listed in an appendix. (A few exceptions applied where an interviewee made an uncontentious or historical point or had made the comment publicly.) I hoped thereby to gain free expression in return for losing the ability to cite a specific source. Whether the trade was worth it—how much less my informants would have said without my assurance—we may never know. In only one case did a financial aid director refuse point-blank to say why a policy had been changed, saying merely that it was no longer "appropriate" and claiming—too modestly, I later discovered—that he or she was not privy to the policy discussions. The policy area, significantly, was the fraught one of race.

At many financial aid offices, I obtained a page from the college's latest FISAP form (Fiscal Operations Report and Application to Participation), filed annually with the federal government (see glossary, Appendix 4). It gives the number of undergraduate applicants eligible for federal aid on campus, broken down by income bands. This enabled me to estimate the proportion of undergraduates with family incomes under the national median, which was about $42,000 in the mid to late 1990s. Virtually all such students got federal aid of one kind or another.

The Spread of Colleges

To distinguish traits and traditions of individual colleges from those of localities and states, I concentrated some of the research on local groups of colleges, such as "Five Colleges" in western Massachusetts (four private colleges and the University of Massachusetts at Amherst); specific areas, such as Chicago and Philadelphia; and specific states, led by Massachusetts, California, New York, and North Carolina. I also studied some leading private and state universities in local pairs: Princeton and Rutgers, Duke and the University of North Carolina at Chapel Hill, Stanford and the University of California at Berkeley.

Despite this spread, there is an inherent northeastern skew in my focus on highly selective private colleges. (Only ten of the thirty-one elite Consortium on Financing Higher Education [COFHE] colleges are outside New England, New York, New Jersey, and Pennsylvania.)

I do not pretend, anyway, that I simply invented and followed an ideal master plan for where to go. Economics and logistics operated here too. Because I did much of the research while traveling for the University of Sussex, England, as a study-abroad representative and adviser, nonuniversity colleges—prime study-abroad clients of British universities—are overrepresented, though not grotesquely so within my elite focus. Private four-year colleges with few if any graduate programs make up 56 percent of all private colleges and universities in my total research sample, and about the same (55 percent) of those where I did archive research. They make up 42 percent (thirteen colleges) of the thirty-one COFHE institutions.[3]

Private undergraduate liberal arts colleges enroll less than a tenth of undergraduates at four-year institutions, but according to various measures and surveys, they are the jewels of college teaching in America.[4] They are relevant, therefore, to questions about who gets what kind of educational opportunity. Historically, too, it is easier to analyze their aid. The financial reports of universities have tended in the past to lump together undergraduate grants and graduate fellowships.

Case Studies

Personal opportunity also played a part in some of the vignettes and case studies of particular colleges. The big Oberlin case study in Chapter 8 reflects personal connections going back to the 1950s, though it also profited from Oberlin's rich archives on admissions and financial aid and from the amount of campus debate on financial aid and related issues. Again, my focus on the Five Colleges of Massachusetts reflects relationships with Smith, where I taught in the mid-1980s, and with Mount Holyoke, which has a student exchange with Sussex. So does the University of Massachusetts nearby. Personal experience of a college obviously helps the researcher to get a feel for the policy environment and to find useful informants in addition to the usual players.

In the case of one institution, though, the personal factor was at first a deterrent. Harvard recurs in so much of the book that this needs an explanation. I knew I had to use the Radcliffe/Molson story in the prologue and recognize the leadership of John U. Monro in shaping modern financial aid (Chapter 6), but I originally planned no extensive research on Harvard. As an alumnus, I had a horror of being tagged with favoritism. Harvard, however, had other plans for me. More books involving student aid have been written on it than on any other college (four volumes on the colonial period alone, and a book on its economic history), and the books led to questions for the archives.[5] Again and again Harvard has been at the center of issues about student aid. Though its growing wealth and selectivity gave it more choices than most colleges, it too has had to ask the central questions about student aid: Who should get what and why?

Appendix 3. Interviews and Archive Research by State and Institution

Geographical Spread

The interview and archive research for this book involved institutions in twenty-five states plus the District of Columbia. The breakdown below gives the number of institutions in each state (and the District of Columbia). Bracketed figures show the number visited for work in their historical archives.

Alabama 1 (1)

Arkansas 1

California 16 (4)

Colorado 1

Connecticut 5 (2)

District of Columbia 7

Georgia 7 (2)

Illinois 8 (3)

Indiana 1

Kentucky 2 (1)

Louisiana 2

Maine 2

Massachusetts 20 (10)

Michigan 1

Minnesota 2

Missouri 2

New Jersey 3 (3)

New York 15 (6)

North Carolina 14 (2)

Ohio 4 (2)

Pennsylvania 8 (3)

Rhode Island 1

Texas 4 (2)

Vermont 1

Virginia 4

Washington 1

Total 133 (41)

The total includes four institutions listed only for archive research (not interviews): Educational Testing Service, Georgia State Archives, New York State Library, and Rockefeller Archive Center.

Interviews and Archive Visits by Institution

The entries below list in alphabetical order the institutions covered. Asterisks indicate where archive research was done. (In-house reports provided by interviewees and archive material sent by archives not visited are not counted as archive research.) Dates give the period in which archive work and interviews were done, including interviews away from the campus and with people who had left the institution; some of these interviews were conducted by telephone. Substantial correspondence and informal but informative conversations are counted as "interviews." Due to space limitations, I do not give the date of each interview or the official status of the interviewee, but the names of financial aid, admissions, and enrollment officials are italicized. See Appendix 2 on the interviewees. Middle names and initials are omitted except where helpful for identification.

Access Program, Lorain, OH   2000–04
     Carol Hoffman.

Agnes Scott College, Decatur, GA*   1992
     Deborah Gaudier.

Alabama, University of [incl. Carl Elliott Papers], Tuscaloosa, AL*   1996
     Clark Centers, *Molly Lawrence.*

Amherst College, Amherst, MA*   1992–2004
     Joe Case, Peter Pouncey, *Jane Reynolds*, Peter Shea, Marisol Thomer.

Barnard College, New York, NY   1998
     Suzanne Clair Guard.

Bates College, Lewiston, ME   1995, 1999
     David Das, *William Hiss.*

Berea College, Berea, KY*   1994, 1996, 2000
     Lance Bryant, *John Cook*, Sarah Douthitt, Sidney Farr, Loyal Jones, Tony Kent, Nanci McLean, Jacqueline Price, William Ramsay, John Stephenson, Robert Stuckert, Janet Tronc, Kevin Williams, *Hazel Wehrle.*

Boston College, Chestnut Hill, MA   1996
     Robert Lay, Nancy Netzer, *Bernie Pekala.*

Bowdoin College, Brunswick, ME   2000, 2002
     Stephen Joyce, James Miller, Walter Moulton.

Brandeis University, Waltham, MA 1994, 1996
Peter Giumette, Duane Quinn.

Brown University, Providence, RI 1996–99
Anthony Canchola Flores, Michael Goldberger, Emery Walker, Eric Widmer, Heather Woodcock.

Bryn Mawr College, Bryn Mawr, PA 1994, 1999
Erika Behrand, *Nancy Monnich,* Wendy Tiffin.

California, University of [UC system], Oakland, CA 1997, 2000–01
Kate Jeffery.

California, University of, Berkeley, CA* 1997, 2001
Richard Black.

California, University of, Davis, Ca 1992
Ronald Johnson.

California, University of, at San Diego, La Jolla, CA 1992, 1999
Vincent De Anda, Thomas Rutter.

California, University of, Santa Barbara, CA 1992
Gene Awakuni, William Villa.

California, University of, Santa Cruz, CA 1992
Ann Draper.

California Student Aid Commission, Sacramento, CA 1997, 2001
Dana Callihan.

Carleton College, Northfield, MN 2003
David Davis-Van Atta.

Carnegie-Mellon University, Pittsburgh, PA 1999–2000, 2002
William Elliott.

Cherokee Tribal Council, Cherokee, NC 2001
Sam Lambert.

Chicago, University of, Chicago, IL* 1993–97, 2000
Andrew Abbott, Dennis Barden, *Michael Behnke,* John Boyer, Lewis Fortner, Lawrence Furnstahl, Rebecca Janowitz, *Theodore O'Neill, Alicia Reyes.*

Claremont Mckenna College, Claremont, CA 1998
Georgette DeVeres, Nicole Hamon.

Clark University, Worcester, MA*   1994
   Susan Baughman, James Collins, William Koelsch, *Duane Quinn*.

College Board, New York, NY*   1995, 1997–99
   George Hanford, Janet Hansen, Hal Higginbotham, Michael Johanek, Kathleen Little, Donald Stewart, *William Van Dusen*.

Colorado, University of, Boulder, CO   1997–98, 2000
   Lou McClelland, *Jerry Sullivan*.

Connecticut College, New London, CT   1997
   Elaine Solinga.

Consortium On Financing Higher Education, Washington, DC   2001
   Ted Bracken.

Cooper Union, New York, NY*   1995
   Richard Bory, Peter Buckley, Robert Hawks, Linda Lemiesz, *Mary Ruokonen*.

Cornell University, Ithaca, NY*   1992–93, 1995, 1996
   Gould Colman, *Urbain (Ben) DeWinter*, Ronald Ehrenberg, Elaine Engst, *Susan Murphy*.

Davidson College, Davidson, NC   1998
   Louis Ortmayer, *Gordon Peck*.

Duke University, Durham, NC*   1995, 1998–2000
   James Belvin, William Chafe, Sara Dumont, Robert Durden, *Christoph Guttentag*, William King, John Piva, Mary Semans.

Educational Testing Service, Princeton, NJ*   1993

Elon University, Elon, NC   1999
   Susan Klopman, Joel Speckhard.

Emory University: see Oxford College

Evergreen State College, Olympia, WA   1999
   James Neitzel, *Marla Skelley*.

Fordham University, New York, NY   1999, 2001
   Peter Stace, Angela Van Dekker.

George Washington University, Washington, DC   1994
   Linda Salamon.

Georgia State Archives, Atlanta, GA*   1992

Georgia State Governor's Office, Atlanta, GA   1999
  Tom Wade.

Guilford College, Greensboro, NC   1999
  Anthony Gurley.

Hampshire College, Amherst, MA*   1991, 1993
  Larry Beede, Jack Fortier, Penina Glaser, *Kathleen Methot, Audrey Smith.*

Hartford, University of, Hartford, CT   1994
  Charles Colarulli, *Joe Kovic.*

Harvard University, Cambridge, MA*   1992, 1996–98, 2002, 2004
  Timothy Alborn, *Sally Donahue,* Robert Donin, *William Fitzsimmons,*
  Fred Glimp, Janet Irons, Fred Jewett, David Karen, Morton Keller,
  Phyllis Keller, *Martha Lyman, Wallace McDonald, James Miller, John*
  Monro, Henry Rosovsky, *George Sanchez,* Daniel Steiner.

Harvey Mudd College, Claremont, CA   1997–98
  Youlonda Copeland-Morgan, Henry Riggs, *Emery Walker.*

Haverford College, Haverford, PA*   1993–96
  Edwin Bronner, Stephen Carey, *David Hoy,* Donna Mancini, Diana
  Peterson, *Dana Swan.*

Hendrix College, Conway, AR   1996–97
  John Churchill, *Rock Jones, Carlia Sproles.*

Holy Cross, College of the, Worcester, MA   1996
  John Brooks, *Frank Delaney,* Frank Miller.

Illinois State University, Normal, IL   1993, 2000
  Stephen Adams, David Krueger, Tom Wallace.

Illinois Wesleyan University, Bloomington, IL   1996, 2000
  Jack Field, Chris Clayton, Melanie Keller, Pamela Muirhead, *Lynn*
  Nichelson.

Johnson C. Smith University, Charlotte, NC   1999
  Cynthia Anderson, Deborah Carter, Jesse Dent.

Kenyon College, Gambier, OH*   1994
  Craig Bradley.

Knox College, Galesburg, IL   1994–95, 1997
   Stephen Bailey, *Janet Hunter*, John Mohr.

Lafayette College, Easton, PA   2000
   Barry McCarty.

Loyola University of Chicago, Chicago, IL   1996–98
   Robert Bucholz (incl. clippings and reports collection), *Joe Burkhart*,
   Michael Minnice.

Macalester College, St. Paul, MN   1994, 2002
   David Busse, Michael McPherson.

Maguire Associates, Concord, MA   1996
   Jack Maguire.

Massachusetts, University of, Amherst, MA*   1990, 1993, 1996, 2000
   Burt Batty, Ken Burnham, Timm Rhinehart.

Massachusetts Institute of Technology, Cambridge, MA   1996, 2000
   Michael Behnke, Paul Gray, *Stanley Hudson,* Charles Vest, Mark
   Wrightman. See also PALMER AND DODGE.

Michigan, University of, Ann Arbor, MI   1996
   Robert Holbrook, George Sanchez.

Missouri, University of, St. Louis, MO
   Anthony Georges, Blanche Touhill.

Morehouse College, Atlanta, GA   1992
   Johnny Nimes.

Mount Holyoke College, South Hadley, MA*
   1993–94, 1996–97, 1999–2000, 2004
   Patricia Albright, Kay Althoff, Peter Berek, *Jennifer Blake, Jane Brown*,
   Janet Collett, *Kim Condon*, Carolyn Dietel, Stephen Ellenburg, Joseph
   Ellis, Janice Gifford, *Clara Ludwig*, Mary Jo Maydew, Joane Picard,
   Michael Robinson, Bea Szekely, Elaine Trehub, *Patricia Waters.*

National Association of College Admission Counselors,
   Alexandria, VA   1995
   Mary Lee Hoganson.

National Association of Student Financial Aid Administrators,
   Washington, DC   1994
   Dallas Martin.

National Merit Scholarship Corporation, Evanston, IL   1993, 2000
Elaine Detweiler, *Marianne Roderick*.

New York, State University of [SUNY system], Albany, NY   1992, 1995
Jane Graham.

New York, State University of, Stony Brook, NY   1993
Marilyn Goodman, Norman Goodman, *Theresa LaRocca-Meyer, Anna Torres*.

New York State Higher Education Services Corporation,
Albany, NY   1995
Francis Hynes, Peter Keitel

New York State Library, Albany, NY*   1995

New York University, New York, NY   1995
Patricia Carey, Ann Marcus, *MaryBeth McMurphy*.

North Carolina, University of, Asheville, NC   1998
John White.

North Carolina, University of, Chapel Hill, NC*   1995, 1998
Michael Martin, Richard McCormick, *Eleanor Morris*, Kenneth
Reckford, Timothy Sandford, June Steel, *William Wells*.

North Carolina, University of, General Administration [UNC system],
Chapel Hill, NC   1998, 2001
Gary Barnes.

North Carolina, University of, Pembroke, NC   1999
Bruce Blackmon, Jacqueline Clark.

North Carolina State Education Assistance Authority, Chapel Hill,
NC   1995
Stan Broadway.

Northern Kentucky University, Highland Heights, KY   1994
Michael Adams, Jessica Bailey, Sandra Easton, Susan Kissel, *Jackie Marshall*.

Northwestern University, Evanston, IL*   1993–96
Kirstie Andrews, Rebecca Dixon, Ronald Dorpel, *William Ihlandfeldt*,
Carolyn Lindley, John Margolis, Marilyn McCoy, Charles Moskos, Scott
Payton, Patrick Quinn, Arnold Weber, Jeremy Wilson.

Notre Dame, University of, Notre Dame, IN   1994–98, 2000, 2002
    Theodore Hesburgh, Ned Joyce, Dan Reagan, *Ken Rooney, Joseph Russo.*

Oberlin College, Oberlin, OH*   1991–2001
    George Andrews, *David Arredondo*, Marian Baum, Roland Baumann,
    Carl Bewig, Marc Blecher, Geoffrey Blodgett, Andrew Bongiorno,
    Norman Care, Sam Carrier, *Debra Chermonte*, David Clark, Yolanda
    Cruz, Young Dawkins, Nancy Dye, Andrew Evans, Lee Fortes, Melissa
    Gottwald, Catharine Gowers, Lisa Halpern, *Thomas Hayden*, Carol
    Hoffman, Lionel Hollins, Chris Howell, Ronald Huiatt, Clayton
    Koppes, Gary Kornblith, Anthony Lanyi, Susan Lanyi, Carol Lasser,
    Virginia Levi, Brian Lindeman, Robert Longsworth, David Love, Alfred
    Mackay, Albert McQueen, Gilbert Meilander, Phyllis Palmer, Ross
    Peacock, Booker Peek, Donald Reutener, Nicholas Riccardi, William
    Robinson, Richard Schoonmaker, Sharon Smith, Tim Smith, Susan
    Sprigge, *Howard Thomas*, Jonathan Thurn, *James White*, Harlan Wilson,
    Milton Yinger, Grover Zinn.

Occidental College, Los Angeles, CA   1998–99
    Youlonda Copeland-Morgan, Robin Craggs, Cecila Fox, *Sean Logan*,
    Pati Pineiro-Goodenberger, Karen Schoenrock, John Slaughter, Woody
    Studenmund, *William Tingley*.

Oxford College of Emory University, Oxford, GA [2-year]   1999
    Beth Cleaveland, Leigh Simmons.

Pacific, University of the , Stockton, CA   1999
    Stephan Coggs.

Paine College, Augusta, GA   1997
    Claudia Jones.

Palmer And Dodge [MIT lawyers], Boston, MA*   1996, 1997, 2003
    Thane Scott.

Pennsylvania, University of, Philadelphia, PA   1994
    William Schilling.

Pitzer College, Claremont, CA   1998
    Margaret Carothers.

Pomona College [incl. J. Edward Sanders Papers c/o Jane Sanders],
Claremont, CA*   1997–99, 2001

David Alexander, *Patricia Coye*, Jane Sanders, Herbert Smith, Peter Stanley.

Princeton University, Princeton, NJ*   1993, 1995, 1998, 2000, 2002–03
Don Betterton, James Compton, Bradford Craig, Jeremiah Finch, Robert Goheen, Nancy Malkiel, *Spencer Reynolds*, Richard Spies.

Rensselaer Polytechnic Institute, Troy, NY   1995, 1999
James Stevenson, Jack Wilson.

Rice University, Houston, TX*   1996, 2000
Dean Currie, Chandler Davidson, Alan Grob, Amita Kamath, *Ann Wright*.

Rochester, University of, Rochester, NY   1995, 1999
Brent Bernard, *Kathy Kurz, Neill Sanders, James Scannell*, Harold Wechsler, *Ryan Williams*.

Rockefeller Archive Center, Sleepy Hollow, NY*   1994

Roosevelt University, Chicago, IL*   1993
Stephen Bellin, Edith Ehrlich, Leonard Ehrlich, Rebecca Jeffords, Herbert Slutsky, Mary Sonada.

Rutgers University, New Brunswick, NJ*   1991, 1993, 1996, 1998
John Brugel, Carl Buck, John Creeden, *Louise Duus*, Thomas Frusciano, Mary Hartman, Francis Lawrence, Richard P. McCormick, Elizabeth Mitchell, Michael Moffatt, *Stephen Rouff*.

Sallie Mae [Student Loan Association], Washington, DC   1995
Jerry Davis.

Scripps College, Claremont, CA*   1997–98
Betty Johnson, Pati Pineiro-Goldberger.

Smith College, Northampton, MA*   1992–94, 1996–2002
Donald Baumer, *Lorna Blake*, Susan Bourque, Maira Carland, John Connolly, Jill Conway, Rick Fantasia, Edward Feld, Christine Forgey, Rosemarie Freeland, Susan Grigg, Charlotte Heartt, Daniel Horowitz, Helen Horowitz, Mentha Hynes, Charles Johnson, Jefferson Hunter, *Pamela Hunter,* Erika Kates, Roger Kaufman, *Anne Keppler*, Lori Krase, Erika Laquer, Eleanor Lincoln, Florence Macdonald, Maureen Mahoney, Sherry Marker, Amanda Martinson, Howard Nenner, Pat Olmstedt, William Oram, Donald Reutener, Donald Robinson, Eleanor Rothman, *Audrey Smith, Myra Smith, Susan Stano*, Lee Taylor,

Susan Toth, Richard Unsworth, Amber Watt, Susan Webster, *Ann Wright*, Nanci Young.

Southern California, University of, Los Angeles, CA   1998–99
Guy Hunter, Davon Ramos, Doan Le, Morton Schapiro.

Spelman College, Atlanta, GA   1992
Brenda Banks, Johnetta Cole.

Stanford University, Stanford, CA*   1992, 1997–98, 2000, 2003
Jean Fetter, Robert Huff, Mary Morrison, James Montoya, John Pearson, *Jon Reider.*

Swarthmore College, Swarthmore, PA*   1994–96, 1999–2001
Wallace Ayres, Mary Ellen Chijioke, Martha Dean, Ed Fuller, Susan Hodge, *Robin Mamlet*, John Nason, Adam Rabinowitz, John Rosselli, William Stanton, *Laura Talbot.*

Syracuse University, Syracuse, NY   1999, 2001
David Smith.

Temple University, Philadelphia, PA*   1994–95
Harry Bailey, Edwin Bronner, *John Morris, Timm Rinehart.*

Texas, University of, Austin, TX*   1992, 1996
Don Davis, Don Stallings (incl. "SFA Scrapbook"), Joe Wilcox.

Texas Higher Education Coordinating Board, Austin, TX   1996, 1999
Mack Adams, Jane Caldwell.

Texas State Senate, Austin, TX   1996
Gonzalo Barrientos.

Trinity College, Hartford, CT   1997
Kelly O'Brien, Christopher Small.

Tufts University, Medford, MA   1993
Daniel Richards.

Tulane University, New Orleans, LA   1995
Elaine Rivera.

U.S. House of Representatives [incl. staff], Washington, DC
1995–96, 1998, 2004
Carl Elliott, Thomas Wolanin. See also Alabama, University of.

U.S. Department of Justice, Washington, DC   1998–99, 2000
John Hoven, Robert Litan, Bruce Pearson.

U.S Senate [staff], Washington, DC   1998, 2004
David Evans, Nick Littlefield.

Vassar College, Poughkeepsie, NY*   1995
Elizabeth Daniels, *Michael Fraher*, *Mary Alice Hunter*.

Vermont, University of, Burlington, VT   1993
Howard Ball.

Villanova University, Villanova, PA   1994, 2000
David Contosta, Sally Griffith, Mario D'Ignazio, *George Walter*.

Virginia Military Institute, Lexington, VA   1999
Timothy Golden.

Wake Forest University, Winston-Salem, NC   1998
William Wells.

Warren Wilson College, Asheville, NC   2001
Ian Robertson.

Washington And Lee University, Lexington, VA   1999
John DeCourcy, William Klingelhofer.

Washington University, St. Louis, MO   1996, 2000
Dennis Martin, Richard Ruhland, Mark Wrightman.

Wellesley College, Wellesley, MA   1999–2000, 2004
Sylvia Hiestand, Wilma Slaight, Diane Triant.

Wesleyan University, Middletown, CT*   1970, 1994, 1996
Edwin Below, Joanne Creighton, *Donald Eldridge*, Fred Greenstein
(1970), Stanley Lebergott (1970), Donald Moon, John Spaeth (1970),
William Wasch (1970), *Barbara-Jan Wilson*, Lauren Wolfe. (This list
includes interviews in 1970 during research for the Wesleyan Alumni
Relations Office.)

Western Carolina University, Cullowhee, NC   2001
Trina Orr.

Westfield State College, Westfield, MA   2000
Angela Nunes.

Wheaton College, Norton, MA*   1996–97
  Gail Berson, Robin Randall, Zephorene (Zeph) Stickney.

Wheelock College, Boston, MA   1998
  Betty Fuchs.

William and Mary, College of, Williamsburg, VA   2004
  Stacy Gould.

Williams College, Williamstown, MA   1993, 2000–01
  Linda Hall, Harry Payne, *Philip Wick.*

Wooster, College of, Wooster, OH   1991
  David Miller.

Worcester Polytechnic Institute, Worcester, MA*   1994, 1996
  Lora Brueck, *Michael Curley.*

Xavier University of Louisiana, New Orleans, LA   1998
  Kenneth Boutte.

Yale University, New Haven, CT   1990, 1993, 2001–02
  Daniel Horowitz, George Pierson, *Donald (Skip) Routh.*

Appendix 4.
Watch Your Language:
A Glossary of Financial Aid

This glossary includes organizations and other entities as well as technical terms broadly associated with financial aid. To save space and avoid invidious selection, the glossary does not list specific statutes, or state and nongovernmental programs and organizations other than college associations. The one exception is American College Testing (**ACT**). Cross-references to other glossary entries are in **boldface** type, and items usually referred to by abbreviations are listed under their abbreviations. Most of the items are current, but the glossary also includes a few archaic terms.

Acceptance rate, admit rate. The percentage of applicants that a college admits (offers a place to). Cf. **yield.**

ACE. Founded in 1918, the American Council on Education has served as an umbrella organization of colleges and college associations but has developed its own voice. Its mission statement stresses the equalizing of educational opportunity and the promotion of a stronger higher-education system as "cornerstones of a democratic society."

ACT. American College Testing administers national college admissions tests; it started up in 1959 in competition with **College Board's SAT**s. Based in Iowa City, ACT is strong in the Midwest and Southeast.

Admit (noun). An admit is a college applicant to whom the college has offered a place (applicant has been admitted). The student has not necessarily said yes and enrolled. Cf. **yield.**

Admit-deny. The practice of admitting a student but denying college grant aid, though the student qualifies for it on the basis of financial need. Grant aid is reserved for those considered more meritorious. This was common practice till the 1970s, but the term was more common before the 1990s, when alternatives appeared. College aid policies today are usually more flexible. Cf. **gap, need-aware, need-blind,** and **preferential packaging.**

AmeriCorps, or the Corporation for National and Community Service, is the federal agency administering awards for community work given under the National Community Services Trust Act of 1993. The awards include small stipends during service plus grants to pay for college or repay student loans.

Athletic scholarships are muscular **merits,** awarded on the basis of athletic prowess, not **financial need.**

Beneficiary aid. A nineteenth- and early-twentieth-century term for **need-based aid.**

BEOG. See **Pell grant.**

Campus-based aid. Federal or state aid provided to colleges to distribute according to colleges' discretion but within set guidelines.

COFHE (pronounced "co-fi"). The Consortium on Financing Higher Education is an elite association of thirty-one highly selective private universities and liberal arts colleges. Created in 1974 out of a smaller group, it is much concerned with financial aid policy and practices. (COFHE should not be confused with the temporary Commission on Financing Higher Education, funded by the Rockefeller Foundation in the 1950s.)

College Board. Founded in 1900 as the College Entrance Examination Board, the board is today a testing body (it owns the **SAT**s), an association of colleges and schools, a research sponsor, and an educational publisher. Dedicated to "equity" as well as "excellence," it has been much concerned with financial aid, especially since the 1940s.

Consolidated loans. Like some other bodies, the federal government enables graduates to replace various federal loans, including "**unsubsidized**" ones, with a single loan, at a relatively low fixed interest rate. (At the time of writing, the program's survival is uncertain.)

CSS. The College Scholarship Service, an arm of the **College Board,** was created in 1954 to help colleges process aid applications and apply **need analysis** to them. CSS also promoted **need-based aid** through conferences and training. The CSS's financial aid processing is now done by a differently named part of the College Board—College and University Enrollment Solutions, or CUES—but CSS remains an oddly named committee within the board bureaucracy.

CSS/Financial Aid Profile (or CSS/Profile) is the **College Board'**s equivalent of **FAFSA,** a financial aid application and assessment form used by some colleges in allocating nonfederal aid.

CWS. See **FWS.**

Dependent students. The traditional undergraduate population, at least since the mid-nineteenth century. By legal definition they depend on parents for over half their financial support, are under twenty-four, and fulfill other criteria indicating that they are not **independent** students.

Differential packaging. See **preferential packaging.**

Direct lending. See **Ford Direct Loans.**

Discount rate. A college's total spending on grant aid in relation to its tuition revenue. It is usually expressed as a percentage of *gross* tuition revenue—what the college would have received if all students had paid full tuition without college grant aid. The grant aid, however, may not all come out of tuition revenue. Some or most of it may be funded by gifts and **endowment** income. Cf. **net tuition.**

Early-decision. An admission policy that allows some applicants to obtain early acceptance by a college if they then commit to that college. "ED" is controversial in several respects including its effect on financial aid, as it prevents the student from effectively comparing different aid offers. Less restrictive "early-action" variants let the student apply early to one or several colleges, but do not bind the student to an early acceptance by a college.

EFC. The expected family contribution (or "calculated" family contribution, as it was originally called in the 1950s) is the assessment of what a student and family can pay toward college out of income and assets. Government and college aid providers use EFC in determining a student's **financial need,** though EFC depends on the **need-analysis methodology** used and on whether the individual is a **dependent** or **independent** student.

Endowment. College assets, usually income-producing and mostly held in stocks, resulting from gifts and bequests. Endowed scholarships are a form of *restricted* endowment: their use is meant to be confined to donors' specified purposes ("restrictions"), as opposed to *unrestricted* endowment.

FAFSA. The Free Application for Federal Student Aid is the form on which students give financial information, enabling the government to tell them what they will be expected to pay toward college costs (their **EFC**) before qualifying for Federal **need-based aid.** The FAFSA Web site amiably warns that filling it out is "unfortunately . . . a lot like filling out your income taxes."

FFEL. Federal Family Education Loans are an umbrella category for several federal **indirect loan** programs.

Financial need. The estimated difference between what a student can afford and the costs of attending a college (charges and living costs). Cf. **EFC.**

FISAP. The Fiscal Operations Report and Application to Participation is a federal form by which a college gives the government annual data on its participation in federal aid programs, including information about applicants for federal aid and recipients of **campus-based aid.**

FM (Federal Methodology). See **need-analysis methodology.**

Ford Direct Loans. Started in 1994, these loans go directly from the federal government to the borrower, rather than via other providers (**indirect student loans**) or allocation by colleges (**campus-based aid**). They include the direct versions of **Stafford loans** and **PLUS.** Congressman William D. Ford (D., MI) was a key figure in the program's enactment.

Front-loading. Putting less grant money into a student's financial aid **package** after the first year of college. Some federal loan programs support this practice by setting higher borrowing limits in later years.

FSEOG. Federal Supplemental Educational Opportunity Grants are federal **campus-based aid:** the money is allocated to colleges to distribute among students with "exceptional **financial need.**" To encourage aid by the college itself, FSEOGs cannot exceed 75 percent of grant aid disbursed to the students by the college. Originally known as Educational Opportunity Grants (EOGs) in 1965, they became "Supplemental" (SEOGs) when **Pell grants** started in the early 1970s, and "Federal" was added to the official term later.

FWS. The Federal Work-Study program, created in 1964 as College Work-Study, gives money to colleges for student employment The federal government usually may not provide more than 75 percent of the funds for a student.

Gap, gapping. Colleges gap students when financial aid from all sources does not meet all their **financial need.**

Geodemographic targeting seeks college applicants who can pay full tuition, often by using zip codes. This marketing consultants' term emerged in the 1990s. (My own preferred term is "zip-coding.")

GSLs. Guaranteed Student Loans. These federal **indirect loans** (federally sponsored through other lenders) started in 1965. GSLs later gave way to **FFELs,** which cover other indirect loans as well.

Hope Scholarships (federal). See **tax credits.**

IM (Institutional Methodology). See **need-analysis methodology.**

Independent students are over twenty-four years old or meet various other criteria indicating financial independence of their parents—as opposed to **dependent students.**

Indirect student loans are sponsored and guaranteed against default by the federal government, but the loan money actually comes from other providers. The federal government, however, gives incentive payments ("special allowances") to the lenders. This applies to both **subsidized** and **unsubsidized** loans.

Institutional aid. Aid funded by colleges, as opposed to state and federal programs.

Ivy League, Ivies. Eight highly prestigious and selective old universities: Brown, Dartmouth, Columbia, Cornell, Harvard, Pennsylvania, Princeton, and Yale. All are private except for Cornell, some of whose schools are state. The league emerged out of intercollegiate athletics in New England in the 1920s and 1930s but did not crystallize as an association with a clearly defined membership till after World War II. Between 1958 and 1991, the Ivies and MIT regularly met to agree on their charges to aided students (see Appendix 1). The Council of Ivy Group Presidents maintains an office in Princeton, New Jersey.

LEAP. Through the Leveraging Educational Assistance Partnership, the federal government gives scholarship money to states on a "matching" basis: the states contribute too; it is supposed to "lever" up state aid. The program started in 1974 as the State Student Incentive Grants (SSIGs).

Lifelong Learning credits. See **tax credits.**

Loan forgiveness lets a recipient off repaying some or all of a loan, usually for specified social service.

Merit scholarships, merits. Known till the 1940s as "Honors," "prize," and "open competition" scholarships, merits are awarded on the basis of academic or other ability, not on **financial need.**

NACAC. Founded in 1937, the National Association of College Admission Counselors brings together high-school college counselors with college admissions officers. It has expressed strong views on admissions and financial aid.

NACUBO. The National Association of College and University Business Officers addresses many aspects of college administration and budgeting, including tuition revenue and tuition discounting through aid. It grew out of a looser federation that evolved in the 1950s.

NASFAA. The National Association of Financial Aid Administrators was formed out of regional associations in 1966. Its ethos stresses **need-based aid.**

National Defense Student Loans. Established by the National Defense Education Act (NDEA) of 1958, these federal loans were **campus-based aid** (allocated by the colleges) and the direct precursor of **Perkins loans.** Unlike Perkins loans, however, they were meant to go to students with a "superior capacity" in science, mathematics, engineering, or a "modern foreign language," or to academically "superior" students planning to teach school. They carried low fixed interest rates (zero while the student was in college) and required **financial need.**

NCAA. The National Collegiate Athletic Association is the body by which member colleges and athletic conferences regulate college athletics. NCAA closely restricts **athletic scholarships** in Division I and II sports and bans them in Division III. Its origins go back to 1905 when President Theodore Roosevelt, outraged at football deaths and injuries, called for collective reform of the game's rules.

Need. See **financial need.**

Need-analysis (or needs-analysis) methodology. The system used to determine **financial need** by assessing what students and families can pay toward college ("expected family contribution" or **EFC**). Since the early 1990s, many private colleges have used an "Institutional Methodology" (IM) for their own financial aid (though the **Ivy League** and some other elite colleges had developed their own methodologies as early as 1958). IM is distinct from **FM,** used for federal aid and many state programs. Cf. **CSS/Financial Aid Profile** and **FAFSA.**

Need-aware (or **need-conscious**) admissions exclude some students (usually less-qualified ones) because they have high **financial need,** expensive to fill. Although the practice occurred sporadically from the late nineteenth century on, the term emerged in the 1960s to distinguish such practices from **need-blind** and **admit-deny** policies. It was sometimes called "deny-deny" (denying aid by denying admission).

Need-based aid. Aid requiring **financial need,** though it may also be subject to other factors.

Need-blind admissions policies are meant to ignore ability to pay in selecting applicants, though many "need-blind" colleges do not apply the principle to foreign students, and some don't do it for students admitted from their admissions waiting lists. As used by nonexperts, the term also implies that the college guarantees meeting all **financial need.**

Negotiation. On financial aid, this refers to conversations that ensue (if they do) when an admitted student tries to get the college to raise its initial aid offer. Negotiation may involve "new information" ("We're having to pay big hospital bills for Uncle Jonah") or competitive offers elsewhere ("Majestic U. will give me more") or both. Cf. **professional judgment.**

Net tuition, net tuition revenue. For a student, net tuition (or net charges) is what he or she pays after subtracting grant aid received from all sources. (Some economists also subtract the subsidy element of loans.) For a college, net tuition *revenue* is what it gets after subtracting its own grant-aid spending. Cf. **discount rate.**

Outside scholarships. Grants by private donors (today usually charitable agencies) to individually chosen students, either directly to them or through their colleges.

Package, packaging. The careful construction by a college of a student's financial aid, usually combining grant, loan, and employment. The practice started in the 1950s. Cf. **preferential packaging.**

Pell grants. The main federal grants, starting in 1973–74 as Basic Educational Opportunity Grants (BEOGs) for needy students. They were later named after Sen. Claiborne Pell (D., RI), their leading architect in Congress.

Perkins loans are **campus-based** federal aid: government loan money is allocated to colleges to distribute to students with "exceptional **financial need.**" The college has to contribute a quarter of the Perkins total. Perkins loans are **subsidized** (interest-free while the student is in college). They increase the amount of subsidized loan that recipients can get by supplementing the main **Stafford**

loans. Unlike many other federal loans, their interest rate is fixed. The 5 percent rate has often been below that of Staffords but is currently higher. The program basically started with the 1958 **National Defense Student Loans.** It was renamed in honor of Congressman Carl D. Perkins (D., KY), a big player in student-aid legislation of the 1970s and 1980s.

PLUS. Parents of students going to college can take out these federal Parent Loans for Undergraduate Students. The loan is **unsubsidized** and cannot exceed the difference between the cost of attending college and (other) financial aid received by the student.

Preferential packaging. A college policy of sweetening a financial aid **package** for favored students by increasing the grant element and reducing the **self-help** element (loan and/or job). When it is applied to socioeconomic groups (low-income or first-generation-college), financial aid professionals usually call it "differential packaging."

Professional judgment. In college financial aid offices, this means the discretion allowed an officer to alter a student's aid on the basis of specific personal circumstances not fully picked up by computerized **need analysis** of the student's ability to pay. Officials often have more latitude to do this with the college's own aid.

ROTC scholarships, offered by the Reserve Officer Training Corps, are among many aid programs involving military service.

SATs. Scholastic Aptitude Tests for college admission are owned by the **College Board.** They started on a small, experimental basis in 1925 and expanded in the 1940s.

Selectivity is a college's academic choosiness in admissions and the measurable quality of its students. Sometimes it is gauged simply by the college's **acceptance rate**—the percentage of applicants it admits—but often it also includes entering students' test scores and class rank in high school.

Self-help is financial aid–speak for the loan and job components of an aid **package.** This usage originated in the 1890s when colleges set up bureaus of "self-help" to assist students in getting jobs.

SEOG. See **FSEOG.**

SSIG. See **LEAP.**

Stafford loans. These are the main federal loans, initiated in 1965. They now include **subsidized** and **unsubsidized** versions, and direct loans (falling under the **Ford Direct Loans** program) as well as **indirect loans.** They are named after Sen. Robert Stafford (R., VT), an important figure in student-aid legislation.

Subsidized student loans. Loans whose provider or sponsor reduces or eliminates the interest charged. Federal subsidized loans require financial need and carry no interest while the student is in college and for a short "grace period" thereafter; their rates are then the same as **unsubsidized** (student) **loans.** Both kinds involve "origination fees," but these can be reduced on various conditions.

Tax credits. Dollar amounts that can be subtracted from income tax to help repay the family for college expenses. Federal tax credits, created in 1997, consist of "Hope Scholarships" for the first two years of college, and Lifelong Learning credits for the last two and graduate school.

Underrepresented minorities. A term, most common in the 1990s, for ethnic groups statistically underrepresented in the college population. It usually means African, Hispanic, and Native Americans, who often receive **preferential packaging** of aid.

Unmet need. The difference between a student's resources (including **EFC** and financial aid) and the cost of attending college. It is very like the concept of **gapping,** but "unmet need" is the term used more in national surveys.

Unsubsidized loans. Federal loans to students or their families that are not interest-free during college (unlike federal **subsidized loans**). Their interest rates, however, are less than ordinary market rates, in part because the rates are restricted: they are linked to Treasury-bill rates and cannot exceed maximum limits. They do not require **financial need.** Best practice—not followed by all colleges—does not count unsubsidized student loans as part of the financial aid **package** used to fill financial need, unless it is in the student's interest to do so.*

Work-study. College or government support for term-time paid employment of students. Cf. **FWS.**

Yield. The percentage of **admits** who enroll at a college. Yield often influences a college's **acceptance rate.** It is also used by colleges to measure the effects of different financial aid offers on different groups and types of students.

---

*Because of differing methods of need analysis, the federal estimates of financial need that govern federal loans have often been higher than the estimates used by leading private colleges for their own aid. When, however, the federal estimate of need is lower for a particular student, a private college, using a higher estimate of need, may give the student so much grant aid that there is little or no "need" left under the federal estimate to qualify for a federal subsidized loan. The college must therefore either reduce the grant aid, making more room for a subsidized loan under federal requirements of financial need, or include in the student's aid package an unsubsidized loan that does not require federally defined need. The latter option is usually of more benefit to the student.

Notes

Full references are in the bibliography except for archive records, internal office papers, court cases and papers, and *Chronicle of Higher Education* Almanac issues. All of these are fully cited in the notes.

Acknowledgments

1. Allmendinger, *Paupers and Scholars* (1975). Other writing on poor and aided students includes Hayes, "Can a Poor Girl Go to College?" (1891); Fallows, "Working One's Way through College" (1901) and "Working One's Way through Women's Colleges" (1901); Gordon, "Smith College Students" (1975); Wechsler, "An Academic Gresham's Law" (1981); LeTendre, "The Working-Class Student at Harvard" (1983); Horowitz, *Campus Life* (1987), esp. chaps. 1–3, 8. Various nineteenth- and early twentieth-century autobiographies describe poor students' experiences. More modern memoirs include Theodore White, *In Search of History* (1978), 35–53; Bergin, "My Native Country" (1982); Toth, *Ivy Days* (1984); Mar, "Blue Collar, Crimson Blazer" (1995). On black students and colleges, Olivier, "Stony Path to Learning" (1945); Moody, *Coming of Age in Mississippi* (1987), Part 3; Suskind, *A Hope in the Unseen* (1999); hooks, "Learning in the Shadow of Race and Class" (2000).

Prologue

1. Wilbur K. Jordan, "Ann Radcliffe" (1959). Morison, *The Founding of Harvard College* (1935), 307–8.
2. Morison, *The Founding of Harvard College* (1935), Appendix D, contains the 1643 text of "First Fruits," which may have been written wholly or partially by Weld and Hugh Peter; it was sent to the mission after it had left. The mission

also included Peter and William Hibbens, but Weld seems to have been the most active in England. Weld's letter (June or July 1632) to Essex, his former parishioners at Tarling, is in Emerson, ed., *Letters from New England* (1976), 93–98. Emerson's collection of letters suggests that Weld's account was more glowing than that of others at the time. On Weld, see *Dictionary of National Biography*, vol. 20 (1909), 1071–72, and *American National Biography*, vol. 22 (1999), 929–31. I am grateful to Roger Thompson for background on Weld and other aspects of the Radcliffe-Mowlson gift.

3. Morison, *Founding* (1935), 303–14, including text of the Radcliffe-Weld covenant.

4. Sibley, *Biographical Sketches of Graduates of Harvard University* (1873), vol. 1, 121–22. Morison, *Founding* (1935), misstates Joseph's name as John. The exact stipend amount is unclear, but I assume a minimum annual payout of 6 percent on the £100 donated endowment. Cf. Foster, *"Out of Smalle Beginnings"* (1962), 66, 158.

5. Moran and Vinovskis, *Religion, Family, and the Life Course* (1992), chap. 6.

6. Quincy, *History of Harvard University* (1840), 182–83, 462–65. Davis, "Ann Radcliffe—Lady Mowlson" (1894). Jordan, "Ann Radcliffe" (1959). Foster, *"Out of Smalle Beginnings"* (1962), 138–39.

7. Morison, *Founding* (1935), 314–21. Foster, *"Out of Smalle Beginnings"* (1962), 88–90, 139; also 93–96, 139n on the apparent diversion of other scholarship money. Some requests for corn money did mention "fellows," but the main and most effective pitch was for "poor, pious and learned students." We do not know if too few poor students applied at this early point to use all the corn money; plenty did twenty years later.

8. Holtschneider, "Institutional Aid to New England College Students" (1997), 19–20, 33–52.

9. *Chronicle of Higher Education,* Almanac issue (Aug. 27, 2004), 12. The total of $105.1 billion in 2002–03 included $5.4 billion in federal tax credits for college d $25.4 billion in "unsubsidized" loans (accruing interest while the student is in college), which are often not counted as part of financial aid packages. The total included Federal Work-Study money paid to colleges for student employment but not colleges' own spending on student jobs.

10. Foster, *"Out of Smalle Beginnings"* (1962), 139.

11. Cf. Hoffman, *Gulliver's Troubles* (1968), 179–94; Wilkinson, *American Tough* (1984), 23–27.

1. Setting the Record Straight

1. Lapovsky and Hubbell, "Positioning for Competition" (2000), 20. This book does not cover the rise of for-profit institutions, competing mainly at the more

vocational and lower-price end of the higher education market. Cf. Kirp, *Shakespeare, Einstein, and the Bottom Line* (2003), chap. 13, and Vedder, *Going Broke by Degree* (2004), 151–62.

2. J. Edward Sanders, Interview (1982). Finn, "Why Do We Need Financial Aid?" (1985), 6. Hauptman, *Tuition Dilemma* (1990), 162. Kurz, "The Changing Role of Financial Aid and Enrollment Management" (1995), 25. Mumper, *Removing College Price Barriers* (1996), 170. Doti, "Tuition Discounting" (2000), 25. Redd, "Discounting toward Disaster" (2000), 1. On the myth of historically dominant merits as a "common belief," Wick, "No-Need/Merit Scholarships" (1997), v, 1–2.

3. Rauh, "The Relation of Student Programs to Institutional Finances" (1972), 77. William Frank Elliott, "Management of Admissions and Financial Aid" (1974). Finn, "Why Do We Need Financial Aid?" (1985), 9. McPherson and Schapiro, *The Student Aid Game* (1998), 15–16.

4. Kane, *The Price of Admission* (1999), 83, and Gose, "Measuring the Value of an Ivy Degree" (2000), summarize and discuss several studies. The research included controls for test-score ability. The study that found a particular payoff for low-income students partially controlled for student ambition in that it followed graduates, each of whom had applied to and been accepted by both more- and less-selective colleges. Dale and Krueger, "Estimating the Payoff to Attending a More Selective College" (2000). Krueger to author, e-mail, Oct. 15, 2002.

5. Reich, "How Selective Colleges Heighten Inequality" (2001). Mishel et al., *The State of Working America* (2001), chap. 1. Schmidt, "Noted Higher-Education Researcher Urges Admissions Preference for the Poor" (2004). Leonhardt, "As Wealthy Fill Top Colleges, Concerns Grow over Fairness" (2004). On four American fears, Wilkinson, *The Pursuit of American Character* (1988), chaps. 5, 6.

6. Cf. Redd, "Discounting toward Disaster" (2000), 15, and Hubell and Lapovsky, "Tuition Discounting in Challenging Times" (2002), 25, 26, 29.

7. Whitehead, *The Separation of College and State* (1973), 92–93, 226–27. On public-private evolution, Herbst, "Eighteenth-Century Origins of the Split between Public and Private Higher Education" (1975); Whitehead and Herbst, "How to Think about the Dartmouth College Case" (1986).

8. Cf. Carnegie Commission on Higher Education, *Higher Education* (1973), 90, 176–77; Minnesota Private College Research Foundation, "Ways and Means" (1992), 117; Cooper, "The Well-to-Do at the Public U" (1999); Gottlieb, "Need Blind" (2000).

9. U.S. Dept. of Interior, *Biennial Survey of Education* (1921, 1925): my count. Cf. Schmidt, *The Liberal Arts College* (1957), 15, 77–78, 148, and Woodward, *Origins of the New South* (1951), 437, which include discussion of low public

support and higher tuition in the South. On fluctuating tuition and aid policies at Massachusetts Agricultural College (today's University of Massachusetts
at Amherst), see Wilkinson, "Plural Ends, Contested Means" (2001), 319. A
variation on low tuition for access is charging per course to part-time students. In the private sector, endowed colleges for "working men and women"
developed this in the late nineteenth century. A leading practitioner today is
Roosevelt University, dramatically founded in 1945 when sixty-nine faculty
and administrators broke away from Chicago's Central YMCA College over its
restrictive racial policies. Gowran, "Roosevelt Entry Policy Aims at 'Culturally
Deprived'" (1963). Lelon, "The Emergence of Roosevelt College of Chicago"
(1973). Interviews, Roosevelt University.

10. Berea does use merit scholarships as well as state and federal student aid. In
different molds, New York's Cooper Union (free tuition) and Houston's Rice
(free till the 1960s and charging a third less tuition than its elite peers since
then) give a lot of aid on a financial-need basis. They are also more academically and nationally selective than Berea, though both were founded as local
working-people's institutes in the late nineteenth century.

11. Allmendinger, *Paupers and Scholars* (1975), 11–12. Redd, "Discounting toward
Disaster" (2000), 11–13. Hubell and Lapovsky, "Tuition Discounting in Challenging Times" (2000), 25. But Breneman, *Liberal Arts Colleges* (1994), found
that a middling-tuition group of liberal arts colleges gave the most aid from
general funds as a percentage of tuition—due, he suggested, to a competitive
squeeze from cheaper colleges below and more prestigious ones above: 58–59.

12. Cf. Breneman, *Liberal Arts Colleges* (1994), 61–62, and Drewry and Doermann,
Stand and Prosper (2001), 252, table. Also freshman surveys comparing sources
of "educational expenses": Cooperative Institutional Research Program, *The
American Freshman,* annual volumes. In the 1920s and 1930s, student aid at the
leading black college, Morehouse, was almost entirely employment. General
Education Board, box 61, folder 538 (Rockefeller Archive Center). An exception in the 1960s was Fisk, the top black college in student SAT scores, which
increased its tuition as well as it scholarships from general funds. Doermann,
Crosscurrents in College Admissions (1968), 45–53. Historical causes of the general
pattern include racial stigma, low black incomes, and underfunded facilities
compared with other colleges. Cf. McGrath, *The Predominantly Negro Colleges
and Universities in Transition* (1965); Curti and Nash, *Philanthropy in the Shaping of American Higher Education* (1968), chap. 8; Jencks and Riesman, *The
Academic Revolution* (1968), chap. 10. Interviews, Johnson C. Smith University,
Morehouse College, Paine College, Spelman College, Xavier University. There
is some more-qualified evidence, too, that Catholic colleges have tended to
charge lower tuition and discount it less with aid, at least since 1920. Cf. Nash
et al., "Financial Aid Policies and Practices" (1967), III-4; Breneman, *Liberal*

Arts Colleges (1994), 61–62; Landy, "The Colleges in Context" (2002), 87–89, 92; Cooperative Institutional Research Program, *The American Freshman* (annual volumes). One can speculate about historical causes (including the austerity pay of clerical faculty, subsidizing lower tuition), but the matter needs more study.

13. On the issue in modern state policy and politics, see Eldon L. Johnson, "Is the Low-Tuition Principle Outmoded?"(1959); Carnegie Commission on Higher Education, *The Capitol and the Campus* (1971), chap. 9; Carnegie Commission, *Higher Education* (1973), 48–49; Breneman and Finn, "An Uneasy Future" (1978), 12–13; Fischer, "State Financing of Higher Education" (1990); Blumenstyk, "States Wrestle with Proposals for Higher Tuition" (1992); Wallace, "The Inequities of Low Tuition" (1992); Johnstone, "The 'High Tuition–High Aid' Model" (1993); Mumper, *Removing College Price Barriers* (1996), 147–69. On the issue in a low-tuition state, as it then was, Task Force on Tuition Policy, "Policy Framework for Student Tuition and Fees in UNC," by Gary Barnes (Chapel Hill: University of North Carolina, General Administration Office, 1998). In the private sector, see Gantz, "On the Basis of Merit Alone"(1991), chaps. 3 and 4, on Rice's decision to end free tuition in the 1960s.

14. *Oxford English Dictionary,* 15th ed., s.v. "scholarship."

15. I owe the basic idea of service-related aid as a third category to the military sociologist Charles Moskos, an author of President Clinton's national service program. Interview, Northwestern University (Charles Moskos). Cf. Moskos, *A Call to Service* (1988).

16. Van Dyke, "Government Experience with the Student War Loan Program" (1949). See also Potter, "The Wrong Kind of Incentive?"(2003), on current federal loan forgiveness and arguments about their funding and efficacy.

17. U.S. Dept. of the Interior, "Self-Help for College Students" (1929), 60–61, 64–74. The percentage "earning entire way" was about the same for undergraduates, who made up the great bulk of the students, as it was for graduate students. It was much less for women students and for leading private colleges, where it was often zero, but ranged as high as 14 percent, at Stanford, for example.

18. My calculations from *Chronicle of Higher Education,* Almanac issue (Aug. 30, 2002), 21. The loan data included "unsubsidized" loans (interest not waived while the student is in college). Federal sponsorship includes direct federal lending as well as private lending with federal subsidies and guarantees against default. See Mumper, "The Student Aid Industry" (1999).

19. Finn, "Why Do We Need Financial Aid?" (1985), 1–3, and Wilkinson, "Plural Ends, Contested Means" (2001), 311–12, classify student-aid purposes.

20. Pulley, "Fund-Raising Efforts Proliferate for Families of Terrorists' Victims" (2001).

21. Powell, *Lessons from Privilege* (1996), makes a similar point about prep schools:

91. See also Goldin, "Full-Tuition Students Increasingly Pay for Others" (1995).

22. On American history, see Bruce Collins, "The Ideology of the Ante-bellum Northern Democrats" (1977), 115–18, and Wilkinson, *American Tough* (1984), 26.

23. Trow, "Class, Race, and Higher Education in America" (1992). Even the nineteenth-century movement to extend college education to the "industrial classes" meant thereby a horizontal extension, beyond the learned professions, as well as an extension down the social scale.

24. Examples and quotations in Wilkinson, "Plural Ends, Contested Means" (2001), 312, 327 n. 18, including earlier class realism by Mary Lyon at Mount Holyoke in the 1830s.

25. This is a huge subject, involving America's dense history of immigration and racial and sectional (regional and urban-rural) conflict. Cf. Trow, "Class, Race, and Higher Education" (1992), and Rauchway, "More Means Different" (2002), 510, 515. In the 1990s, elite New England college administrators sometimes used sectional terms for white low-income families and students, e.g. "Maine potato farmers," "Dorchester kids." But see Schmidt, "Poll Finds Wide Support for Bush's Stance on University of Michigan Case" (2003), and Dworkin, "The Court and the University" (2003), 8–9, on recent popular support for class preferences in college admissions versus elite support for racial preferences.

26. Wechsler, *The Qualified Student* (1977), chap. 7. See also Oren, *Joining the Club* (1985), esp. 41, 48–53, 181–82, 338.

27. Cf. Duffy and Greenberg, *Crafting a Class* (1998), 155. Also the Supreme Court cases *Regents of the University of California v. Bakke* (1978), esp. Justice Powell's opinion, and *Grutter v. Bollinger* and *Gratz v. Bollinger* (2003).

28. Cf. Ehrenberg and Murphy, "What Price Diversity?" (1993), 70–71, and Bowen and Bok, *The Shape of the River* (1998), 50, 51.

29. North Carolina State Education Assistance Authority, *Student Financial Aid for North Carolinians* (annual), describes the NC Legislative Tuition Grant Program and the State Contractual Scholarship Fund Program: 32, 38 in the 1998–99 edition.

30. "Mission and market" may have been coined by Lagemann, *The Politics of Knowledge* (1989), 257–58, but she applied it to all "institutions of education and culture" in a somewhat different way. See also Winston, "Subsidies, Hierarchies, and Peers" (1999), on the modern college as "church" and "car dealer." One should distinguish here between a college's overall mission and its perceived mission for student aid. The overall mission is likely to stress various kinds of *good learning* (a term which can include research) regardless of whether widened access is deemed necessary to that. The student-aid mission is more likely to stress widened access ("opportunity") as a goal. Though widened access may

also be a *means* to good learning by recruiting talent and obtaining educational diversity, it is true to an old definition of "mission" as "sending forth." *Webster's Collegiate Dictionary* (1941). On ideas of mission and merit aid at three liberal arts colleges, see Eames, "Financial Aid Policy Development" (2002), 71–72, 121, 167. Massy, "Collegium Economicum" (2004), gives a short bibliography on the economic behavior of private colleges as nonprofit institutions 35.

31. Today's highly selective stratum corresponds to the "highly selective" through "most selective" categories used by the perennial *Cass and Birnbaum's Guide to American Colleges* before it ceased publication in the late 1990s. It also corresponds roughly to the "very highly selective" college category in annual freshman surveys: Cooperative Institutional Research Program, *The American Freshman.*

32. Bowen and Breneman, "Student Aid" (1993). McPherson and Schapiro, *The Student Aid Game* (1998), 16–17. The latter is a variation on the former, which was a defense of the Ivies and MIT against U.S. Justice Department charges of price-fixing market behavior: see Appendix 1. William G. Bowen had been president of Princeton. The original argument conceded that a middling selective group of colleges combined market with educational motives, but it confined the market motive simply to getting enough students, not getting impressively good ones.

33. See Hubell and Lapovsky, "Tuition Discounting in Challenging Times" (2002), 29–30, on the continued widespread potency of the "Chivas Regal" principle: high sticker price (if not *too* inflated) signals quality; only a few, unselective colleges have tried cutting full tuition. The Chivas Regal term was first applied to colleges in the 1980s by Joseph Ellis, Jr., when he was Mount Holyoke's dean of the college. Werth, "Why Is College So Expensive?" (1988). An e-mail marketing report in *Copernicus Mzine* has sharply observed that tuition and total charges do not correlate closely with private-college quality status as measured by *U.S. News and World Report* college ratings: "The Cost of Private Universities and Colleges"(2003). So Stanford and the University of Southern California charge about the same full tuition. This is only true, though, for colleges within a broad prestige band. According to a national survey, 54 percent of Americans between twenty-five and sixty-five did not agree that "high-cost colleges and universities are generally also of higher quality," but most of those who had gone to college had themselves attended low-tuition institutions and so might have had a loyal and defensive bias in answering the question. See Selingo et al., "What Americans Think about Higher Education" (2003), A11, 12.

34. Cf. U.S. Court of Appeals, Third Circuit, cited in Appendix 1. Interviews and correspondence, Amherst College, Stanford University. Legally, a college can forgo giving generally funded aid but usually not its donated scholarships. In the 1990s, Washington and Lee, with a southern conservative clientele, did the

former, earning bad marks in *Princeton Review*'s college directories and student surveys for having a "country club" homogeneity.

35. On early state aid, see Giddens, "The Origins of State Scholarship Programs" (1970). On Rutgers's complex evolution to fully state status, see George P. Schmidt, *Princeton and Rutgers* (1964), chaps. 4–6.

36. On California, see Drury, *Rudolph James Wigg* (1968), 240 ff., and Sanders and Palmer, *The Financial Barrier to Higher Education in California* (1965). Also, J. Edward Sanders to Sheridan N. Hegland (Feb. 10, 1986) in Sanders papers, courtesy Jane Sanders, Pomona. Jane Sanders to author (Feb. 10, 1996). Interview, Pomona College (Herbert Smith). On trends and private-college concerns in the 1960s and 1970s, Fenske and Boyd, "State Need-Based College Scholarship and Grant Programs" (1981), 26–27; Breneman, *Liberal Arts Colleges* (1994), 27–28; Duffy and Goldberg, *Crafting a Class* (1998), 186. Also, State of New York, Report of the Select Committee on Higher Education (1974), including hearings and bill, on the 1970s origins of New York's Tuition Assistance Program, the nation's biggest state scholarship system.

37. Jerry Davis (Sallie Mae Corp.) to author, Jan. 29, 1995. Stan Broadway (North Carolina State Education Assistance Authority) to author, July 6, 1995.

38. *Time* (March 18, 1946), quoted in Olson, *The G.I. Bill, the Veterans, and the Colleges* (1974), 45–46.

39. Estimate based on a $4,000 Pell grant and $4,000 Supplementary Educational Opportunity Grant (allocated by campuses in varying ways and amounts).

40. Cf. McPherson and Schapiro, *The Student Aid Game* (1998), 371, table. Some states have reciprocal agreements letting some or all of their aid be taken to partner states. Since 2000, the federal and state proportions of need-related grant aid was about 7 percent at Harvard and Oberlin but about 14 percent at Stanford, largely because of its high in-state enrollment, like other leading California colleges. Data from Harvard Admissions Office, Oberlin Office of Institutional Research, and Stanford Office of Financial Aid. At *all* four-year private colleges in 2003–04, 62 percent of student grant aid was federal, 17 percent state (College Board data).

41. McPherson and Schapiro, *The Student Aid Game* (1998), 84–85. See also Sarah Turner, "The Vision and Reality of Pell Grants" (1998). The much more generous GI Bill did reduce college spending on aid. And Stanford found a few years ago that an admissions shift from low-income to middle-income students increased its own financial aid bill due to loss of public grant aid. Interview, Stanford University.

2. Aid in History: Who Got It, What Shaped It

1. The nearest to this for a single college is Seymour Harris's economic history of Harvard (*The Economics of Harvard,* 1970), an informative but jumpy book that gives much data on aid and charges but does not systematically relate trends in aid spending to total charges or budget totals. Holtschneider, "Institutional Aid to New England College Students"(1997) does do this for the colonial period. On the limits of historical college data generally, see Appendix 2.

2. Carnegie Commission, *Higher Education* (1973), 32, Table 6. The data trawl started with 1929–30. There are no exactly comparable published data after 1969–70, but see Hauptman, *The Tuition Dilemma* (1990), 9, on the period 1970–87.

3. Reeves et al., *The Liberal Arts College* (1932), introduction and chaps. 65, 71. It is not clear if the data included rebates for ministers' children (usually 50 percent off tuition) and other ministerial and faculty categories. Levine, *The American College and the Culture of Aspiration* (1986) gives unclear data from the Association of American Universities, stressing lack of scholarships and college loan funds in the 1920s: 188. Federal college-by-college surveys of spending on scholarships and fellowships for 1916–18 and 1920–22 (surveys not continued in the 1920s) indicate that at least half of all colleges (about the same proportions for public and private) gave scholarships and fellowships. The reports confused absence of scholarships with none reported. At fifteen leading liberal arts colleges, where graduate fellowships would not apply, scholarship spending was usually about 4 percent of total college spending income (excluding additions to capital endowment). As an average discount on full tuition for all students, scholarships ranged from 4 percent to over 30 percent. My calculations from U.S. Dept. of Interior, *Biennial Survey of Education* (1921, 1925), tables on college properties and receipts.

4. On early Harvard and subsequent trends, see Foster, *"Out of Smalle Beginnings"* (1962), 141, 206; Harris, *The Economics of Harvard* (1970), xxxi and chap. 8; Veysey, *The Emergence of the American University* (1965), 290n. On Amherst, Tyler, *History of Amherst College* (1873), chap. 14 and p. 396; Allmendinger, *Paupers and Scholars* (1975), 12, 50. On NYU, Frusciano and Pettit, *New York University and the City* (1997), 9.

5. President's Report, 1983–84 (Swarthmore College President's Office), 3. A Swarthmore pamphlet of 1934, "Trusts and Bequests," showed a sharp decline from 1906 to 1934 in the student-aid proportion of endowments bestowed on the college (Swarthmore College, Friends Historical Library).

6. Cf. Spady, "Educational Mobility and Access in the United States "(1967–68).

7. Data from Harris, *A Statistical Portrait of Higher Education* (1972), 138–39. The

student quartiles were of all college students, who had higher incomes than the national population.

8. My calculations from McPherson and Schapiro, *The Student Aid Game* (1998), 31–32. The authors defined low family income in 1992–93 as under $30,000 (well under the national median). Middle income was $30,000 to $70,000. Recent reports have highlighted much less adequate aid for lower-income students: e.g., Archibald, *Redesigning the Financial Aid System* (2002), 3, graph.

9. We have little data on long-term trends in gross costs (before financial aid) of going to college relative to incomes, still less on net costs (after financial aid) and on "opportunity costs" (earnings foregone while attending college). Studies of America's oldest college indicate that tuition, room, and board (TRB) at Harvard relative to national average per-capita income did not increase and probably fell from the 1650s, and from the 1860s to the 1960s, because of the real decline of room and board costs offsetting increases in tuition. More general studies have found shorter-term fluctuations, including a rise in TRB at liberal arts colleges relative to manual workers' wages, 1800–1860s; a rise in TRB at private and public colleges relative to depressed incomes in the 1930s; a sharp rise at private colleges relative to per-capita disposable and post-tax income in the 1950s and 1960s; and another sharp rise at private colleges relative to median household income in the 1980s and 1990s. Foster, *"Out of Smalle Beginnings"* (1962), 83–84. Harris, *The Economics of Harvard* (1970), xxviii, 39, 44–48. Harris, *A Statistical Portrait of Higher Education* (1972), 111. Burke, *American Collegiate Populations* (1982), 50. Cartter, "Pricing Policies for Higher Education" (1966), 7–8. Baum, "Access, Choice, and the Middle Class" (1994), 17.

10. Hayes, "Can a Poor Girl Go to College?" (1891), makes all these points except that women had fewer scholarships. On that, see Solomon, *In the Company of Educated Women* (1985), 72. Gender differences in the history of college access and student aid merit their own full study, but see Solomon, esp. chap. 5, and Newcomer, *A Century of Higher Education for Women* (1959), esp. 130–45 and chap. 8.

11. Gordon, "Smith College Students" (1975). Rhees, *Laurenus Clark Seelye* (1929). President's reports by Seelye (Smith College Archives). Using information from the Smith College Archives, I reanalyzed Gordon's data on the first ten classes, devised my own categories based on father's occupation, and excluded the first two, smaller classes, in case the earliest years were atypical. The data on grants seemed to include both outright scholarships and more informal tuition remissions.

12. Smith College, Official Circular no. 7 (1880), no. 17 (1890), Smith College Neilson Library. Gordon, "Smith College Students" (1975), 150–51.

13. Data from U.S. Bureau of the Census, *The Statistical History of the United States* (1976), 168, and Veysey, *The Emergence of the American University* (1965), 390. The estimate for artisans is from 1893, a depression year, so it may actually be too low. In the Smith data, I classified artisans (e.g., carpenters, bakers, builders) somewhat arbitrarily as working class / lower class, as distinct from merchants and dealers (middle class). Children of parents with lower-paying occupations, however, did not get bigger average grants. Most of the differences in grant amounts between aided individuals over the four years were due to a student's getting or not getting any grant in a given year.

14. Holtschneider, "Institutional Aid to New England College Students" (1997), 33n. King, "Financial Thresholds to College" (1957), 22. Harris, *The Economics of Harvard* (1970), 97–98.

15. Survey of University of Michigan parents in 1886 by President James B. Angell in Sagendorph, *Michigan* (1948), 164–65; percentage whose fathers were "mechanics," "laborers," or "lumbermen" was calculated by me. Michigan and Harvard surveys for 1870s and 1902–03 in Thernstrom, "'Poor but Hopefull Scholars'" (1986), 124–25. At the University of Texas in 1892–93, when fees were ten dollars, 2 percent of students were children of workers in the "mechanical trades," 2.4 percent clerks and other service workers, and 12 percent widows. Benedict, *A Source Book* (1917), appendix.

16. My calculations from Potthoff, "Who Goes to College?" (1931). Cf. Nidiffer, "Poor Historiography" (1999), 335.

17. Schudson, "Organizing the 'Meritocracy'" (1972), 40.

18. For comparisons with European higher education and its tighter governance, see Trow, "American Higher Education" (1991), 140–44. On nineteenth-century college closures, Burke, *American Collegiate Populations* (1982), 23.

19. Cf. McPherson and Schapiro , Selective *Admission and the Public Interest* (1990), 9, and Duffy and Greenberg, *Crafting a Class* (1998), chap. 1.

20. On trends, causes, and examples, see George P. Schmidt, *The Liberal Arts College* (1957), 78; Doermann, *Crosscurrents in College Admissions* (1968), 31–38 (1999); Aldersley, "Upward Drift Is Alive and Well" (1995); Hoxby, "Where Should Federal Education Initiatives Be Directed?" (1999), 29–30; Brewer et al., *In Pursuit of Prestige* (2002), 33–34, 140–43, 149–50.

21. Story, *The Forging of an American Aristocracy* (1982). Thernstrom, "'Poor but Hopefull Scholars'" (1986).

22. Cf. Levine, *The American College and the Culture of Aspirations* (1986), chap. 4; Hoxby, "Where Should Federal Education Initiatives Be Directed?" (1999), 38; Brewer et al., *In Pursuit of Prestige* (2002), 27–31, 43–44.

23. On Temple, including racial and academic issues, see Gose, "Temple U. Raises Standards to Woo Suburban Students" (1998). Much earlier, though, Roosevelt

resisted raising admission test standards to the point of disadvantaging poorer students. Gowran, "Roosevelt Entry Policy Aims at 'Culturally Deprived'" (1963).

24. Interviews, Oberlin College.

25. Quotations on national-regional balance are from Paul Gross, memo to Willis Smith, chairman of trustees, May 24, 1947 (Duke University Archives). Also A. Kenneth Pyle, "Directions for Progress," Report by the Chancellor to the Trustees, Sept. 26, 1980; Mary D. B. T. Semans, "Remarks [on] Benjamin N. Duke and Other Scholarships," Scholarship Candidates' Dinner, Duke University, Feb. 14, 1986 (all in Duke University Archives). Interviews, Duke University, Wake Forest University. In 2000, Duke substituted for the loan-replacement grants a small special scholarship program for North Carolina students, based on merit but with extra grants according to need, as the former program had done little to attract students from the region.

26. Horowitz, *Campus Life* (1987), 4–6; U.S. Dept. of Education, *120 Years of American Education* (1993), 76–77.

27. Kett, *The Pursuit of Knowledge under Difficulties* (1994), esp. 89–93, 107–25, including observations by Alexis de Tocqueville. Howe, *Making the American Self* (1997). Howe does not distinguish enough between elite ideas for ordinary people and ideas held by them—the latter not documented.

28. Kerns, "Farmers' Daughters" (1986), 14–15, 20–21.

29. Aronson, *Status and Kinship in the Higher Civil Service* (1964), chap. 6 and p. 204. Kett, "A Class Act" (2001).

30. Cf. Hofstadter, *Anti-intellectualism in American Life* (1962), 253–64; Randall Collins, "Functional and Conflict Theories of Educational Stratification" (1971); Bledstein, *The Culture of Professionalism* (1978); Levine, *The American College and the Culture of Aspiration* (1986), chap. 3; Halsey and Leslie, "Historical Sociology Meets the Credentialing Society" (1997).

31. Using father's educational level as a class indicator, Spady, "Educational Mobility and Access" (1967–68), found that, among both white and black male students, the proportion of lower-class high school graduates who went to college and the proportion of lower-class freshmen who got bachelor's degrees declined between the early 1920s and late 1950s. He attributed this hypothetically to a disadvantaged, "left-behind" population of poor rural southerners. Overall, lower-class rates of going to college and graduating from college still increased, as growing proportions of all classes graduated from high school.

32. On making up for poor preparation in the late-nineteenth and early-twentieth centuries, see Sharpless, *The Story of a Small College* (1918); on Haverford, 77, 136. Also David Starr Jordan, *The Days of a Man* (1922), on Leland Stanford, 485, and Porter, *Trinity and Duke* (1964), 87, on concerns for leaving out the poorly prepared poor boy by academic upgrading at Trinity (Duke). Elsewhere,

the high opinions of poor students did not just apply to highly selected scholarship winners, but unusual Harvard scholarship data from the 1920s supports those opinions. At two high scholarship levels, students without financial need received honorary, nonmonetary scholarships but were fewer at the top level than at the lower level, relative to needy students. My analysis from catalogs for 1920–21, 1929–30 (Harvard University Archives). Studies of students before 1930 point in the same direction, when put together: Orlando F. Lewis, "The Self-Supporting Student" (1904), 725–28. Bailey, "College Life and the Social Order" (1914). E. L. Clark, "Family Background and College Success" (1927). Witty and Foreman, "Self-Support and College Attainment" (1930). Jencks and Riesman, *The Academic Revolution* (1968), 95. See also Report of the President, April 1983 (Princeton Manuscript Library), 8, for statistics on Princeton in 1911 and the 1930s. Other observations, not distorted by scholarship selectivity, include Report of the President for 1903–1904 (Stanford University Archives); Yale President James B. Angell, 1926, quoted in Reynolds, *The Social and Economic Status of College Students* (1927), 29; Annual Report of the President to the Trustees for 1927–1928 (Oberlin College Archives). Several reports from the late nineteenth century to the 1940s said that public-school students tended to do better than private-school students. However, the whole thesis of a poorer-to-richer shift in student academic achievement needs a broader and more precise comparison of socioeconomic classes over time.

33. Dunham, "A Revolution in Admissions" (1966). King, "Financial Thresholds to College" (1957). Doermann, *Crosscurrents in College Admissions* (1968), 28–29. Rauh, "The Relation of Student Aid Programs to Institutional Finances" (1972). Doermann noted similar correlations between family income and test scores on intelligence and aptitude tests from 1900, but many of these tests were even more class and ethnically biased than SATs, and they were not confined to would-be college students.

34. Mumper, *Removing College Price Barriers* (1996), citing research by T. Mortenson and Z. Wu, 60. Interviews, Mount Holyoke College and Wheaton College. Cf. Werth, "Why Is College So Expensive?" (1988), 37. In 1989–90 and 1995–56, the top and bottom income quartiles of college students were both underrepresented in the distribution of merit aid: Heller, "Merit and Need-Based Aid" (2000), 42 More recently, however, merit aid has shifted toward the rich.

35. Horowitz., *Campus Life* (1987), makes the basic distinction between "collegians" and poorer, more dedicated students from the eighteenth century on: chap. 1. For a qualifying portrait of debonair but thinking funsters, see Owen Wister's novel *Philosophy 4: A Story of Harvard University* (1903), though it is subtly anti-Semitic.

36. Cf. Theodore White, *In Search of History* (1978), 41–50; Wechsler, "An Academic Greshman's Law" (1981); Bergin, "My Native Country" (1982); Horowitz,

Campus Life (1987), chaps. 1, 2, 8. But see Kett, *Rites of Passage* (1977), 55–56, on nineteenth-century revolts by older, poorer students against college discipline.

37. Lynn and Lynn, *Middletown* (1929), described considerable working-class family aspirations for college in 1920s "Middletown" (Muncie, Indiana), though going to college was a much more assumed route among the middle classes: 182–87.

38. Herrnstein and Murray, *The Bell Curve* (1994), 25 and chap. 1.

39. But see Flacks and Thomas, "Among Affluent Students, a Culture of Disengagement" (1998), on a reversion to older ways among rich students at UC Santa Barbara.

40. Mary Mensel, director of financial aid, taped interview by Helen Millbank, 1977 (Smith College Archives). Lucas, *American Higher Education* (1994), describes the prewar growth of student administration, 203–4.

41. Nash et al., "Financial Aid Policies" (1967), II-3, II-4.

42. Brooks, "NASFAA" (1986), esp. 1–18. Cf. Russo, "The Financial Aid Professional" (1995). Interviews, Smith College.

3. Enter Uncle Sam

1. Cf. Keppel, "The Higher Education Acts Contrasted" (1987), on provision by the 1965 Higher Education Act (Title III) for aid to "developing [disadvantaged] institutions." This was intended to favor black colleges but included some general community colleges and small church colleges. Keppel, 53–56.

2. *Chronicle of Higher Education*, Almanac issue (Aug. 30, 2002), 18, 21: state data for 2001–02, federal for fiscal year 2000. This included "unsubsidized" loans to students and parents as aid but excluded federal and state tax revenue lost through tuition tax credits and tax-subsidized college savings plans.

3. Kimberling, "Federal Student Aid" (1995), 71. Hoxby, "Where Should Federal Aid Initiatives Be Directed?" (1999), esp. 43.

4. See Archibald, *Redesigning the Financial Aid System* (2002), 37, on aid to church colleges and the constitutional separation of church and state.

5. Cf. Woodhall, "International Experience of Financial Support for Students" (1989), 70–77; Woodard, "Worldwide Tuition Increases Send Students into the Streets" (2000); Bollag, "Student Loans" (2001).

6. Quattlebaum, *Federal Educational Activities* (1952), 40–41. Mosch, *The GI Bill* (1975), 14–16.

7. Lyon, "The Federal Government and College Students during the Great Depression" (1969), esp. 46–63, 118–21. Levine, *The American College and the Culture of Aspiration* (1986), chap. 9. Also Lindley and Lindley, *A New Deal for Youth* (1935), esp. 12. Johnson and Willey, "Backgrounds of College NYA

Students," (1939), esp. 254, 255–56. A recent study argues that the New Deal program generally reoriented college leaders to the idea of federal student aid. Bower, "'A Favored Child of the State'" (2004).

8. Olson, *The G.I. Bill, the Veterans, and the Colleges* (1974), discusses liberal interpretations of the amount of college time funded and different college options for getting back added costs of taking in the veterans: 61–62, 87–88.

9. Data from U.S. Bureau of the Census, *A Statistical History of the United States* (1976), 1116.

10. On early American attitudes, Ward, *Andrew Jackson* (1953), chaps. 1, 2; Cunliffe, *Soldiers and Civilians* (1968).

11. On veterans and pensions, McConnell, *Glorious Contentment* (1992); Skocpol, *Protecting Soldiers and Mothers* (1992); Amenta, *Bold Relief* (1998). On military-related state student aid, Giddens, "The Origins of State Scholarship Programs" (1970); Bullock, *History of Emory University* (1936), 51; Ratcliffe, "State Scholarships Increase" (1936); Willey, *Depression, Recovery, and Higher Education* (1937), 300–301.

12. Hansen, "The :Politics of Federal Scholarships" (1977), 87. See also Ross, *Preparing for Ulysses* (1969); Brinkley, *The End of Reform* (1995), chap. 10; Bennett, *When Dreams Came True* (1996), esp. chaps. 4–6.

13. "Fireside chat" address to the nation, July 28, 1943, in Roosevelt, *Papers and Addresses* (1950), 334.

14. Bennett, *When Dreams Came True* (1996), 90.

15. Olson, "The G.I. Bill and Higher Education" (1973), stresses the economic motive.

16. U.S. Congress, House, Armed Forces Committee, *Preliminary Report to the President* (1943), 8–11. Olsen, "The G.I. Bill and Higher Education "(1973), 47–48.

17. See esp. House floor debate, May 14–15, 1944, *Congressional Record,* 78th Cong., 2nd sess., 1944, vol. 90, pt. 4. Also Sen. Claude Pepper, quoted in Rivlin, *The Role of the Federal Government in Financing Higher Education* (1961), 66.

18. Mulligan, "Socio-Economic Background and College Enrollment" (1951). Cohen, *A Consumer's Republic* (2003), 156–60. Approximately 3.5 million GI Bill veterans attended high schools or trade schools in addition to the 2.2 million at colleges. Rivlin, *The Role of the Federal Government* (1961), 67.

19. Reginald Wilson, "GI Bill Expands Access for African Americans" (1994). Hartmann, *The Home Front and Beyond* (1982), chap. 6. Willenz, "Invisible Veterans" (1994). Cohen, *A Consumer's Republic* (2003), stresses racial obstacles to college-seeking black veterans, including the saturated capacity of black colleges: 166–73. But the GI Bill itself deliberately bypassed state controls in the South and elsewhere, and the supporting Lanham Act disproportionately funded black-college buildings and equipment: Reginald Wilson, 34–35.

20. Montgomery, "The Montgomery GI Bill" (1994). The impact of student aid on military recruitment and social composition needs a major study.

21. Herrnstein and Murray, *The Bell Curve* (1994), 31–32.

22. Olson, "The G.I. Bill and Higher Education" (1973), 602–5.

23. Warner et al., *Who Shall Be Educated?* (1944). Different views of the Commission's political makeup are given by Kerr-Tener, "From Truman to Johnson" (1985), 56–62, and Freeland, *Academia's Golden Age* (1992), 75. On Zook, see Hawkins, *Banding Together* (1992), 153, 167–69; Bennett, *When Dreams Came True* (1996), 133, 161; and *American National Biography*, vol. 24 (1999), 255–56.

24. U.S. President's Commission, *Higher Education for Democracy*, vols. 1, 2 (1947). College attendance data from U.S. Bureau of the Census, *A Statistical History of the United States* (1976), 383.

25. Kennedy, ed., *Education for Democracy* (1953). Ravitch, *The Troubled Crusade* (1983), 17–18. Kerr- Tener, "From Truman to Johnson" (1985), 87–103. Hawkins, *Banding Together* (1992), chap. 8.

26. Kerr-Tener, "From Truman to Johnson" (1985), chap. 2.

27. Interview, U.S. House of Representatives (Carl Elliott). Cf. Elliott and D'Orso, *The Cost of Courage* (1992), chaps. 8, 9.

28. On science scholarships, see Axt, *The Federal Government and Financing Higher Education* (1952), 234–35.

29. Hansen, "The Politics of Federal Scholarships" (1977), chap. 3. Clowse, *Brainpower for the Cold War* (1981). Kerr-Tener, "From Truman to Johnson" (1983), chap. 3. Ravitch, *The Troubled Crusade* (1983), 228–30. The House hearings chaired by Rep. Carl Elliott, Sr., across the country in 1957 are a rich repository of policy attitudes: U.S. Congress, House, Committee on Education and Labor, *Scholarship and Loan Program* (1957). On state colleges, interview, Stanford (Robert Huff). Elliott and Sen. Lister Hill, both Alabama progressives who championed federal scholarships, did not want them officially need-related because of uncertainty about how much to allow for neediness at high-cost colleges.

30. Cf. William J. Lederer and Eugene Burdick's bestseller of 1958, *The Ugly American*.

31. Rivlin, *The Role of the Federal Government in Financing Higher Education* (1961), 75–77. See also Morse, "How We Got Here from There" (1977), 4–7. Presidents' reports and papers at Princeton, Rutgers, and Swarthmore, 1958–59, and Oberlin, 1962, contain useful policy discussions of the loyalty oath and affidavit.

32. See Mumper, "The Student Aid Industry" (1999), on federal subsidies and loan guarantees to private lenders.

33. Cf. Hansen, "The Politics of Federal Scholarships" (1977), chaps. 4, 5. Various concerns are collected in U.S. Congress, Legislative Reference Service,

Guaranteeing an Opportunity for Higher Education (1963). Amber Watt helpfully analyzed these in an undergraduate paper, Smith College History Dept., 1999.

34. Sundquist, "Origins of the War on Poverty" (1969), shows that no one influence or factor led to President Kennedy's call for facts and figures on poverty in December 1962, moving toward action in 1963. Cf. Schlesinger, *A Thousand Days* (1965), 1009–12; Matusow, *The Unraveling of America* (1984), chap. 4; Lagemann, *The Politics of Knowledge* (1989), 217.

35. Cf. Chafe, *The Unfinished Journey* (1986), 236–46.

36. E.g., Johnson, message to Congress on education, Jan. 12, 1965, reprinted in Gettelman and Mermenstein, eds., *The Great Society Reader* (1967), 186–97. On "manpower" needs and on equity, Keppel, "The Higher Education Acts Contrasted" (1987), quotes 1965 Senate and House committee reports: 56–57.

37. Isaac Becher in U.S. Congress, House, Committee on Education and Labor, *Higher Education Act of 1965* (1965), hearings before subcommittee on education, part 3, 1115–16. Among other issues, the hearings exposed differences between government and business views on how to handle student loans. See also Hansen, "The Politics of Federal Scholarships" (1977), chap. 5.

38. Carnegie Commission, *Quality and Inequality* (1968), esp. 18–19. The percentage figure is mine, based on total enrollment data from U.S. Bureau of the Census, *A Statistical History of the United States* (1976), 383. On the Carnegie Commission's reorientation to poverty in the 1960s and its influence on discussions of federal student aid, see Lagemann, *The Politics of Knowledge* (1989), 217–21, 226–30, 262.

39. Hansen, "The Politics of Federal Scholarships" (1977), 167–68, summarized by Mumper, *Removing College Price Barriers* (1996), 80–81. Unusual and lucid detail on the working and reach of EOGs via state allotments is in J. Edward Sanders, "The Origins of Student Financial Aid in California," 1972 (Sanders Papers, courtesy Jane Sanders, Pomona).

40. U.S. Dept. of Health, Education, and Welfare, *Toward a Long-Range Plan for Federal Financial Support of Higher Education* (1969), vi.

41. Hansen, "The Politics of Federal Scholarships" (1977), chap. 6. Fischer, "State Financing of Higher Education" (1990), 50. Gladieux and Hauptman, *The College Aid Quandary* (1995), 16–17. Mumper, *Removing College Price Barriers* (1996), 80–85. Kramer, "Linking Access and Aspirations" (1997). Wolanin, "Pell Grants" (1997). Gladieux and Wolanin, *Congress and the Colleges* (1976), gives a detailed political history of the road to Pell grants: see esp. 50–53 on the role of Clark Kerr. On Pell and SEOG benefits and income groups covered in the 1980s, see Johnstone, *Sharing the Costs of Higher Education* (1986), 126–27.

42. Janet Hansen, "Origins and Development of the SSIG Program," 1979 (Educational Testing Service Archives, Princeton). On the SSIG program generally,

see Gladieux and Hauptman, *The College Aid Quandary* (1995), 10–11, tables, and 17; Mumper, *Removing College Price Barriers* (1996), 83–84; Duffy and Goldberg, *Crafting a Class* (1998), 186.

43. Gladieux and Wolanin, *Congress and the Colleges* (1976), 42–43. Alice Rivlin's 1969 government report positively contemplated that federal student aid would provide general budget assistance to private colleges by enabling them to raise tuition. U.S. Dept. of Health, Education, and Welfare, *Toward a Long-Range Plan* (1969), 29. The Carnegie Commission report *Quality and Inequality* (1968) asked for increased federal student aid *plus* "cost-of-education" supplements to colleges for the added costs of enrolling and caring for disadvantaged students: 30–32. Senator Pell's original bill included this, but it was never funded. Wolanin, "Pell Grants" (1998). On relative shifts from federal grants for colleges to federal student aid between 1965 and 1972, see Kimberling, "Federal Student Aid" (1995), 71–72.

44. McPherson and Schapiro, *Keeping College Affordable* (1991), 13, 68–69, 72–73. Astin, "Tying Tuition to the CPI" (2004). McPherson and Schapiro noted that above the tuition levels of most private colleges and major state universities, tuition increases did not qualify students for increased Pell grants. A market-oriented scholar has recently claimed that federal loans and other government aid boost college prices by inflating consumer demand; yet he also favors free, income-related government "vouchers" for college, while ignoring the burden and deterrence of loans. Vedder, *Going Broke by Degree* (2004), 20-21, 196-204.

45. The 1980s, not the 1990s, saw the big growth of *subsidized* loans (interest-free while the student is enrolled in college); borrowing limits for them did not change in the 1990s. The big 1990s growth was in *un*subsidized loans. The decline in veterans' grant aid after the 1970s, though still a big item, magnified the overall shift from grants to loans. See glossary (Appendix 4), on "unsubsidized loans"; their interest rates, too, are held down by the federal government.

46. It is seldom noted that spending on Social Security college grants for the surviving dependents of a deceased provider was over 80 percent as much as Pell grants from the mid-1970s till the program was phased out between 1982 and 1985. The program was regressive, too: like other Social Security benefits, the payments went up according to the deceased's income. When Reagan budget cuts killed the program in the 1980s, it was already under attack from Republicans for giving too much benefit to one group. On complex issues concerning Pell grant coverage and types of loans, see Brademas, *The Politics of Education* (1987), 20–22; Mortenson, "Refocusing the Pell Grant from Poverty to Higher Income Applicants" (1988); Orfield, "Money, Equity, and College Access" (1992); Gladieux and Hauptman, *The College Aid Quandary* (1995),

15–18; "Federal Student Aid" (1995); Mumper, *Removing College Price Barriers* (1996), esp. 86–106; Wolanin, "Pell Grants" (1998).

47. Selingo, "AmeriCorps at 5 Years" (1998). Cf. Mumper, *Removing College Price Barriers* (1996), 242–44. See Waldman, *The Bill* (1995), on the "national service" bill's politics.

48. As of September 2002, the main federally subsidized Stafford loans (interest-free during college) could not exceed 8.25 percent interest per annum and were actually at a historic low of 3.46 percent. On different income-contingent loan plans, see Rauh, "The Relation of Student Aid Programs to Institutional Finances" (1972), 34–36; Friedman and Friedman, *Free to Choose* (1979), 183–85; Hauptman, *The Tuition Dilemma* (1990), 47–54; Mumper, *Removing College Price Barriers* (1996), 232–36; Burd, "Few Borrowers Repay Loans through 'Income-Contingent' System" (1998); Lawrence A. Juhlin, letter, *Chronicle of Higher Education* (Mar. 3, 1993), B4.

49. Data from Mumper, *Removing College Price Barriers* (1996), 206, 214; Hartle and King, "The End of Equal Opportunity in Higher Education?" (1997); McPherson and Schapiro, *The Student Aid Game* (1998), 38; "College Enrollment Rises," *USA Today* (1999); "Family Education and Higher Education Opportunity," *Postsecondary Education Opportunity Research Newsletter* (2001); "Educational Attainment," *Postsecondary Education Opportunity Research Newsletter* (2003).

50. See Archibald, *Redesigning the Financial Aid System* (2002), 63–66, for a basic description of the Federal Hope and Lifetime Learning credits and a chart showing who received benefits. For political background, see Spencer, "The New Politics of Higher Education" (1999), esp. 113–17; Burd, "Rift Grows over What Keeps Low-Income Students Out of College" (2002); Longanecker, "Is Merit-Based Aid Really Trumping Need-Based Aid?" (2002), 36–37. For a sophisticated history of federal student aid from a critical, conservative standpoint, see Kimberling, "Federal Student Aid" (1995).

51. Millard, "Governance, Quality and Equity" (1991), esp. 59–67, stresses alternating shifts toward "access" and "quality" in public higher-education policy.

52. Eames, "Financial Aid Policy Development" (2002), 50. My percentage calculation. One program, the Morris K. Udall Scholarships, is for Native Americans as well as environmental study and health care. The only federal merits for general "excellence" have been the Robert C. Byrd Scholarships established in 1987. At the time of writing, it looks likely that Pell grants will acquire a merit element: they will give an extra amount during the first two years of college to students who maintain a B average and have gone through a demanding high school program sponsored by schools and businesses (the State Scholars program currently operating in fourteen states). This couples the old state-merit concept of using college aid to stimulate better high school work with

the modern idea of "front-loading" grant aid to encourage college enrollment and give extra help while students are new to college.

53. Cf. Lawrence, "The University in State and Church" (1984), esp. 97–98, 115, 150. See also Clark Kerr, ca. 1988, on early European academic markets, quoted in Massy, "Collegium Economicum" (2004), 28.

4. The Roots of Student Aid

1. The Oxford story is told in slightly different versions by Rashdall, *The Universities of Europe in the Middle Ages* (1895), chap. 12; Mallet, *History of the University of Oxford* (1924), 31–34; and Aston and Faith, "The Endowments of the Universities and Colleges to Circa 1348" (1984). It involved the killing of a town woman by a clerk in unclear circumstances and the changing relationship between King John and the pope, whose demands were made and effected five years later.

2. Oxford and Cambridge colleges grew out of groups of clerks taught by masters. The first college—University College, Oxford—was founded in 1249. On medieval student aid, I have used the writers in note 1 above; Catto, "Citizens, Scholars and Masters" (1984); Southern, "From Schools to University" (1984); Lucas, *American Higher Education* (1994), chap. 2; and an informative letter from Dr. Roger Highfield of Merton College, Oxford (Aug. 28, 1998).

3. The story of William of Wykeham, fourteenth-century bishop of Winchester and lord chancellor (a high royal administrator) says much about the politics of creating free school and college places for "poor scholars." See Moberly, *Life of William of Wykeham* (1887), esp. chap. 9; *Dictionary of National Biography*, vol. 21 (1909), 1140–46; T. J. H. Bishop and Wilkinson, *Winchester and the Public School Elite* (1967), 83–84; Tapper, *Fee-Paying Schools and Educational Change in Britain* (1997), 30–33.

4. A proposal in 1583 by Sir Humphrey Gilbert, Elizabethan explorer, soldier, and intellectual, for a national leadership academy giving a wide education and vigorous training to young aristocrats, accused them of using up places at Oxford and Cambridge that should have gone to poor scholars. Furnival, ed., *Queen Elizabethes Achademy* [and other tracts] (1869), 10.

5. Jordan, *Philanthropy in England* (1959) and *The Charities of London* (1960). Jordan stresses the philanthropic expansion of education in sixteenth- and seventeenth-century England. On its limits, see Cressy, "Educational Opportunity in Tudor and Stewart England" (1976). Cf. Stone, "The Size and Composition of the Oxford Student Body" (1995), and Potter, "University and Society" (1997). I am grateful to Michael Hawkins and Howard Nenner for observations on this period.

6. Corporation Records, 1818, vol. 8 re. UAT.5.1 (Harvard University Archives).

Also Holtschneider, "Institutional Aid to New England College Students"(1997), chap. 2, esp. 35n. Holtschneider's dissertation is the fullest study of student aid in colonial New England.

7. Morison, *Three Centuries of Harvard* (1936), 73.

8. Of twenty-five major donated scholarships given before 1776, twenty required neediness, "indigence," etc.; nine preferred kin; five made some religious reference; and four specified a student's hometown or local area. (Many donors gave more than one preference.) Three mentioned scholarly dedication or industry, but only one specified high academic ability. This figured more in later periods but did not rise above 10 percent of scholarships till after World War I. My survey of donors' "restrictions" (specifications) covered those scholarship endowments large enough to survive into Harvard's *Donation Book of 1844* or a 1948 sequel, *Endowment Funds of Harvard University* (Harvard University Archives). The survey included about half of all scholarships donated to Harvard in the colonial period. Cf. Holtschneider, "Institutional Aid to New England College Students" (1997), 33–34.

9. Quotations from Harvard fund-raising circular by Rev. Jonathan Mitchell, ca. 1663, in Curti and Nash, *Philanthropy in the Shaping of American Higher Education* (1965), 8, and Allmendinger, *Paupers and Scholars* (1975), 47–48. See also Shipton, "The New England Frontier" (1937). On Harvard and other colonial college missions, see Morison, *Three Centuries of Harvard* (1936), 23–24, and George P. Schmidt, *The Liberal Arts College* (1957), 23–27.

10. Morison, *Harvard College in the Seventeenth Century* (1936), 107–8. Foster, *"Out of Smalle Beginnings"* (1962), chap. 7. Holtschneider, "Institutional Aid" (1997), 28–31.

11. My estimate from Morison, *Harvard College in the Seventeenth Century* (1936), 74–75, 450–51, comparing the classes of 1636–54 and 1661–75. The nonelite fathers made up 18 percent of known occupations, but Morison judged they would include nearly all the "unknown" occupations, comprising a fifth of the whole. In that era, though, a tradesman might be rich: John Harvard, the young divine who left the college its first big legacy when he died in 1638, was the son of a London butcher.

12. Thernstrom, "'Poor but Hopefull Scholars'" (1986), 116–17. Holtschneider, "Institutional Aid" (1997), explores economic stresses of the times and Harvard's choices: chap. 2. There is no direct data on what happened to the student social mix, but there are some indications that it became narrower in the nineteenth century after a delayed effect: in the late eighteenth century, students made up for reduced financial aid by going to Harvard at an older age, presumably having saved some money first. See Thernstrom above. By 1700, Harvard was denying scholarships to freshmen.

13. Holtschneider, "Institutional Aid" (1997), chap. 4. See also Richardson, *History*

of Dartmouth College, vol. 1 (1932), and Allmendinger, *Paupers and Scholars* (1975), 49–50. See also picture caption on Samson Occom following p. **???** above and Morison, *Harvard College in the Seventeenth Century* (1936), 340–42, on Harvard's abortive Indian College. Holtschneider explores Wheelock's complex attitudes toward Indian assistance and education.

14. Mission statements in Hofstadter and Smith, eds., *American Higher Education* (1961), including William and Mary's Statutes of 1727: 2, 39, 47–48. An established scholarship fund secured the ministerial places in the 1720s: Godson, *The College of William and Mary,* vol. 1 (1993), 62–63. The College of New Jersey (later Princeton, founded 1746) had special funds for "poor and pious youth" from at least the 1750s. At Queen's College (Rutgers, founded 1766), early aid was church-oriented, too, but endowed scholarships did not start there till 1814. "Undergraduate Financial Aid at Princeton," report of the president, April 1983, by William G. Bowen (Princeton University Archives). Committee on Beneficiary Funds, report including history, Oct. 21, 1891 (Rutgers University Special Collections).

15. Quotation in Holtschneider, "Institutional Aid" (1997), from a typical annual Yale application to the state general assembly, 1727: 203. On Rhode Island and Yale, Holtschneider, above, chaps. 2, 5. At Rhode Island, the college and individual faculty helped students in various informal ways, from loans to living and working arrangements. The college also experimented with accelerated programs to save the students money, though not for as long as the College of Philadelphia (later University of Pennsylvania), which did not settle permanently on four years till 1825. Cheyney, *History of the University of Pennsylvania* (1940), 82, 84–85, 186, 194. McAnear, "College Founding in the American Colonies" (1955), 32, 36. Holtschneider's appendix gives student charges, 1740–1800, for the four colonial New England colleges—Dartmouth, Harvard, Rhode Island, Yale—but the data are spotty and confusing, not always yielding comparisons of like with like. It seems that Harvard's total charges were by far the highest but not its basic tuition.

16. McAnear, "College Founding" (1955), 40. The nine colonial colleges were Dartmouth, Harvard, King's, College of New Jersey (Princeton), College of Philadelphia (Penn), Queen's (Rutgers), Rhode Island (Brown), William and Mary, and Yale.

17. My main source on King's is Humphrey, *From King's College to Columbia* (1976), esp. 73–100, 267–84. According to Jesse Brundage's history of college philanthropy for the Department of the Interior, no private donor gave to King's/Columbia for student aid till the Civil War. U.S. Dept. of Interior, "Philanthropy in the History of American Higher Education" (1922), 26, table.

18. Letters and memos by Antill, 1757–61, quoted in Humphrey, *From King's College*

(1976), 87–88. See also speech by Archibald Kennedy, New York, 1755, quoted in McAnear, "College Founding" (1955), 41.

19. In the eighteenth century, the evangelical "low" churches were more apt to support college access for poor students. McAnear, "College Founding" (1955), 339–41. But William and Mary, with its free places for poor ministerial and missionary students, was high-church Anglican like King's. Proximity to the "Indian frontier" encouraged the missionary motive. In the case of Baptist Rhode Island, a history of nonsectarian tolerance may have inhibited the use of aid to recruit a proselytizing ministry, but that is my conjecture.

20. Quincy, *History of Harvard University* (1860), 277. Seymour Martin Lipset cited Quincy, 280–81, in claiming that Harvard students complained at the unfairness of examinations to the underprivileged and underprepared. Quincy makes no such statement there. Lipset in Lipset and Riesman, *Education and Politics at Harvard* (1975), 50. Cf. Novak, *The Rights of Youth* (1977); Hessinger, "'The Most Powerful Instrument of College Discipline'" (1999).

21. Cf. Robson, "College Founding in the New Republic"(1983); Hessinger, "'The Most Powerful Instrument'" (1999), 237–38. Historians disagree about the extent and variety of democratic attitudes before and immediately after the Revolution. See Neem, "Early Modern Postmodern Polities" (2004).

22. Rudolph, *Mark Hopkins and the Log* (1956), 8. Holtschneider, "Institutional Aid" (1997), 68–69. Williamstown Historical Commission, *Williamstown* (1974), summarizes the complex relation of the Free School to the academy and local population: 186–87. Cf. Durfee, *A History of Williams College* (1860), 66, 79. My account of Williams draws largely on Rudolph, 6–14, 64–72. I am grateful to Linda Hall at Williams College Archives for sending photocopies and background information.

23. Gift and legacy statements by Woodbridge Little in "Gifts to Williams College, 1789–1911," 3–4 (Williams College Archives and Special Collections). On Woodbridge Little, see Durfee, *Williams Biographical Annals* (1871), 100.

24. My calculation based on cost and enrollment data from Linda Hall at Williams College Archives, the total Little gift and legacy of $3,500, and 8 percent return per year on inherited estates in rural Massachusetts. Rothenberg, "The Emergence of a Capital Market in Rural Massachusetts" (1985), esp. 790. I am grateful to James Henretta for this source.

25. Rudolph, *Mark Hopkins and the Log* (1956), quotes Hawthorne, *American Notebooks,* and Mark Hopkins, who showed some ambivalence towards country and mountain boys: 55–56.

26. Cf. Richardson, *History of Dartmouth College,* vol. 2 (1932), 711; George P. Schmidt, *The Liberal Arts College* (1957), 78; Leslie, *Gentlemen and Scholars* (1992), 239–41.

27. My estimate from data in U.S. Bureau of the Census, *A Statistical History of the United States* (1976), 10, 368–69. See Rudolph, *The American College and University* (1962), 48-49, on American expansive optimism and college founding.

28. Geiger, *The American College in the Nineteenth Century* (2000), 133.

29. Boorstin, *The Americans* (1965), 152.

30. Schmidt, *The Liberal Arts College* (1957), 64–65. Cf. Curti, *American Paradox* (1956); Hofstadter, *Anti-intellectualism in American Life* (1962).

31. Cheyney, *History of the University of Pennsylvania* (1940), 186. Hofstadter and Metzger, *The Development of Academic Freedom in the United States* (1955), 212. Novak, *The Rights of Youth* (1977), 10. Wechsler, *The Qualified Student* (1977), 7. Geiger, *The American College in the Nineteenth Century* (2000), 147, 150–51.

32. Rudolph, *The American College and University* (1962), 190–92. Rudolph dates perpetual scholarships back to at least 1789 at the University of North Carolina. On Americans' gullible fascination with new "facts" and figures, see Neil Harris's life of P. T. Barnum, *Humbug* (1973).

33. Columbia University, *A History of Columbia University* (1904), 112–17.

34. Trustees' minutes, Feb. 13, 1896, and Catalogue for 1895–96, 156 (Princeton University Manuscript Library). Wertenbaker, *Princeton 1746–1896* (1946), 315, 330–32, 385. Leslie, *Gentlemen and Scholars* (1992), 118–20.

35. On shifts, stages, and differences among the churches, see Schmidt, *The Liberal Arts College* (1957), 29–33; Rudolph, *The American College and University* (1962), 54–58; Hofstadter, *Anti-intellectualism in America* (1962), 95–106; Geiger, *The American College in the Nineteenth Century* (2000), 21–23.

36. Pell to Craven (Sept. 16, 1854), quoted with background by Chaffin, *Trinity College* (1950), 114–16.

37. Allmendinger, *Paupers and Scholars* (1975).

38. Allmendinger, *Paupers* (1975), 65. In general, though, Naylor, "The Ante-Bellum College Movement" (1973) has stressed inter-sect cooperation rather than competition in the early expansion of American colleges, against the older view of Tewksbury, *The Founding of American Colleges* (1932), and its followers.

39. Allmendinger, *Paupers* (1975), including the defense of AES by Moses Stewart, who also used familial language: 72–75.

40. Allmendinger, *Paupers* (1975), summarizes the AES's twilight years, including its merger with the Society for the Promotion of Collegial and Theological Education in the West: 76. The inference about secularization is mine.

41. Greek professor Theodore Wolsey, a colleague of Day, quoted on Day's attitudes by Kingsley, *Yale College,* vol. 1 (1879), 142.

42. Beecher, *A Plea for Colleges* (1836), quoted in Rudolph, *The American College and University* (1962), 63. Tewksbury, *The Founding of American Colleges* (1932), quotes a similar statement twenty years later by Theron Baldwin, general secre-

tary of the Society for the Promotion of Collegial and Theological Education in the West: 5. In a southern version, the minister at the founding dedication of North Carolina Normal College in 1854 lambasted "haughty wealth." Chaffin, *Trinity College* (1950), 115.

43. Stuart C. Henry, *Unvanquished Puritan* (1973), 174–76.

44. On the origins and development of manual-labor institutions, including the influence of the Swiss Philipp von Fellenberg and J. H. Pestalozzi, see Fletcher, *A History of Oberlin College*, vol. 1 (1943), chap. 5, and Kett, *The Pursuit of Knowledge under Difficulties* (1994), 128–31. See also Allmendinger, *Paupers and Scholars* (1977), 57.

45. Kenyon College circular and catalogs, 1829–1854, and *Kenyon Book* ca. 1880 (all in Kenyon College Special Collections). First Annual Report of the Oberlin Collegiate Institute, Nov. 1834 (Oberlin College Archives and Special Collections).

46. Weld, "Report to the Executive Committee" (1833). This was part of Weld's first and only official report as general agent of the Society for Promoting Manual Labor in Literary Institutions.

47. Paul E. Johnson, *A Shopkeeper's Millennium* (1978), chap. 2. Cf. Kett, *The Pursuit of Knowledge under Difficulties* (1994), 140.

48. Schmidt, *The American Liberal Arts College*(1957), 86–87, 277 n. 16. Rudolph, *The American College and University* (1962), 216–17.

49. On agriculture and education, see Veysey, *The Emergence of the American University* (1965), 71, 85–86, and Kett, *Pursuit of Knowledge* (1994), 132–33, 140–41. See Green, *Mary Lyon and Mount Holyoke* (1979), esp. chap. 5, on Lyon's "domestic work" concept at Mount Holyoke, including her wariness of manual-labor college enterprises. See also Findlay, *Dwight L. Moody* (1969), chap. 9, on late nineteenth-century religious and social origins of Northfield Mount Hermon School's present-day "work program." Arthur Morgan, creator of the Antioch approach, laid out its holistic philosophy in "The Antioch Program" (1930), but "co-operative education" was started more prosaically by University of Cincinnati engineering faculty and local factories in 1906–07.

50. Peck, *Berea's First 125 Years* (1982), chaps. 4, 6. Bobbitt, *The Impact of Berea College on Student Characteristics* (1969). Abramson, "From the Beginning Berea Nurtured Those Most in Need" (1993). President Francis S. Hutchins, "The Berea Idea," Address to General Faculty, Mar. 12, 1951 (Berea College Archives). Strategic Planning Committee, "Being and Becoming: Berea College in the 21st Century," June 1996 (Berea College, President's Office), 29–35. Interviews, Berea College. The economic survival of Berea's employment programs, unlike the old manual-labor programs, is beyond this book's scope, but it involves lessons learned from the failure at Oberlin, the development of more scientific farming, the aptitudes of the student workforce, and recently a trade-off between small

losses and the attractiveness of the work system to big donors. Five other four-year colleges (three Presbyterian) have integral work programs for all students, done concurrently with courses: Alice Lloyd, KY; Blackburn, IL; College of the Ozarks, AR; Warren Wilson, NC; and Sterling, VT. See Gose, "A College Returns to Its Roots" (1998). A sixth college, Goddard, VT, ended its program in 2002. By strict definition, these work programs are not financial aid, as they are not targeted on specific students; they reduce costs for everyone. But two of the colleges (Berea and Ozarks) restrict admissions to low-income students, and two (Berea and Alice Lloyd) restrict most admissions to a poor local region (Appalachia).

51. Quoted in Conant, *Thomas Jefferson and the Development of American Public Education* (1963), 16. On Jefferson's basic scheme, see Jefferson, *Notes on the State of Virginia* (1785), 193, 196–98.

52. Conant, "Education for a Classless Society" (1940). On the scheme's history and politics, see Conant, *Thomas Jefferson* (1963), chaps. 1, 2; Honeywell, "A Note on the Educational Work of Thomas Jefferson" (1969); Cremin, *American Education* (1970), 443; Peterson, *Thomas Jefferson and the New Nation* (1970), 149–52, 965–67. Conant's book explored possible influence from the proposals of John Knox, the sixteenth-century Scottish Presbyterian: 8–19, 70–71. William and Mary did not officially become a state college till 1906.

53. William Manning, "The Key of Libberty" (1798), and Jonathan Baldwin Turner, "Plan for an Industrial University, for the State of Illinois"(1851) in Crane, ed., *The College and the Public* (1963). Foner, *Free Soil, Free Labor, Free Men* (1970), chap. 1. Kett, *The Pursuit of Knowledge under Difficulties* (1994), 102–4.

54. Bulletin of Information for Prospective Students, Normal College, 1850–51 (Duke University Archives). On the New York people's colleges, see Rogers, "The People's College Movement in New York State" (1945); Wright, *Pre-Cornell and Early Cornell* (1958); Lang, "The People's College" (1978).

55. Ezra Cornell, "Opening Address" at President Andrew White's inauguration, 1868, and "General Announcement" in *Cornell University to 1872*, undated (both in Cornell University Rare and Manuscript Collections). Veysey, *The Emergence of the American University* (1965), quotes Cornell's famous remark, made at least twice in the 1860s: 63n, 82.

56. Chronological table in Annual Report of the President for 1892–93, plus catalog cost data kindly sent me by Elaine Engst (Cornell University Rare and Manuscript Collections). When Cornell ended tuition fees at the College of Agriculture in 1874, it raised tuition elsewhere from $45 to $65. See Morris Bishop, *Early Cornell* (1962), 55–68, 309–14, on disputes about the land-grant and scholarships; the state insisted on a new four-year scholarship per district every year.

57. Quotations in Smythe, *Kenyon College* (1924), 42–44. Other information is in

an unpublished book-length account, "Kenyon College," ca. 1882, and early catalogs (all in Kenyon College Special Collections). Ministerial aid started at about a third off total costs. By the 1850s it was free tuition, room, and board.

58. Battle, *History of the University of North Carolina* (1912), 214–15, 220–30. Also "Act to transfer the land scrip . . ." (1867), and Code of North Carolina for 1883, section 2633 (both in University of North Carolina–Chapel Hill Library, North Carolina Collection). For class and sectional quarrels in Texas, see Lane, *History of the University of Texas* (1891), 26–29, and Benedict, *A Source Book* (1917), 37–44.

59. Weld, "Report to the Executive Committee" (1833), 41. Carmichael, *New York Establishes a State University* (1955), 11, on New York state politics in the 1850s. President F. A. P. Barnard, "Analysis of Some Statistics of Collegiate Education: A Paper Read before the Trustees of Columbia College," Jan. 3, 1870, 18–19 (Columbia University Archives). William Allan Neilson to Jean Campbell, Dec. 16, 1925, in President Neilson's papers, office series, box 401 (Smith College Archives). On high southern state tuition in the nineteenth century, see George P. Schmidt, *The Liberal Arts College* (1957), 78.

60. Letter in *New York Journal of Commerce* (July 7, 1847), quoted with context by Rudy, *The College of the City of New York* (1977), 15–21. For attitudes toward the free academy, see also Kaestle, *The Evolution of an Urban School System* (1973), 100–109.

61. Jefferson, *Notes on the State of Virginia* (1785), 193, 196–98.

62. Rudolph, *The American College and University* (1962), chaps. 6, 14. Rudolph, *Curriculum* (1977).

63. On the Yale Report, see Rudolph, *Curriculum* (1977), 65–75. On Wayland, see Rudolph, *American College* (1962), 237–40, and Schmidt, *Liberal Arts College* (1957), 60–63. On Cornell, Stanford, etc., see Veysey, *Emergence of the American University* (1965), 63, 63n. Also Leland Stanford, "Speech for Opening Day" (Oct. 1, 1891), and press interviews, 1880s–1890s (Stanford University Special Collections). On different but overlapping concepts of democratic "utility," including east-west differences, see Veysey, 63–66, 98–113.

64. On Peter Cooper's founding ideas for Cooper Union, see Nevins, *Abraham S. Hewitt* (1935), 82, 113–15, 270–78. On its influence and other institutions, see Meiners, *A History of Rice University* (1982), 11, 15–16. On the rise of low-tuition night schools and YMCA colleges, see Lelon, "The Emergence of Roosevelt College" (1973), and Kett, *The Pursuit of Knowledge under Difficulties* (1994), chap. 7.

65. J. Douglas Perry, "Incredible University: A Story of Temple University" (undated book-length manuscript on Conwell and Temple), and Catalogue and Prospectus, 1888 (all in Temple University Conwellana-Templana Collection).

Conwell, *Acres of Diamonds* (1905), elaborates on his basic lecture of the same title. Temple did not become a fully public institution till the early 1960s.

66. Jencks and Riesman, *The Academic Revolution* (1968), 383. On Temple's student makeup, see Angelo, "The Students of the University of Pennsylvania and the Temple College" (1979), 191, Table 3.

67. On Harvard Catholics, see Thernstrom, "'Poor but Hopefull Scholars'" (1986), 123, and Gleason, "American Catholic Higher Education" (1967), 28. According to Gleason, Valparaiso University, Indiana, known as the "poor man's Harvard," had the next highest Catholic proportion among non-Catholic colleges.

68. George P. Schmidt, *The Liberal Arts College* (1957), 275. Thernstrom, "'Poor but Hopefull Scholars'" (1986), 122–23. Thwing, *American Colleges* (1878), 36.

69. Quoted in Thernstrom, "'Poor but Hopefull Scholars'"(1986), 119–20. See also Harris, *The Economics of Harvard* (1970), 92–93.

70. Worcester, *Ballad* (Jan. 22, 1845), quoted in Gilmore, "Jacksonians and Whigs at Harvard" (1970).

71. On general Democrat/Whig differences, see Ashworth, *"Agrarians" and "Aristocrats"* (1983), chaps. 1, 2. Pessen, *Jacksonian Democracy* (1969), finds more overlaps. The party analysis of Harvard issues is mine, but political background is given by Gilmore, "Jacksonians and Whigs" (1970), and Lipset in Lipset and Riesman, *Education and Politics at Harvard* (1975), 72–81. Key statements are in Harris, *The Economics of Harvard* (1970), 92–94, and Andrew Peabody's address reported largely verbatim in Andrew P. White, "The Condition and Wants of Harvard College" (1845). Also "Extracts from the Diaries of John Quincy Adams . . . Relating to Harvard College," Sept. 1834 to Aug. 1835; George Bancroft and Linus Child, "Report on Diminishing the Cost of Instruction at Harvard College, together with a Minority Report," Feb. 25, 27, 1845; Massachusetts House of Representatives, special committee on Harvard University [chairman George Boutwell], majority and minority reports, Apr. 15, 1850 (all in Harvard University Archives). The issues included whether advanced-placement students should pay less than others for a Harvard degree.

72. Annual Reports of the President . . . to the Overseers [including Treasurer's report] for 1848–49 through 1852–53 (Harvard University Archives).

73. Hawkins, *Between Harvard and America* (1972), 8.

74. Eliot, Inaugural Address (1869). Veysey, *The Emergence of the American University* (1965), 86–98, brilliantly summarizes Eliot's complex ideology and temperament. On changes in his attitudes, see Hawkins, *Between Harvard and America* (1972), esp. chaps. 3–6.

75. Adams, "The Proposed Increase of the Tuition Fee" (1904); Board of Overseers, Report of Special Committee on the Financial Requirements of the University . . . (1904); Annual Reports of the President and Treasurer for 1904–05, 1905–06, and 1907–08; Eliot to Charles Francis Adams, Jr., June 4, 1904 (all in

Harvard University Archives). At Berkeley in 1899, Governor Henry T. Gage blocked a proposal by the University of California—a free-tuition institution that was financially hard-pressed—to introduce a twenty-five-dollar tuition fee along with seventy-five new scholarships for "worthy" students who were unable to pay it and needed more help. Opponents declared that free tuition put all students, many of them poor, "on the same footing," whereas charging tuition would "estrange" the university from the people whose tax support it needed (Eliot's large middle class). Others, including senior faculty, argued that tuition fees would actually relieve taxpayers while encouraging students to appreciate "the advantages of college" and not think "the world owed them a living." Ferrier, *Origins and Development of the University of California* (1930), 389–93. Stadtman, *The University of California* (1968), 120–25.

76. Thwing, *American Colleges* (1878), chap. 2. Veysey, *Emergence* (1965), 290n. Harris, *The Economics of Harvard* (1970), 95. Thernstrom, "'Poor but Hopefull Scholars'" (1986), 123. Overseers Special Committee (note 75 above) and Report of the Dean of the College for 1998–99 by L. B. R. Briggs (both in Harvard University Archives). Briggs reported the restriction on freshman scholarships without explanation except to say approvingly that most scholarships were competed for by students already in the college.

77. Eliot, Inaugural Address (1869). Fallows, "Working One's Way through College" (1901), 166. Annual Report of the President for 1898–99, including provision for cheaper dining facilities and a "Cooperative Society" discount store (Harvard University Archives).

78. James McCosh, cited by Hawkins, *Between Harvard and America* (1972), 172. Views vary on whether Eliot encouraged and increased public-school admissions amid the expansion and upgrading of public schools. See Morison, *Three Centuries of Harvard* (1936), 421; Veysey, *Emergence* (1965), 326; Hawkins, *Between Harvard and America* (1972), 171–72; Thernstrom, "'Poor but Hopefull'" (1986), 122. Also Annual Reports of the President for 1889–90, 1894–95, 1902–03 (Harvard University Archives).

79. Slosson, *Great American Universities* (1910), 361–63. Veysey, *Emergence* (1965), 288–89. Angelo, "The Students at the University of Pennsylvania" (1975). For different views of Harvard and a more communal but conformist Yale, see Fallows, "Working One's Way" (1901); Morrison, *Three Centuries* (1936), 418–22; Wechsler, "An Academic Greshman's Law" (1981), 418–19. Also Owen Johnson's *Stover at Yale* (1912), a searching and sensitive novel beneath its eastern upper-class heartiness.

80. Report of the President for 1877–78 and Report of Dean of the College for 1898–99 (both in Harvard University Archives).

5. Merit and "Self-Help"

1. On anxieties of the time, see Wilkinson, *American Tough* (1984), 63–65, 94–99. On varieties of social Darwinism, Himmelfarb, *Victorian Minds* (1970), chap. 12.

2. Hadley, "Inaugural Address" (1899) and "Alleged Luxury among College Students" (1901).

3. Pierson, *Yale* (1952), chap. 6 and pp. 35–37, 411–14. Veysey, *The Emergence of the American University* (1965), 236–37. Schiff, "A Century of *Stover*" (1997). See also *American National Biography*, vol. 19 (1919), 775–76, on Hadley as president and economist.

4. Barnard, "Annual Report" (1879), 190.

5. See Maclean, *History of the College of New Jersey*, vol. 2 (1877), 330–34, 434, for ambiguities at Princeton in the 1850s. At Yale in the 1840s, President Theodore Dwight Woolsey introduced exam-based merits, some paid by himself, along with published lists of prize-winning and high-ranked students, to promote "sound scholarship." This followed what may have been America's first fellowships for graduates only, the Berkeley Scholarships, established in the 1830s and competed for by Yale undergraduates. Kelley, *Yale* (1974), 38–39, 174–75. Historical Register of Yale University, 1701–1937, 117 (Yale University Manuscripts and Archives).

6. Rudolph, *Mark Hopkins and the Log* (1956), 7n. Catalogs and Annual Reports of the President, 1880s to 1930s (Oberlin College Archives).

7. Annual Report of the President for 1884–85 (Cornell University Rare and Manuscript Collections). Cf. Beadie, "From Student Markets to Credential Markets" (1999).

8. "An act to increase the efficiency of the public school system . . . ," in *Laws of New Jersey: Acts of the 114th Legislature of the State of New Jersey* (Trenton, 1890), and "An act appropriating scrip for the public lands . . ." (New Jersey land-grant agreement, 1864), both in Rutgers University Library, New Jersey Documents section. The state merits were scrapped in 1929 but restored in the late 1930s with a financial-need requirement. Wilkinson, "Plural Ends, Contested Means" (2001), 309, 321.

9. New York State Department of Education, Annual Reports for 1912–13, 1915 (New York State Library, Albany). The Regents scholarships were scaled by need beginning in the late 1950s. On agriculture-college problems and pricing, see Wilkinson, "Plural Ends" (2001), 319.

10. Annual Report of the President for 1892–93 (Cornell University Rare and Manuscript Collections), 4.

11. Richardson, *History of Dartmouth College* (1932), 711. Data on charges from the Dartmouth College Catalogue for 1895–96, kindly sent me by Mary S. Donin, Dartmouth College Archives.

12. President's Report for 1899: Report of Dean Benjamin Terry for the Senior College (University of Chicago Special Collections).

13. "Statement by the President of the University for the Quarter Ending July 1, 1893"; Presidents' papers, 1893–1925, box 60, letters in folders 3, 11, 13 (1893–1906); Circulars of Information for the Colleges, June 1, Sept. 15, 1901; "Awards and Aids," Jan. 25, 1925 (all in University of Chicago Special Collections). Also Storr, *Harper's University* (1966), 20–21. On Harper, organization, and access, Veysey, *The Emergence of the American University* (1965), 326, 366–80.

14. Burton R. Clark, *The Distinctive College* (1970), chap. 8. Annual Reports of the President for 1921–22, 1923–24 (Swarthmore College Archives). Pamphlets listing endowments in 1906 and 1934 show declines in the scholarship proportion of all endowments and the need-related proportions of scholarships (Swarthmore College Archives)

15. "Announcement of Scripps College, 1927–28"; Board of Trustees Minutes, June 18, 1927; folder on Scholarships: Historical Information (all in Scripps College Archives). Cf. Horowitz, *Alma Mater* (1984), 339–43.

16. Annual Reports of the President for 1927–28, 1930–31 (Oberlin College Archives).

17. Bishop J. B. Kerfoot to Rev. William Bodine, Mar. 27, 1879, in *The Kenyon Book* (ca. 1890), 76–77 (Kenyon College Special Collections). On British origins and meanings of the term "muscular Christianity," see Newsome, *Godliness and Good Learning* (1961), 198–99; Vance, *The Sinews of the Spirit* (1985), 2–3.

18. Opinion of seminary scholarships as described by L .R. Briggs in his Report of the Dean of the College for 1898–99 (Harvard University Archives). In 1899, a seasoned college observer made what today might be called an anti-affirmative-action criticism of colleges for elevating a group category—a church-based "professional . . . class"—above individual needs and merits. Thwing, "Pecuniary Aid for Poor and Able Students" (1899). On the secularizing of American colleges and their presidents, see Rudolph, *The American College and University* (1962), 419–20; Veysey, *The Emergence of the American University* (1965), 202–3, 373; Marsden, *The Soul of the American University* (1994).

19. Register . . . for 1884–85; Annual Report of the President for 1884–85 (Cornell University Rare and Manuscript Collections).

20. Catalogues of Yale University for 1900–01 to 1904–05 (Yale University Manuscripts and Archives). Cf. Pierson, *Yale* (1952), 413; Oren, *Joining the Club* (1985), 53.

21. Reports of the Director of the Bureau of Self-Help and Appointments (its exact name varied), in Reports of the President, 1900–21, esp. Kitchel's long, philosophical report for 1904–05 (Yale University Manuscripts and Archives). See Kelley, *Yale* (1973), 322–23, on Hadley's unforceful leadership.

22. Martin, "An Historical Analysis of Financial Aid at Wellesley College" (1973). "A

Chain of Alumnae Helping Students," *Wellesley* magazine (1999). Diane Speare Truant (Wellesley SAS secretary) to author, Jan. 28, April 24, 1999. Henry Durant became Wellesley's treasurer when Massachusetts chartered it as a college, but Ada Howard, the first president, was really his deputy.

23. Veysey, *The Emergence of the American University* (1965), 99–100. Barnard, "Annual Report" (1879), 181, 186–87.

24. Barnard, "Annual Report" (1879), 187–90.

25. Ibid., 181. T. Cushing, "Undergraduate Life Sixty Years Ago," *Harvard Graduates' Magazine* (1893), 555–56, quoted in Harris, *The Economics of Harvard* (1970), 93–94. Thwing, *American Colleges* (1878), chap. 2. Harvard catalogs do not show whether this scaling of grants was done before 1830.

26. See page 247 n.8. Annual Reports of the President for 1893–94, 1877–78 (Harvard University Archives). J. D. Greene to President A. L. Lowell, Feb. 15, 1910, quoted in Harris, *Economics* (1970), 89. The complexity of attitudes toward scholarship policies was demonstrated by the maverick Charles Francis Adams, Jr., historian, investor, railroad expert, and leader of the Harvard overseers who unsuccessfully called for a big tuition increase coupled with more spending on scholarships (see chap. 4 above). Adams believed that students from rich families tended to be abler than those from poor families because of natural selection. Speaking out to his diary in the early 1900s, he inaccurately debunked Eliot's concern for a large middling stratum of students as democratic cant, a weak-minded leveling down. Yet his own ideas about tuition and aid left no place for merit scholarships. Harvard, in his view, should be proud to levy the rich through high tuition fees, providing scholarships (scaled by ability) for the "capable poor." Admitting he was "socialistic" about this, he nonetheless declared that it was in line with "the great natural law of the survival of the fittest" and would mean that tuition income was spent "most profitably" for students and "the community." Adams's social Darwinism was not just about individual winning but about the efficient advance of a whole society. As president of the Union Pacific Railroad, he extended workers' benefits and job security, believing from his military Civil War days in the effectiveness of group morale and loyalty. Adams, "The Proposed Increase of the Tuition Fee" (1904). Eliot to Adams, May 27, June 4, 1904 (Harvard University Archives). Adams, "Memorabilia," 1901–1905, entry Jan. 11, 1905 (Massachusetts Historical Society, Boston). Kirkland, *Charles Francis Adams, Jr.* (1965).

27. Annual Reports of the President, 1887–88, 1890–99; Overseers, Report of the Committee on Free Scholarship, 1892 (all in Harvard University Archives).

28. Annual Report of the President for 1890–91, quoted in Harris, *Economics* (1970), 99. Hawkins, *Between Harvard and America* (1972), notes Eliot's shift away from seeing free-tuition public colleges as communistic "pensioners of the state": 152–56.

29. Neilson to R. H. Girard, Dec. 22, 1920, and to Fowler, Bauer, and Kenny, Dec. 5, 1924, in President Neilson papers, office series, box 421, folder on Scholarships, 1918–39 (Smith College Archives).

30. President's Report of 1903 (University of Chicago Special Collections).

31. Fallows, "Working One's Way through College" (1901), 166. Orlando F. Lewis, "The Self-Supporting Student" (1904), 723.

32. Slosson, *Great American Universities* (1910), 269–70. On the development of university administration, Rudolph, *The American College and University* (1962), chap. 2; Veysey, *The Emergence of the American University* (1965), 302–17; Lucas, *American Higher Education* (1994), 191–94.

33. John F. Crowell, "The Education of Poor Boys," c1890 (Duke University Archives). J. Douglas Perry, "Incredible University," undated, chap. 9 (Temple University Conwellana-Templana Collection). U.S. Dept. of Interior, "Self-Help for College Students" (1929), part 2.

34. Nellie Sanford Webb et al., "Alumnae Fund . . . for Students' Aid Society," 1904; "Students' Aid Society," *Smith College Weekly* (Sept. 25, 1912), 2 (all in Smith College Archives).

35. Bailey, "College Life and the Social Order" (1914); Myer, "What Would You Do for an Education?" (1922); Greenleaf, "Self-Supporting Students" (1926); Witty and Foreman, "Self-Support and College Attainment" (1930); Howes, "The Student Works His Way" (1930).

36. Crowell, "Education of Poor Boys." Fallows, "Working One's Way through College" (1901). Slosson, *Great American Universities* (1910), 268–71. Owen Johnson, *Stover at Yale* (1912). U.S. Dept. of Interior, "Self-Help for College Students" (1929), part 2. General support for working through college was not enough to save Mount Holyoke's communal and cost-saving system of "domestic work," required of all students. Mary Lyon, the college's founder, had established it right at the beginning, in 1837, as an explicit alternative to higher charges and targeted aid. In response to a new, richer clientele and some student dislike of compulsory chores, Mount Holyoke ended the system in 1913, replacing it with higher tuition and "co-op" dorms and other work opportunities for needy students. The move involved keen debate among faculty, students, and alumni, including the question of whether needy students would be too set apart by special arrangements. Student employment per se was not criticized. Cole, *A Hundred Years of Mount Holyoke College* (1940), 26, 241 ff. Folder on "Domestic Work" (Mount Holyoke College Archives).

37. On Stanford's founding with free tuition, see Orrin Leslie Elliott, *Stanford University* (1937), 20–21, 56–57, 154–56.

38. Herbert Hoover, "Hoover on Tuition Fees" (1919). Mitchell, *Stanford University* (1958), 31–32. Annual Reports of the President, 1919, 1920, 1921; University Clippings, General, Oct.–Dec. 1919, Jan. 1920 (all in Stanford University Special

Collections). On Hoover at Stanford, Nash, *The Life of Herbert Hoover* (1983), chaps. 2, 3. There was some similarity with Rice's ending of free tuition in the 1960s. Gantz, "On the Basis of Merit Alone" (1991), chaps. 3, 4.

39. My calculation from catalog data kindly sent by Polly Armstrong (Stanford University Special Collections).

40. Similar statements are in Harvard Corporation Records for 1818, vol. 8, ref. UAT.5.31 (Harvard University Archives), and Cornell's Annual Report of the President [for] 1884–85, section on student loan fund (Cornell University Rare and Manuscript Collections). Also Chaffin, *Trinity College* (1950), on Trinity (later Duke) in 1891: 454–55.

41. Harold H. Swift papers, box 140, folder 9, "Student Costs" (University of Chicago Special Collections).

42. As listed by U.S. Dept. of Interior, "Self-Help for College Students" (1929), 14–18.

43. "Advocates Loans for Scholarships," *New York Times* (1926). Monro, "Untapped Resource" (1956), 15.

44. Quarterly Calendars and Circulars of Information (University of Chicago Special Collections).

45. Trevor Arnett, "Cost of Higher Education and How It Should Be Met," ca. 1925, in Harold W. Swift papers, box 40, folder 9 (University of Chicago Special Collections). Arnett's advocacy included a survey of private college presidents, who gave mixed and cautious responses to his plan: Arnett, *Trends in Tuition Fees* (1939), 56–75. See also Arnett, *Recent Trends in Higher Education* (1940), chap. 4.

46. President Neilson papers, office series, box 418, folder on circular, "To the Parents of the Class of 1925 . . . ," May 25, 1926, and related correspondence with parents and other colleges (Smith College Archives).

47. See Fels, "Charging the Full Cost of Education" (1958), on postwar proposals and efforts to charge full costs with added aid.

6. Seeking Equity and Order

1. U.S. Dept. of Commerce, *Historical Statistics of the United States* (1960), 202. Levine, *The American College and the Culture of Aspiration* (1986), chap. 9. See Ratcliffe, "State Scholarships Increase" (1936), and Willey, *Depression, Recovery, and Higher Education* (1937), 301–2, on the mixed and modest response of state governments, caught between rising student need for aid and falling tax revenue.

2. Karabel, "Status-Group Struggle" (1984), 19 ff.

3. Willey, *Depression, Recovery* (1937), chap. 13. Porter, *Trinity and Duke* (1964),

57–59. Levine, *American College* (1986), 192–93. General Information Number for 1934–35 (Cornell University Rare and Manuscript Collections).

4. Neilson to Oberlin president Ernest Wilkins, Nov. 18, 1935, in President Neilson papers, office series, box 404, folder 32 (Smith College Archives). "Princeton and the FERA," *Princeton Alumni Weekly* (1937). See also Lipset in Lipset and Riesman, *Education and Politics at Harvard* (1975), 161–62, on Harvard trustee resistance to federal work-study, and Bower, "'A Favored Child of the State'" (2004), 370, 378, on other elite colleges' objections.

5. Committee on Undergraduate Scholarships, Report, Mar. 12, 1935; Melby to Personnel Director Elias Lyman, June 2, 1935, and A .H .Hibbard to Lyman, May 8, 1936, both in President Scott papers, box 38, folder 9 (all in Northwestern University Archives). On Melby's progressive background and disputes at Northwestern, see Colwell, "The Study of Education at Northwestern University" (1988).

6. Annual Reports of the President, 1933, 1934; catalogs 1920s–50s (Swarthmore College Archives). Announcements, 1920s–1950s (University of Chicago Special Collections).

7. Pierson, *Yale College* (1955), chap. 22.

8. Harris, *The Economics of Harvard* (1970), 99.

9. President's Report to the Overseers, Feb. 1934; Dean of the College A. C. Hanford, "Development of the Harvard National Scholarship Plan," 1937 (Harvard University Archives). Harris, *Economics* (1970), 99. Conant, "Education for a Classless Society" (1940). Conant, *My Several Lives* (1970), chap. 12. Karabel, "Status-Group Struggle" (1984), 23. Hershberg, *James B. Conant* (1993), 56–59. Interviews, Princeton University.

10. "Scholarships in a Privately Endowed University," 1936 (Princeton University Archives).

11. Karabel, "Status-Group Struggle" (1984), 24. Keller and Keller, *Making Harvard Modern* (2001), 33–34. Bowen and Bok, *The Shape of the River* (1998), xxviii–xxix, 4. of the 161 Harvard Nationals, only 10 went to farmers' sons, 24 to sons of teachers and school superintendents. Nearly all the rest went to other professional and business families.

12. Brett, "Colleges as Salesmen" (1938), esp. 200. Arnett, *Recent Trends in Higher Education* (1940), 41. Pierson, *Yale College* (1955), 491. McDonald, "Equalizing Scholarship Opportunities"(1957), 30. Thelin, *The Cultivation of Ivy* (1976), 30–31.

13. Blum, *V Was for Victory* (1976), 141–44. Hartmann, *The Home Front and Beyond* (1982), 103–4. Keller and Keller, *Making Harvard Modern* (2001), 29.

14. This showed up when I compared financial reports for male Amherst with those of neighboring female Smith, which trained wartime WAVEs but had few GI veterans (Amherst College Archives and Smith College Archives).

15. College application and admissions trends in the late 1940s and early 1950s were volatile and complex. Duffy and Goldberg, *Crafting a Class* (1998), chap. 1. See also Commission on Financing Higher Education, *The Nature and Needs of Higher Education* (1952), 78, on the temporary effect of low Depression birthrates.

16. Clark, "The Two Joes Meet"(1998). See also Godson, *The College of William and Mary*, vol. 2 (1992), 492, on financial aid to prevent a decline in good applicants at an elite state college.

17. J. Edward Sanders, "Visiting the Colleges" (1953). W. J. Bender, memo to members of Association of Colleges in New England, Aug. 14, 1953 (Amherst College, Office of Financial Aid). Frank H. Bowles, 53rd Report of the Director, College Entrance Examination Board, 1954 (Educational Testing Service Archives, Princeton), 35–36. James Perkins at hearings, Aug. 12, 1957, in U.S. Congress, House, Committee on Education and Labor, *Scholarship and Loan Program* (1957). King, "Financial Thresholds to College" (1957). Duffy and Goldberg, *Crafting* (1998), 170–71.

18. Sanders, "Visiting" (1953). Bender (note 17 above). King, "The Educational Function of Financial Aid" (1955), 9.

19. John W. Nason in Carrell and Carrell, eds., *A Singular Time, A Singular Place* (1992), 13–19. David W. Fraser, "Conversation with John Nason . . ," Apr. 4, 1989; Dick and Jean Burrowes, eds., "The Fractured 'Forties: Together Again after Five Decades; Memories of the War Years at Swarthmore College," June 1992 (all in Swarthmore College Archives). Interviews, Swarthmore College (Mary Ellen Chijioke, John Nason). John Rosselli (alumnus) to author, Mar. 17, 2000.

20. Annual Reports of the President for 1945–51; Presidential papers, John W. Nason, box 1, folders on Admissions; box 3, folders on "Open Scholarships, 1941–1949" and "The Negro Question"; Corporation Minutes, Executive Committee of Board of Managers, Nov. 5, 1946, and Board of Managers' meeting, June 13, 1947 (all in Swarthmore College Archives). Also Howard C. Johnson, "On Buying Students," 1952, in Harold H. Swift papers, box 141, folder on "Scholarships and Fellowships" (University of Chicago Special Collections).

21. "The Impact of Inflation upon Higher Education," Feb. 1951, cited by Commission on Financing Higher Education, *The Nature and Needs of Higher Education* (1952), x.

22. Commission on Financing, *Nature and Needs* (1952). Axt, *The Federal Government and Financing Higher Education* (1952); Hollinshead, *Who Should Go to College?* (1952). Millett, *Financing Higher Education* (1952).

23. For more comparisons between the two commissions, see David D. Henry, *Challenges Past, Challenges Present* (1975), 79–84, and Freeland, *Academia's Golden Age* (1992), 73–77.

24. Conant, "Wanted: American Radicals" (1943), 45. Harvard provost Paul Buck, a leading commissioner, was a Conant protégé.

25. Commission on Financing, *Nature and Needs* (1952), 135–36.

26. Hollinshead, *Who Should Go to College?* (1952), 95. Millett, *Financing Higher Education* (1952), 382. Hayes, "Can a Poor Girl Go to College?" (1891): see p. **???** above.

27. Hollinshead, *Who Should Go to College?* (1952), esp. preface and 72–73.

28. Ibid., 107–8.

29. Ibid., 103–4, 116–17.

30. Bowles (note 17 above), 35.

31. Stalnaker, "The National Merit Scholarship Program" (1956). Also F. D. Danielson, "Merit Scholarship Corporation," July 11, 1958, report from information by Edward C. Smith, National Merit vice president, in President J. Roscoe Miller papers, box 2, folder 6 (Northwestern University Archives). On concepts of general education at the time, see Freeland, *Academia's Golden Age* (1992), 77–80.

32. Danielson (note 31 above) gives a detailed layout of National Merit's early selection and financial systems. Scholarship America, an umbrella organization of local and other scholarship-giving foundations, is today a leading advocate for awards given on merit but scaled by need. Nelsen, "Use Both Merit and Need" (2003).

33. Stalnaker, "National Merit" (1956), 166.

34. Thresher, "Sponsored Scholarships and the Student" (1955). Hansen, "The Politics of Federal Scholarships" (1977), 92–93.

35. Fuess, "The College Board"(1967), 1–17. Schudson, "Organizing the 'Meritocracy'"(1972).

36. Quotations from Annual Reports of the College Entrance Examination Board (College Board Archives, New York). Cf. Whyte, *The Organization Man* (1956). On College Board history and scholarships, Bowles (note 17 above), 33–34.

37. Interview, Harvard University (John Monro). On Monro's background and career, see Kahn, *Harvard through Change and through Storm* (1969), 36–39, and Woodcock, "The Experiences of John Usher Monro" (1999). Also "Oral History Interview with John Monro" by John Aubry, Tougaloo College, July 26, 1989 (College Board Archives, New York); and Provost Paul Buck papers, folder on "Monro, J. U., 1950–51" (Harvard University Archives).

38. Monro, "Helping Him Pay His Way" (1950), and "Helping the Student Help Himself" (1953).

39. Interview, Harvard University (Fred Jewett).

40. *Harvard College Class of 1934—25th Anniversary Report,* quoted in Woodcock, "The Experiences of John Usher Monro" (1999), 1.

41. "Oral History Interview with John Monro" (note 37 above).

42. Reed, "Student Civil Rights Activism" (1983).

43. Thelin, *The Cultivation of Ivy* (1976), 30–32.

44. J. Edward Sanders, Interview (1982), citing Monro.

45. Geiger, *The American College in the Nineteenth Century* (2000), 17–18.

46. Emery Walker (former Brown admissions director) to author, Nov. 6 and Nov. 28, 1997. Interview, Wesleyan University (Donald Eldridge). Cf. Bowles (note 17 above), 36. It is unclear when Eldridge and Wilson teamed up, but it may have been as early as 1949, on a train to New York to meet with the College Board.

47. Bowles (note 17 above), 38. Two boxes on "Intercollegiate: Five/Seven Sisters Colleges," incl. folder on scholarships (Smith College Archives). On Sisters' activities, see also Walton, "Cultivating a Place for Selective All-Female Education" (2001).

48. Sanders, "Visiting the Colleges" (1953).

49. Interview, Pomona College (Jane Sanders). Sanders, "Are Scholarships Improving Education?" (1953), in *College Board Review*'s special issue reporting the symposium.

50. Monro, "Helping the Student Help Himself" (1953).

51. Hollinshead, *Who Should Go to College?* (1952), 108. Millett, *Financing Higher Education* (1952), 135–36. Also Report of the Scholarship Committee, May 2, 1934, discussing Princeton's War Memorial Scholarships in 1921, box 2 on "Student Aid and Employment" (Princeton University Archives). Committee on Scholarships, Annual Report for 1952–53, in Financial Aids Office Records, 1940–1970, box 1 (Stanford University Special Collections). In Britain, by the 1920s, some local authorities were scaling scholarships by need, others by academic merit. Ellis, *The Poor Student and the University* (1925), 33–40.

52. Clara Ludwig (former Mount Holyoke admissions director) to author, Feb. 17, 1994; her letter corrected Bowles (note 17 above), 38, on some details. See also Report of the President for 1953–1954 by Acting President Meribeth Cameron (Mount Holyoke Archives).

53. Bowles (note 17 above), 35–40, gives a more detailed chronology of the founding of CSS. Monro put his reservations to Harvard's president Nathan Pusey, Nov. 20, 1953. Box on "John Usher Monro: College Scholarship Service: Correspondence etc.," April 1953–54 (Harvard University Archives).

54. College Board's College and University Enrollment Solutions now does the financial aid processing.

55. CSS stopped providing this information in 1981 for reasons of confidentiality, but it helped groups of colleges to share it. Joe Case (former CSS officer) to author, July 17, 2001, e-mail.

56. On CSS early operations and principles, see Bowles (note 17 above), 39; Fels, "The College Scholarship Service" (1954); Bacon, "Financial Aid" (1959); Col-

lege Scholarship Service, *CSS Need Analysis* (1980), 5–6; J. Edward Sanders, Interview (1982); Nelson, "The Role of the College Scholarship Service" (1985), 154–56.

57. On CSS purposes, Monro wrote a remarkably intemperate attack on a Sept. 1954 proposal for research on "the Role of Scholarships," which stressed the bidding war (Monro box, Harvard Archives, note 53 above). Interview, Harvard University (John Monro). "Oral History Interview with John Monro" (note 37 above), 7.

7. Choosing the Best

1. Kemeny, "The First Five Years" (1975), 28. Klitgaard, *Choosing Elites* (1983), 26, 75. Oren, *Joining the Club* (1985), 211–12. Kabaservice, "The Birth of a New Institution" (1999), 37–38. Keller and Keller, *Making Harvard Modern* (2001), 293, 295. Presidents' papers, John W. Nason, paper received from Amherst, April 25, 1947; Barclay White, Jr., et al. to John .W. Nason, Nov. 24, 1952 (all in Swarthmore College Archives). William Ihlandfeldt, annual report on admissions and financial aid, 1968, in President J. Roscoe Miller papers, box 2, folder 6 (Northwestern University Archives).

2. Klitgaard, *Choosing Elites* (1985), 159–65.

3. Nash et al., "Financial Aid Policies" (1967), II-6, 13, 16–17, 21. Hansen, "The Politics of Federal Scholarships" (1977), 140. But see Kelley, *Yale* (1973), 450, 452–53, on Yale's move in the 1960s against freshman jobs as a deterrent to top students and a "hardship" for the less well-prepared.

4. Cf. Monro, "Untapped Resource" (1956), 14; Bacon, "Financial Aid" (1959); Rivlin, *The Role of the Federal Government in Financing Higher Education* (1961), 77; Doermann, *Crosscurrents in College Admissions* (1968), 49–51, 98; Morse, "How We Got Here from There" (1977), 6–7, 10. Reports of the President for 1957–63 (Mount Holyoke College Archives) and for 1966–67 (Smith College Archives). Breneman, *Liberal Arts Colleges* (1994), claimed that the economist Gary Becker's *Human Capital* (1964) caused wider acceptance of student loans as personal and public investment: 23. I doubt that this had much effect on trends to packaging, which were already under way.

5. Sanders, Interview (1982). Interview, Harvard University (Wallace McDonald). From the state sector, there were double-barreled attacks on heavy loans coupled with high tuition. Eldon L. Johnson, "Is the Low-Tuition Principle Outmoded?" (1959). President's Report for 1958, by Jean Paul Mather (University of Massachusetts Archives, Amherst).

6. Morse, "How We Got Here" (1977), 7.

7. The College Board published the "Principles" in an annual guide, *Financing a College Education.*

8. Moon, "Student Financial Aid" (1962), 9. Brown, "Equity Packaging of Student Financial Aid" (1976), 3. Steering Committee, "Study of Education at Stanford," Report 4, Dec. 1968, 74–75 (Stanford University Archives).

9. "Principles of Financial Aid Administration," 1961 (note 7 above). *U.S. v. Brown University et al.,* U.S. Court of Appeals for the Third Circuit, "Brief for the Defendant-Appellate," no. 92–1911 (Dec. 14, 1992), 8.

10. Nash et al., "Financial Aid Policies" (1967), II-6, 8. Van Dusen and O'Hearne, *An Idealization of a Collegiate Financial Aid Office* (1968), 12. Minutes of the Duke University Scholarship Committee, 1948–1967: entries for June 25, 1956, and May 18, 1965; southern-college "Scholarship Agreement," ca. 1956, attached to the Minutes (Duke University Archives). College Compact [midwestern] on Financial Aid (Oberlin College Archives). Interviews, Harvey Mudd College (Emery Walker), Northwestern University (Rebecca Dixon), Pomona College (Herbert Smith), Stanford University (Robert Huff). There is very little record of how most cooperative agreements ended.

11. See Appendix 1 on the two college groups and the antitrust case.

12. Thelin, *The Cultivation of Ivy* (1976). Interviews, Cornell University (Ben DeWinter), Harvard University (Fred Glimp).

13. Jencks and Riesman, *The Academic Revolution* (1968), 138. Wortman, "Can Need-Blind Survive?"(1993). Duffy and Greenberg, *Crafting a Class* (1998), 190–91. Sources also include a prepublication book manuscript by Jerome Karabel on Harvard, Yale, and Princeton admissions, 1900–present (University of California, Berkeley, Dept. of Sociology), and a letter, David Karen to author, Oct. 2, 1991, on his study of Harvard admissions. Interviews, Harvard University (Fred Glimp, Fred Jewett), Northwestern University (William Ihlandfeldt). Phillips Academy started need-blind/need-met in the late 1950s.

14. King, "Financial Thresholds to College" (1957). Mensel, "Changing Picture of Financial Aid" (1962). Nash et al., "Financial Aid Policies" (1967), II-11, 15. Steering Committee, "The Study of Education at Stanford," Dec. 1966, Report 4, 73–74 (Stanford University Special Collections). Report of Financial Aid Office, June 1969 (Mount Holyoke College Archives). Herbert Smith (former financial aid director, Pomona) to author, Oct. 8, 2001.

15. Interview, Bowdoin College (Walter Moulton).

16. Interviews, Harvard University (Fred Glimp), Pomona College (Herbert Smith), Smith College (Anne Keppler). See Nash et al., "Financial Aid Policies" (1967), I-13, I-22 through I-25, on elite-college removal of high grade requirements for retaining scholarships in college.

17. Cf. Rauh (1972), 40. Some colleges combined admit-deny policies with need-aware exclusion when an applicant was admissible but weak. Smith did this in the 1970s in admitting a few students from the admissions waiting list. Interviews, Smith College.

18. Duffy and Greenberg, *Crafting a Class* (1998), 20–21, 191. Cf. Kemeny, "The First Five Years" (1975), 29.

19. Quoting Report of the President, Feb. 1976; cf. President's Reports for 1957–58, 1968–69, 1970–71 (all in Princeton University Archives).

20. Dean of the College, Report to the Faculty on Undergraduate Admission and Financial Aid, Sept. 20, 1971, by Edward D. Sullivan, 10; Report of the President, April 1983, by William G. Bowen, 10–11 (both in Princeton University Archives). Interviews, Princeton University (Bradford Craig, Robert Goheen).

21. Gardner Patterson, "The Education of Women at Princeton," July 12, 1968, chap. 4, in "Coeducation Reports" box; President's Report for 1967–68 (both in Princeton University Archives). Interview, Princeton University (Robert Goheen). Moves to coeducation elsewhere seldom involved just *adding* students.

22. Report by Director of Admission, John Osander, for 1970–71; Dean of the College's report (note 20 above), 13; Report of the President, April 1983, 13–14, 14n (all in Princeton University Archives).

23. Herrnstein and Murray, *The Bell Curve* (1994), 32, 34. Norton et al., *A People and a Nation* (1982), 868, graph.

24. My calculations from data in U.S. Bureau of the Census, *A Statistical History of the United States* (1976), 382–83. The *number* of community colleges went up by a third.

25. Dunham, "A Revolution in Admissions"(1966). Herrnstein and Murray, *The Bell Curve* (1994), chap. 1. Fetter, *Questions and Admissions* (1995), 71, 72. Duffy and Goldberg, *Crafting a Class* (1998), 4–5. Geiger, "The Ten Generations of American Higher Education" (1999), sees academic stratification starting between the World Wars: 57–61.

26. Brint and Karabel, *The Diverted Dream* (1989), 86–89. Harvard president A. Lawrence Lowell took a similar position in 1932. Lucas, *American Higher Education* (1994), 221.

27. Differing ideas about modern mobility, achievement, and education are explored by Erickson and Goldthorpe, *The Constant Flux* (1992), chap. 1. The term "meritocracy" was coined by the great British sociologist, Michael Young, who envisaged what we might call a *testocracy*. In his book *The Rise of the Meritocracy* (1958), a satirical "history" as narrated in 2033, British society comes to select its leaders and professionals largely on the basis of IQ tests. The key formula is "IQ + effort = merit," and even "effort" is subject to pen and paper tests of "work patterns." Young's book is full of sly jokes. Near the end he gives the c.v. of a modern labor leader, recording his IQ at each stage of his career. If you peer closely at the numbers you will see that his IQ falls, never to recover, from 123 to 115 when he goes to Harvard on a Commonwealth Fellowship. Young's narrator, an enthusiast for the system, makes no comment on this, though

earlier he notes the low standards of American public education despite the "extraordinary prescience" of U.S. Army intelligence testing in World War I.

28. Jencks and Riesman, *The Academic Revolution* (1968), chap. 1 and p. 114. Freeland, *Academia's Golden Age* (1992), 85–97. Wilkinson, *American Social Character* (1994), 15, 337–38. Reuben, "Merit, Mission, and Minority Students" (2001), 201. But see Conway, *True North* (1994), 58–59, on a gender gap in faculty meritocracy.

29. Jencks and Riesman, *Academic Revolution* (1968), 24–25. Geiger, "The Ten Generations of American Higher Education" (1999), 57–61.

30. Interviews in 1970, Wesleyan University. Opinions differed on whether the new Wesleyan faculty really promoted graduate study. On Wesleyan's fluctuating fortunes, see Keller, *Academic Structure* (1987), 45–49, and Steinberg, *The Gatekeepers* (2002), xix–xxi.

31. Cf. Doermann, *Crosscurrents in College Admissions* (1968), 54, and Kabaservice, "The Birth of a New Institution" (1999). Also Karabel (note 13 above).

32. Dunham, "A Revolution in Admissions" (1966), 6. Jencks and Riesman, *Academic Revolution* (1968), 121–25. Lemann, "The Structure of Success in America" (1995) and "The Great Sorting "(1995). Reuben, "Merit, Mission, and Minority Students" (2001), 201–2.

33. Jencks and Riesman, *Academic Revolution* (1968), 122n. Powell, "Notes on the Origins of Meritocracy in American Schooling" (2001), 77. Keller and Keller, *Making Harvard Modern* (2001), 291–96.

34. Quotations from Doermann, *Crosscurrents in College Admissions* (1968), 75. See also Doermann, "Crosscurrents in Admissions" (1965), and Cartter, "Pricing Policies for Higher Education" (1966), 7–8. Also William Ihlandfeldt, "Report on Freshman Admission at Northwestern," Jan. 4, 1974, box on Admissions, Financial Aid, and Student Records (Northwestern University Archives).

35. Jencks and Riesman, *Academic Revolution* (1968), 122.

36. Doermann, "Crosscurrents" (1965), 463. Doermann, *Crosscurrents* (1968), 62–64. See also Bender (note 37 below).

37. King, "Financial Thresholds to College"(1957). Final Report of W. J. Bender, Admission and Scholarship Committee, 1952–1960, esp. 6, 9, in Report of the President . . . [with] Reports of Departments, 1959–1960 (Harvard University Archives). Bender also claimed that increases in total charges exceeded increases in the average college scholarship. This was true, but the percentage of students on college grant aid rose from 19 percent to 26 percent: 9, table. On Bender versus faculty over admissions, see Kahn, *Harvard through Change and through Storm* (1969), 34–36, and Keller and Keller, *Making Harvard Modern* (2001), 34–35, 293–96.

38. Esty, "Does Financial Aid Come Too Late?" (1961). Moon, "Student Financial Aid in the United States" (1962), 10.

39. Kabaservice, "The Birth of a New Institution" (1999), 32–33. For a complex view of Jews, learning, and occupations, see Slater, "My Son the Doctor" (1969). Amherst's leaflet on "Aid to Transfer Students," 1972, folders on "Admissions and Financial Aid" (Amherst College Archives), gives a medley of social, academic, and market reasons for targeting older community-college students, including veterans. For differing stances on community-college transfers, see Nash et al., "Financial Aid Policies" (1967), I-14, 18, and Steering Committee, Stanford (note 14 above), 66, 68–69.

40. Committee on Admissions and Enrollment, Berkeley Division, Academic Senate, "Freshman Admissions at Berkeley" [Jerome Karabel, Chair], May 19, 1989 (University of California, Berkeley, Archives). University of Michigan Institute of Social Research, "White Institutions' Response to Black Students' Entry: Report on Northwestern University," 1975, in President Robert H. Strotz papers, box 47, folder 1 (Northwestern University Archives). Kabaservice, "'Something Special to Offer'"(2001), 86. Kemeny, "The First Five Years" (1975), 29, 31–32.

41. Williamson and Wild, *Northwestern University* (1976), 322–23, 329, 332–38. Interview, Northwestern University (William Ihlandfeldt). Stanford Steering Committee (note 14 above), esp. 73–74; Committee on Undergraduate Admission and Financial Aid, report for 1976–77, 3 (both in Stanford University Archives). On minorities and admit-deny policies, see Duffy and Goldberg, *Crafting a Class* (1998), 181, and Reports of Office of Financial Aid, June 1969 and Dec. 1973 (Mount Holyoke College Archives). On special programs, Keller and Keller, *Making Harvard Modern* (2001), 276; Patterson and Longsworth, *The Making of a College* (1975), 239–41, and box on "Early Identification Program" (Hampshire College Archives).

42. Duffy and Goldberg, *Crafting a Class* (1998), 151–54. Reuben, "Merit, Mission, and Minority Students" (2001), 224–45. Keller and Keller, *Making Harvard Modern* (2001), 466. Cf. Doermann, *Crosscurrents in College Admissions* (1968), 47, 50.

43. Doermann, *Crosscurrents* (1968), 63–66. LeTendre, "The Working-Class Student at Harvard" (1983). Freeland, *Academia's Golden Age* (1992), 402–3. Also Report for Office of Admissions and Financial Aid to Dean of the Faculty for 1981–82 (Harvard University Admissions and Financial Aid Office).

44. My analysis of data in Cooperative Institutional Research Program, *The American Freshman* (1975), 58, 70; (1980), 71, 87, 94, on father's occupation and education by selectivity level of institution. The same decline did not occur at highly selective public universities. The published data did not go back before 1974 and did not separate low-level white-collar workers or "*very* highly selective" universities. Trends after 1980 were more varied and complex.

8. New Strategies

1. On Oberlin radicalism, see Blodgett, "Oberlin Fever"(1995). On early gender attitudes, Conway, "Perspectives on the History of Women's Education" (1974); Ginzberg, "The Joint Education of the Sexes" (1987). On race, Fletcher, *A History of Oberlin College* (1943), esp. 75–78, 451; Bigglestone, "Oberlin College and the Negro Student" (1971); Brandt, *The Town That Started the Civil War* (1990), chap. 1; Diepenbrock, "Black Women and Oberlin College" (1993); Waite, *Permission to Remain among Us* (2003); Roland Baumann, "Constructing Black Education at Oberlin College: A Documentary History, 1834–2003" (Oberlin College Archives, publication pending). On economic access and openness, see Fallows, "Working One's Way through College" (1901), 174, and Burke, *American Collegiate Populations* (1982), 126–33. Interviews, Oberlin College (Roland Baumann, Geoffrey Blodgett, Andrew Bongiorno, Albert McQueen, Milton Yinger).

2. Bennett, *When Dreams Came True* (1996), 117–20. Baumann (note 1 above), esp. document 16.

3. Comparative Ph.D. surveys by Carol Fuller for Great Lakes Association (1985) and Franklin and Marshall College (1990), cited by Alfred F. MacKay, dean of the college of arts and sciences, in "Academic Quality and Admissions," undated report, ca. 1991 (Oberlin College Archives). In fall 2001, Oberlin enrolled 2,840 students, almost all undergraduates, including 374 in the conservatory and 194 taking double majors in both the conservatory and the College of Arts and Sciences.

4. In its early years Oberlin attracted money from rich slavery abolitionists, but it also fell on good fortune in the late 1920s. From 1929 to after World War II, it had one of the biggest endowments in the country. This was largely due to one alumnus, Charles M. Hall, of a local Oberlin family. The year after he graduated, in 1896, he developed in his family's woodshed an electrical process for producing aluminum. He went on to help found Alcoa. A bequest by Hall in the late 1920s increased Oberlin's endowment sevenfold; the college immediately expanded its operating budget by 50 percent. By 1993, however, Oberlin's endowment per student had fallen behind that of its midwestern competitor Carleton and leading eastern colleges. This was due to overcautious investment decisions in the late 1960s and early 1970s and a traditional tendency for its alumni to become teachers and social-service professionals rather than the corporate rich. J. G. Cowles to John D. Rockefeller, Jr., Nov. 26, 1900, in Board of Trustees, Miscell. History folders; Treasurer's statements for 1925–26, 1929–30; Treasurer's comparison of "Endowments and Plant," 1946–47, in Board of Trustees, Documentary folder for 1949 (all in Oberlin College Archives). See also *Chronicle of Higher Education* (Feb. 4, 1994), A44

ff, for college endowment totals as of June 30, 1993. Interview, Oberlin College (David Clark).

5. Brewer et al., *In Pursuit of Prestige* (2002), 40–41.

6. On student demography and preferences, Breneman, *Liberal Arts Colleges* (1994), 9, 31–32, and Annual Report of the President for 1991–92, by S. Frederick Starr (Oberlin College Archives). The leveling off in "college-age" numbers was offset by an increase in older students, but they were largely concentrated in public colleges and the less-selective private ones.

7. General Faculty Planning Committee, "Discussion of Financial Aid Policy, Budget, and Priorities," Nov. 1, 1993, circular to College of Arts and Sciences Faculty (Oberlin College Archives).

8. Maguire Associates, "Oberlin College: A Marketing Opportunity and Image Analysis," Apr. 1, 1992, vol. 1; twenty-year data in Oberlin College Financial Report for Year Ended June 30, 1991, 87 (all in Oberlin College Archives).

9. Oberlin administrators differ on when the 10 percent addition started and what preceded it, but it antedated the departure of College Board and leading private colleges from the "Federal Methodology" of assessing financial need to a largely less generous formula, though the Ivies had already discontinued it. On Oberlin planning in the 1980s, see Virginia F. Levi to Carl Bewig, "Financial Aid Awards," Admissions Office memo, Dec. 9, 1981; David Davis-Van Atta (Institutional Research) to Acting President James L. Powell, "Comments on a Proposed Administration of Limited Scholarship Funds," Dec. 30, 1981; Carl W. Bewig, Director of Admissions, to Admissions Committee, "Draft Motion," Oct. 17, 1985 (all in Oberlin College Archives). Interviews, Oberlin College (Howard Thomas, James White).

10. "More Full-Paying Students?" *Oberlin College Observer* (1989). Interview, Oberlin College (Ross Peacock). It was later claimed that the plan itself, supplied by college marketing consultants, targeted the wrong populations.

11. The merits debate went back at least to 1981. "Forum: Merit Scholarships at Oberlin?" *Oberlin College Observer* (1981), 2–3. Carl W. Bewig for Committee on Admissions, "Report on No-Need Financial Grants," March 20, 1981 (Oberlin College Archives). See also MacKay, "Private-College Education" (1990), and letters in the *Oberlin Alumni Magazine* (Fall 1990), 1–2.

12. MacKay, "Improving Yield with Merit Scholarships" (1992).

13. My report of attitudes and events from 1993 is partly based on extensive interviews, listed in Appendix 3. I am especially indebted to Ross Peacock (director of institutional research) for many hours of open discussion as well as data. This is not an organizational study of how policies were changed (see my caveat in Appendix 2), but the role of Zinn and his committee was enhanced by Oberlin traditions of faculty involvement and open policy debate, as well as widespread

distrust of President S. Frederick Starr, a brilliant but difficult man. He left office in 1994.

14. On "early decision" admissions, see glossary (Appendix 4) and Eric Hoover, "New Attacks on Early Decision" (2002).

15. Riccardi, "Trustees Split on Painful Budget"(1993). On the changes, see Ganzel "College Changes Financial-Aid Policy" (1993).

16. Howell, "Race Issues Are Important, but Class Issues Can't Be Ignored" (1993). Subsequent student press articles raised the class issue too but less intensively than about minorities.

17. Debra Chermonte, dean of admissions and financial aid, "Admissions and Financial Aid Report to the Board of Trustees," Sept. 25, 2001 (Oberlin College Archives). In 1991 and 2001, just over 17 percent of Oberlin students were low-income Pell grant recipients, a percentage putting it in the top three on that criterion in both years among twenty-five liberal colleges given the highest quality ratings by *U.S. News and World Report.* More than half of the other colleges, including several with high numbers of Pell grants, increased their Pell percentages; Oberlin's slightly fell. These comparisons hold when foreign students, not eligible for Pell, are taken out. Basic data in *Journal of Blacks in Higher Education,* "Pell Grants as a Measure of Student Diversity" (2002). According to one Oberlin administrator, the need-aware policy decreased the number of lower-middle-income rather than low-income students because of admissions decisions.

18. Unlike many other colleges, Oberlin did not "front-load" aid, giving freshmen more grant aid and a lighter loan burden. In 2001–02 its standard loan "expectation" of $4,000 per year was higher for aided freshmen and sophomores but lower for juniors and seniors than the median at Oberlin's fellow elite colleges in the Consortium on Financing Higher Education (COFHE). Consortium on Financing Higher Education, *Tuition, Student Budgets, and Self-Help* (2001), Tables 7, 8A. Oberlin's merit scholarships, some tilted to minorities, replaced preferential packaging, but the college negotiated some better financial aid deals individually for strong and demanding admits.

19. McPherson and Schapiro, "The Future Economic Challenges for the Liberal Arts Colleges" (1999).

20. See esp. Clotfelter, *Buying the Best* (1996); Ehrenberg, *Tuition Rising* (2000). Vedder, *Going Broke by Degree* (2004), gives the widest-ranging and most provocative explanations of college cost and price inflation, though his research and analysis have many gaps: see chaps. 1-4.

21. On trends from the 1970s, Baum, "Access, Choice, and the Middle Class" (1994); Clotfelter, *Buying* (1996), 1–9; Ehrenberg, *Tuition* (2000), chap. 1. Consortium, *Tuition, Budgets, and Self-Help* (2001), showed continued elite-college

tuition rises above income increases for the "college-parent" age group (forty-five to fifty-four): 12.

22. Clotfelter, *Buying* (1996), separated out the elite COFHE group of colleges: 250. See also Ehrenburg, *Tuition* (2000), 81–82. On family size, see Cook and Frank, "The Economic Payoff of Attending an Ivy League Institution" (1996). On upper-class parents, Toor, "Pushy Parents" (2000); Skinner, "Designer Parents" (2000); Flanaghan, "Confessions of a Prep School College Counselor" (2001). See also Gladieux, "Low-Income Students and the Affordability of Higher Education" (2004), 36, on different causes of public- and private-college price increases.

23. Clotfelter, *Buying* (1996), 12–13, 52–53, 73–74, 146–47, 150. McPherson and Schapiro, *The Student Aid Game* (1998), 68. Archibald, *Redesigning the Financial Aid System* (2002), claimed that college grant aid increases led to greater tuition increases, but his statistics fit the reverse just as well: chap. 5.

24. Dog analogy from Robert Atwell, president of the American Council on Education, quoted in Duffy and Greenberg, *Crafting a Class* (1998), 194, and repeated to me in interviews. See also Werth, "Why Is College So Expensive?" (1988); Hauptman, "Why Are College Charges Rising?" (1989); and Breneman, *Liberal Arts Colleges* (1994), reporting such anxieties going back to the 1970s: 26. Even when measured against consumer prices in general, not inflated college charges, maximum Pell grants in 1995–96 had fallen by 25 percent from 1980–81, 40 percent from 1975–76. Other federal grants fell even more. St. John, *Refinancing the College Dream* (2003), 19, 20. My percentage calculations.

25. Clotfelter, *Buying* (1996), 4. Redd, "Discounting toward Disaster" (2000), 17. Redd showed that about a quarter of private colleges—mostly unselective ones—between 1990 and 1997 increased their grant-aid discounts to the point of reducing their net tuition revenue per student. For many unselective liberal arts colleges, freshman enrollment declined, especially among high-income students, who could most afford full tuition. McPherson and Schapiro, "The Future Economic Challenges for the Liberal Arts Colleges" (1999). In effect, therefore, the most vulnerable colleges cut their net prices.

26. National Association and College Board, *The Financial Aid Profession at Work* (2000), 7; *Financial Aid Professionals* (2002), 23–25. The early 1990s recession had ended by 1993. The estimates of financial need used the federal method, which often gives a higher "need" figure than the College Scholarship Service method. But the survey included unsubsidized student and parent loans as aid; many selective private colleges do not. Data showing higher unmet need for lower-income students are in Archibald, *Redesigning the Financial Aid System* (2002), 3, 60, and Fitzgerald, "Missed Opportunity" (2004), 12. Their data slightly exaggerate unmet need by not including student jobs paid for by colleges themselves (as opposed to federal work-study payments).

27. McPherson and Schapiro (1998), *The Student Aid Game*, 31–32. Jerry Sheehan Davis, "College Affordability" (2000), 13. U.S. Dept. of Education, *What Students Pay for College* (Sept. 2002), esp. v–vi, 10, 41–43. On more-progressive trends in the 1970s, see McPherson and Schapiro, *Keeping College Affordable* (1991), 35, 36. At both private and public four-year colleges in the mid to late 1990s, net costs of going to college declined, especially for low-income students. This seems to contradict other findings that richer students' aid increased the most over roughly the same period. My speculative explanation: although rising tuitions continued to qualify richer students for need-related aid and there was more spending on merits in addition to need-related aid, lower-income students were concentrated at less-selective private colleges, which made the biggest increases in price-discounting, and working-class students shifted from highly selective state universities to lower-tuition state universities and colleges. Data in Cooperative Institutional Research, *The American Freshman* (1992, 2000), tables on father's educational level and occupation by selectivity and type of institution.

28. On "entitlement" versus sacrifice, see Kurz, "The Changing Role of Financial Aid and Enrollment Management" (1995), 29. Cf. Lasch, *The Culture of Narcissism* (1979); Horowitz, *Campus Life* (1987), chap. 12; Ehrenreich, *Fear of Falling* (1989); Sanders and Henson, "Financial Aid in 2010" (2000), 23–24.

29. Appendix 1.

30. Cf. . Delbanco, "The Struggle of All against All" (2002). Also Monks and Ehrenberg, "The Impact of *U.S. News and World Report* College Rankings" (1999). Among colleges generally in the 1980s and 1990s, students made multiple applications to more and more colleges, lowering colleges' yield rates (proportions of admission offers accepted). This drove colleges to more intensive recruiting. Eric Hoover, "The Changing Environment for College Admissions" (2002).

31. On the nature of enrollment management, see Scannell, *The Effect of Financial Aid Policies on Admission and Enrollment* (1992), 31–32; Dixon, *Making Enrollment Management Work* (1995), 5; Hossler, "How Enrollment Management Has Transformed—or Ruined—Higher Education" (2004). For specimens of how its thinking evolved, see William Frank Elliott, "Management of Admissions and Financial Aid" (1974); Ihlandfeldt, *Achieving Optimal Enrollments and Tuition Revenues* (1981), esp. chap. 6; and Scannell above (1992). The term "leveraging," borrowed from business finance, often refers to levering *money*, but enrollment consultants to colleges have sometimes used it more widely to mean levering *students*, based on "yield analysis" of what aid it takes to attract them.

32. Stephen R. Lewis, "Ensuring Access, Strengthening Institutions" (1995), 12. Steinberg, *The Gatekeepers* (2002), 258. Toor, *Admissions Confidential* (2001), esp. 209–12, on tensions at Duke about "development admits."

33. I know of no recent or systematic report of the number of highly selective private colleges that are need-blind/need-met. Thirty was the estimate of an informed source in the COFHE in 2002; it included four or five colleges that go need-aware when admitting from their waiting list and also included colleges that are need-aware in admitting foreign students. A 1994 survey across all colleges found that under 10 percent reported need-aware admissions; they were nearly all private and tended to be higher-tuition. National Association of College Admission Counselors, "Executive Summary" (1994), 5–8.

34. Betsy White, "The Policy of Admission"(1992–93). Woodcock, "The Evolution of Need Aware Admission and Financial Aid Policies at Brown University" (1997). Brown's choice of need-aware admissions (it did meet all need) was a matter of policy preference as well as economics. It often cited its low endowment and small amount of endowed scholarships, compared to other Ivies, but its total endowment *per student* was above that of Cornell and Penn. Its officials defensively accused other Ivies of covert need-aware practices, and I found the administration unusually resistant to revealing its federally filed Fiscal Operations Report and Application to Participation (FISAP) data on aided students' family incomes (see Appendix 2). In the 1990s, well under 40 percent of Brown's undergraduates were on grant aid, less than at the other Ivies, but it reached out to inner-city schools and was dedicated to class equity in the way it allocated aid.

35. Mulvihull, "Competition Also at Odds over Aid" (1993). Interviews, Amherst College (Joe Case, Peter Pouncey); Wesleyan (Donald Moon). At both colleges, the issues were mainly about admitting need-aware when it came to taking applicants from the admissions waiting list.

36. "Under 20 percent" is my inference from colleges' FISAP data: see Appendix 2. The displaced percentage of *enrolled* students is probably higher than for admits, as students at the low end of a college's admits are more likely to accept an admissions offer, having less choice of comparable colleges. The term "low-income" is more often used than defined in the educational press. For high-tuition colleges since 1990, I count as "low income" a family income under the national median, about $42,000 in the late 1990s, which was well under the $60,000 median for families with "householders" aged forty-five to fifty-four (the age of most parents of dependent college students). Some studies, however, use "low-income" to mean the poorest quarter or third of students, or Pell grant recipients (with family incomes usually under $35,000 since 2000).

37. Interviews, University of Chicago, Clark University, Knox College, Mount Holyoke College.

38. NACAC Member Communiqué (National Association of College Admission Counselors, Alexandria, VA, Nov. 1995). Interview, NACAC (Mary Lee Hoganson).

39. Director of Financial Aid, Reports to the President, Jan. 30, 1970, and Dec. 3, 1973 (Mount Holyoke College Archives).

40. Stephen R. Lewis, "Ensuring Access, Strengthening Institutions" (1995). Gose, "A College Sees Benefits in Admissions Policy That Considers Families' Ability to Pay" (1997).

41. Massa, "Merit Scholarships and Student Recruitment" (1991). Scannell, *The Effect of Financial Aid Policies* (1992), 44–45. Masters, "Area Colleges Turn Student Aid into Bait" (1994). A research proposal for Columbia's Bureau of Applied Social Research briefly suggested a revenue motive as early as 1954: John Usher Monro papers, box on College Scholarship Service Correspondence, Sept. 1954 (Harvard University Archives; no author given). However, against the widespread operating assumption that merits tend to go to students with little or no need, the National Postsecondary Student Aid Survey for 1995–96 indicated that at *higher-tuition* private colleges (above $14,665), middle- and low-income students got more merit aid per student than upper-middle- or upper-income students. It is not clear, though, whether the reported merit amounts actually included need-based aid that merit receivers also got. Tables in McPherson and Schapiro, "The Blurring Line between Merit and Need" (2002), esp. 43. Michael S. McPherson, e-mail correspondence with author, April 19–20, 2002.

42. Duffy and Greenberg, *Crafting a Class* (1998), 205–6. National Association and College Board, *The Financial Aid Profession at Work* (2000), 52–53. National Association of Student Financial Aid Administrators, news release, "2001 SU-FAPPP Results" (Washington, DC: May 12, 2002). The college response rate, however, was only 30 percent for the 2001 SUFAPPP (Survey of Financial Aid Policies, Practices, and Procedures).

43. McPherson and Schapiro, *The Student Aid Game* (1998), 105. U.S. Dept. of Education, *What Students Pay for College* (2002), 6–10. Eames, "Financial Aid Policy Development" (2002), 330–31, 334–35.

44. Duffy and Greenberg, *Crafting* (1998), chap. 7. A source in the elite COFHE association of colleges estimated that 19 of its 31 members, plus 10–15 other private colleges, gave only need-related grant aid in 2002. About 10 percent of four-year colleges gave no merits in the early to mid 1990s, but most of these were probably low-tuition state colleges. National Association of College Admission Counselors, "Report" (1994), 14. National Association and College Board, *Financial Aid Profession* (2000), 52; (2002), 19–20. A recent study of college pricing wrongly portrays Columbia and Northwestern as giving academic merits, though the author is a Northwestern alumnus! Vedder, *Going Broke by Degree* (2004), 71–72.

45. Winston, "Subsidies, Hierarchy, and Peers" (1999), 19. Ehrenberg, *Tuition Rising* (2000), 10–11.

46. In support of state merits, the seventeenth-century notion that scholarships should not subsidize those who left the colonies has joined up with the nineteenth-century idea that merits could motivate better work in the schools. Both ideas found new expression when state economic development seemed to depend more and more on nurturing and retaining "human capital." Still most direct state spending on student aid has remained need-related, despite big regional differences (merits are strong in the South). There has been some argument as to whether state merits have depleted assistance to low-income and minority students, whether they develop talent and keep it for long in the state, and what income groups pay most for them as taxpayers and state lottery players. Healy, "HOPE Scholarships Transform the University of Georgia" (1997). Selingo, "For Fans of Merit Scholarships: A Cautionary Tale" (1999), "Questioning the Merit of Merit Scholarships" (2001), and "Researchers Square Off on State-Based Merit Scholarships"(2002). Longanecker, "Is Merit-Based Student Aid Really Trumping Need-Based Aid?" (2002). Heller, "State Aid and Student Access" (2002). Grant aid given by state colleges themselves is about three-quarters as much as direct state grant aid. Doyle et al., "Institutions Amplifying State Policy" (2004), show that where states give more merits in relation to need-related aid, public colleges tend to do the same with their own aid. The authors assume without evidence that the colleges simply imitate their respective states' policies.

47. These notes do not cite numerous articles written on merits in this period, but see the exchange in *Change* between Haines, "Wrong for Society, Wrong for Institutions" (1984), and Jones, "Merit Aid Is an Investment for American Leadership" (1984). Some pros and cons of merits are also summed up by Finn, "Why Do We Need Financial Aid?" (1985), 15–17; Archibald, *Redesigning the Financial Aid System* (2002), 82–86; and Eames, "Financial Aid Policy Development" (2002), 66–67. The discussion that follows is adapted from Wilkinson, "Quarreling about Merits" (2004).

48. Supporters of attaching merits to special programs include enrollment directors who don't really like merits and seek to rescue them with program "enhancement." The nearest I have heard to Alison Antimerit's criticism is the position taken by Mount Holyoke students and faculty in 2000–01. Given a choice between introducing straight merits and creating merits with special academic "experienceships," they chose the former—and prevailed. Reflecting an old Mount Holyoke value on community, they saw the latter as "divisive" and "elitist."

49. On budget threats, see King, "Financial Thresholds to College" (1957); Robert K. Durkee and Peter Berek, letters to editor, *Chronicle of Higher Education* (Feb. 7, 1990); Chase, "Trouble in River City" (2000); Redd, "Discounting

toward Disaster" (2000); Winston and Zimmerman, "Where Is Aggressive Price Competition Taking Higher Education?"(2000).

50. Eames, "Financial Aid Policy Development" (2002), 66–67, 135, 250–51.

51. McPherson and Schapiro, *Keeping College Affordable* (1991), 149–52, "Merit Aid: Students, Institutions, and Society." (1994), and *The Student Aid Game* (1998), 109–15. Almost none of my many interviewees in admissions and financial aid seemed to know of this argument. Baum and Schwartz, "Merit Aid to College Students" (1988) presented a more regressive model in which merits displaced talented *needy* students downwards.

52. Arenson, "To Raise Its Image, CUNY Pays for Top Students" (2002). Selingo, "Mission Creep" (2002).

53. U.S. Dept. of Education, "What Students Pay for College" (2002), 9. In 1999–2000, an estimated 58 percent of private-college students receiving non-need-based college grants had financial need, based on the relatively generous federal methodology for assessing need. National Association of Student Financial Aid Administrators, "Highlights of the 2001 SUFAPPP," research news release (Washington, DC: Sept. 3, 2002).

54. For differing views of this, see Gose, "Colleges Turn to 'Leveraging'" (1996); Baum, "Equity and Enrollment Management" (2000).

55. On widespread use of preferential packaging, see McPherson and Schapiro, "The Blurring Line between Merit and Need" (2002). Preferential packaging usually assumes a reduced loan burden, not reduced work earnings, but in fact the individual student has some choice.

56. This generally applies, though some preferential awards carry honorific names like merits, especially ones introduced in the 1990s by colleges that did not have merits (e.g. Smith's Dunn Scholars' awards and Penn's Trustee Scholars).

57. National Association of College Admission Counselors, "Executive Summary" (1994), 11–12.

58. National Association, "Report on the Results of the Membership Survey" (1994), 14. It is not clear whether the 29 percent for lower-income students included aid favoring *middle*-income over high-income students. About 4 percent of private colleges reported preferential packaging for first-generation college students. Ethnicity was the top reason at public colleges. The survey's response rate for all colleges was only 44 percent, less than the 51 percent obtained by a 1996–97 survey that also found academically based preferential packaging to be the commonest kind. National Association and College Board, *The Financial Aid Profession at Work* (2000), 44.

59. McPherson and Schapiro, "The Blurring Line" (2002), esp. 40, 43, 45. On elite trends, Consortium, *Tuition, Student Budget, and Self-Help* (annual from 1982), tables on "self-help."

60. Ehrenberg, *Tuition Rising* (2000), 86–88. Consortium (note 59 above). Inter-

views, Harvard University, University of Pennsylvania, Yale University. In the late 1960s, Stanford, an increasingly strong competitor against the Ivies, started limiting its academic preferential packaging to a more select few, at least partly on the grounds that it could distinguish these more clearly and fairly. Steering Committee, "Study of Education at Stanford, "1968, Report 4; Committee on Undergraduate Admission and Financial Aid, Report for 1976–1977 (all in Stanford University Archives). Interview, Stanford University (Robert Huff).

61. Interviews, Smith College, Wheaton College.

62. Extra loan requirements usually entail a "double loan"—a standard federal Stafford loan and a Perkins loan (federal but allocated by the college). Colleges giving merit scholarships to students with financial need often fold them regressively into preferential packaging: the merit is applied against the student's need-based grant so that only a lower-need student whose need-based grant is less than the merit gets added money from the merit.

63. Data from Ross Peacock (Institutional Research, Oberlin) and Prof. Michael Robinson (Economics Dept., Mount Holyoke). See Gose, "Changes at Elite Colleges" (1999) on uneasiness at Swarthmore about new preferential packaging. Interviews, Swarthmore College.

64. There is not space here to review the diverse biases and issues involved in favoring specific fields, talents, and home-state residence or college tuition assistance for faculty and staff. Ihlandfeldt, *Achieving Optimal Enrollments and Tuition Revenues* (1981), 112–13. Gose, "Colleges Turn to 'Leveraging'" (1996).

65. On phases in minority admissions, see Duffy and Greenberg, *Crafting a Class* (1998), chap. 5, and Reuben, "Merit, Mission, and Minority Students"(2001).

66. On Hispanics, Flint, "The Influence of Job Prospects on Student Debt Levels" (1998), 10, 17–19.

67. On federal restriction of state minority scholarships, see Jaschik, "Department Tells How Colleges Must Justify Minority Scholarships" (1994); Healy, "Education Department Sends Strong Warning on Race-Exclusive Scholarships" (1997); Lederman, "University Alters Minority Scholarships" (1997). The Constitution (Article I, Section 8) has in effect protected state and federal scholarships for Native Americans by recognizing them as special, treaty-making tribal entities. On scholarships and effective anti-affirmative-action pressures at private Washington University in Missouri, see *Chronicle of Higher Education*, Almanac issue (Aug. 27, 2004), 67.

68. Interviews, Oberlin College, Smith College. Smith's effort included three merit scholarships for disadvantaged schools in Springfield, Mass. Oberlin's president Nancy Dye continued to support minority preferences at the admissions stage, for "educational diversity and to . . . redress inequalities." Letter to *Oberlin Alumni Magazine* (Winter 2002–03).

69. Interviews, Stanford University. In the late 1990s, Stanford's categories of ex-

pected self-help levels (loan and job), as reported in elite colleges' annual "Yellow Book," dropped minorities as an officially favored category but retained a low-income category and started referring briefly to a Special Recognition category. Consortium, *Tuition, Student Budgets, and Self-Help* (1996, 2000), Table 10. On California, see Healy, "U of California to Admit Top 4% from Every High School" (1999), and Peter Schmidt, "U of California Ends Affirmative-Action Ban" (2001).

70. Elite-college data in Consortium (note 69 above), compared with the national college surveys (note 58 above). The 1996 survey found more differential packaging than minority packaging among private colleges generally, but its questionnaire about differential packaging did not clearly confine it to reductions of expected self-help, as opposed to simply giving more grant aid to poorer students on the basis of need. National Association and College Board, *The Financial Aid Profession at Work* (2000), 44–45 and appendix p. 5.

71. Press releases from Princeton University Office of Communications, Jan. 1998 and Jan. 2001. Gose, "Princeton Plans Major Increase in Aid for Middle- and Low-Income Students" (1998).

72. In June 1997, Princeton's endowment of $4.94 billion was fourth after Harvard, the University of Texas, and Yale, but Princeton had far fewer students and, comparatively, even fewer graduate students. Its endowment per student was approximately $784,000 per student, compared with Harvard's $609,000. My calculations using "Fact File: 495 College and University Endowments," *Chronicle of Higher Education* (Feb. 20, 1998), A49.

73. Interviews, Princeton University. See Part III on results.

74. Crenshaw, "Finding a Way through the College Aid Maze" (1994), gives an unusually clear account, with a chart, of how income and assets were supposedly "taxed" before the changes by Princeton and others.

75. Gose, "Recent Shifts on Aid by Elite Colleges" (1998). Brownstein, "Upping the Ante for Student Aid" (2001). Also various press releases from Brown, Dartmouth, Harvard, Stanford, Yale, 1998 and 2001. An added concession at many elite colleges was letting students keep all scholarship money given them directly by outside donors without subtracting any of it from their college grants.

76. A common method is to put some grant money into a student's aid package before filling in the rest of the student's need with self-help and further grants.

77. Stecklow, "Colleges Manipulate Financial-Aid Offers" (1996). Interviews, Bowdoin College, Guilford College, University of Hartford, Maguire Associates, Mount Holyoke College, University of Rochester, Wheaton College. Since 2001, even the College Board has marketed a data-processing "Financial Aid Strategy Tool" (FAST) that helps colleges predict the admissions "yield" of different grant-aid offers to different kinds of students and the effects on student

"quality," "diversity," and "revenue." But yield-based discounting does not always work against poorer students. Colleges that, controversially, give less grant aid to the most interested applicants on the grounds that they need less inducement may reduce aid to those who visit the campus, and these tend to be richer students who can afford to do campus tours. A few state universities do yield-based discounting, especially when their tuition income comes directly back to them rather than going to the state. Here, too, a policy can favor lower-income students. In the late 1990s the University of Colorado, Boulder, found that it increased yield and net tuition revenue when it altered its preferential packaging for high-GPA out-of-state students so that those with low need got less extra grant and those with high-need got more. Lou McClelland, "1997–98 Financial Aid Experiment" (University of Colorado Student Affairs Research Services, Jan. 6, 1999). As public colleges come to depend more on tuition-fee income, enrollment consultants are promoting their use of yield-based pricing and aid. See Kurz and Scannell, "How Should Public Colleges Price Their Product?" (2004).

9. Containing the Market

1. College Board, "A Report on the College Board Colloquium" (1997). At College Board's National Forum, Oct.–Nov. 2000, speakers at the panel session "A Delicate Balance: Financial Aid Modeling and Institutional Values" expressed a range of guilt, heroic anguish, and aggressive defensiveness. Taped session T-12, Oct. 31, New York. My interview research did not systematically tap for and quantify expressions of ambivalence and discomfort. I do not claim that most of my interviewees in admissions and financial aid (Appendix 3) clearly expressed those feelings, but they recurred often enough to be noteworthy.

2. The "Statement of Ethical Principles" on the National Association of Student Financial Aid Administrators (NASFAA) Web site declares that the financial aid professional's "primary goal" should be to "help students achieve their educational potential by providing appropriate financial resources." It goes on to stress the importance of removing "financial barriers" to college and the assistance of students with financial need. An earlier NASFAA statement in the 1990s urged that merit aid, where substantial, should be targeted on needy students. A transition from this ethos to one that views colleges as businesses can be seen in Scannell, *The Effect of Financial Aid on Admission and Enrollment* (1992). The author, at the time a college enrollment manager and now an enrollment consultant, respectfully quotes College Board's strictly need-based financial aid "Principles" before laying out with gusto the arithmetic of leveraging and the realities that drive it.

3. Toor, *Admissions Confidential* (2001). "The Challenged Integrity of the Admis-

sions Process," taped panel session M-13, College Board National Forum, Oct. 30, 2000, New York.

4. See McPherson and Schapiro, "The End of the Student Aid Era?" (2001), 352–33, on the lack of middle-class or rich "melt" at these colleges in the 1980s and 1990s. Redd, "Discounting toward Disaster" (2000), shows that students poor enough to qualify for federal Pell grants ranged from 24 percent to 12 percent at private colleges in 1996–97 according to college selectivity: 15.

5. At selective colleges in the 1980s and 1990s, responsiveness to increased grant aid tended to be greater for lower-income students, controlling for academic ability, but was also greater for strong academic students, controlling for income. Not all studies, however, agreed on all these results. Ehrenberg and Sherman, "Optimal Financial Aid Policies for a Selective University" (1984), esp. 217–18n, 224. Moore et al., "The Effect of the Financial Aid Package on the Choice of a Selective College" (1991), esp. 311, 315–16, 320 n. 7.

6. Finn, "Why Do We Need Financial Aid?" (1985), 6–8. Less discussed is the leeway colleges have in estimating students' living -costs over and above fixed charges.

7. E.g., Davis and Kennedy, *College Financial Aid for Dummies* (1997), esp. chap. 8.

8. "Request a Review of Your Financial Aid Package," Carnegie Mellon University Office of Admission, 1999. Elliott to author, Nov. 8, Nov. 29, 1999, e-mails, and phone, Aug. 15, 2002.

9. The Ivies did this competing more than MIT or the small-college overlap group. Interviews, Amherst College, MIT, Yale University. Harr, "The Admissions Circus" (1984).

10. My interviews repeatedly found this, even at state universities. An Ivy counsel affirmed to me the factor of legal uncertainty. The MIT-Justice settlement and the legislation required need-blind admissions as a demonstration of good faith that colleges were consulting on aid for social and educational purposes and not just doing it as a form of business price-fixing. The settlement actually required that cooperating colleges meet all need too, but the legislation dropped that. The need-blind proviso included students admitted from admissions waiting lists, but not foreign students. See Appendix 1 on the settlement and legislation.

11. Putka, "Arithmetic on College Aid Varies Widely" (1993). Massa, "Financial Aid in Selective Colleges" (1995), 4. College Scholarship Service, *The History of Need Analysis* (1993), gives a chronology of need-analysis methodologies. Prior to FM, the federal government and colleges had more similar assessments of financial need, though the Ivies had already evolved their own. In 1996, over 60 percent of private four-year and over 90 percent of state colleges used FM to allocate their own ("institutional") aid. National Association and College Board, *The*

Financial Aid Profession at Work (2000), 33–34. But the highly selective private colleges I visited after 1992 almost all used IM or their own version of it.

12. Both phrases were probably coined by James Miller, dean of admission and financial aid at Bowdoin, formerly director of financial aid at Harvard. Nothing, of course, is entirely new. Through the seventeenth century, and perhaps later, colleges sometimes exaggerated the neediness of ministers' children; they assumed that "church mice" were poor as well as deserving.

13. A survey found no increase in reported "negotiation" (review of aid offers after queries or challenges) among private colleges as a whole between 1988 and 1996, and a sequel survey in 1999–2000 found that even fewer private-college financial aid officers said they altered aid in response to competitive offers: 2 percent, down from 19 percent in 1995–96. National Association and College Board, *Financial Aid Profession* (2000), 47–51; *Financial Aid Professionals* (2002), 11–12. Though the earlier report said that more-selective colleges did less negotiation, I believe that, among top colleges, competitive offers were increasingly masked by "new information." In the 1999–2000 survey, 46 percent of private-college financial aid offices said they reviewed their aid offers when applicants appealed against them, and half increased the awards after "professional judgment" reviews. My interviewees at highly selective colleges (and a few prep schools) reported an increasing variety of supposedly need-based offers to the same students in the 1990s. Hoxby, "Benevolent Colluders?" (2000), found a decreased correlation between grant aid and family income among overlap colleges after the overlap cooperation ended, though aid to low-income students did not fall, and the change might have reflected increased preferential packaging rather than "negotiation": see esp. 28. Colleges in a control group of highly selective, well-endowed non-overlap colleges showed no change. A more recent study indicated that about 15 percent of high-GPA high school applicants for aid at highly selective colleges reported getting their aid offers revised—almost always for grant increases of less than a thousand dollars over four years. Avery and Hoxby, "Do and Should Financial Aid Packages Affect Students' College Choices?" (2003), 8, 9, 12, 14. The authors' numbers were less than my interviewees indicated. See also Steinberg in note 14 below.

14. Interviews, Harvard University, Yale University. "Special Announcement" in Schools and Scholarship Committee, Chairperson's Newsletter, April 1998; "College Admission Yield Rises . . . ," Harvard-Radcliffe *Gazette*, May 14, 1998 (Harvard-Radcliffe Office of Admissions and Financial Aid). Steinberg, *The Gatekeepers* (2002), gives a vivid account of a star applicant and the overlap between "new information" and competitive bidding, in this case by Yale and Harvard against Stanford, involving offered grant increases ranging from $1,500 to $6,500: 204–6, 243–49.

15. Massa, "Financial Aid in Selective Colleges" (1995), 4.

16. Russo, "The Financial Aid Professional: An Endangered Species?" (1995), esp. 42. College Board, "A Report on the College Board Colloquium" (1997). Monks, "Is This the Beginning of the End of Need-Based Aid?" (2000). McPherson and Schapiro, "The Blurring Line between Merit and Need" (2002), 45.

17. Quotations from College Scholarship Service, "CSS Council Resolution: Independent Methodology" (New York: College Board, 1999). Scannell, "Development of Optimal Financial Aid Strategies" (1980), heralded a modern wave of criticism of need analysis for being insensitive to middle-income families.

18. Crenshaw, "Finding a Way through the College Aid Maze"(1994). Feldstein, "College Scholarship Rules and Private Savings" (1995).

19. On community and four fears in American history, Wilkinson, *The Pursuit of American Character* (1988), chaps. 4–6.

20. Clayton Spencer, "Antitrust Exemption for Need-Based Financial Aid: Extension of 'Section 568,'" briefing memo, 2 (Harvard University President's Office, June 11, 1997).

21. Section 568 was part of the Improving America's Schools Act (1994): see Appendix 1. The CSS revision, too, was led by officials of colleges legally qualified to consult, but it had further legal protection in that CSS, which supplied important staff work, was a separate entity from the colleges as an arm of College Board. It did not represent just one group of competing colleges.

22. Virtually all New IM revisions were backed by arguments stressing what was reasonable and fair. In the siblings case, the committee argued that, regardless of spacing, families usually financed college from past as well as current income and assets. The revisions also protected richer families from what, under old IM, seemed a double jeopardy in which high income, heavily "taxed" already, triggered extra high tax rates on assets.

23. I have used the following CSS papers from College Board, New York: "The New Institutional Methodology: Bridging the Needs of Families and Institutions," Fall 1998, and Jan. 1999 drafts, with joint cover letters to colleges by Donald A. Saleh, chair, CSS Council (dean of admission and financial aid, Cornell) and Edwin G. Below, chair, CSS Financial Aid Standards and Services Advisory Committee. CSS Council Resolution, " Institutional Methodology," 1999. The second New IM draft incorporated feedback from colleges, especially concerned with counterbalance for low-income students. I am indebted to Kathleen Little (College Board) for a detailed question-and-answer e-mail about the revisions, July 15, 1999. Interviews, Amherst College (Joe Case), Pomona College (Patricia Coye).

24. My sources include two memos of 1998 and 1999 from a COFHE presidents' "Working Group on Financial Aid," a precursor to the 568 group.

25. On "568," see note 21 above and Appendix 1. The twenty-eight institutions were Amherst, Boston College, Bowdoin, Chicago, Claremont McKenna, Colum-

bia, Cornell, Davidson, Duke, Emory, Georgetown, Haverford, Macalester, MIT, Middlebury, Northwestern, Notre Dame, Pennsylvania, Pomona, Rice, Stanford, Swarthmore, Vanderbilt, Wake Forest, Wellesley, Wesleyan, Williams, and Yale. Harvard and Princeton did not join, on the grounds that their aid was already more generous than the 568 group's formulas. Arenson, "Leading Colleges Adopt New Guidelines" (2001).

26. Press release, "Group of 28 university presidents affirm commitment to financial aid based on need," July 6, 2001 (Cornell University News Office). Report of the Common Standards Subcommittee to the 568 Presidents' Working Group, June 2001 (Cornell University President's Office). For background, see Arenson, "Leading Colleges" (2001) and Burd, "Private Colleges Seek Antitrust Exemption for Aid Talks" (2001). Interviews, Consortium on Financing Higher Education (Ted Bracken), Williams College (Harry Payne).

27. Arenson, "Leading Colleges" (2001).

28. Justifications for factoring home equity into EFC are that it reflects a family's financial strength and can often provide cash through a second mortgage or home-equity credit line. On the other hand, the report recognized that it is still an illiquid asset: you can't just sell off a chimney to pay some college costs. The 568 group also introduced adjustments for different family living costs across the country.

29. See Conway, *A Woman's Education* (2001), 110.

30. Asinof, "Colleges Clamp Down on Financial Aid" (2002). A wire-service article in June 2004 implied that the IM revisions did not have a wide influence on colleges generally. Citing a study by Harvard's Susan Dynarski, the author, Janet Kidd Stewart, stressed that saving for college (still) often reduced a student's financial aid. The article mainly criticized federal need analysis, but it included financial aid at the "360 best colleges." Some of them may have used FM rather than IM for their own aid (see note 11 above), but no mention was made of the IM revisions. Stewart, "Save a Lot for College? Expect to Pay More" (2004).

31. Carstensen, "Colleges and Student Aid" (2001).

32. *Talk of the Nation,* National Public Radio, July 17, 2001.

Part III. Reforming the System

1. Late-1980s data showed that elite private colleges tended to give no admissions preference to lower-income students among their high-test-score applicants. McPherson and Schapiro, *Keeping College Affordable* (1991), 92, table. Even where selective colleges do not preferentially package aid for minorities, admissions and enrollment directors have told me that poor non-Hispanic whites, as a constituency, come after academic stars, athletes, alumni "legacies," and

minorities. When this book was in press, William Bowen *et al* published similar findings in *Equity and Excellence* (University of Virginia Press).

2. See Katz, *The Price of Citizenship* (2001), on the capitalist "marketization" of welfare.

3. Comments in interviews. See also chap. 5, note 26 above, quoting Charles Francis Adams, Jr., in 1905. It is sometimes argued, wrongly in my view, that charging rich students more than poorer ones is not a "Robin Hood" transfer from rich to poor because all students at most colleges are subsidized by college endowment and gift income and/or state appropriations (in the case of state colleges). Cf. Strosnider, "A University Relies on Its Endowment to Cover the Costs of Financial Aid" (1998). At most private colleges today, however, the college's general revenue, including tuition revenue, funds some need-related student aid. So richer students, paying higher tuition fees, are helping to pay for the education of poorer students. At state colleges, the issue is more complicated as it involves the distribution of state taxes (between richer and poorer families, and college and noncollege families) that pay the state-appropriation subsidies to colleges. Robin Hood operates where richer families pay higher state taxes and state tuition in toto.

4. Cf. Johnstone, *Sharing the Costs of Higher Education* (1985), 147, graphs. Today Canada's leading universities (public) come close to the in-state tuition of America's leading state universities. A comparison of Canadian and U.S. tuition and aid policies, and their funding, would be very useful.

5. Woodhall, "Human Capital Concepts" (1987), 21–22, citing the landmark works of Theodore Schultz and Gary Becker. See also Leslie and Brinkman, *The Economic Value of Higher Education* (1988), 5–7, citing precursor studies published by J. R. Walsh in 1938 and Jacob Minur in 1958.

6. Institute for Higher Education Policy, *The Policy of Choice* (2003), 15.

7. Ralph H. Turner, "Modes of Ascent through Education" (1960), expounded a somewhat similar concept of "sponsored mobility" though he applied it too crudely to the British school system as opposed to the American. See also William Julius Wilson, *The Truly Disadvantaged* (1987), chap. 5, on affirmative action.

8. The best estimate was 80 percent.

9. Report of the Summer Working Group 2000 for the Ada Comstock Scholars Program, Dec. 12, 2000, esp. 18 (copy from Association of Low-Income Students, Smith College). Consortium, *Tuition, Student Budgets, and Self-Help* (1996, 2001), tables on "self-help expectations by admissions ratings." Interviews, Smith College.

10. On inequality, see Mishel et al., *The State of Working America* (2001), 386, 396–97; "Would You Like Your Class War Shaken or Stirred, Sir?" *Economist* (2003), 47, table. Comparative-mobility findings vary according to method and

to types of mobility: movement between income levels, between occupational classes, within a lifetime, and between generations. Erickson and Goldthorpe, *The Constant Flux* (1992), chaps. 1, 6, 9. Solon, "Cross-Country Differences in Intergenerational Earnings Mobility" (2002).

11. Cohen, *A Consumer's Republic* (2003), chap. 5. Carnevale and Rose, "Socioeconomic Status, Race/Ethnicity, and Selective College Admissions" (2004), 127–29.

12. Warner et al., *Who Shall Be Educated?* (1944). Esty, "Does Financial Aid Come Too Late?" (1961).

13. Cameron and Heckman, "Can Tuition Policy Combat Rising Wage Inequality?" (1999). St. John, *Refinancing the College Dream* (2003), chap. 8. Findings have differed as to whether families, and which families, significantly exaggerate college costs. McPherson and Schapiro, *Keeping College Affordable* (1991), 101. Mumper, *Removing College Price Barriers* (1996), 198–201. U.S. Dept. of Education, *Getting Ready to Pay for College* (2003), esp. 29–30, 42–43. Sanoff, "Americans See Money for College Somewhere over the Rainbow" (2004), B7. More recent studies have shown that, among low-income young Americans, rising college aspirations—driven in part by loss of good blue-collar jobs—have far outstripped preparation for college. Toppo and DeBaros, "Reality Crashing Down on Dreams of College" (2005).

14. Reynolds, *The Social and Economic Status of College Students* (1927), 6, 15, 42. Burke, *American Collegiate Populations* (1982), 228.

15. McPherson and Schapiro, *Keeping College Affordable* (1991), 91, table on students with high Preliminary Scholastic Aptitude Test (PSAT) scores.

16. The effect of Pell grants on low-income students has been much debated. Some research suggests that the establishment of Pell grants, and their subsequent real decrease in the late 1970s, affected low-income student enrollment in colleges, especially for older students and at two-year community colleges. They did not seem to affect the proportion of low-income people earning four-year degrees by age twenty-four. Mumper, *Removing College Price Barriers* (1996), 207, 214. Sarah Turner, "The Vision and Reality of Pell Grants"(1998). St. John, *Refinancing the College Dream* (2003), chap. 5.

17. Leslie and Fife, "The College Grant Study" (1974). Tierney, "The Impact of Financial Aid on Student Demand for Public/Private Higher Education" (1980). Moore et al., "The Effect of the Financial Aid Package on the Choice of a Selective College" (1990). Avery and Hoxby, "Do and Should Financial Aid Packages Affect Students' College Choices?" (2003).

18. "Pell Grants as a Measure of Student Diversity," *Journal of Blacks in Higher Education* (2002), Web site update, Feb. 12, 2004, on top twenty-five universities as rated by *U.S. News and World Report;* it gave a separate ranking for the top twenty-five liberal arts colleges. Ranks recalculated by me, excluding public

universities, foreign students, and Harvard's part-time extension-course students. Princeton data with comment from its financial aid office, July 2003.

19. Data on each institution in Higher Education Management Statistics for 1996, University and College Admissions Service, London, kindly provided by Liz Viggars. For the United States, see Cooperative Institutional Research, *The American Freshman* (annual), tables on parents' occupation and education by college selectivity.

20. The data, admittedly, are quite old: late 1980s and early 1990s. McPherson and Schapiro, *Keeping College Affordable* (1991), 91. Carnevale and Rose, "Socioeconomic Status, Race/Ethnicity, and Selective College Admissions" (2004), 135–38. See also Hearn, "Pathways to Attendance at the Elite Colleges" (1990): among top students in the 1980s, he found that rich ones were far more likely than the others to go to highly selective colleges: 131. In McPherson and Schapiro's data, lower-income students were even more underrepresented at top state universities.

21. Rodriguez, *Hunger of Memory* (1982), 57–58. McDonough, *Choosing Colleges* (1997), esp. chap. 5. Arnone, "A Texas-Size Challenge" (2003). I am grateful to John Douglass for reminding me of Rodriguez's story.

22. U.S. Dept. of Education, *Programs at Higher Education Institutions for Disadvantaged Precollege Students* (1995). Perna, "Precollege Outreach Programs" (2002).

23. Cage, "University of Southern California Reaches Out" (1992). Final Report, 1987–1992, on Middlebury's SCIENS program with comments from Prof. Craig Landgren, Biology department, Nov. 1992. Information from Smith College Media Relations and Student Affairs offices, 2002. Interviews, Smith College. SUCCESS was aimed at students who had already applied, but it promised to have a ripple effect on potential applicants. See also Web site of the Posse Foundation, founded 1989 and working with about twenty very selective colleges. A "College Horizons" summer program for Native Americans at Carleton, St. John's (Santa Fe), and Whitman is described by Eric Hoover, "For American Indians, the Keys to College" (2004).

24. "Selectivity" contributes 15 percent of *U.S. News's* college ranking. The entering class's test scores provide half of the ranking. Percentage in the top 25 percent of their high school class (10 percent for "national" colleges) provides 40 percent, and percentage of applicants admitted, 10 percent. The magazine's printed listing of college SAT scores gives the SAT range of the middle half of the class, thus omitting the lowest quarter. SUCCESS enrollment in a given year did not exceed a dozen students. Smith's student body was about 2,600. The Kaplan test preparation company has recently offered low-cost services for college access programs.

25. This list excludes many other proposals, including better accommodation of

college study by welfare benefits. Perhaps the most radical approach, standing outside the usual run of commentators, is by Archibald, *Redesigning the Financial Aid System* (2002). He argues, not always cogently, that colleges should do all the lending and government almost all the giving, with better advance information about what grants students can expect.

26. The most effective, sometimes draconian, cost controls seem to have been at state colleges. National Commission, *Straight Talk about College Costs and Prices* (1998), 14–21, 233–41. Cf. Council for Aid to Education, *Breaking the Social Contract* (1997), 18–22, and Ehrenberg, *Tuition Rising* (2000), chap. 19. Also several Democratic and Republican bills, U.S. Congress, 2003–04. The most wide-ranging and challenging proposals for curbing college costs and prices are made by Vedder, *Going Broke by Degree* (2004), chaps. 8–10.

27. Hoxby, "Where Should Federal Education Initiatives Be Directed?" (1999). Leslie and Brinkman, *The Economic Value of Higher Education* (1993), summarize many studies showing higher-education benefits. Studies of economic payoffs to college graduates allow for their precollege cognitive and academic abilities rather than other, less testable qualities. On payoffs to a local community's economic well-being, see Morin, "The Spillover Effect" (2002), reporting a study by Enrico Moretti. On noneconomic payoffs, Mumper, *Removing College Price Barriers* (1996), 8–10, 14–15, and Behrman and Stacey, eds., *The Social Benefits of Education* (1997). On "credentialism," Berg, *Education and Jobs* (1970); Michael Lewis, *Liar's Poker* (1989), 94–95; Randall Collins, "The Dirty Little Secret of Credential Inflation" (1999). On the counterweight of noneducational factors in general earnings and social improvements, Levin and Kelley, "Can Education Do It Alone?" (1994), 107; Putnam, *Bowling Alone* (2000), esp. 186–87; Mishel et al., *The State of Working America* (2001), 152–55, 156. And important new research puts into question the general economic payoff of expanding higher education and giving it more state support. Vedder, *Going Broke by Degree* (2004), chap. 7.

28. King, "Financial Thresholds to College" (1957). Mumper, *Removing College Price Barriers* (1996), 4, 250–52. Cf. Hutton, *The World We're In* (2002), 154, and "Educational Attainment," *Postsecondary Educational Opportunity Research Newsletter* (March 2003).

29. Institute for Higher Education Policy, *The Policy of Choice* (2002). Carnevale and Rose, "Socioeconomic Status, Race/Ethnicity, and Selective College Admissions" (2003), 107–15. Glenn, "Minority Students Fare Better at Selective Colleges" (2004).

30. Hall, "The Biggest Barrier to College Isn't Race" (2003).

31. *Chronicle of Higher Education,* Almanac issue (Aug. 29, 2003), A12. Loans including "unsubsidized" ones were 53 percent of the total including federal tax credits. Grant aid increased more than loans after 2000, slightly offsetting a

much bigger long-term trend of faster loan growth. Federal "subsidized" loans (interest-free while the recipient is in college) were 43 percent of all federal loans. My percentage calculations.

32. From Jan. 2003 to Jan. 2004, the Consumer Price Index for All Urban Consumers rose by 1.9 percent. The interest rate after graduation for federal Stafford subsidized loans was 3.42 percent.

33. Winter, "Rich Colleges Receive Richest Share of U.S. Aid" (2003). Also letters in *Chronicle of Higher Education* (July 21, 2000), B9.

34. Interview, Barnard College. Cf. McPherson and Schapiro, *The Student Aid Game* (1998), 89–90, 140. They, too, proposed new campus-based federal grants as a lever for more college aid and later, on a College Board panel, added the idea of a cost-of-education supplement to the colleges. Michael S. McPherson to author, e-mail, Feb. 24, 2004.

35. Hubbell and Lapovsky, "Tuition Discounting in Challenging Times" (2002), 29. Loren Loomis Hubbell to author, e-mail, May 23, 2003. Archibald, *Redesigning the Financial Aid System* (2002), stressed that higher-rated colleges gave larger grants on average to the students they aided, offsetting their higher charges, but he did not note in this context that they had fewer students needing aid: 108.

36. *U.S. v. Brown University et al.,* U.S. Court of Appeals for the Third Circuit, (1993).

37. An alternative would be to use "FISAP" data on student incomes submitted annually by colleges government on their federal aid applicants. See Appendix 2. Foreign students should be excluded, as they do not get federal aid. Four-year colleges should be listed separately from universities, as the latter's endowments have to cover more expenses, especially graduate programs.

38. See note 18 above. The *Chronicle of Higher Education* annually ranks hundreds of colleges by market value of their endowments.

39. See Appendix 1, on NCAA, antitrust, and legislation.

40. The revised law should probably not get into technical detail about how merits might be limited. One model is the system operated by the University of California in the 1990s. In requiring that its different UC campuses spend a third of tuition fee increases on aid, the Oakland head office allowed a small percentage of that aid to be merits.

41. Riesman, "On Discovering and Teaching Sociology" (1988).

Appendix 1. The Case of the Charitable Price Fixers

1. *U.S. v. Brown University et al.,* U.S. District Court for Eastern District of Pennsylvania, "Complaint for Equitable Relief for Violation of 15 U.S. Code Section 1, Sherman Antitrust Act." The complaint alleged conspiracy as well

as combination, but the colleges had not concealed what they were doing, though they did not publicize it. The Sherman Act is printed in, e.g., Gellhorn, *Antitrust Law and Economics* (1976), 375–79.

2. On origins of the usage "overlap," see College Scholarship Service, *CSS Need Analysis* (1980), 5. Hoxby, "Benevolent Colluders?" (2000), attributed it to aid agreements between overlapping athletic associations before World War II (24–25), but she gave no source and did not answer my inquiries. The overlap sessions also included bilateral meetings when just two colleges were offering aid to the same student. The allied colleges group started as the "Pentagonal" group of five: Amherst, Bowdoin, Dartmouth (also in the Ivy group), Wesleyan, Williams. It is not clear when it started meeting alongside the Ivies, but it became the "Pentagonal Plus" group when several others joined, including Tufts University and Harvard (like Dartmouth in both groups, due to overlapping "admits"). In the late 1970s, the group became the "Pentagonal Sisters" when they were joined by the former "Seven Sisters" women's colleges, including Vassar, which had started admitting men. As the Pentagonals, traditionally male only, had gone coed too, they all had more overlapping applicants. Interview, Amherst College (Joe Case). Anne Keppler (former Smith College financial aid director) to author, April 2, 2000. On early developments, especially among the Ivies, see McDonald, "Equalizing Scholarships" (1957), and Reports to the President for the Bureau of Student Aid and Employment for 1957–58 through 1959–60 by W. Bradford Craig (Princeton University Manuscript Library).

3. *U.S. v. Brown University et al.,* U.S. Court of Appeals for the Third Circuit, "Brief for Appellee" (Sept. 1992), 12. Also court deposits. Stanford gave athletic scholarships, but no other merits. The Ivy Needs Analysis Agreements, used by the overlap groups for assessing what families could pay, usually expected bigger contributions than the more widely endorsed "Uniform Methodology," created in 1974–75." The Ivy analysis was tougher on families with tax shelters and manipulated income from assets, and it was also harder on single parents. Overlap cooperation itself tended to increase individual EFCs by bringing pooled information to bear on financial misreporting by families.

4. Putka, "Do Colleges Collude on Financial Aid?" (1989). "OPEC" referred to the Organization of Petroleum Exporting Countries. The Justice Department investigation was also provoked by a student's confidential report of intercollegiate collusion on tuition, though there had been earlier reports of the overlap operations. See Butterfield, "Student Bonuses End at Two Colleges" (1983), and Harr, "The Admissions Circus" (1984). The delayed response of the Justice Department does not seem to have been due to any shift on antitrust policy between the Reagan and Bush administrations. Interviews, U.S. Dept. of Justice.

5. U.S. Dept. of Justice, press release, "Consent Decree Settles Charge of

Conspiracy"(May 22, 1991). *U.S. v. Brown University et al.,* U.S. District Court for the Eastern District of Pennsylvania, "Stipulation" and "Competitive Impact Statement" (May 1991).

6. Putka, "Ivy League Discussions on Finances Extend to Tuition and Salaries" (1992).

7. This and other parts of the story are based on interviews at Amherst (Joe Case), Harvard, MIT, Palmer and Dodge (MIT's lawyers), and U.S. Dept. of Justice. I am grateful to John Margolis, associate provost of Northwestern, for first telling me of the overlap case and providing copies of his many press clippings on it; to Joe Case, Amherst dean of financial aid, for copies of court briefs, opinions, and other papers; and to MIT, Palmer and Dodge, and the U.S. Justice Department for trial exhibits, including college memos.

8. Susan Lewis, "The Side of the Angels" (1994), 1.

9. *Chronicle of Higher Education,* Almanac issue (Aug. 28, 1991), 65.

10. Interviews, U.S. Dept. of Justice.

11. No study at the time fully controlled for distinctive socioeconomic traits of overlap college students that might affect charges. Later findings favored both sides in different respects. See esp. Hoxby, "Benevolent Colluders?" (2000), including her bibliography.

12. *U.S. v. Brown University et al.,* U.S. District Court for the Eastern District of Pennsylvania, "Decision and Order," no. 91-3274 (Sept. 2, 1992). All the Ivies' names had been entered into the title of the case, though MIT was the sole defendant.

13. *U.S. v. Brown University et al.,* U.S. Court of Appeals for the Third Circuit, "Opinion" [with dissent], no. 92-1911 (Sept. 17, 1992). The court did not clearly say here whether it meant competition between students (consumers) or between colleges for more students. The "procompetitive" effects of some price-fixing has been an issue in antitrust law.

14. Antitrust law requires different amounts of "industry" analysis according to obviousness of wrongdoing and other considerations. The amount required was contested in this case. See Gellhorn, *Antitrust Law and Economics* (1976), on the evolution of "per se" and "rule of reason" levels of analysis.

15. For the settlement, see Jaschik, "Antitrust Case Closed "(1994).

16. Section 1544 of the 1992 Higher Education Act Amendments was succeeded by Section 568 of the Improving America's Schools Act of 1994, followed by the 1997 act as mentioned. The legislation developed provision for limited and controlled exchanges of information on awards and aided students between colleges through a third party. The MIT/Justice settlement gave MIT somewhat more scope than Section 1544 to exchange financial aid data with another college if that college met all need and practiced need-blind admissions. MIT could also

join other colleges in following the legislation rather than the settlement, as it subsequently did.

17. Gellhorn, *Antitrust Law and Economics* (1976), 188–92; see also 167–68, 221–22.

18. The actual price paid by an aided student was the expected family contribution (EFC) plus "self-help" (expected loan and job earnings). Despite some efforts to standardize self-help requirements, the Ivies and MIT accepted differences between them in their "typical" self-help requirements as well as in the concessions they made (bigger grants, lower loans) to select categories of students such as academic stars, minorities, and low-income students. MIT's expected self-help levels were usually higher than the others', as it believed engineering students could more easily find well-paid jobs in the summer and after graduation. (In 1989–90, MIT's standard self-help expectation for freshmen was $5,300 a year, compared with $5,150 at Penn, the next highest, and $4,000 at Dartmouth, Harvard, and Yale, the lowest.) MIT did not press the point, as it did not want to distance itself from the others or imply that differences in the self-help part of price were legally virtuous. To do so would weaken MIT's claim that its price-fixing was legal. The Justice Department, for its part, focused on the EFC part of price, as this was where the Ivies and MIT openly tried to agree most closely. Though its court briefs did note the attempts to standardize self-help, members of the Justice Department argued to me later that illegal price-fixing did not necessarily mean total price conformity. In a price-fixing ring, different parties could still give some special deals and discounts.

19. Report of the President for 1952–1953 by Rosewell G. Hamm (Mount Holyoke College Archives). The Justice Department's Investigative Demand for college memos and papers did not go back before the 1980s, allegedly to save the colleges from further burdens of collecting information.

Appendix 2. Research Strategy and Limits

1. Eames, "Financial Aid Policy Development" (2000).

2. The closest to this are probably the data in Behle and Maxwell, "The Social Origins of Students at the Illinois Industrial University" (1998). Foster, *"Out of Smalle Beginnings"* (1962), does give, separately, college charges and daily wages of unskilled laborers around Cambridge in the mid-1600s: 56 and chap. 4.

3. In my own sample, I count Worcester Polytechnic Institute as a primarily undergraduate college, but Rensselaer Polytechnic Institute as a university. Some liberal arts colleges, most notably Wesleyan, that are named "University" are counted here as undergraduate colleges. So is Washington and Lee University, though it has a law school. Boston College, on the other hand, is very much a university.

4. Bourque, "Reassessing Research"(1999). Cech, "Science at Liberal Arts Colleges" (1999). Reisberg, "Are Students Actually Learning?" (2000).

5. Morison, *The Founding of Harvard College* (1935). Morison, *Harvard College in the Seventeenth Century,* 2 vols. (1936). Foster, *"Out of Smalle Beginnings"* (1962). Harris, *The Economics of Harvard* (1970).

Bibliography

Abramson, Rudy. "From the Beginning Berea Nurtured Those Most in Need." *Smithsonian* (Nov./Dec. 1993): 92–104.

Adams, C. F. "The Proposed Increase of the Tuition Fee." *Harvard Graduates' Magazine* 13 (Sept. 1904): 6–22.

"Advocates Loans for Scholarships." *New York Times* (Aug. 2, 1926): 11.

Aldersley, Stephen F. "'Upward Drift' Is Alive and Well." *Change* (Sept./Oct. 1995): 51–56.

Allmendinger, David F., Jr. *Paupers and Scholars: The Transformation of Student Life in Nineteenth-Century New England.* New York: St. Martin's, 1975.

———. "Mount Holyoke Students Encounter the Need for Life-Planning, 1837–1850." *History of Education Quarterly* 19 (Spring 1979): 27–46.

Amenta, Edwin. *Bold Relief: Institutional Politics and the Origins of Modern American Social Policy.* Princeton: Princeton University Press, 1998.

American National Biography. New York: Oxford University Press, 1999.

Angelo, Richard. "The Students at the University of Pennsylvania and the Temple College of Philadelphia, 1873–1906: Some Notes on Schooling, Class and Social Mobility in the Late Nineteenth Century." *History of Education Quarterly* 19 (1979): 179–205.

Archibald, Robert B. *Redesigning the Financial Aid System: Why Colleges and Universities Should Switch Roles with the Federal Government.* Baltimore: Johns Hopkins University Press, 2002.

Arenson, Karen W. "Leading Colleges Adopt New Guidelines for Awarding Financial Aid." *New York Times* (July 6, 2001): A11.

———. "To Raise Its Image, CUNY Pays for Top Students." *New York Times* (May 11, 2002): A16.

Arnett, Trevor. *Trends in Tuition Fees in State and Endowed Colleges and Universities in the United States from 1928–29 through 1936–37.* New York: General Education Board, 1939.

———. *Recent Trends in Higher Education in the United States; with Special Reference to Financial Support for Private Colleges and Universities.* New York: General Education Board, 1940.

Arnone, Michael. "A Texas-Size Challenge." *Chronicle of Higher Education* (Nov. 2003): A13–14.

Aronson, Sidney H. *Status and Kinship in the Higher Civil Service: Standards of Selection in the Administrations of John Adams, Thomas Jefferson, and Andrew Jackson.* Cambridge: Harvard University Press, 1964.

Ashworth, John, *"Agrarians" and "Aristocrats": Party Political Ideology in the United States, 1837–1846.* Atlantic Highlands, NJ: Humanities Press, 1983.

Asinov, Lynn. "Colleges Clamp Down on Financial Aid." *Wall Street Journal* (Apr. 11, 2002): D1–2.

Astin, Alexander W. "Tying Tuition to the CPI: Why It Doesn't Add Up." *Chronicle of Higher Education* (Feb. 20, 2004): B20.

Aston, T. H., and Rosamond Faith. "The Endowments of the University and Colleges to circa 1348." In *History of the University of Oxford,* Vol. 1, *The Early Oxford Schools,* ed. J .I. Catto. Oxford: Clarendon Press, 1984.

Avery, Christopher, and Caroline M. Hoxby. "Do and Should Financial Aid Packages Affect Students' College Choices?" NBER Working Paper no. 9482. Cambridge: National Bureau of Economic Research, Feb., 2003.

Axt, Richard G. *The Federal Government and Financing Higher Education.* New York: Columbia University Press for the Commission on Financing Higher Education, 1952.

Bacon, Theodore S., Jr. "Financial Aid." *Amherst Alumni News,* 11 (Apr. 1959): 6–7.

Bailey, William B. "College Life and the Social Order." *Religious Education* 9 (1914): 243–50.

Barnard, Frederick A. P. "Annual Report of the President" (1879). In *The Rise of a University,* vol. 1, *The Later Days of Old Columbia College, From the Annual Reports of Frederick A .P. Barnard, President of Columbia College, 1864–1889,* ed. William F. Russell. New York: Columbia University Press, 1937.

Barton, Paul. "Wealth Likely to Continue Separating Blacks, Whites." *Asheville Citizen-Times* (Apr. 13, 1998, Gannet News Service): 1.

Battle, Kemp D. *History of the University of North Carolina.* 2 vols. Raleigh: Broughton, 1907, 1912.

Baum, Sandra. "Access, Choice and the Middle Class." *Journal of Student Financial Aid* 24 (1994): 17–25.

———. "Equity and Enrollment Management: Conflicting Goals?" In National

Association of College and Business Officers, *Proceedings from the NACUBO Forum on Tuition Discounting* (Dallas: Feb. 3–4, 2000): 45–48.

Baum, Sandra, and Saul Schwartz. "Merit Aid to College Students." *Economics of Education Review* 7 (1988): 127–34.

Beadie, Nancy. "From Student Markets to Credential Markets: the Creation of the Regents Examination System in New York State, 1864–1890." *History of Education Quarterly* 39 (Spring 1999): 1–30.

Becker, Gary S. *Human Capital: A Theoretical and Empirical Analysis with Special Reference to Education.* 3rd edition. Chicago: University of Chicago Press, 1993.

Beecher, Lyman. *On the Importance of Assisting Young Men of Piety and Talents in Obtaining an Education for the Gospel Ministry.* Andover: Flagg and Gould, 1815.

———. *A Plea for Colleges: an address before the Union literary society of Miami University, Ohio.* Cincinnati: Truman and Smith, 1836.

Behle, J. Gregory, and William Edgar Maxwell. "The Social Origins of Students at the Illinois Industrial University, 1868–1894." *History of Higher Education Annual* 18 (1998): 93–109.

Behrman, Jere R., and Nevzer Stacey, eds. *The Social Benefits of Education.* Ann Arbor: University of Michigan Press, 1997.

Benedict, H. Y., ed. *A Source Book Relating to the History of the University of Texas.* Bulletin no. 1757. Austin: University of Texas, Oct. 10, 1917.

Benjamin, Roger W. *Breaking the Social Contract: The Fiscal Crisis in California Higher Education.* New York: Council for Aid to Education, 1997.

Bennett, Michael J. *When Dreams Came True: The GI Bill and the Making of Modern America.* Washington, DC: Brassey's, 1996.

Berg, Ivar. *Education and Jobs: The Great Training Robbery.* New York: Praeger, 1970.

Bergin, Thomas. "My Native Country." In *My Harvard, My Yale,* ed. Diana Dubois. New York: Random House, 1982.

Bigglestone, W. E. "Oberlin College and the Negro Student, 1865–1940." *Journal of Negro History* 56 (1971): 198–219.

Bishop, Morris. *Early Cornell, 1865–1900.* Ithaca: Cornell University Press, 1965.

Bishop, T. J. H., with Rupert Wilkinson. *Winchester and the Public School Elite: A Statistical Portrait.* London: Faber, 1967.

Bledstein, Burton J. *The Culture of Professionalism: The Middle Class and the Development of Higher Education in America.* New York: Norton, 1978.

Blodgett, Geoffrey. "Oberlin Fever: Improving Each Other for 16 Decades." *Oberlin College Observer* (Jan. 19, 1995): 4–5.

Blum, John Morton. *V Was for Victory: Politics and Culture during World War II.* New York: Harcourt Brace Jovanovich, 1976.

Blumenstyk, Goldie. "States Wrestle with Proposals for Higher Tuition." *Chronicle of Higher Education* (Mar. 25, 1992): A28–29.

Bobbitt, James R. *The Impact of Berea College on Student Characteristics.* Berea: Berea College Press, 1969.

Bollag, Burton. "Student Loans: A Slippery Lifeline." *Chronicle of Higher Education* (Dec. 7, 2001): A34–36.

Boorstin, Daniel J. *The Americans: The National Experience.* New York: Random House, 1965.

Bourque, Susan C. "Reassessing Research: Liberal Arts Colleges and the Social Sciences." *Daedalus* 128 (Winter 1999): 265–72.

Bowen, William G., and Derek Bok. *The Shape of the River: Long-Term Consequences of Considering Race in College and University Admissions.* Princeton: Princeton University Press, 1998.

Bowen, William G., and David W. Breneman. "Student Aid: Price Discount or Educational Investment?" *Brookings Review* 11 (Winter 1993): 28–31.

Bower, Kevin P. "'A Favored Child of the State': Federal Student Aid at Ohio Colleges and Universities, 1934–1943." *History of Education Quarterly* 44 (Fall 2004): 364-87.

Brademas, John, with Lynne Brown. *The Politics of Education: Conflict on Capitol Hill.* Norman: University of Oklahoma Press, 1987.

Brandt, Nat. *The Town That Started the Civil War.* Syracuse: Syracuse University Press, 1990.

Breneman, David W. *Liberal Arts Colleges: Thriving, Surviving, or Endangered?* Washington, DC: Brookings, 1994.

Breneman, David W., and Chester Finn. "An Uneasy Future." In *Public Policy and Private Education,* ed. Breneman and Finn. Washington, DC: Brookings, 1978.

Brett, Albert. "Colleges as Salesmen." *Harper's* 177 (July 1938): 194–201.

Brewer, Dominic J., Susan M. Gates, and Charles A. Goldman. *In Pursuit of Prestige: Strategy and Competition in U. S. Higher Education.* New Brunswick, N.J.: Transaction, 2002.

Brinkley, Alan. *The End of Reform: New Deal Liberalism in Recession and War.* New York: Knopf, 1995.

Brint, Steven, and Jerome Karabel. *The Diverted Dream: Community Colleges and the Promise of Educational Opportunity in America, 1900–1985.* New York: Oxford University Press, 1989.

Brooks, Steven. "NASFAA: The First Twenty Years." Washington, DC: National Association of Student Financial Aid Administrators, 1986.

Brown, Ronald M. "Equity Packaging of Student Financial Aid." Paper distributed to Regional Meetings of CEEB/CSS. New York: College Scholarship Service of the College Board Entrance Examination Board, 1976.

Brownstein, Andrew. "Upping the Ante for Student Aid." *Chronicle of Higher Education* (Feb. 16, 2001): A47–49.

Bullock, Henry Morton. *History of Emory University.* Nashville: Parthenon, 1936.

Burd, Stephen. "Few Borrowers Repay Student Loans through 'Income-Contingent' System." *Chronicle of Higher Education* (Sept. 25, 1998): A40–41.

———. "Private Colleges Seek Antitrust Exemption for Aid Talks." *Chronicle of Higher Education* (Mar. 16, 2001): A25.

———. "Rift Grows over What Keeps Low-Income Students Out of College." *Chronicle of Higher Education* (Jan. 25, 2002): A18–19.

Burke, Colin B. *American Collegiate Populations: A Test of the Traditional View.* New York: New York University Press, 1982.

Butchart, Ronald E. "Mission Matters: Mount Holyoke, Oberlin, and the Schooling of Southern Blacks, 1861–1917." *History of Education Quarterly* 42 (Spring 2002): 1–17.

Butterfield, Fox. "Students' Bonuses End at Two Colleges." *New York Times* (July 10, 1983), section 1, p. 17.

Caestle, Carl F. *The Evolution of an Urban School System: New York City, 1750–1850.* Cambridge: Harvard University Press, 1973.

Cage, Mary Crystal. "University of Southern California Reaches Out to Riot-Torn South Central Los Angeles." *Chronicle of Higher Education* (Dec. 2, 1992): A35–36.

Cameron, Stephen V., and James J. Heckman. "Can Tuition Policy Combat Rising Wage Inequality?" In *Financing College Tuition: Government Policies and Educational Priorities,* ed. Marvin H. Kosters. Washington, DC: AEI Press, 1999.

Carmichael, Oliver Cromwell. *New York Establishes a State University.* Nashville: Vanderbilt University Press, 1955.

Carnegie Commission on Higher Education. *Quality and Inequality: New Levels of Federal Responsibility for Higher Education.* New York: McGraw-Hill, 1968.

———. *The Capitol and the Campus: State Responsibility for Postsecondary Education.* New York: McGraw-Hill, 1971.

———. *Higher Education: Who Pays? Who Benefits? Who Should Pay?* New York: McGraw-Hill, 1973.

Carnevale, Anthony P., and Stephen J. Rose. "Socioeconomic Status, Race/Ethnicity, and Selective College Admissions." In *America's Untapped Resource: Low-Income Students in Higher Education,* ed. Richard D. Kahlenberg. New York: Century Foundation, 2004.

Carrell, Jeptha J., and Demaris Affleck Carrell, eds. *A Singular Time, a Singular Place: Swarthmore College and World War II, 1941–1949.* Swarthmore: Swarthmore College, 1994.

Carstensen, Peter. "Colleges and Student Aid: Collusion or Competition?" *Chronicle of Higher Education* (Aug. 10, 2002): B24.

Cartter, Allan M. "Pricing Policies for Higher Education." Lake Geneva, WI: College Scholarship Colloquium on the Economic Aspects of Education, 1966.

Cass-Liepmannn, Julia, ed. *Cass and Birnbaum's Guide to American Colleges.* New York: HarperCollins, annual editions, formerly edited by James Cass and Max Birnbaum as *Comparative Guide to American Colleges.*

Catto, J. I. . "Citizens, Scholars and Masters." In *History of the University of Oxford,* vol. 1, *The Early Oxford Schools,* ed. J. I. Catto. Oxford: Clarendon Press, 1984.

Cech, Thomas R. "Science at Liberal Arts Colleges: A Better Education?'" *Daedalus* 128, (Winter 1999): 195–216.

Chafe, William H. *The Unfinished Journey: America since World War II.* New York: Oxford University Press, 1986.

Chaffin, Nora C. *Trinity College, 1839–1892: The Beginnings of Duke University.* Durham: Duke University Press, 1950.

"A Chain of Alumnae Helping Students." *Wellesley* alumnae magazine (Winter 1999): 6.

Chase, Hank. "Trouble in River City." In National Association of College and University Business Officers, *Proceedings from the NACUBO Forum on Tuition Discounting* (Dallas: Feb. 3–4, 2000): 13–17.

Cheney, Edward Potts. *History of the University of Pennsylvania, 1740–1940.* Philadelphia: University of Pennsylvania Press, 1940.

Clark, Burton R. *The Distinctive College: Antioch, Reed, and Swarthmore.* Chicago: Aldine, 1970.

Clark, Daniel A. "The Two Joes Meet—Joe College, Joe Veteran: The GI Bill, College Education, and Postwar American Culture." *History of Education Quarterly* 38, (Summer 1998): 165–89.

Clark, E. L. "Family Background and College Success." *School and Society* 25 (1927): 237–38.

Clotfelter, Charles T. *Buying the Best: Cost Escalation in Elite Higher Education.* Princeton: Princeton University Press, 1996.

Clowse, Barbara Barksdale. *Brainpower for the Cold War: The Sputnik Crisis and National Defense Act of 1958.* Westport: Greenwood, 1981.

Cohen, Lizabeth. *A Consumer's Republic: The Politics of Mass Consumption in Postwar America.* New York: Knopf, 2003.

Cole, Arthur. *A Hundred Years of Mount Holyoke College.* New Haven: Yale University Press, 1940.

College Board. *Financing a College Education: A Guide for Counselors.* New York: College Entrance Examination Board, various years.

———. *A Report on the College Board Colloquium on the Role of Ethics in Enrollment Management and Financial Aid.* New York: College Entrance Examination Board, 1997.

————. *Trends in Student Aid.* New York: College Entrance Examination Board, annual.

"College Enrollment Rises in '90s." *USA Today* (Oct. 28, 1999): 1A.

College Scholarship Service. *CSS Need Analysis: Theory and Computation Procedures for the 1981–82 FAF.* New York: College Entrance Examination Board, 1980.

————. *The History of Need Analysis.* New York: College Entrance Examination Board, 1993.

Collins, Bruce. "The Ideology of the Ante-bellum Northern Democrats." *Journal of American Studies* 11 (1977): 103–21.

Collins, Randall. "Functional and Conflict Theories of Educational Stratification." *American Sociological Review* 36 (1971): 1002–18.

————. "The Dirty Little Secret of Credential Inflation." *Chronicle of Higher Education* (Sept. 27, 2002): B20.

Collison, Michael N.-K. "Private Colleges Unveil Tuition Discounts and Loans to Woo Middle-Income Students." *Chronicle of Higher Education* (June 24, 1992): A27–28.

Columbia University. *A History of Columbia University, 1754–1904.* New York: Columbia University Press, 1904.

Colwell, Bruce William. "The Study of Education at Northwestern University, 1900–1945: Conflicts of Mission and Men." Ph.D. diss., Northwestern University, 1988.

Commission on Financing Higher Education. *The Nature and Needs of Higher Education.* New York: Columbia University Press, 1952.

Comstock, Ada Louise. "College Scholarships in Relation to Students' Aid" [ca. 1915]. In *The Evolution of an Educator: an Anthology of Public Writings of Ada Louise Comstock,* ed. Barbara Solomon. New York: Garland, 1987.

Congressional Record. 78th Cong., 2nd sess., 1944. Vol. 90, pt. 4.

Conant, James B. "Education for a Classless Society: The Jeffersonian Tradition." *Atlantic Monthly* 166 (May 1940): 593–602.

————. "Wanted: American Radicals." *Atlantic Monthly* 171 (May 1943): 41–43.

————. *Thomas Jefferson and the Development of American Public Education.* Berkeley: University of California Press, 1963.

————. *My Several Lives: Memoirs of a Social Inventor.* New York: Harper and Row, 1970.

Consortium on Financing Higher Education. *Tuition, Student Budgets, and Self-Help at the Consortium Institutions.* Washington, DC: COFHE, annual editions.

Contosta, David R. *Villanova University, 1842–1992: American—Catholic—Augustinian.* University Park: Pennsylvania State University Press, 1995.

Conway, Jill Ker. "Perspectives on the History of Women's Education in the United States." *History of Education Quarterly* 14 (Spring 1974): 1–30.

————. *True North: A Memoir.* New York: Knopf, 1994.

————. *A Woman's Education*. New York: Knopf, 2001.

Conwell, Russell. *Acres of Diamonds*. New York: Harper, 1905.

Cook, Philip J., and Robert H. Frank. "The Economic Payoff of Attending an Ivy-League Institution." *Chronicle of Higher Education* (Jan. 5, 1996): B3.

Cooper, Kenneth. "The Well-to-Do at the Public U." *Washington Post* (Nov. 25, 1999): A103.

Cooperative Institutional Research Program. *The American Freshman: National Norms*. Los Angeles: University of California Higher Education Research Institute, annual editions.

"The Cost of Private Universities and Colleges: A Pricing Paradox." *Copernicus Mzine* (Apr. 2003), www.copernicusmarketing.com/about/mzine/backissues.htm.

Crane, Theodore Rawson, ed. *The College and the Public*. New York: Teachers College, Bureau of Publications, 1963.

Cremin, Lawrence A. *American Education: The Colonial Experience, 1607–1783*. New York: Harper and Row, 1970.

Crenshaw, Albert B., "Finding a Way through the College Aid Maze." *Washington Post* (Jan. 30, 1994): H1, 3.

Cressy, David. "Educational Opportunity in Tudor and Stewart England." *History of Education Quarterly* 16 (Fall 1976): 301–20.

Cunliffe, Marcus. *Soldiers and Civilians: The Martial Spirit in America, 1775–1865*. Boston: Little, Brown, 1968.

Cunningham, Alisa Frederico. *The Policy of Choice: Expanding Student Options in Higher Education,* by Washington, DC: Institute for Higher Education Policy, 2002.

Curti, Merle. *American Paradox: The Conflict of Thought and Action*. New Brunswick: Rutgers University Press, 1956.

Curti, Merle, and Roderick Nash. *Philanthropy in the Shaping of American Higher Education*. New Brunswick: Rutgers University Press, 1965.

Dale, Stacy Berg, and Alan B. Krueger. "Estimating the Payoff to Attending a More Selective College." NBER Working Paper no. 7322. Cambridge: National Bureau of Economic Research, Jan. 2000.

Davis, Andrew McFarland. "Ann Radcliffe—Lady Mowlson." *New England Magazine* (Feb. 1894): 773–79.

Davis, Herm, and Joyce Lain Kennedy. *College Financial Aid for Dummies*. Foster City, CA: IDG Books, 1997.

Davis, Jerry Sheehan. "College Affordability: Overlooked Long-Term Trends and Recent 50-State Patterns." *USAGroup Foundation New Agenda,* Series 3 (Nov. 2000): 1–75.

Delbanco, Andrew. "The Struggle of All against All." *New York Times Book Review* (Sept. 29, 2002): 13.

Dictionary of National Biography. London: Smith Elder, 1909.

Diepenbrock, David. "Black Women and Oberlin College in the Age of Jim Crow." *UCLA History Journal* 13 (1993): 27–59.

Dixon, Rebecca R. *Making Enrollment Management Work.* San Francisco: Jossey-Bass, 1995.

Doermann, Humphrey. "Crosscurrents in Admissions." *Harvard Alumni Bulletin* (Mar. 20, 1965): 460–63.

———. *Crosscurrents in College Admissions: Institutional Response to Student Ability and Family Income.* New York: Teachers College Press, 1968.

———. *Toward Equal Access.* New York: College Entrance Examination Board, 1978.

Doti, James L. 'Tuition Discounting—Its Causes and Effects." In National Association of College and University Business Officers, *Proceedings from the NACUBO Forum on Tuition Discounting* (Dallas: Feb. 3–4, 2000): 25–34.

Doyle, William R., Jennifer A. Delaney, and Blake Alan Naughton. "Institutions Amplifying State Policy: How Public Colleges Award Institutional Aid." *Change* (July/Aug. 2004): 36–41.

Drewry, Henry N., and Humphrey Doermann. *Stand and Prosper: Private Black Colleges and Their Students.* Princeton: Princeton University Press, 2001.

Drury, Clifford Merrill. *Rudolph James Wigg.* Glendale, CA: Clark, 1968.

Duffy, Elizabeth A., and Idana Goldberg. *Crafting a Class: College Admissions and Financial Aid, 1955–1994.* Princeton: Princeton University Press, 1998.

Dunham, E. Alden. "A Revolution in Admissions." *Princeton Alumni Weekly* (Nov. 15, 1966).

Durfee, Calvin. *A History of Williams College.* Boston: Williams College, 1860.

———. *Williams Biographical Annals.* Boston: Lee and Shephard, c. 1871.

Dworkin, Ronald. "The Court and the University." *New York Review of Books* (May 15, 2003): 8–11.

Eames, Angeles Lacomba. "Financial Aid Policy Development: An Analysis of Merit Policy at Selected Liberal Arts Colleges in the Midwest." Ph.D. diss., Loyola University Chicago, 2002.

"Educational Attainment, 1940 to 2002." *Postsecondary Education Opportunity Research Newsletter* no. 129 (Mar. 2003).

Ehrenberg, Ronald G. *Tuition Rising: Why College Costs So Much.* Cambridge: Harvard University Press, 2000.

Ehrenberg, Ronald G., and Susan M. Murphy. "What Price Diversity? The Death of Need-Based Financial Aid at Selective Private Colleges and Universities?" *Change* (July/Aug. 1993): 64–73

Ehrenberg, Ronald G., and Daniel R. Sherman. "Optimal Financial Aid Policies for a Selective University." *Journal of Human Resources* 19 (1984): 202–30.

Ehrenreich, Barbara. *Fear of Falling: The Inner Life of the Middle Class.* New York: Pantheon, 1989.

Eliot, Charles William, Inaugural Address (1869). In *American Higher Education: A Documentary History,* vol. 1, ed. Richard Hofstadter and Wilson Smith. Chicago: University of Chicago Press, 1961.

Elliott, Carl, Sr., and Michael D'Orso. *The Cost of Courage: The Journey of an American Congressman.* New York: Doubleday, 1992.

Elliott, Orrin Leslie. *Stanford University: The First Twenty-Five Years.* London: Stanford University Press, 1937.

Elliott, William Frank. "Management of Admissions and Financial Aid." Ph.D. diss., University of Pittsburgh, 1974.

Ellis, G. S. M. *The Poor Student and the University: A Report on the Scholarship System, with Particular Reference to Awards Made by Local Educational Authorities.* London: Labour Publishing, 1925.

Emerson, Everett, ed. *Letters from New England: The Massachusetts Bay Colony.* Amherst: University of Massachusetts Press, 1976.

Erickson, John, and John H. Goldthorpe. *The Constant Flux: A Study of Class Mobility in Industrial Societies.* Oxford: Oxford University Press, 1992.

Esty, John C., Jr. "Does Financial Aid Come Too Late?" *College Board Review* 44 (Spring 1961): 17–18.

Fallows, Alice Katharine. "Working One's Way through College." *Century Magazine* 62 (June 1901): 163–77.

———. "Working One's Way through Women's Colleges." *Century Magazine* 62 (July 1901): 323–41.

"Family Income and Higher Education Opportunity, 1970 to 2000." *Postsecondary Education Opportunity Research Newsletter* no. 112 (Oct. 2001).

Feldstein, Martin. "College Scholarship Rules and Private Saving." *American Economic Review* 85 (June 1995): 552–66.

Fels, William C. "The College Scholarship Service." *College Board Review* (May 1954): 428–35.

———. "Charging the Full Cost of Education." *College Board Review* (Fall 1958): 17–19.

Fenske, Robert H. "Student Aid Past and Present." In *Handbook of Student Financial Aid,* edited and written by Robert H. Fenske et al. San Francisco: Jossey-Bass, 1983.

Fenske, Robert H., and Joseph D. Boyd. *State Need-Based College Scholarship and Grant Programs: A Study of Their Development, 1969–1980.* College Board Report no. 81-7. New York: College Entrance Examination Board, 1981.

Ferrier, William Warren. *Origins and Development of the University of California.* San Francisco: Southern Gate, 1930.

Fetter, Jean H. *Questions and Admissions: Reflections on 100,000 Admissions Decisions at Stanford.* Stanford: Stanford University Press, 1995.

Findlay, James F., Jr. *Dwight L. Moody: American Evangelist, 1837–1899.* Chicago: University of Chicago Press, 1969.

Finn, Chester, Jr. "Why Do We Need Financial Aid? Or Desanctifying Student Assistance." In *An Agenda for the Year 2000,* ed. College Scholarship Service. New York: College Entrance Examination Board, 1985: 1–23.

Fischer, Fred J. "State Financing of Higher Education: A New Look at an Old Problem." *Change* (Jan./Feb. 1990): 42–56.

Fitzgerald, Brian K. "Missed Opportunity: Has College Opportunity Fallen Victim to Policy Drift?" *Change* (July./Aug. 2004): 10–19.

Flacks, Richard, and Scott L. Thomas. "Among Affluent Students, a Culture of Disengagement." *Chronicle of Higher Education* (Nov. 27, 1998): A48.

Flanagan, Caitlin. "Confessions of a Prep School College Counselor." *Atlantic Monthly* (Sept. 2001): 53–61.

Fletcher, Robert Samuel. *A History of Oberlin College From Its Foundation through the Civil War.* Oberlin: Oberlin College, 1943.

Flint, Thomas A. "The Influence of Job Prospects on Student Debt Levels of Traditional and Adult Undergraduates." *Journal of Student Financial Aid* 28 (Spring 1998): 7–28.

Foner, Eric. *Free Soil, Free Labor, Free Men: The Ideology of the Republican Party before the Civil War.* New York: Oxford University Press, 1970.

"Forum: Merit Scholarships at Oberlin?" *Oberlin College Observer* (Feb. 26, 1981).

Foster, Margery Somers. *"Out of Smalle Beginnings . . .": An Economic History of Harvard College in the Puritan Period (1636–1712).* Cambridge: Belknap Press of Harvard University Press, 1962.

Fox, Dixon Ryan. *Union College: An Unfinished History.* Schenectady: Union College Graduate Council, 1945.

Freeland, Richard M. *Academia's Golden Age: Universities in Massachusetts 1945–1970.* New York: Oxford University Press, 1992.

Friedman, Milton, and Rose Friedman. *Free to Choose: A Personal Statement.* New York: Harcourt Brace Jovanovich, 1979.

Frusciano, Thomas J., and Marilyn Petit. *New York University and the City: An Illustrated History.* New Brunswick: Rutgers University Press, 1997.

Fuess, Claude Moore. *Amherst: The Story of a New England College.* (Boston: Little, Brown, 1935).

———. *The College Board: Its First Fifty Years.* New York: College Entrance Examination Board, 1967.

Furnival, F. J., ed., for the Early English Text Society. *Queen Elizabethes Achademy* [and other tracts]. London: Kegan Paul, 1869.

Gantz, Kerri D. "On the Basis of Merit Alone: Integration, Tuition, Rice University, and the Charter Change Trial, 1963–1966." M.A. thesis, Rice University, 1991.

Ganzel, Carol. "College Changes Financial-Aid Policy." *Oberlin College Observer* (Nov. 25, 1993): 1.

Geiger, Roger. "The Ten Generations of American Higher Education." In *American Higher Education in the Twenty-First Century: Social, Political, and Economic Challenges,* ed. Philip G. Altbach. Baltimore: Johns Hopkins University Press, 1999.

———. *The American College in the Nineteenth Century.* Nashville: Vanderbilt University Press, 2000.

Gellhorn, Ernest. *Antitrust Law and Economics.* St. Paul: West, 1976.

Gettleman, Marvin E., and David Mermelstein, eds. *The Great Society Reader: The Failure of American Liberalism.* New York: Vintage, 1967.

Giddens, Thomas R. "The Origins of State Scholarship Programs." *College and University* 46 (1970): 37–45.

Gilmore, John A. D. "Jacksonians and Whigs at Harvard: The Politics of Higher Education." Undergraduate honors thesis. Cambridge: Harvard University, 1970.

Ginzberg, Lori D. "The 'Joint Education of the Sexes': Oberlin's Original Vision." In *Educating Men and Women Together: Coeducation in a Changing World,* ed. Carol Lasser. Urbana: University of Illinois Press, 1987.

Gladieux, Lawrence E. "Low-Income Students and the Affordability of Higher Education." In *America's Untapped Resource: Low-Income Students in Higher Education,* ed. Richard D. Kahlenberg. New York: Century Foundation, 2004.

Gladieux, Lawrence E., and Arthur M. Hauptman. *The College Aid Quandary: Access, Quality, and the Federal Role.* Washington, DC, and New York: Brookings/College Board, 1995.

Gladieux, Lawrence E., and Thomas R. Wolanin. *Congress and the Colleges: the National Politics of Higher Education.* Lexington, MA: Heath, 1976.

Gleason, Philip. "American Catholic Higher Education: A Historical Perspective." In *The Shape of Catholic Higher Education,* ed. Robert Hassenger. Chicago: University of Chicago Press, 1967.

Glenn, David. "Minority Students Fare Better at Selective Colleges, Sociologists Find." *Chronicle of Higher Education* (Sept. 3, 2004): A41.

Godson, Susan H. *The College of William and Mary: A History.* Williamsburg: King and Queen Press for College of William and Mary Society of Alumni, 1993.

Godzicki, Ralph J. "A History of Financial Aids in the United States." In *Money, Marbles, or Chalk: Student Financial Support in Higher Education,* ed. Roland Keene. Carbondale: Southern Illinois University Press, 1975.

Goldin, Davidson. "Full-Tuition Students Increasingly Pay for Others." *New York Times* (Mar. 22, 1995): A1, B7.

Goodwin, Doris Kearns. *No Ordinary Time: Franklin and Eleanor Roosevelt: The Home Front in World War II.* New York: Simon and Schuster, 1994.

Gordon, Sarah H. "Smith College Students: The First Ten Classes, 1879–1888." *History of Education Quarterly* 15 (Summer 1975): 147–67.

Gose, Ben. "Colleges Turn to 'Leveraging' to Attract Well-Off Students." *Chronicle of Higher Education* (Sept. 13, 1996): A45–46.

———. "A College Sees Benefits in Admissions Policy That Considers Families' Ability to Pay." *Chronicle of Higher Education* (Mar. 28, 1997): A47–48.

———. "A College Returns to Its Roots by Recruiting Appalachia's Poorest." *Chronicle of Higher Education* (Jan. 9, 1998): A55–56.

———. "Princeton Plans Major Increase in Aid for Middle- and Low-Income Students." *Chronicle of Higher Education* (Jan. 30, 1998): A35–36.

———. "Recent Shifts on Aid by Elite Colleges Signal New Push to Help the Middle Class." *Chronicle of Higher Education* (Mar. 6, 1998): A43–44.

———. "Temple U. Raises Standards to Woo Suburban Students." *Chronicle of Higher Education* (Dec. 11, 1998): A61–63.

———. "Changes at Elite Colleges Fuel Intense Competition in Student Aid." *Chronicle of Higher Education* (Feb. 5, 1999): A42–43.

———. "Measuring the Value of an Ivy Degree." *Chronicle of Higher Education* (Jan. 14, 2000): A52–53.

Gottlieb, Bruce. "Need Blind: Is Berkeley too Cheap?" *New Republic* 222 (June 19, 2000): 22–24

Gowran, Clay. "Roosevelt Entry Policy Aims at 'Culturally Deprived.'" *Chicago Tribune* (Mar. 24, 1963).

Green, Elizabeth Alden. *Mary Lyon and Mount Holyoke: Opening the Gates.* Hanover: University Press of New England, 1979.

Greenleaf, Walter J. "Self-Supporting Students in Colleges and Universities." *School Life* 11 (June 1926): 188–89.

Hackett, Alice Payne. *Wellesley: Part of the American Story.* New York: Dutton, 1949.

Hadley, Arthur Twining. "[Inaugural] Address." *Yale Alumni Weekly* (Oct. 18, 1899): 33–36.

———. "Alleged Luxury among College Students." *Century Magazine* 62 (June 1901): 313–14.

Haines, Richard W. "Wrong for Society, Wrong for Institutions, and Wrong for Students." *Change* 16 (Sept. 1984): 25–34.

Hall, Kermit L. . "The Biggest Barrier to College Isn't Race." *Chronicle of Higher Education* (June 20, 2003): Review section, end page ("Point of View").

Halsey, John F. P. and W. Bruce Leslie. "Historical Sociology Meets the Credentialing Society." *History of Higher Education Annual* 17 (1997): 113–21.

Hansen, Janet S. "The Politics of Federal Scholarships: A Case Study of the Development of General Grant Assistance for Undergraduates." Ph.D. diss., Princeton University, 1977.

Harr, John. "The Admissions Circus." *New England Monthly* (Apr. 1984): 49–55.

Harris, Neil. *Humbug: The Art of P. T. Barnum.* Boston: Little, Brown, 1972.

Harris, Seymour E. *The Economics of Harvard.* New York: McGraw-Hill, 1970.

———. *A Statistical Portrait of Higher Education: A Report for the Carnegie Commission on Higher Education.* New York: McGraw-Hill, 1972.

Hartle, Terry W., and Jacqueline E. King. "The End of Equal Opportunity in Higher Education?" *College Board Review* 181 (July 1997): 8–15.

Hartmann, Susan M. *The Home Front and Beyond: American Women in the 1940s.* Boston: Twayne, 1982.

Hauptman, Arthur A. "Why Are College Charges Rising?" *College Board Review* (Summer 1989): 11–17, 32–34.

———. *The Tuition Dilemma: Assessing New Ways to Pay for College.* Washington, DC: Brookings, 1990.

Hawkins, Hugh. *Between Harvard and America: The Educational Leadership of Charles William Eliot.* New York: Oxford University Press, 1972.

———. *Banding Together: The Rise of National Associations in American Higher Education, 1887–1950.* Baltimore: Johns Hopkins University Press, 1992.

Hayes, Alice, "Can a Poor Girl Go to College?" *North American Review* 152 (1891): 624–31.

Healy, Patrick. "Education Department Sends Strong Warning on Race-Exclusive Scholarships." *Chronicle of Higher Education* (Oct. 31, 1997): A47–48.

———. "HOPE Scholarships Transform the University of Georgia." *Chronicle of Higher Education* (Nov. 7, 1997): A32–34.

———. "U of California to Admit Top 4% from Every High School." *Chronicle of Higher Education* (Apr. 2, 1999): A36–38.

Hearn, James C. "Pathways to Attendance at the Elite Colleges." In *The High-Status Track: Studies of Elite Schools and Stratification,* ed. Paul William Kingston and Lionel S. Lewis. Albany: State University Press of New York, 1990.

Heller, Donald E. "Merit and Need-Based Aid." In National Association of College and University Business Officers, *Proceedings from the NACUBO Forum on Tuition Discounting* (Dallas: Feb 3–4, 2000): 35–44.

———. "State Aid and Student Access: The Changing Picture." In *Condition of Access: Higher Education for Lower Income Students,* ed. Donald E. Heller. Westport: Praeger, 2002.

Henry, David D. *Challenges Past, Challenges Present: An Analysis of American Higher Education since 1930.* San Francisco: Jossey-Bass, 1975.

Henry, Stuart C. *Unvanquished Puritan: A Portrait of Lyman Beecher.* Grand Rapids, MI: Eerdmans, 1973.

Herbst, Jurgen. "The Eighteenth-Century Origins of the Split Between Public and Private Higher Education in the United States." *History of Education Quarterly* 15 (Fall 1975): 273–80.

Herrnstein, Richard J., and Charles Murray. *The Bell Curve: Intelligence and Class Structure in American Life.* New York: Free Press, 1994.

Hershberg, James G. *James B. Conant: Harvard to Hiroshima and the Making of the Nuclear Age.* New York: Knopf, 1993.

Hessinger, Rodney, "'The Most Powerful Instrument of College Discipline': Student Disorder and the Growth of Meritocracy in the Colleges of the Early Republic." *History of Education Quarterly* 39 (Fall 1999): 237–62.

Himmelfarb, Gertrude. *Victorian Minds: A Study of Intellectuals in Crisis and of Ideologies in Transition.* New York: Harper and Row, 1970.

Hoffman, Stanley. *Gulliver's Troubles, or the Setting of American Foreign Policy.* New York: McGraw-Hill, 1968.

Hofstadter, Richard. *Anti-intellectualism in American Life.* New York: Vintage, 1962.

Hofstadter, Richard, and Walter P. Metzger. *The Development of Academic Freedom in the United States.* New York: Columbia University Press, 1955.

Hofstadter, Richard, and Wilson Smith, eds. *American Higher Education: A Documentary History.* Chicago: University of Chicago Press, 1961.

Hollinshead, Byron S. *Who Should Go to College?* New York: Columbia University Press, for the Commission on Financing Higher Education, 1952.

Holtschneider, Dennis Henry. "Institutional Aid to New England College Students, 1740–1800." Ph.D. diss., Harvard University, 1997.

Honeywell, Roy J. "A Note on the Educational Work of Thomas Jefferson." *History of Education Quarterly* 9 (Spring 1969): 64–72.

hooks, bell. "Learning in the Shadow of Race and Class." *Chronicle of Higher Education* (Nov. 17, 2000): B14–16.

Hoover, Eric. "New Attacks on Early Decision." *Chronicle of Higher Education* (Jan. 11, 2002): A45–46.

———. "The Changing Environment for College Admissions." *Chronicle of Higher Education* (Nov. 29, 2002): A30.

———. "For American Indians, the Keys to College." *Chronicle of Higher Education* (July 23, 2004): A11–12.

Hoover, Herbert. "Hoover on Tuition Fees." *Stanford Illustrated Review* (Nov. 1919): 88–89, 104–5.

Horowitz, Helen Lefkowitz. *Alma Mater: Experience and Design in Women's Colleges from Their Nineteenth-Century Beginnings to the 1930s.* Boston: Beacon, 1984.

———. *Campus Life: Undergraduate Cultures from the Eighteenth Century to the Present.* Chicago: University of Chicago Press, 1987.

Hossler, Donald R. "How Enrollment Management Has Transformed—or Ruined—Higher Education." *Chronicle of Higher Education* (Apr. 30, 2004): B3–5.

Howe, Daniel Walker. *Making the American Self: Jonathan Edwards to Abraham Lincoln.* Cambridge: Harvard University Press, 1997.

Howell, Chris. "Race Issues Are Important, but Class Issues Can't Be Ignored." *Oberlin Review* (Dec. 3, 1993).

Howes, Raymond F. "The Student Works His Way." *Outlook and Independent* (Sept. 3, 1930): 20–22, 36–38.

Hoxby, Caroline M. "Where Should Federal Education Initiatives Be Directed?" In *Financing College Tuition: Government Policies and Educational Priorities,* ed. Marvin H. Kosters. Washington, DC: AEI Press, 1999.

———. "Benevolent Colluders? The Effects of Antitrust Action on College Financial Aid and Tuition." NBER Working Paper no. 7754. Cambridge: National Bureau of Economic Research, June 2000.

Hubbell, Loren Loomis, and Lucie Lapovsky. "Tuition Discounting in Challenging Times." *NACUBO Business Officer* (National Association of College and University Business Officers, Feb. 2002): 24–33.

Humphrey, David C. *From King's College to Columbia, 1746–1800.* New York: Columbia University Press, 1976.

Hutton, Will. *The World We're In.* London: Little, Brown, 2002.

Ihlandfeldt, William. *Achieving Optimal Enrollments and Tuition Revenues.* San Francisco: Jossey-Bass, 1981.

Jaschik, Scott. "Antitrust Case Closed." *Chronicle of Higher Education* (Jan. 5, 1994): A24, 38.

———. "Department Tells How Colleges Must Justify Minority Scholarships." *Chronicle of Higher Education* (Mar. 2, 1994): A25.

Jefferson, Thomas. *Notes on the State of Virginia.* 1785. In *The Portable Jefferson,* ed. Merrill D. Peterson. New York: Viking, 1975.

Jencks, Christopher, and David Riesman. *The Academic Revolution.* New York: Doubleday, 1968.

Johnson, Dorothy, and Malcolm M. Willey. "Backgrounds of College NYA Students." *School and Society* 50 (Aug. 19, 1939): 252–56.

Johnson, Eldon L. "Is the Low-Tuition Principle Outmoded?" *College Board Review* (Spring 1959): 16–18.

Johnson, Owen. *Stover at Yale.* New York: Stokes, 1912.

Johnson, Paul E. *A Shopkeeper's Millennium: Society and Revivals in Rochester, New York, 1815–1837.* New York: Hill and Wang, 1978.

Johnstone, D. Bruce. *Sharing the Costs of Higher Education: Student Financial Assis-*

tance in the United Kingdom, the Federal Republic of Germany, France, Sweden, and the United States. New York: College Entrance Examination Board, 1986.

———. "The 'High Tuition–High Aid' Model of Public Higher Education Finance: The Case Against." New Orleans: Annual Meeting of National Association of System Heads, Apr. 1993.

Jones, Gary L. "Merit Aid Is an Investment for American Leadership." *Change* (Sept. 1984): 24–31.

Jordan, David Starr. *The Days of a Man.* Yonkers: World, 1922.

Jordan, Wilbur K. *Philanthropy in England, 1480–1660: A Study of the Changing Pattern of English Social Aspirations.* London: Allen and Unwin, 1959.

———. "Ann Radcliffe." Lecture Series no. 3. Cambridge: Radcliffe Institute, 1959.

———. *The Charities of London, 1480–1660: The Aspirations and the Achievements of the Urban Society.* London: Allen and Unwin, 1960.

Jump, James W. "The Policy of Admission." *Journal of College Admission* 12 (Spring, 1995): 12–15.

Kabaservice, Geoffrey. "The Birth of a New Institution." *Yale* (alumni magazine, Dec. 1999): 26–41.

———. "'Something Special to Offer': Meritocracy in the Universities." *History of Education Quarterly* 41 (Spring 2001): 81–88.

Kaestle, Carl F. *The Evolution of an Urban School System: New York City, 1750–1850.* Cambridge: Harvard University Press, 1973.

Kahlenberg, Richard D. *The Remedy: Class, Race, and Affirmative Action.* New York: Basic Books, 1996.

Kahn, E. J., Jr. *Harvard through Change and through Storm.* New York: Norton, 1969.

Kane, Thomas J. *The Price of Admission: Rethinking How Americans Pay for College.* Washington, DC: Brookings, 1999.

Karabel, Jerome. "Status-Group Struggle, Organizational Interests, and the Limits of Institutional Autonomy: The Transformation of Harvard, Yale, and Princeton, 1918–1940." *Theory and Society* 13 (1984): 1–40.

Katz, Michael B. *The Price of Citizenship: Redefining the American Welfare State.* New York: Metropolitan Books, 2001.

Keller, George. *Academic Structure: Management Revolutions in American Higher Education.* Baltimore: Johns Hopkins University Press, 1987.

Keller, Morton, and Phyllis Keller. *Making Harvard Modern: The Rise of America's University.* New York: Oxford University Press, 2001.

Kelley, Brooks Mather. *Yale: A History.* New Haven: Yale University Press, 1974.

Kemeny, John G. "The First Five Years: A Report by the Thirteenth President." *Dartmouth Alumni Magazine* (Apr. 1975): 14–49.

Kennedy, Gail, ed. *Education for Democracy: The Debate over the Report of the President's Commission.* Boston: Heath, 1952.

Keppel, Francis. "The Higher Education Acts Contrasted, 1965–1986: Has Federal Policy Come of Age?" *Harvard Educational Review* 57 (Feb. 1987): 49–67.

Kerns, Kathryn. "Farmers' Daughters: The Education of Women at Alfred Academy and University before the Civil War." *History of Higher Education Annual* 6 (1986): 11–28.

Kerr-Tener, Janet. "From Truman to Johnson: Ad Hoc Policy Formation in Higher Education." Ph.D. diss., University of Virginia, 1985.

Kett, Joseph F. *Rites of Passage: Adolescence in America, 1790 to the Present.* New York: Basic Books, 1977.

———. *The Pursuit of Knowledge under Difficulties: From Self-Improvement to Adult Education in America, 1750–1990.* Stanford: Stanford University Press, 1994.

———. "A Class Act: Collegiate Competition and American Society." In *The Faithful Mirror: Reflections on the College Board and American Education,* ed. Michael C. Johanek. New York: College Entrance Examination Board, 2001.

Kimberling, C. Ronald. "Federal Student Aid: A Critical History." In *The Academy in Crisis: The Political Economy of Higher Education,* ed. John W. Sommer. New Brunswick: Transaction, 1995.

King, Richard G. "The Educational Function of Financial Aid." *College Board Review* (Spring 1955): 9–10.

———. "Financial Thresholds to College." *College Board Review* (Spring 1957): 21–24.

Kingsley, William Lathrop. *Yale College: A Sketch of Its History.* New York: Henry Holt, 1879.

Kirkland, Edward Chase. *Charles Francis Adams, Jr., 1835–1915: The Patrician at Bay.* Cambridge: Harvard University Press, 1965.

Kirp, David L. *Shakespeare, Einstein, and the Bottom Line: The Marketing of Higher Education.* Cambridge: Harvard University Press, 1965.

Klitgaard, Robert. *Choosing Elites: Selecting the "Best and the Brightest" at Top Universities and Elsewhere.* New York: Basic Books, 1985.

Kramer, Martin. "Linking Access and Aspirations: the Dual Purpose of Pell Grants." In *Memory, Reason, Imagination: A Quarter Century of Pell Grants,* ed. Lawrence E. Gladieux et al. New York: College Entrance Examination Board, 1998.

Kurz, Kathy A. "The Changing Role of Financial Aid and Enrollment Management." In *Making Enrollment Management Work,* ed. Rebecca R. Dixon. San Francisco: Jossey-Bass, 1995.

Kurz, Kathy, and Jim Scannell. "How Should Public Colleges Price Their Product?" *Chronicle of Higher Education* (Dec. 17, 2004): B12.

Lagemann, Ellen Condliffe. *The Politics of Knowledge: The Carnegie Corporation, Philanthropy, and Public Policy.* Middletown: Wesleyan University Press, 1989.

Landy, Thomas M. "The Colleges in Context." In *Catholic Women's Colleges in America*, ed. Tracy Scheir and Cynthia Russett. Baltimore: Johns Hopkins University Press, 2002.

Lane, J. J. *History of the University of Texas Based on Facts and Records.* Austin: Hutchings State Printer, 1891.

Lang, Daniel. "The People's College, the Mechanics' Mutual Protection, and the Agricultural College Act." *History of Education Quarterly* 18 (Fall 1978): 295–321.

Lapovsky, Lucie, and Loren Loomis Hubbell. "Positioning for Competition." In National Association of College and University Business Officers, *Proceedings from the NACUBO Forum on Tuition Discounting* (Dallas: Feb. 3–4, 2000): 19–24.

Lasch, Christopher. *The Culture of Narcissism: American Life in an Age of Diminishing Expectations.* New York: Norton, 1979.

Lawrence, T. H. "The University in State and Church." In *History of the University of Oxford*, vol. 1, *The Early Oxford Schools*, ed. J. I. Catto. Oxford: Clarendon Press, 1984.

Lederer, William J., and Eugene Burdick. *The Ugly American.* New York: Norton, 1958.

Lederman, Douglas. "University Alters Minority Scholarships on the Advice of the Education Department." *Chronicle of Higher Education* (Apr. 11, 1997): A30.

Lelon, Thomas Charles. "The Emergence of Roosevelt College of Chicago: A Search for an Ideal." Ph.D. diss., University of Chicago, 1973.

Lemann, Nicholas. "The Structure of Success in America." *Atlantic Monthly* 276 (Aug. 1995): 41–50.

———. "The Great Sorting." *Atlantic Monthly* 276 (Sept. 1995): 84–100.

Leonhardt, David. "As Wealthy Fill Top Colleges, Concerns Grow over Fairness." *New York Times* (Apr. 22, 2004): A1, 22.

Leslie, Larry L., and Paul T. Brinkman. *The Economic Value of Higher Education.* New York: American Council on Education/Macmillan, 1988; revised edition, [Washington, DC]: American Council on Education; Phoenix, AZ : Oryx Press, 1993.

Leslie, Larry L., and Jonathan Fife. "The College Grant Study: The Enrollment and Attendance Impacts of Student Grant and Scholarships Programs." *Journal of Higher Education* 45 (1974): 651–74.

Leslie, W. Bruce. *Gentlemen and Scholars: College and Community in the "Age of the University," 1865–1917.* University Park: Pennsylvania State University Press, 1992.

LeTendre, Gerald Kenneth. "The Working-Class Student at Harvard: A Study of Socialization and Adaption in the University." Undergraduate honors thesis, Harvard University, 1983.

Levin, Henry, and Carolyn Kelley. "Can Education Do It Alone?" *Economics of Education Review* 13 (1994): 97–108

Levine, David O. *The American College and the Culture of Aspiration, 1915–1940.* Ithaca: Cornell University Press, 1986.

Lewis, Michael. *Liar's Poker: Rising through the Wreckage on Wall Street.* New York: Norton, 1989.

Lewis, Orlando F. "The Self-Supporting Student in American Colleges." *North American Review* 179 (1904): 718–30.

Lewis, Stephen R. "Ensuring Access, Strengthening Institutions." *College Board Review* (Spring 1995): 12–17.

Lewis, Susan. "The Side of the Angels." *Technology Review* (MIT, Apr. 1994): 1–8.

Lindley, Betty, and Ernest K. Lindley, *A New Deal for Youth.* New York: Viking, 1935.

Lipset, Seymour Martin, and David Riesman. *Education and Politics at Harvard: Two Essays Prepared for the Carnegie Commission on Higher Education.* New York: McGraw-Hill, 1975.

Longanecker, David. "Is Merit-Based Student Aid Really Trumping Need-Based Aid?" *Change* (Mar./Apr. 2002): 30–37.

Lucas, Christopher J. *American Higher Education: A History.* New York: St. Martin's, 1994.

Lukens, Lewis N., and Philip Wallis." How Scholarships Are Granted." *Princeton Alumni Weekly* (Mar. 12, 1937): 2, 16.

Lundstrom, Meg. "Intro to Haggling." *Business Week* (Mar. 15, 1999): 104–6.

Lynd, Robert S., and Helen Merrell Lynd. *Middletown: A Study in American Culture.* New York: Harcourt, Brace, 1929.

Lyon, Bruce Wayne. "The Federal Government and College Students during the Great Depression: A Study of the College Student and Program of the Federal Emergency Relief Administration and the National Youth Administration." Ph.D. diss., Ohio State University, 1969.

MacKay, Alfred F. "Private-College Education: Why Not Give It Away?" *Oberlin Alumni Magazine* (Spring 1990): 16–19.

———. "Improving Yield with Merit Scholarships: A One-Year Experiment." *Oberlin College Observer* (Jan. 16, 1992): 6.

Maclean, John. *History of the College of New Jersey from its Origins in 1746 to the Commencement of 1854.* Philadelphia: Lippincott, 1877.

Mallet, C. E. *History of the University of Oxford.* Vol. 1, *The Mediaeval University.* London: Methuen, 1924.

Mar, M. Elaine. "Blue Collar, Crimson Blazer." *Harvard Magazine* (Nov./Dec., 1995): 47–51.

Marmaduke, Arthur S. "State Student Aid Programs." In *Handbook of Student Financial Aid,* ed. Robert S. Fenske et al. San Francisco: Jossey-Bass, 1987.

Marsden, George M. *The Soul of the American University: From Protestant Establishment to Established Nonbelief.* New York: Oxford University Press, 1994.

Martin, Mary Ellen. "An Historical Analysis of Financial Aid at Wellesley College." Undergraduate honors thesis, Wellesley College, 1973.

Massa, Robert J. "Merit Scholarships and Student Recruitment." *Journal of College Admission* (Spring 1991): 10–14.

———. "Financial Aid in Selective Colleges: Toward 2000." *Journal of College Admission* (Summer 1995): 4–5.

Massy, William F. "Collegium Economicum: Why Institutions Do What They Do." *Change* (July/Aug. 2004): 27–35.

Masters, Brooke A. "Area Colleges Turn Aid into Student Bait." *Washington Post* (May 20, 1994): A1, 10.

Matusow, Allen J. *The Unraveling of America: A History of Liberalism in the 1960s.* New York: Harper and Row, 1984.

McAnear, Beverly. "College Founding in the American Colonies, 1745–1775." *Mississippi Valley Historical Review* 42 (1955): 24–44.

McConnell, Stuart. *Glorious Contentment: The Grand Army of the Republic, 1865–1900.* Chapel Hill: University of North Carolina Press, 1992.

McDonald, Wallace. "Equalizing Scholarship Opportunities." *College Board Review* (Fall 1957): 29–32.

McDonough, Patricia M. *Choosing Colleges: How Social Class and Schools Structure Opportunity.* Albany: State University of New York Press, 1997.

McGrath, Earl J. *The Predominantly Negro Colleges and Universities in Transition.* New York: Columbia University, Teachers College, Bureau of Publications, 1965.

McPherson, Michael S., and Morton Owen Schapiro. *Selective Admission and the Public Interest.* New York: College Entrance Examination Board, 1990.

———. *Keeping College Affordable: Government and Educational Opportunity.* Washington, DC: Brookings, 1991.

———. "Merit Aid: Students, Institutions, and Society." CPRE Research Report Series, no. 30. Consortium for Policy Research in Education, Aug. 1994.

———. "Financing Undergraduate Education: Designing National Policies." *National Tax Journal* 50 (Sept. 1997): 557–71.

———. *The Student Aid Game: Meeting Need and Rewarding Talent in American Higher Education.* Princeton: Princeton University Press, 1998.

———. "The Future Economic Challenges for the Liberal Arts Colleges." *Daedalus* 128 (Winter 1999): 47–75.

———. "The End of the Student Aid Era? Higher Education Finance in the United States." In *A Faithful Mirror: Reflections on the College Board and Education in America,* ed. Michael C. Johanek. New York: College Entrance Examination Board, 2001.

———. "The Blurring Line between Merit and Need in Financial Aid." *Change* (Mar./Apr. 2002): 39–46.

Meiners, Frederick. *A History of Rice University: The Institute Years, 1907–1963.* Houston: Rice University Studies, 1982.

Mensel, Mary E. "Changing Picture of Financial Aid." *Smith Alumnae Quarterly* (July 1962): 219–20.

Millard, Richard M. "Governance, Quality and Equity in the United States." In *Quality and Access in Higher Education: Comparing Britain and the United States,* ed. Robert O. Berdahl. Buckingham, UK: Open University Press, 1991.

Millett, John D. *Financing Higher Education in the United States: The Staff Report of the Commission on Financing Higher Education.* New York: Columbia University Press, 1952.

Minnesota Private College Research Foundation. "Ways and Means: How Minnesota Families Pay for College." St. Paul, 1992.

Mishel, Lawrence, Jared Bernstein, and John Schmitt. *The State of Working America 2000/2001.* Ithaca: Cornell University Press, 2001.

Mitchell, J. Pearce. *Stanford University, 1916–1941.* Stanford: Stanford University, 1958.

Moberly, George Herbert. *Life of William of Wykeham.* Winchester, UK: Warren, 1887.

Monks, James. "Is This the Beginning of the End of Need-Based Financial Aid?" *College Board Review* (Aug. 2000): 12–15.

———, and Ronald G. Ehrenberg. "The Impact of *U.S. News and World Report* College Rankings on Admissions Outcomes and Pricing Policies." NBER Working Paper no. 7227. Cambridge: National Bureau of Economic Research, July 1999.

Monro, John U., "Helping Him Pay His Way." *Harvard Alumni Bulletin* (Feb. 1950): 378–81.

———. "Helping the Student Help Himself." *College Board Review* (May 1953): 351–57.

———. "Untapped Resource: Loans for Student Aid." *College Board Review* (Winter 1956): 14–18.

Montgomery, G. V. "Sonny." "The Montgomery GI Bill: Development, Implementations, and Impact." *Educational Record* 75 (Fall 1994): 49–55.

Moody, Ann. *Coming of Age in Mississippi.* New York: Doubleday, 1965.

Moon, Rexford G. "Student Financial Aid in the United States: Administration and Resources." Report for *Economist* Intelligence Unit and the International Study on College Admissions. New York: UNESCO, 1962.

Moore, Robert L., A. H. Studenmund, and Thomas Slobko. "The Effect of the Financial Aid Package on the Choice of a Selective College." *Economics of Education Review* 10 (1991): 311–21.

Moran, Gerald F., and Maris A. Vinovskis. *Religion, Family, and the Life Course:*

Explorations in the Social History of Early America. Ann Arbor: University of Michigan Press, 1992.

"More Full-Paying Students?" *Oberlin College Observer* (Oct. 12, 1989): 1–2.

Morgan, Arthur E. "The Antioch Program." *Journal of Higher Education* 1 (1930): 497–502.

Morin, Richard. "The Spillover Effect." *Washington Post* (Aug. 18, 2002): B5.

Morison, Samuel Eliot. *The Founding of Harvard College*. Cambridge: Harvard University Press, 1935.

———. *Harvard College in the Seventeenth Century*. Cambridge: Harvard University Press, 1936.

———. *Three Centuries of Harvard, 1636–1956*. Cambridge: Harvard University Press, 1936.

Morse, John F. "How We Got Here from There." In *Student Loans: Problems and Policy Alternatives*, ed. Lois D. Rice. New York: College Entrance Examination Board, 1977: 3–15.

Mortenson, Thomas G. . "Refocusing the Pell Grant from Poverty to Higher Income Applicants: 1979–80 to 1986–87." *Journal of Student Financial Aid* 18 (Fall 1988): 5–11.

Mosch, Theodore. *The GI Bill: A Breakthrough in Educational and Social Policy in the USA*. New York: Exposition Press, 1975.

Moskos, Charles C. *A Call to Service: National Service for Country and Community*. New York: Free Press, 1988.

Mulligan, Raymond E. "Socio-Economic Background and College Enrollment." *American Sociological Review* 16 (Apr. 1951): 188–96.

Mulvihull, Geoff. "Competition Also at Odds over Aid." *Oberlin Review* (Dec. 3, 1993): 5.

Mumper, Michael. *Removing College Price Barriers: What Government Has Done and Why It Isn't Working*. Albany: State University of New York Press, 1996.

———. "The Student Aid Industry." In *Financing a College Education: How It Works, How It's Changing*, ed. Jacqueline E. King. Westport: ACE/Oryx, 1999.

Myer, Sylvia. "What Would You Do for an Education?" *Woman's Home Companion* 49 (1922): 42–44.

Nash, George, Patricia Nash, and Martin M. Goldstein. "Financial Aid Policies and Practices at Accredited Four-Year Universities and Colleges." New York: Bureau of Applied Social Research for the College Entrance Examination Board, Feb. 1967.

Nash, George H. *The Life of Herbert Hoover: The Engineer, 1874–1914*. New York: Norton, 1983.

National Association of College Admission Counselors. "Report on the Results of the Membership Survey of Need-Blind and Need-Conscious Admission Practices." Alexandria, VA: NACAC, May 1994.

———. "Executive Summary: 1994 Survey of Admission Practices." Alexandria, VA: NACAC, Sept. 1994.

National Association of Student Financial Aid Administrators and the College Board. *Financial Aid Professionals at Work: The 1996 Survey of Undergraduate Financial Aid Policies, Practices, and Procedures.* Washington, DC, and New York: NASFAA and College Entrance Examination Board, 2000.

———. *The Financial Aid Profession at Work in 1999–2000: Results from the 2001 Survey.* Washington, DC, and New York: NASFAA and College Entrance Examination Board, 2002.

National Commission on the Cost of Higher Education. *Straight Talk about College Costs and Prices.* Westport: ACE/Oryx, 1998.

Naylor, Natalie A. 'The Ante-Bellum College Movement: A Reappraisal of Tewksbury's *Founding of American Colleges and Universities.*" *History of Education Quarterly* 13 (Fall 1973): 261–74.

Neehy, Paul. 'The Threats to Liberal Arts Colleges." *Daedalus* 128 (1999): 28–45.

Neem, Johann N. "Early Postmodern Polities: The Narratives of Colonial Political Development." *Reviews in American History* 32 (Dec. 2004): 478–85.

Nelsen, William C. "Use Both Merit and Need in Awarding Scholarship Aid." *Chronicle of Higher Education* (July 4, 2003): B20.

Nelson, James E. "The Role of the College Scholarship Service in the Year 2000." In *An Agenda for the Year 2000: Thirtieth Anniversary Colloquia Proceedings.* New York: College Scholarship Service, College Entrance Examination Board, 1985.

Nevins, Allan. *Abram S. Hewitt, with Some Account of Peter Cooper.* New York: Harper, 1935.

New York State. Report of the Select Committee on Higher Education. Legislative Document no. 6. Albany: 1974.

Newcomer, Mabel. *A Century of Higher Education for Women.* New York: Harper, 1959.

Newsome, David. *Godliness and Good Learning: Four Studies on a Victorian Ideal.* London: Murray, 1961.

Nidiffer, Jana. "Poor Historiography: The 'Poorest' in American Higher Education." *History of Education Quarterly* 39 (Fall 1999): 321–36.

Nitowski, Mark. "Financial Aid Tilts toward Merit to Help Middle Income Families." *Carnegie Mellon Magazine* (Fall 1994): 17–19.

North Carolina State Education Assistance Authority. *Student Financial Aid for North Carolinians.* Chapel Hill: annual editions.

Norton, Mary Beth, et al. *A People and a Nation: A History of the United States.* Complete ed. Vol. 2, *Since 1865.* Boston: Houghton Mifflin, 1982.

Novak, Steven. *The Rights of Youth: American Colleges and Student Revolts.* Cambridge: Harvard University Press, 1977.

O'Connell, Charles. "Complex Purposes Lead to Diverse Practices." In *Proceedings from College Scholarship Service Colloquium on Student Financial Aid and Institutional Purpose.* New York: College Entrance Examination Board, 1963.

Olivier, Warner. "Stony Path to Learning." *Saturday Evening Post* (Apr. 14, 1945): 22–23, 48, 52.

Olson, Keith W. "The G.I. Bill and Higher Education: Success and Surprise." *American Quarterly* 25 (Dec. 1973): 596–610.

———. *The G.I. Bill, the Veterans, and the Colleges.* Lexington: University Press of Kentucky, 1974.

Oren, Daniel A. *Joining the Club: A History of Jews and Yale.* New Haven: Yale University Press, 1985.

Orfield, Gary. "Money, Equity, and College Access." *Harvard Educational Review* 62 (Fall 1992): 337–72.

Patterson, Franklin, and Charles R. Longsworth. *The Making of a College: A New Departure in Higher Education.* Cambridge: MIT Press, 1966; expanded ed., 1975.

Peck, Elizabeth S. *Berea's First 125 Years, 1855–1980.* Lexington: University Press of Kentucky, 1982.

"Pell Grants as a Measure of Student Diversity at America's Highest-Ranked Colleges and Universities." *Journal of Blacks in Higher Education* 37 (Autumn 2002): 105–7.

Perna, Laura W. "Precollege Outreach Programs." *Journal of College Student Development* 43 (Jan./Feb. 2002): 64–83.

Pessen, Edward. *Jacksonian Democracy: Society, Personality, and Politics.* Homewood, IL: Dorsey, 1969.

Peterson, Merrill D. *Thomas Jefferson and the New Nation: A Biography.* New York: Oxford University Press, 1970.

Pierson, George W. *Yale: College and University, 1871- 1937.* Vol. 1, *Yale College: An Educational History.* New Haven: Yale University Press, 1952.

———. *Yale: College and University, 1871- 1937.* Vol. 2, *Yale College: The University College, 1921–1937.* New Haven: Yale University Press, 1955.

Porter, Earl W. *Trinity and Duke, 1892–1921.* Durham: Duke University Press, 1964.

———. Potter, Stephen. "University and Society." In *History of the University of Oxford,* vol. 4, *Seventeenth-Century Oxford,* ed. Nicholas Tyacke. Oxford: Clarendon Press, 1997.

Potter, Will. "The Wrong Kind of Incentive? Critics Fault Plan to Expand Loan-forgiveness Program." *Chronicle of Higher Education* (Mar. 21, 2003): A27.

Potthoff, Edward F. "Who Goes to College?" *Journal of Education* 2 (1931): 294–97.

Powell, Arthur G. *Lessons from Privilege: the American Prep School Tradition*. Cambridge: Harvard University Press, 1996.

———. "Notes on the Origins of Meritocracy in American Schooling." *History of Education Quarterly* 41 (Spring 2001): 72–100.

"Princeton and the FERA." *Princeton Alumni Weekly* (Dec. 7, 1934).

Pulley, John L. "Fund-Raising Efforts Proliferate for Families of Terrorists' Victims." *Chronicle of Higher Education* (Nov. 2, 2001): A35–36.

Putka, Gary. "Do Colleges Collude on Financial Aid?" *Wall Street Journal* (May 2, 1989): B1.

———. "Ivy League Discussions on Finances Extend to Tuition and Salaries." *Wall Street Journal* (May 8, 1992): B1, 2.

———. "Arithmetic on College Aid Varies Widely." *Wall Street Journal* (Nov. 11, 1993): B2.

Putnam, Robert D. *Bowling Alone: The Collapse and Revival of American Community.* New York: Simon and Schuster, 2000.

Quattlebaum, Charles A. *Federal Educational Activities and Educational Issues before Congress.* Report for U.S. House Committee on Education and Labor. 82nd Cong., 2nd sess., 1952. H. Doc. 423.

Quincy, Josiah. *History of Harvard University.* Vol. 1. Cambridge: Owen, 1840.

———. *History of Harvard University.* Vol. 2. Boston: Crosby, 1860.

Rashdall, Hastings. *The Universities of Europe in the Middle Ages.* Vol. 3, *English Universities—Student Life.* Oxford: Oxford University Press, 1895; new ed., 1936, ed. F. M. Powick and A .B. Emden.

Ratcliffe, Ella B. "State Scholarships Increase." *School Life* 21 (1936): 171–72, 192.

Rauchway, Eric. "More Means Different: Quantifying American Exceptionalism." *Reviews in American History* 30 (Sept. 2002): 504–16.

Rauh, Morton A. "The Relation of Student Aid Programs to Institutional Finances." Report to the Associated Colleges of the Midwest and the Great Lakes Colleges. Yellow Springs, OH: Aug. 1972.

Ravitch, Diane. *The Troubled Crusade: American Education, 1945–1980.* New York: Basic Books, 1983.

Redd, Kenneth E. "Discounting toward Disaster: Tuition Discounting, College Finances, and Enrollments of Low-Income Undergraduates." *USAGroup Foundation New Agenda,* Series 3 (Dec. 2000): 1–38.

Reed, John. "Student Civil Rights Activism: Northwestern University,1945–1968; A Case Study." Undergraduate honors thesis, Northwestern University, 1983.

Reeves, Floyd W., et al. *The Liberal Arts College: Based upon Surveys of Thirty-Five Colleges Related to the Methodist Episcopal Church.* Chicago: University of Chicago Press, 1932.

Reich, Robert B. "How Selective Colleges Heighten Inequality." *Chronicle of Higher Education* (Sept. 13, 2000): B7–10.

Reisberg, Leo. "Are Students Actually Learning?" *Chronicle of Higher Education* (Nov. 17, 2000): A67–68.

Reuben, Julie A. "Merit, Mission, and Minority Students: The History of Debate over Special Admission Programs." In *A Faithful Mirror: Reflections on the College Board and Education in America,* ed. Michael C. Johanek. New York: College Entrance Examination Board, 2001.

Reynolds, O. Edgar. *The Social and Economic Status of College Students.* New York: Columbia University, Teachers College, Bureau of Publications, 1927.

Rhees, Harriet Seelye. *Laurenus Clark Seelye, First President of Smith College.* Boston and New York: Houghton Mifflin, 1929.

Riccardi, Nicholas. "Trustees Split on Painful Budget." *Oberlin Review* (Dec. 10, 1993): 1.

Richardson, Leon Burr. *History of Dartmouth College.* Hanover: Dartmouth College, 1932.

Riesman, David. "On Discovering and Teaching Sociology: A Memoir." *Annual Review of Sociology* 14 (1988): 1–24.

Rivlin, Alice. *The Role of the Federal Government in Financing Higher Education.* Washington, DC: Brookings, 1961.

Robson, David W. "College Founding in the New Republic 1776–1800." *History of Education Quarterly* 23 (Fall 1983): 323–41.

Rodriguez, Richard. *Hunger of Memory: The Education of Richard Rodriguez.* Boston: Godine, 1982; Bantam ed., New York: 1983.

Rogers, Warren P. "The People's College Movement in New York State." *New York History* 26 (1945): 415–46.

Roosevelt, Franklin D. *Public Papers and Addresses.* Vol. 12. Ed. Samuel I. Rosenman. New York: Harper, 1950.

Ross, David R. *Preparing for Ulysses: Politics and Veterans during World War II.* New York: Columbia University Press, 1969.

Rothenberg, Winifred B. "The Emergence of a Capital Market in Rural Massachusetts." *Journal of Economic History* 45 (Dec. 1985): 781–808.

Rudolph, Frederick. *Mark Hopkins and the Log: Williams College, 1836–1872.* New Haven: Yale University Press, 1956.

———. *The American College and University: A History.* New York: Knopf, 1962.

———. "The Origins of Student Aid in the United States." In *Student Financial Aid and the National Purpose,* ed. James E. Allen. Princeton: College Entrance Examination Board, 1962.

———. *Curriculum: A History of the American Undergraduate Course of Study since 1636.* San Francisco: Jossey-Bass, 1977.

Rudy, S. Willis. *The College of the City of New York: A History, 1847–1947.* New York: Arno, 1977.

Russo, Joseph A. "The Financial Aid Professional: An Endangered Species?" *College Board Review* (1995): 40–43, 63–64.

Sagendorph, Kent. *Michigan: The Story of the University.* New York: Dutton, 1948.

St. John, Edward P. *Refinancing the College Dream: Access, Equal Opportunity, and Justice for Taxpayers.* Baltimore: John Hopkins University Press, 2003.

Sanders, J. Edward. "Visiting the Colleges." *College Board Review* (Feb. 1953): 336–40.

———. "Are Scholarships Improving Education?" *College Board Review* (May 1953): 358–64.

———. "Financial Aid to Fill the Pool with Talent." In *Proceedings from College Scholarship Service Colloquium on Financial Aid and Institutional Purpose.* New York: College Entrance Examination Board, 1963: 36–39.

———. Interview for the National Association of Student Financial Aid Administrators Oral History Series. Tape recording. Washington, DC, Feb. 22, 1982..

Sanders, J. Edward, and Hans C. Palmer. *The Financial Barrier to Higher Education in California: A Study Prepared for the California State Scholarship Commission.* Pomona: Pomona College, 1963.

Sanders, Neill, and James Henson. "Financial Aid in 2010: A Cloudy Crystal Ball." *College Board Review* (Jan. 2000): 20–25.

Sanoff, Alvin P. "Americans See Money for College Somewhere over the Rainbow." *Chronicle of Higher Education* (Apr. 30, 2004): B6–8

Scannell, James J. "Development of Optimal Financial Aid Strategies." Ph.D. diss., Boston College, 1980.

———. *The Effect of Financial Aid Policies on Admission and Enrollment.* New York: College Entrance Examination Board, 1992.

Schiff, Judith Ann. "A Century of Stover." *Yale Alumni Magazine* (Oct. 1997): 112.

Schlesinger, Arthur M., Jr. *A Thousand Days: John F. Kennedy in the White House.* Boston: Houghton Mifflin, 1965.

Schmidt, George P. *The Liberal Arts College: a Chapter in American Cultural History.* New Brunswick: Rutgers University Press, 1957.

———. *Princeton and Rutgers: The Two Colonial Colleges of New Jersey.* Princeton: Van Nostrand, 1964.

Schmidt, Peter. "U of California Ends Affirmative-Action Ban." *Chronicle of Higher Education* (May 25, 2001): A39–40.

———. "Poll Finds Wide Support for Bush's Stance on University of Michigan Case." *Chronicle of Higher Education* (Mar. 7, 2003): A23.

———. "Noted Higher-Education Researcher Urges Admissions Preferences for the Poor." *Chronicle of Higher Education* (Apr. 16, 2004): A26–27.

Schudson, Michael S. "Organizing the 'Meritocracy': A History of the College

Entrance Examination Board." *Harvard Educational Review* 42 (Feb. 1972): 34–69.

Selingo, Jeffrey. "AmeriCorps at 5 Years." *Chronicle of Higher Education* (Sept. 25, 1998): A38–39.

———. "For Fans of State Merit Scholarships: A Cautionary Tale from Louisiana." *Chronicle of Higher Education* (Apr. 16, 1999): A36–39.

———. "Questioning the Merit of Merit Scholarships." *Chronicle of Higher Education* (Jan. 19, 2001): A20–22.

———. "How California's Ambitious Aid Program Stumbled Badly and Disappointed Many." *Chronicle of Higher Education* (Mar. 15, 2002): A23–24.

———. "Mission Creep?" *Chronicle of Higher Education* (May 31, 2002): A19–22.

———. "Researchers Square Off on State-Based Merit Scholarships." *Chronicle of Higher Education* (Sept. 13, 2002): A26.

Selingo, Jeffrey, et al. "What Americans Think about Higher Education." *Chronicle of Higher Education* (May 2, 2003): A10–17.

Sharpless, Isaac. *The Story of a Small College.* Philadelphia: Winston, 1918.

Shea, Christopher. "Sweetening the Pot for the Best Students." *Chronicle of Higher Education* (May 17, 1996): A39–40.

Shipton, Clifford. "The New England Frontier." *New England Quarterly* 10 (1937): 25–36.

Sibley, John Langdon. *Biographical Sketches of Graduates of Harvard University in Cambridge, Massachusetts.* Vol. 1, *1642–1658.* Cambridge: Sever, 1873.

Skinner, Rod. "Designer Parenting: Are Parents Packaging Their Children for College Admissions?" *College Board Review* (Jan. 2000): 6–11.

Skocpol, Theda, *Protecting Soldiers and Mothers: The Political Origins of Social Policy in the U.S.A.* Cambridge: Harvard University Press, 1992.

Slater, Mariam K. "My Son the Doctor: Aspects of Mobility among American Jews." *American Sociological Review* 34 (June 1969): 359–73.

Slosson, Edwin E. *Great American Universities.* New York: Macmillan, 1910.

Smythe, George Franklin. *Kenyon College: Its First Century.* New Haven: Yale University Press, 1924.

Solomon, Barbara. *In the Company of Educated Women: A History of Women and Higher Education in America.* New Haven: Yale University Press, 1985.

Solon, Gary. "Cross-Country Differences in Intergenerational Earnings Mobility." *Journal of Economic Perspectives* 16 (Summer 2002): 59–66.

Southern, R. W. "From Schools to University." In *History of the University of Oxford,* vol. 1, *The Early Oxford Schools,* ed. J. I. Catto. Oxford: Clarendon Press, 1984.

Spady, William G. "Educational Mobility and Access in the United States: Growth and Paradoxes." *American Journal of Sociology* 73 (1967–68): 273–86.

Spencer, A. Clayton. "The New Politics of Higher Education." In *Financing a College*

Education: How It Works, How It's Changing, ed. Jacqueline E. King. Westport: ACE/Oryx, 1999.

Stadtman, Verne A. *The University of California, 1868–1968.* New York: McGraw-Hill, 1968.

Stalnaker, John M. "The National Merit Scholarship Program." *Journal of the National Association of Deans of Women* 19 (June 1956): 166–68.

Stecklow, Steve. "Colleges Manipulate Financial-Aid Offers, Shortchanging Many." *Wall Street Journal* (Apr. 1, 1996): A1, 7.

Steinberg, Jacques. *The Gatekeepers: Inside the Admissions Process of a Premier College.* New York: Viking, 2002.

Stewart, Janet Kidd. "Save a Lot for College? Expect to Pay More." *Cleveland Plain Dealer* (June 3, 2004, Tribune Media Services).

Stone, Lawrence. "The Size and Composition of the Oxford Student Body." In *The University in Society,* vol. 1, *Oxford and Cambridge,* ed. Lawrence Stone. Princeton: Princeton University Press, 1975.

Storr, Richard J. *Harper's University: The Beginnings; A History.* Chicago: University of Chicago Press, 1966.

Story, Ronald. *The Forging of an American Aristocracy: Harvard and the Boston Upper Class* . Middletown: Wesleyan University Press, 1982.

Strosnider, Kim. "A University Relies on Its Endowment to Cover the Costs of Financial Aid." *Chronicle of Higher Education* (June 12, 1998): A37–39.

Sundquist, James L. "Origins of the War on Poverty." In *On Fighting Poverty: Perspectives from Experience,* ed. James L. Sundquist. New York: Basic Books, 1969.

Suskind, Ron. *A Hope in the Unseen: An American Odyssey from the Inner City to the Ivy League.* New York: Broadway, 1999.

Tapper, Ted. *Fee-Paying Schools and Educational Change in Britain: Between the State and the Marketplace.* London: Woburn, 1997.

Tewksbury, Donald G. *The Founding of American Colleges and Universities before the Civil War.* New York: Columbia University, Teachers College, Bureau of Publications, 1932.

Thelin, John R. *The Cultivation of Ivy: A Saga of the College in America.* Cambridge, MA: Schenkman, 1976.

Thernstrom, Stephan. "'Poor but Hopefull Scholars.'" In *Glimpses of the Harvard Past,* ed. Bernard Bailyn et al. Cambridge: Harvard University Press, 1986.

Thresher, B. Alden. "Sponsored Scholarships and the Student." *College Board Review* (Fall 1955): 8–12.

Tierney, Michael L. "The Impact of Financial Aid on Student Demand for Public/Private Higher Education." *Journal of Higher Education* 51 (1980): 527–45.

Thwing, Charles F. *American Colleges: Their Students and Work.* New York: Putnam's, 1878.

———. "Pecuniary Aid for Poor and Able Students." *Forum* 27 (1899): 179–89.

Toor, Rachel. "Pushy Parents and Other Tales of the Admissions Game." *Chronicle of Higher Education* (Oct. 6, 2000): B18–19.

———. *Admissions Confidential: An Insider's Account of the Elite College Selection Process.* New York: St. Martin's, 2001.

Toppo, Greg, and Anthony DeBarros. "Reality Crashing Down on Dreams of College." *USA Today* (Feb. 2, 2005): A1–2.

Toth, Susan Allen. *Ivy Days: Making My Way Out East.* Boston: Little, Brown, 1984.

Trow, Martin. "American Higher Education: Exceptional or Just Different?" In *Is America Different? A New Look at American Exceptionalism,* ed. Byron E. Shafer. Oxford: Oxford University Press, 1991.

———. "Class, Race, and Higher Education in America." *American Behavioral Scientist* 35 (Mar./June 1992): 344–59.

Turner, Ralph H. "Modes of Ascent through Education: Sponsored and Contest Mobility." *American Sociological Review* 25 (1960): 121–39.

Turner, Sarah. "The Vision and Reality of Pell Grants: Unforeseen Consequences for Students and Institutions." In *Memory, Reason, Imagination: A Quarter Century of Pell Grants,* ed. Lawrence E. Gladieux et al. New York: College Entrance Examination Board, 1998.

Tyler, W. S. *History of Amherst College during Its First Half Century, 1821–1871.* Springfield, MA: Bryan, 1873.

U.S. Bureau of the Census. *The Statistical History of the United States, from Colonial Times to the Present.* With an Introduction and User's Guide by Ben J. Wattenberg. New York: Basic Books, 1976.

U.S. Congress. House. Armed Forces Committee on Postwar Educational Opportunities for Service Personnel. *Preliminary Report to the President.* 78th Cong., 1st sess., July 30, 1943.

———. Committee on Education and Labor. *Scholarship and Loan Program.* Hearings before Special Education Subcommittee. 85th Cong., 1st ses., Aug.–Nov. 1957.

———. Committee on Education and Labor. *Higher Education Act of 1965.* Hearings before Subcomittee on Education. 89th Cong., 1st sess., 1965.

U.S. Congress. Legislative Reference Service. *Guaranteeing an Opportunity for Higher Education to All Qualified High School Graduates: Should the Federal Government Participate?* Doc. 164. 88th Cong., 1st sess., 1963.

U.S. Department of Commerce, Bureau of the Census. *Historical Statistics of the United States, from Colonial Times to 1957.* Washington: U.S. Government Printing Office, 1960.

U.S. Department of Education, National Center for Education Statistics (NCES).

120 Years of American Education, ed. Thomas D. Snyder. Jessup, MD: ED Pubs, 1993.

———. *Programs at Higher Education Institutions for Disadvantaged Precollege Students,* by B. Chancy et al. Jessup, MD: ED Pubs, 1995.

———. *What Students Pay for College: Changes in Net Price of College Attendance between 1992–93 and 1999–2000,* by Laura Horn et al. Jessup, MD.: ED Pubs, 2002.

———. *Getting Ready to Pay for College: What Students and Their Parents Know about the Cost of College Tuition and What They Are Doing to Find Out,* by Laura Horn et al. Jessup, MD: ED Pubs, 2003.

U.S. Department of Health, Education, and Welfare. *Toward a Long-Range Plan for Federal Financial Support of Higher Education: A Report to the President,* by Alice A. Rivlin et al. Washington, DC: U.S. Government Printing Office, 1969.

U.S. Department of the Interior, Bureau of Education. *Biennial Survey of Education.* Washington, DC: U.S. Government Printing Office, 1921, 1925.

———. "Philanthropy in the History of American Higher Education." Bulletin no. 26, by Jesse Brundage. Washington, DC: U.S. Government Printing Office, 1922.

———. "Self-Help for College Students." Bulletin no. 2, by Walter J. Greenleaf. Washington, DC: U.S. Government Printing Office, 1929.

U.S. President's Commission on Higher Education. *Higher Education for Democracy.* 5 vols. Washington, DC: U.S. Government Printing Office, 1947, 1948; reprint, New York: Harper, 1952.

Vance, Norman. *The Sinews of the Spirit: The Ideal of Christian Manliness in Victorian Literature and Religious Thought.* Cambridge: Cambridge University Press, 1985.

Van Dusen, William D., and John O'Hearne. *An Idealization of a Collegiate Financial Aid Office.* Austin: Coordinating Board, Texas College and University System, 1968.

Van Dyke, George E. "Government Experience with the Student War Loan Program." *Higher Education* 6 (Nov. 15, 1949): 61–63.

Vedder, Richard. *Going Broke by Degree: Why College Costs Too Much.* Washington, DC: American Enterprise Institute Press, 2004.

Veysey, Laurence R. *The Emergence of the American University.* Chicago: University of Chicago Press, 1965.

Waite, Cally C. *Permission to Remain among US: Education for Blacks in Oberlin, Ohio, 1880–1914.* Westport: Bergin and Garvey, 2003.

Waldman, Steven. *The Bill: How Legislation Really Becomes Law; A Case Study of the National Service Bill.* New York: Penguin, 1995.

Wallace, Thomas P. "The Inequities of Low Tuition." *Chronicle of Higher Education* (Apr. 1, 992): A48.

Walton, Andrea. "Cultivating a Place for Selective All-Female Education in a Co-educational World: Women Educators and Professional Voluntary Associations, 1880–1926." In *A Faithful Mirror: Reflections on the College Board and Education in America*, ed. Michael C. Johanek. New York: College Entrance Examination Board, 2001.

Ward, John William. *Andrew Jackson—Symbol for an Age.* New York: Oxford University Press, 1955.

Warner, W. Lloyd, Robert J. Havighurst, and Martin B. Loeb. *Who Shall Be Educated? The Challenge of Unequal Opportunities.* New York: Harper, 1944.

Wechsler, Harold S. *The Qualified Student: A History of Selective Admissions in America.* New York: Wiley, 1977.

———. "An Academic Gresham's Law: Group Repulsion as a Theme in American Higher Education." *Teachers College Record* 82 (1981): 567–88.

Weld, Theodore D. "Report to the Executive Committee." In *Report on Manual Labor in Literary Institutions: First Annual Report.* New York: Society for Promoting Manual Labor in Literary Institutions, 1833.

Wertenbaker, Thomas Jefferson. *Princeton 1746–1896.* Princeton: Princeton University Press, 1946.

Werth, Barry. "Why Is College So Expensive?" *New England Monthly* (Jan. 1988): 35–43, 99.

White, Betsy. "The Policy of Admission." *Brown Alumni Monthly* (Winter 1992–93): 31–37.

White, Daniel Appleton. "The Condition and Wants of Harvard College." *North American Review* 60 (Jan. 1845): 38–63.

White, Theodore. *In Search of History: A Personal Adventure.* New York: Harper and Row, 1978.

Whitehead, John S. *The Separation of College and State: Columbia, Dartmouth, Harvard, and Yale.* New Haven: Yale University Press, 1973.

Whitehead, John S., and Jurgen Herbst. "How to Think about the Dartmouth College Case." *History of Education Quarterly* 26 (Fall 1986): 333–49.

Whyte, William H. *The Organization Man.* New York: Simon and Schuster, 1956.

Wick, Philip G. *No-Need/Merit Scholarships: Practices and Trends.* New York: College Entrance Examination Board, 1997.

Wilkinson, Rupert. *American Tough: The Tough-Guy Tradition and American Character.* Westport: Greenwood, 1984; illustrated edition, New York: Harper and Row, 1986.

———. *The Pursuit of American Character.* New York: Harper and Row, 1988.

———. "Packaging and Equity: Historical Perspectives." *Journal of Student Financial Aid* 28 (Spring 1998): 41–52.

———. "Plural Ends, Contested Means: Student Financial Aid in American History." In *A Faithful Mirror: Reflections on the College Board and American Higher*

Education, ed. Michael C. Johanek . New York: College Entrance Examination Board, 2001.

———. "Quarreling about Merits: The History of a Financial-Aid Debate." *College Board Review* (Winter 2004): 9–13.

———, ed. *American Social Character: Modern Interpretations.* New York: HarperCollins, 1994.

Willenz, June A. "Invisible Veterans." *Educational Record* 75 (Fall 1994): 41–46.

Willey, Malcolm M. *Depression, Recovery, and Higher Education: A Report by Committee Y of the American Association of University Professors.* New York: McGraw-Hill, 1937.

Williamson, Harold F., and Payson S. Wild. *Northwestern University: A History, 1850–1975.* Evanston: Northwestern University, 1976.

Williamstown Historical Commission. *Williamstown: The First Two Hundred Years, 1733–1953, and Twenty Years Later, 1953–1973.* Williamstown: Commission, 1974).

Wilson, Reginald. "GI Bill Expands Access for African Americans." *Educational Record* 75 (Fall 1994): 32–39.

Wilson, William Julius. *The Truly Disadvantaged: The Inner City, the Underclass, and Public Policy.* Chicago: University of Chicago Press, 1987.

Winston, Gordon C. "Subsidies, Hierarchy, and Peers: The Awkward Economics of Higher Education." *Journal of Economic Perspective* 13 (Winter 1999):13–36.

Winston, Gordon C., and David Zimmerman. "Where Is Aggressive Price Competition Taking Higher Education?" *Change* (July/Aug. 2000): 11–18.

Winter, Greg. "Rich Colleges Receive Richest Share of U.S. Aid." *New York Times* (Nov. 9, 2003): 1, 18.

Wister, Owen. *Philosophy 4: A Story of Harvard University.* New York: Macmillan, 1903.

Witty, Paul A., and Luella Foreman. "Self-Support and College Attainment." *Vocational Guidance* (1930): 102–6.

Wolanin, Thomas R. "Pell Grants: A Twenty-Five Year History." In *Memory, Reason, Imagination: A Quarter Century of Pell Grants,* ed. Lawrence E. Gladieux et al. New York: College Entrance Examination Board, 1998.

Woodard, Colin. "Worldwide Tuition Increases Send Students into the Streets." *Chronicle of Higher Education* (May 5, 2000): A54–56.

Woodcock, Heather. "The Evolution of Need Aware Admission and Financial Aid Policies at Brown University." Course paper for Prof. Richard Chait, Harvard University, Graduate School of Education, Dec. 1997.

———. "The Experiences of John Usher Monro at Harvard College and Miles College." Course paper for Prof. Julie Reuben, Harvard University, Graduate School of Education, May 1999.

Woodhall, Maureen. "Human Capital Concepts." In *Economics of Education: Research and Studies,* ed. George Psacharopoulos. Oxford: Pergamon, 1987.

——. "International Experience of Financial Support for Students." In *Financial Support for Students: Grants, Loans or Graduate Tax?,* ed. Maureen Woodhall. London: Kogan Page, 1989.

Woodward, C. Vann. *Origins of the New South, 1877–1913.* Baton Rouge: Louisiana State University Press, 1951.

Wortman, Marc. "Can Need-Blind Survive?" *Yale Alumni* (Oct. 1993): 62–67.

"Would You Like Your Class War Shaken or Stirred, Sir?" *Economist* (Sept. 6, 2003): 46–47.

Wright, Albert Hazen. *Pre-Cornell and Early Cornell.* Vol. 6, *Cornell's Three Predecessors.* Studies in History. Ithaca: New York State College of Agriculture, 1958.

Young, Michael. *The Rise of the Meritocracy: An Essay on Education and Equality.* London: Thames and Hudson, 1958; reprint, Harmondsworth: Penguin, 1961.

Index

568 Presidents' Working Group, 171, 172–74; college members of, 284n25

abolitionists, slavery, 78, 142, 270n4

academies, eighteenth and nineteenth century, 40, 70, 75, 77, 81

access and outreach programs, 55, 60, 185–86; in the 1960s, 130, 142; new proposal regarding, 190–1

ACT (American College Testing) scores, 145, 185, 219. *See also* SAT scores

Adams, Charles Francis, Jr., 258n26

Addams, Jane, 101

Admissions, 87, 112; and admit rates, 36, 136, 143, 219; and "development admits," 150; directors, 124,132, 165; and early decision, 145, 184, 221; recruiting and marketing, 37, 104, 115–16, 141, 144, 149, 165; unselective, 36, 151, 273n75; and yield, 165–66, 226. *See also* admit-deny policy; need-aware admissions; need-blind admissions; selectivity

admit-deny policy, 133, 134, 135, 140, 151–52, 266n17; defined; 219–20

advanced placement and accelerated programs, 73, 248n14, 254n71

affirmative action, 20–21, 159–60, 187–88; extended to economic classes, 186

African Americans, 60; in the nineteenth century, 78; in the 1940s-50s, 50, 51, 104, 114, 116, 121, 122–23, 241n19; in the 1960s-70s; 20–21, 55–56, 61, 129–30 140, 151–52; in the 1990s-2000s, 159–60; as an interest group, 180; at Oberlin, 142, 145, 160

agricultural education, 78, 79–80

Alabama, University of, 111n

Albany, 71

Albion College, 29

Alfred Academy and University, 40

Alice Lloyd College, 251–52n50

Allmendinger, David F., Jr., xiii, 75

alumni, alumnae, 86, 117, 118, 124–25, 132, 179; in the late nineteenth and early twentieth centuries, 101, 103–4, 108, 113; in the 1990s-2000s,